GENERAL MILLER.

London. Published, March by Longman & Co.

MEMOIRS

OF

GENERAL MILLER,

IN THE SERVICE OF

THE REPUBLIC OF PERU.

BY JOHN MILLER.

SECOND EDITION.

IN TWO VOLUMES.

VOL. I.

LONDON:

PRINTED FOR LONGMAN, REES, ORME, BROWN, AND GREEN,
PATERNOSTER-ROW.

1829.

E.H.
3
F

PREFACE

SECOND EDITION.

THE present edition of these Memoirs contains a considerable quantity of new and interesting matter, and the general arrangement of the work has been altogether improved. The portraits of San Martin, Bolivar, and O'Higgins, the three most conspicuous characters of the South American revolution, engraved from original paintings, have been introduced.

The Appendix has been enlarged by the insertion of several documents, in order to elucidate the operations in the Puertos Intermédios, and some others which serve to illustrate more fully the character of persons mentioned in the narrative.

Having published a Spanish edition, I think it due to my friend, the translator, to give that part of his preface which exhibits his own view of the Spanish colonial system, and although I do not concur in the opinions he advances, I cannot express my dissent from them without at the same time acknowledging, that great credit is due to him for the moderation and honourable feeling with which he has advocated the cause of his own country.

After describing the contents of this work, and
paying some compliments, which emanate rather from
the warmth of friendship than the impartiality of
criticism, General Torrijos sketches, in very handsome terms, the character of the subject of the Memoirs, and proceeds as in the annexed translation *.

THE AUTHOR.

Wingham, 1st March, 1829.

---

* The translator, General Don Jose Maria de Torrijos, was born at Madrid
in the year 1791. When ten years old he was made a page to King Charles the
Fourth.   At the age of thirteen he received a captaincy in the Ultonia, a regiment of the Irish brigade.   He prosecuted his military studies at the engineer
academy of Alcala de Henares.   In the course of the war he was appointed to
the command of Doyle's regiment of light infantry, which, in 1812, formed part
of the garrison of Badajoz, where the friendship between General Torrijos and
the subject of these memoirs commenced.   He commanded a Spanish brigade
at the battle of Vitoria, and continued attached to Lord Hill's division until
the peace of 1814.   The valour, talent, zeal, activity, and services of General
Torrijos, during the Peninsular war, are too well known to require detail.   The
liberality of his political sentiments occasioned him to be thrown into the cells
of the inquisition at Murcia, where he remained in solitary confinement from
1817 to 1820, when his prison-doors were thrown open, by the re-establishment
of the constitution.   In 1823, General Torrijos commanded in Carthagena and
Alicant, and maintained those fortresses in behalf of the constitutional government long after the absolute king had re-entered the capital.   When further
opposition had become without an object, the general obtained the most favourable conditions for his army; but, unable himself to reconcile his mind to the idea
of living under a despotic prince, he emigrated, and is now living in London, where
he is respected and esteemed by all who have the pleasure of his acquaintance.

TRANSLATION

PREFACE TO THE SPANISH EDITION.

---

*   *   *   *   *

" THE system of colonial policy by which America
was governed for three centuries has been characterized as disastrous and unjust.   But was this
system peculiar to Spain?   Did not other nations
pursue the same conduct towards their colonies?   If
one nation adopted a more moderate system towards
a portion of her colonies, was not this a consequence
of the greater degree of liberty enjoyed by that
nation?   Did unhappy Spain either enjoy this advantage, or have the means of expressing her inclinations?   Would not those who advance these revolting
accusations be better employed in censuring the
numerous acts of injustice committed by their own
governments upon their present colonial possessions?
Did the colonies established by the republics of an-
tiquity, or the nations they conquered, enjoy greater
happiness?   Do the colonies, from the Indus to
Canada, now under the European yoke, enjoy greater
happiness?   Why then should Spain be exclusively
attacked—Spain, which, ever since the discovery of
her colonies, has been, and still is, as much oppressed
by her kings, as her kings oppressed America?   De-

fective as may be her colonial laws and regulations, are they not adopted by all nations in doubtful cases? Have those islands and Spanish colonies which, in consequence of the war, have passed into the hands of other nations, gained any material advantages in their government and administration? What nation ever gave to her colonies the same means she enjoyed herself, of disseminating knowledge and promoting public instruction? What is the number of their universities, seminaries, councils, and colleges? Did not these abound in the Spanish colonies? America was placed upon a footing with Spain, and this is all that could be expected. To claim for colonies more than the mother country possesses is absurd. North America was doubtless more happy, prior to emancipation, than South America; but was not England a much happier nation than Spain? Did not the independence of these colonies cost rivers of blood? Did England treat all her dependencies alike? Does she at present so treat them? Are her colonies upon a level with the mother country? Does every part of the United Kingdom enjoy equally the advantages of her free institutions? How did republican France treat her colonies? To secure these possessions, did she scruple to immolate thousands of victims, even in the days of unlimited and tumultuous liberty? Have Holland, Genoa, and Venice, exhibited towards the countries they possessed, greater examples of philanthropy and moderation, than England, France, Spain, and Portugal?

All nations have acted with injustice towards their colonies, and continue to do so, by making their interests subservient to the commerce and advantage of the mother country.

" Spain conquered her colonies, by force of arms, at a period when morals were far less clearly defined than in the present age; when a mistaken piety sacrificed its victims without compunction; and when superstition had her altars in all countries. The state of abasement in which the natives were discovered, their manners, customs, religion, sacrifices, and mode of making war, and the doubtful origin of the first settlers, deprived these unhappy people of all consideration in the eyes of their conquerors, and their preservation or annihilation was weighed rather in the scales of utility than of justice. To pass judgment on the conquerors, or on their descendants, with reference to the principles that now govern the world, would be an act of evident injustice. Without going back to the origin of things, without giving to peculiar times and circumstances the weight they are entitled to, previous to the formation of any correct judgment, certain inconsiderate declaimers have accused, and continue to accuse, Spain and the Spaniards of acts of cruelty and barbarity, which, under the same circumstances, they would have committed themselves, and which, in all probability, they would have exceeded.

" No sooner was the dominion of Spain established in a fixed and permanent manner throughout the *extent of the two* Americas, than a complete and

well-constructed code fixed the fate of these countries. Just and salutary laws, founded on natural
rights, the essential basis of all legislation, were compiled or enacted expressly for the future government
of America: but the character of paternal solicitude,
and kingly interference, which they subsequently
assumed, either for the suppression of offences, or
the prevention of irregularities, in conjunction with
the gold which America produced, brought about an
entire change in the fortunes and institutions of unhappy Spain.

" From that moment nothing was intrusted to
individual interests; the hand of government of-
ficiously interfered with the most simple and private
acts of domestic life; and such was the indiscretion
of legislators, that laws were published regulating the
texture and dimensions of the dress of the people,
and the hour at which they were to return home in
the evening, or leave home in the morning. No one
was permitted to exercise his own will; and the
riches which America furnished, by putting it into
the power of government to multiply its agents,
brought about a real and serious oppression. This
progressive increase of oppression and of oppressors
furnished the kings of Spain with the means of
destroying the moderate or representative monarchical government, which had raised the nation
to the summit of greatness and of power, and which
had gained for it the respect of the whole world.
Supported by the clergy, and by a few bold and
venal moralists, and more especially by the detestable

inquisition, they assumed the direction of public opinion; to themselves alone was it permitted to appeal on political subjects; and these false principles being on all occasions repeated and sanctioned by the church, we receive them in our infancy with as much reverence and respect as the sacred doctrines of the consoling religion of Jesus Christ, which we happily profess.

" As America continued to furnish ample supplies of the precious metals, the only wealth at that time considered as such, our kings were able to make themselves independent of the people; they ceased to assemble the national representatives in order to demand their assistance; and succeeding generations, if by chance they ever heard of the natural rights of man, certainly knew nothing of the real enjoyment of liberty. Civil or criminal laws, promulgated upon the spur of the moment, either for America or for Spain, with an ostentatious affectation of watchfulness over, and regard for, the persons and property of their subjects, opened the road to the patriarchal system of our jurisconsults, which is absolute despotism dexterously disguised. Nevertheless, as the happiness of past times was not altogether forgotten, and as the municipal elective system had a tendency to nourish these recollections, and to create a leaning to civil liberty, our kings found it necessary to strengthen themselves by corporations, which might give an appearance of legality to their proceedings. The Council of Castile lent its support to the arm *that oppressed its* country; and the Council of the

Indies, with similar powers, honours, and attributes, performed the same office with respect to America. They became respectively the arbitrators of the fate of Spain and America, in all cases when the will or caprice of the monarch left them unmolested, and assumed all the power and authority of the former national representation. The kings were willing spectators of these usurpations, and showed even an alacrity in presiding over the corporations, as substitutes for the ancient Cortes; reserving, however, to themselves the absolute right of removing, deposing, banishing, imprisoning, or hanging, any individual member.

" Many of the early conquerors, a great proportion of the official functionaries, and not a few of those who went to seek their fortunes in America, becoming accustomed to the climate, and equally pleased with the fertility of the soil, and probably indisposed to expose themselves a second time to the dangers of a sea voyage, at a time when these dangers were more formidable than they are at present, settled in those countries; and as they multiplied, in the course of time, a generation sprung up, for whom it was necessary to find establishments of public instruction, and a liberal plan of education. The defective and vicious establishments of Spain were acordingly transplanted across the Atlantic; and the colonies, like the mother country, remained, in the seventeenth century, stationary in knowledge and intelligence. The spirit *of liberty* which the municipal system had preserved *in both hemispheres*, nourished, however, a certain

germ of independence in the public mind, which gave
the clergy more uneasiness than the government.
Under the pretext of public necessities, the kings of
Spain had sold the regiments and writerships in per-
petuity, to such purchasers as were willing to buy
them, making them transferable by sale or inherit-
ance. This measure was attended with one result
peculiarly unfortunate. It produced a number of
oligarchical governments, who opposed and made
head against the central government of the nation,
and detained it in a system of oppression and usurpation; while the clergy, under shelter of the immunity
afforded by the inquisition, daily increased their
power and influence. This body had already acquired the universal monopoly of public education,
and were masters of the fairest portion of the soil,
obtained as donations or benefactions from the kings
for the purpose of expiating their offences, and by
the system of *mandates*, or testamentary distributions
of property, wrung from parties on the point of death;
while the missions with which they enriched themselves in America rendered them so powerful, that a
despotic government began to tremble for its existence. An absolute theocracy, directed by the supreme
chief of the church, was the scheme attributed to the
Jesuits, the most powerful and the most talented of
the priestly community; those celebrated champions
who, from their station in the lists, proudly challenged whoever dared to attack them.

" The government then appealed to the people
whom it had so unadvisedly degraded, and finding

them slow in discovering their real interests, and in availing themselves of this opportunity of breaking the chains, and terminating the disgraceful thraldom, to which superstition and fanaticism had condemned them, it addressed itself to those illustrious men, who, keeping pace with the progress of knowledge, deplored, in the seclusion of their cabinets, the misfortunes and ignorance of their country. These eminent men listened to the appeal; they wrote upon all branches of the subject; and made every effort in their power to enlighten and to direct public opinion. But though indirectly supported and encouraged by the court, the first who ventured on the arena fell victims to the power of that atrocious arm which sacrificed every thing to its own aggrandizement. Nevertheless a ray of light began to inspire hope and courage; several renowned patriots redoubled their attacks; and at last the government became a party in the strife; decreed the expulsion of the Jesuits; facilitated the means of elemental instruction by laymen; and, as if by enchantment, the enormous body of theocratical preachers retired to their cloisters and catacombs.

" The trammels of superstition being broken, and the inquisition without power and almost nominal, the people enjoyed their triumph; and, with the powerful arms of sarcasm and ridicule, followed up their victory over their enemies, who were afraid to show signs of life, while the government gradually *stripped* them of their ill-gotten wealth. The *opinions and principles* that triumphed in France spread

rapidly in Spain, usefully and judiciously modified by
the good sense of the Spanish people, who demanded
the re-enactment of the ancient Spanish laws, and the
reform of the abuses which had been introduced in
their place: but the government, who were not more
favourable to national liberty than to the preponderance of the clergy, hesitated as to the course they
should adopt; and thus, by their weakness, infused
spirits into both parties, and by their immorality and
bad administration furnished the most plausible pretexts for an attack from each. Detested by the
people, struggling with a thousand privations, which
the general dilapidation had occasioned, and weakened by internal divisions and dissensions, they presented a spectacle of absolute impotence. The per-
fidious invasion of the French caused it to disappear
in the act; but offended national pride called every
Spaniard to arms, and the early efforts of the patriots
were crowned with successes which presaged a happy
termination to so many sacrifices. The clergy then
began to consider that the circumstances of the times
presented a tempting opportunity for regaining their
lost power and influence. They accordingly re-echoed
the national cry, and invoked the names of Ferdinand
and the country, in the base hope of oppressing the
nation and the government. It is owing to this circumstance that foreigners frequently attribute to
fanaticism the glorious struggle undertaken by the
Spaniards for the noblest of causes, which they conducted with so much valour, and which they concluded *so victoriously*; without considering that the

people spontaneously commenced this struggle, stimulated by no motive but offended honour, and that
they continued it solely for the purpose of avenging
their wrongs, of rescuing their monarch, from whom,
after so many solemn promises, they expected a very
different return from that with which he has requited
their services, and of destroying for ever the arbitrary
government which had ruined the nation.

"The clergy soon perceived the new turn that
opinions had taken, and, unable successfully to make
head against it, they withdrew, as a body, their influence and power; and although they did not dare
to co-operate in the views of Napoleon, which me-
naced their interests with so much danger, they
began to conspire against the national government,
which must have terminated with the undue influence it had exercised in civil matters, and with
the abuses with which it had become enriched.   At
this period many worthy and respectable ecclesiastics
separated themselves from the common mass, and,
devoting themselves to the cause of the country,
rendered the most efficient services to the popular
party, and have since distinguished themselves by a
noble disinterestedness in defence of the rights and
liberties of the people.   A great many of them, and
among the number several bishops, have incurred
persecutions, and been obliged to emigrate from their
country; and not a few still groan in the dungeons
with which Ferdinand and his prevaricating satellites
have recompensed their virtues.

"*Spanish America* naturally followed in the steps

of the mother country, with the sole difference, that to the evils common to both countries, was added the greater frequency of local abuses practised by subordinate agents, to whom distance from the seat of government gave encouragement to practices which probably would not have been ventured upon in Spain. Upon the whole, it may be doubted whether the enlightened despotism exercised by the viceroys in America was not, in many instances, of a less oppressive and degrading character than that exercised in Spain by some of her profligate kings, and not unfrequently by ministers and favourites. Be this as it may, one could hardly expect to find in the colonies of a nation enslaved and oppressed either by fanaticism, or by the absolute power of her kings, either good government, or justice, or liberty. America was prohibited from cultivating the natural productions of Spain, and the same barbarous and tyrannical policy forbad Spain to naturalize in her soil the productions of America. In conformity with the colonial system which has been adopted, and which is still acted upon, by all nations towards their colonies, America could trade only with Spain; but the Spanish government, adhering to its restrictive and monopolizing system, confined the trade with America to a few privateers, at first from Seville, under the control of the government, subsequently from Cadiz, and ultimately from a few other ports. Venal and arbitrary as were many of the government agents who went to America, had those who were appointed at home either more honesty or more moderation? What could be expected from a government so demoralized and corrupt? America and Spain, at one and the same period, were exposed to the same calamities; and one caused the ruin of the other. The former, by supplying the precious metals, furnished the arms which despotism needed for oppressing the latter, by means of innumerable agents paid with this wealth, and deprived herself of her youth, who rarely returned to their native country, for the purpose of maintaining slavery in her colonies.

" America, however, has gained during this period the knowledge of the Christian religion, which, independently of its holiness and truth, has full reason to be considered as an inestimable benefit, for the precepts of pure morality which it inculcates. Her real and relative progress in civilization has been infinitely more rapid; and her population, if we include the Indians still in a state of freedom, cannot be much, if at all, diminished. Her agricultural wealth, the only real wealth, has been very considerably increased; her sons, notwithstanding the recent date of their emancipation, have gained the respect of the people of all countries; and illustrious men in all departments, and eminent writers in verse and prose, have conferred honour on America by their works. Spain, in the meanwhile, has fallen from her station among the nations; she has lost her liberal institutions; she has groaned for the space of three centuries, and she still groans, under the weight of a cruel and vindictive despotism. Her population has been reduced one half; her agricultural wealth, her commerce, and industry, are almost nothing, compared to what they were when she conquered America; and her progress in civilization, compared to that of other nations of Europe, has been such that, instead of being ranked among the foremost, she must at present be numbered with those most in arrear. America did not discover that the fault was attributable to these misfortunes of Spain: nor did Spain discover that they resulted from those which America suffered. Both were the victims of the Spanish government which oppressed them, and both sought an opportunity of breaking their chains.

"The invasion of the Peninsula exhibited the force of the national character in both hemispheres; all unanimously cried out for liberty; the sacred names of country, independence, civil and political liberty, resounded on all sides; and the freedom of the press was a common privilege. The rulers of the nation, accustomed to passive obedience from the people, conceived they would submit with perfect indifference to a change of dynasty; and, obliged to decide immediately on the line of conduct to be pursued, they yielded to what they considered the force of circumstances: but a new change of affairs occurring with the general rising of the people against the foreign yoke, they found themselves compromised, many of them in spite of themselves. This circumstance will explain the equivocal or treacherous conduct

pursued by many of the authorities both in America
and Spain, and which has given rise to many erro-
neous conclusions, drawn, as this has been, from false
and incorrect premises. The people trampled upon
every thing; they created provincial juntas which
governed them, and, without knowing it, dissolved
the monarchy. To create it afresh, they established
a central government, composed of two members of
each particular junta; and this assembly, uniting the
parties into which the state was divided, assumed
the direction of affairs; and thus the progress of
dissolution, if not completely arrested, was at least
rendered imperceptible. In America, juntas were
formed on the same footing, and from the same
causes as in Spain, and the division of these states
was also carried into effect; but, as it was not possible that these juntas should be united among themselves, as was the case in the mother country, and as
the central government there thought only of the
best means of obtaining resources from those vast
and rich countries, in order to meet the expenses of
the war, which, for want of systematic management,
amounted to immense sums, the original germ always
existed; it was even acquiring growth and vigour;
and men of intelligence and zeal for their country's
welfare beheld the opportunity they had so long
anxiously desired, and began to labour for its emancipation. The disasters of the campaigns of 1809
and 1810, which endangered the very existence of
Spanish independence, brought great odium upon

the central or federated government that directed them. They finally resigned their functions, and appointed a regency as their substitute, with an express injunction to convoke the Cortes of the kingdom, fixing the bases of the election of deputies on the grounds that the ancient forms were defective and impracticable. America saw the possibility that Spain would succumb; and public enthusiasm provided the means of avoiding a similar fate, and of prolonging resistance in those countries, without considering that this resistance would lead to a separation from the mother country. The public functionaries in America perceived it, and, mistaking causes and names, they characterized as the spirit of faction what was, in fact, dignity; they alarmed the Spanish government, which unadvisedly permitted itself to be drawn aside; and a spirit of division and animosity, which had never before existed, began to exhibit itself very plainly. The government, which, on its part, had made every exertion in its power to repel the French invasion, if sometimes it took into its calculations the possibility of being defeated, adopted measures for subjecting America to the same fate as it had done before to the Canaries, Cuba, &c. &c.; so that, although Spain should undergo a change of dynasty, she should not lose any of her possessions. To measures projected by men without popularity, who formed a weak government, measures which apparently were calculated to injure the cause they sought to defend, it was easy *for the American* patriots to offer the strongest

opposition; to win over the multitude to favour their
designs; and, invoking the name of Ferdinand, to
make themselves independent.

" The Spanish people, on their part, who, after
so many sacrifices, saw the inquisition, though in-
active, still in existence, and found that former governments, after pronouncing anathemas against the
arbitrary character of the ancient administration, had
not broken the chain of abuses on which it was
founded, but, on many occasions, had availed themselves of it, petitioned publicly and unanimously for
fixed, written, and permanent laws, which might
afford them protection against the persecutions of a
capricious monarch, or of a profligate minister, and
against the avarice and rapacity of the agents of despotism. The deputies elected for the Cortes listened
to the voice of the public, declared themselves constituent assemblies, and, compiling the sacred laws,
which for three centuries had been neglected, they
united in one code the rights and privileges inherent
in man, as they had been enjoyed by our ancestors
in the past times of our national prosperity.

" This code contained the virtual independence
of America, since taking the general population for
its basis, and allowing one deputy to Cortes for every
seventy thousand souls; while the population of America exceeded that of Spain by about one half, it is
clear that the measures discussed must always have
had a favourable leaning towards America. To avoid
this inconvenience, it is more than probable that the
plan resorted to would have been the formation of

Cortes, or national assemblies, in various central parts of America, which might thus have governed itself, as did North America previous to its emancipation, and would have learned to sustain and direct itself, and would have consolidated its liberty, prior to declaring itself independent, with the same facility that the latter did so, without passing through the turbulent and bloody scenes which it has finally been doomed to undergo. But America could not confide to the chance of the continuation of the constitutional system the great work she had undertaken, nor leave it in the power of government, on the termination of the war, to direct against her all its power and all its influence, increased by a presentiment of the restoration, and sufferings, of Ferdinand. Buenos Ayres, who had openly manifested her intentions, proceeded fearlessly in her career; declared the regency and the Cortes void, and, consequently, the constitution; and never ceased to implore the provinces to follow her example, offering them the aid of her military force, together with her immediate and effective co-operation.

" Ferdinand returned; but instead of consolidating the national happiness, in return for the costly sacrifices that had been made for him; instead of declaring himself the father of his people, and complying with the solemn promises he had made to the nation when he gained possession of the throne by the revolt of Aranjuez, he annulled the code which secured the liberties of the people; but in order not to outrage public opinion, he offered to

assemble cortes, to study the national happiness, and
promised not to be absolute.   Instead of complying
with these solemn promises, he broke his word as a
prince, his faith as a man of honour, and threw himself into the hands of the priests, who up to that
period had been lying in wait, secretly conspiring
against the government and national institutions;
becoming the agent of his own vindictive passions,
he persecuted those who had best served their country in his absence, and who had most efficaciously
exerted themselves to restore him to his throne.

 " Not content with carrying on these persecutions
in Spain, and instead of sending emissaries to the different provinces of America, for the paternal purpose
of terminating the dissensions there, he was hurried
away by the persuasions of the barbarous and sanguinary fanatics who surrounded him, and immediately
despatched an expedition, dragging from the bosom
of their families thousands of individuals who had
voluntarily taken up arms to serve during the war
with France, and who, on the restoration of peace,
obtained by their blood, hoped, at least, to be permitted to remain in the enjoyment of those domestic
pleasures which they had so patriotically given up
on the national summons, and, by the advice of the
sanguinary Eguia, and of the profligate Ostolaza,
intrusted the command to the atrocious Morillo.

 " About six years succeeded of despotism, of victims, and of persecutions in Spain; and of despotism,
victims, persecutions, and a desolating war in America.   The dawn of liberty beamed again in Spain

on the proclamation of the constitution, on the 1st
of January, 1820, the seasonable fruit of so many
unsuccessful attempts; and hereupon the liberal government renounced the expeditions proposed by the
absolute government, then ready to set sail, and a
general armistice followed, in America, the news of
the liberty of Spain.   Her representatives agreed to
send special commissioners 'to proceed to the different governments established in the two Spanish
Americas, to hear and receive all proposals that
might be made for transmission to the mother country, with the exception of such as might go to deprive the European and American Spaniards residing
in any part of the provinces beyond sea of the absolute liberty of transferring and disposing of their
persons, families, and property, in the manner that
may seem best to them, without being exposed to
any impediment or any measure that may be in-
jurious to their fortunes.   2. The commissioners
shall remain there till replies are furnished, &c. &c.'
If a delicacy, perhaps excessive, in saving the honour
of the Spanish name made them more tardy than
might have been desirable and just, for the purpose
of immediately suspending the effects of that disastrous war, at all events this step displayed, in some
degree, the sentiments of the Spanish nation.   The
first national representation pronounced that the
Americans possessed equal rights with the natives
of Spain.   The second, finding those countries
struggling for their independence, offered to treat
with them, admitting that independence as the basis

of the negotiation; and the third made manifest to a powerful nation their desire of mediation as to the form and manner of the recognition of the independence for which they were struggling. Can Spain, as a nation, be accused of cruelty and oppression towards her colonies? Can it justly be imputed to the liberal party that they opposed American independence, sacrificing to ignorant prejudices the most valuable interests of America and of Spain? How much time was sacrificed, and how much blood wasted, before nations, more advanced in civilization, and better governed, would renounce possession of their colonies, which had not merely proclaimed themselves independent, but which, in fact, were so! The only three Spanish legislatures who were enabled to express the national opinion, did they not differ from the tyrants who had oppressed Spain and America? What has been the past and present conduct of Ferdinand? Repeated expeditions have occasioned an accumulation of force in the islands of Cuba and the Canaries, which continually threatening to disembark, keeps the new states in continual alarm, nourishing that discontent which, in sudden changes of government, is the natural consequence of the change of fortune of individuals who live by abuses; and it is more than probable, that ultimately the troops will disembark, and light up the flames of civil war in those republics, sacrificing to its senseless fury more victims of both hemispheres.

   " What would have happened if liberty had continued to exert her beneficial effects in Spain? What would happen if she should be again restored to her after so many misfortunes? The recognition of American independence is inseparable from the second hypothesis upon a basis liberal, just, and mutually agreed upon; the relations of friendship and consanguinity would assume their ancient force; we should unite with the cordiality to be expected from the natural ties that subsist between us—identity of language, manners, customs, tastes, and even vices; and a free communication and profitable exchange of our mutual superfluities, would raise from insignificance our commerce and mercantile marine to the rank and importance which nature has so benignantly assigned it. If this be as certain as facts themselves prove it; if absolutism in Spain is the obstacle to the happiness and tranquillity of America, and the prosperity and felicity of Spain, why do they not unite to destroy this edifice, ensanguined with the blood of so many victims, and so inconsistent with the light and intelligence of the age in which we live? Can nothing better be done than to bestow names and titles which are not more suitable to one country than the other? What greater right has a Fernandez, a Cordova, a Rodriguez, an Alvarado, &c. &c. born in Spain, to the descent by right or indirect line, from Atalfo, Witiza, or Rodrigo, than a Fernandez, a Cordova, a Rodriguez, an Alvarado, &c. &c. born in America?

" It may have been politic, and even just, during the sanguinary contest which the Americans have conducted with so much glory, that the storehouses of memory should have been opened, and that to in-

flame the ignorant vulgar, who always require the
stimulus of great excitement, a tissue of horrible
accusations should have been brought forward, the
repetition of which might make them fly indignantly
to arms.   But when the war is concluded; when
reason, justice, and sound policy, demand a contrary
proceeding, why perpetuate animosities which cannot
fail of disturbing the good understanding, and cooling
the sympathy which ought to reign between the two
countries?   Should not the Americans recollect that
their fathers, grandfathers, or ancestors, were Spaniards, and that these accusations reflect upon the
memory of those whom they ought to regard with
respect and veneration?   Who were the perpetrators
of the crimes which with so little forbearance they
descant upon—if really these crimes were committed
at all?   If, indeed, very few Americans have occupied
the first places in the civil magistracy in America,
and very few American officers have been commanders
there, how many ministers of state, presidents of colleges, captains general of the provinces and departments of marine, inspectors, viceroys, governors, &c.
have there not been in Spain, and still are to be found
there, who were Americans?   The circumstance of
being an American, does it unfortunately act as a bar
to distinction in Spain?   No—quite the contrary; the
natural vivacity and gentleness of character and manners of the American gain him a ready admission
into society, and open the road to success in whatever
pursuit he may embark.

   " The American most fanatically prejudiced against

Spain will be unable to deny these truths, but must acknowledge the justice of my observations.   Let him call to mind the hospitality and cordial welcome which the Spaniards gave him in Spain; and following the impulse of the heart, and not that of a mistaken policy, let him fix his eye upon the fate of the country of his descent, of his parents and friends; let him extend to it a protecting hand; let him calculate well his own interest in doing so; and let him add to the glory of having won with his sword his own freedom and independence, that of having aided his brothers in making themselves free and independent.

" It is my hope, that the rancorous spirit which civil war has always and everywhere excited, may not be of long duration between Spain and America; and that although previous habits and prejudices may preserve for some time a tendency towards vehement and unfounded accusations, reason will triumph in the end, and both countries will do each other justice. In the mean time, it is most desirable that those Spaniards who do not consider the Americans as re-bellious children, but as patriots who have done that which, under similar circumstances, they themselves would have done; and those Americans who do not look upon the Spaniards as their oppressors, but as victims of the same abuses and of the same govern-ment; should give all their attention to the best means of establishing among themselves, upon the most solid foundation, and with as little delay as possible, that good understanding, which is so con-sistent with good policy, and so essential for pre-

paring the public mind for the oblivion of past misfortunes and ancient disagreements.   In family dissensions there should be a generous forbearance of
offence, and honour and glory should be given to him
who first extends the hand and proffers a sincere reconciliation.   The practical example furnished by the
United States of the greater advantage they afford
the mother country now, than they did as colonies,
should sufficiently convince every Spaniard of the
expediency of co-operating in the establishment of
peace and harmony between Spaniards and Americans; and the Americans should consider the benefits resulting under the same circumstances to
the United States, and the substantial power and
happiness produced within a few years, by the wise
policy which England ultimately adopted towards
them.   While all true statesmen, on each side of
the Atlantic, rejoice in the mutual advantages they
shall have obtained, the philosophic observer will be
cheered with the thought, that the New World, by
means of peace, will acquire, in a short time, that
stability and intelligence which constitute power,
and perpetuate the honour of nations and of the
human race."

End of the Spanish translator's preface.

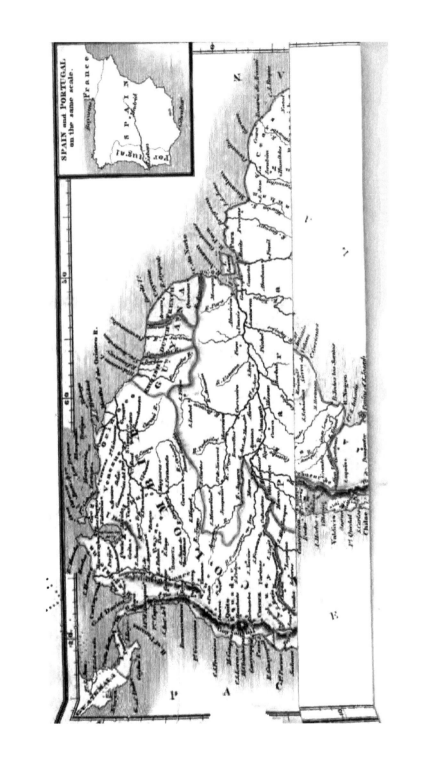

SPAIN and PORTUGAL
on the same scale.

INTRODUCTION.

I HAVE compiled the following work chiefly from the private letters, journals, and recollections of my brother, General Miller, who has been upwards of ten years in the service of South America. These furnish ample materials for an account of the war of independence in the provinces of the Rio de la Plata, Chile, and Peru; and contain numerous remarks and observations on those extensive countries, with incidents and anecdotes illustrative of the character, manners, and customs of the people.

As the geography, and recent political divisions, of the new American states are far from being familiar to the generality of European readers, I have given a concise outline of them, together with an estimate of the population. A glance at the general map, and a reference to the statistical tables, will give a tolerably correct idea of the boundaries and population of the countries treated of. An outline of the map of Spain and Portugal, upon precisely the same scale as the general map, is given, in order to show the insignificance, in territorial extent, of those kingdoms, as compared with the vast regions over which they so long exercised a most baneful dominion. The maps and plans have been executed by Mr. Arrowsmith, who has taken the utmost pains to give them the greatest possible accuracy.

The first chapter contains a brief summary of the Spanish colonial system, drawn from sources of unquestionable authenticity, and corroborated by personal observation. To this succeeds a rapid survey of the effects of such a system, exhibiting the proximate causes of the great political changes that have elevated those former colonies of Spain to the rank of independent nations.

One of the principal objects of the work is to paint in true colours the merit, the valour, the constancy, and the natural benevolence, of the Peruvian, Chileno, and Argentine peasantry and soldiery, who possess these good qualities in spite of the many vices resulting from Spanish contagion and misrule.

To award praise or attach blame justly is a delicate and invidious, if not a dangerous, task. Most of the distinguished actors in the scenes described in the following pages are now living, and some of them in the enjoyment of high civil offices, or important military commands. When any such have received commendation, it is probable they will consider it to have been bestowed much too sparingly. When, on the contrary, any of their actions have been censured, feelings of no friendly nature will, no doubt, be abundantly stirred up. General Miller has no disappointment to complain of: he has received every step of promotion, and every honour that has been conferred upon him, without solicitation, either direct or indirect; and, therefore, there can be no motive for misrepresentation.

It is a source of unfeigned regret, that it has been found impossible to record the services, or even the names, of hundreds of individuals, to whose important aid, in very critical circumstances, General Miller was deeply indebted. Arequipa alone would furnish a long list of names that would do honour to this work.

In the construction of the first four chapters, the " NOTICIAS SECRETAS," of Ulloa, edited by Mr. Barry; "THE LIFE OF DR. MORENO," by his brother; and " THE OUTLINE OF THE REVOLUTION IN SPANISH AMERICA, by a South American" (Dr. Palacios), have been consulted. The long list of patriots murdered without trial, and in violation of solemn capitulations or amnesties, by order of General Morillo, is taken from an interesting pamphlet, entitled " AN APPEAL TO THE BRITISH NATION ON THE AFFAIRS OF SOUTH AMERICA," by Colonel Maceroni. The list was extracted from official documents at Madrid.

I am indebted to Señor Don José Miguel

de la Barra, consul-general for Chile, residing in London, for some interesting data relative to the revolution in his own country. My acknowledgments are equally due to other friends, particularly to Mr. Thomas Williams, formerly secretary of legation to the Colombian embassy, and to Señor Don Vicente Pazos Kanki, a lineal descendant of one of the ancient Peruvian caciques. From this gentleman many curious and interesting particulars, which could not be gleaned in an active military career, have been obtained. I, myself, have travelled in Peru from Payta to Arequipa; crossed the isthmus of Panama; ascended the Orinoco to Angostura; traversed the continent, from Valparaiso to Buenos Ayres; and spent some time at Rio Janeiro and other parts of the Brazils. Having travelled in a neutral capacity, unconnected with military or mercantile pursuits, my account may be thought to have some claim to the merit of impartiality.

THE AUTHOR.

4, *Grove End Place, St. John's Wood.*
    1st September, 1828.

THE NEW GOVERNMENTS OF AMERICA ARE,

		Population.
1. THE REPUBLIC OF THE UNITED PROVINCES OF Río de la Pláta	. . . .	600,000
2. REPUBLIC OF CHÍLE	. . . .	1,200,000
3. REPUBLIC OF PERÚ	. . .	1,736,923
4. DICTATORSHIP OF PARAGÜAY	. .	500,000
5. REPUBLIC OF BOLÍVIA .	. . .	1,200,000
6. REPUBLIC OF COLÓMBIA	. . .	2,711,296
7. REPUBLIC OF MÉXICO .	. .	8,000,000
8. REPUBLIC OF CENTRAL AMÉRICA .	. .	1,700,000
9. EMPIRE OF BRAZÍL	. . .	4,000,000
		21,648,219

TERRITORIAL DIVISIONS.

Provinces.

ARGENTINE REPUBLIC
or
UNITED PROVINCES OF
THE RIO DE LA PLATA

- Buénos Ayres
- Córdova
- Corríentes
- Catamárca
- Mendóza, or Cuyo
- Misiones
- Monte Vidéo, or Banda Oriental
- Riója
- Salta
- Santiágo del Estéro
- Santa Fé
- San Juan
- San Luis
- Tucumán
- Taríja

Capital, BUENOS AYRES.
Inhabitants, 100,000.

Provinces.

CHILE . . . {
Coquímbo
Aconcágua
Santiágo
Colchágua
Măule
Concepcíon
Valdívia
Chilóe

Capital, SANTIAGO.
Inhabitants, 40,000.

Arăuco (the finest part of Chíle, occupied by unsubdued Indians) is not included in this calculation.

Departments.	*Provinces.*
	Cercádo
	Cánta
	Cañéte
LÍMA . . .	Chancăy
	Ica
	Sánta
	Huarochirí
	Yaúyos
	Cajamárca
	Chachapóyas
	Chóta
	Huamachuco
PERU . . TRUXÍLLO . .	Jáen
	Lambayéque
	Măynas
	Patás
	Piúra
	Huánuco
	Huāylas
JUNÍN . . .	Xáuxa
	Pásco
	Huamalíes
	Conchúcos

Departments.	Provinces.
Junín	Huári Cajatámbo Tárma
Púno	Lámpa Azángaro Caraváya Chucuíto Guancaní
Arequípa	Cercádo Moquégua Aríca Tarapacá Condesúyos Cayllóma Camaná
Ayacúcho	Anco Andagüailas Cangállo Guamánga Huancavelíca Guánta Lucánas Tayacája Castroviréyna Parinacóchas
Cúzco	Cercádo Abancáy Aymaräes Cálca Chumbivílcas Cotabámbas Parúro Paucartámbo Quispicánchi Tínta Urubámba

PERU

POPULATION
- Whites - - - - 240,819
- Indians - - - - 998,846
- Meztizos - - - - 383,782
- Free Mulatos - - - 69,848
- Slaves - - - - 43,628

Total 1,736,923

Capital, LIMA.
Inhabitants, 70,000.

Departments.	Provinces.
CHÁRCAS	Zinti
	Yamparães
	Tomína
	Pária
	Orúro
	Carángas
POTOSÍ	Atacáma
	Lípes
	Pórco
	Chayánta
	Chíchas
LA PAZ	Pacájes
	Síca-Síca
	Chulumáni
	Omasúyos
	Larecája
	Apolobámba
COCHABÁMBA	Sacába
	Tapacarí
	Arque
	Pálca
	Clissa
	Mízque
SANTA CRUZ DE LA SIERRA,	Mójos
	Chiquítos
	Válle Gránde
	Pámpas
	Baüres

UPPER PERU or BOLIVIA

Capital, CHUQUISACA.
Inhabitants, 18,000.

PARAGUAY.

Capital, ASUMPCION.

	Departments.	Provinces.
	ORINÓCO	Cumaná Barcelóna Margaríta Guayána
	VENEZŬELA	Carácas Carabóbo
	APURE	Varínas Apúre
	ZÚLIA	Maracăibo Córo Mérida Truxíllo
COLOMBIA	BOYACÁ	Túnja Pamplóna Socórro Casanáre
	CUNDINAMÁRCA	Bogotá Antióquia Maríquíta Neíva
	MAGDALÉNA	Cartagéna Santa Márta Rio de la Hácha
	CAUCA	Popayán Chocó Pásto Buena Ventúra
	ISTMO	Panamá Verágua

	Departments.	Provinces.
COLOMBIA	EQUADÓR	{ Pinchíncha Imbubúra Chimborázo
	ASSUAY	{ Cuénca Lója Jáen Máynas
	GUAYAQUÍL	{ Guayaquíl Manalí

Capital, Bogotá.
Inhabitants, 60,000.

Federal States.

MEXICO	{ Chiápa Chihuahua Coahuila and Téjas Durángo Guanajŭato México Michoacán, or Valladolíd Nuevo-Leon Oajáca Puebla de los Angeles Querétaro San Luis de Potosí Sonóra and Sinaloa Tabásco Tamaulipas Vera-Cruz Xalísco (formerly Guadalajara) Yucatán Zacatécas Territories of Upper and Lower Califórnia Tlascála Colima Santa Fé de Nuevo Mexíco

Capital, MEXICO.
Inhabitants, 170,000.

Federal States.

CENTRAL AMERICA . . {
Guatemála
San Salvadór
Hondúras
Nicarágua
Costa Ríca

Capital, GUATEMALA.

Inhabitants, 36 or 40,000.

Provinces.

BRAZIL . . . . . {
San Pédro
Santa Catalina
San Pablo
Rio Janeiro
Espiritu Santo
Bahía
Sergype
Alagóas
Pernambúco
Minas Geráes
Goyáz
Mata-Grósso
Paraíba
Rio Grande
Ceará
Riaühy
Maranham
Pará

Capital, RIO JANEIRO.

Inhabitants, 200,000.

GLOSSARY.

Alcálde, mayor or municipal officer.

Anden, a terrace.

Andenes, plural of Anden.

Arequipeñas, feminine of Arequipeños.

Arequipeños, inhabitants of Arequipa.

Argentine, appertaining to the river Plata, or its provinces.

Argentínos, inhabitants of the provinces of El Rio de la Plata.

Arróyo, a rivulet.

Asiénto, station.

Asoguéros, mine proprietors.

Audiéncia, court of justice.

Bálsas, a raft, or float.

Bólas, a sort of sling with three balls.

Boliviáno, belonging to Bolivia.

Bombílla, a little tube to suck mäté.

Cabíldo, corporation, or municipal body.

Cacíca, wife or daughter of a cacique.

Cacíque, Indian chief.

Caléta, a creek, or cove, or inlet.

Camótes, a tropical vegetable, a sort of sweet potato.

Cavalládas, drove, or stock of horses, mules, &c.

Cazadóres à caballo, light dragoons.

Cazadóres, light infantry.

Cercádo, environs.

Chásqui, a messenger.

Chiléna, feminine of Chileno.

Chiléno, Chilian.

Chóla, feminine of Cholo.

Chólo, a Chileno or Peruvian peasant of mixed blood.

Contrabandísta, smuggler.

Cordilléra, the great ridges of the Andes.

Corrál, cattle-pen.

Cuésta, a mountain side.

Cúra, the priest of a parish.

Custódia, a casket for the consecrated wafer.

Cuyános, inhabitants of the province of Cuyo.

Cuzquéña, feminine of Cuzqueño.

Cuzquéños, inhabitants of Cuzco.

Desaguadéro, outlet of lake Titicáca, forming a large river, which loses itself in the desert.

Desplobládo, unpeopled tract.

Doctór, a collegial title in theology, jurisprudence, medicine, &c. sometimes *satirically* applied to those learned quacks who veer about with every political breeze.

Estáncia, grazing farm.

Estanciéro, grazier.

Fiscál, legal adviser, or attorney-general.

Garúa, heavy mists prevalent on the coast of Peru.

Gáuchos, peasantry of the Pampas.

Granadéros à cabállo, heavy dragoons.

Grémio, a trading company.

Guáca, Indian burial-place.

Guanáco, animal peculiar to the Andes.

Guápo, brave, daring.

Guásos, peasantry of Chile.

Hacendádo, a landed proprietor.

Haciénda, an estate.

Iqueños, inhabitants of Ica.

Júnta Gubernatíva, governing council.

Limeña, feminine of Limeño.

Limeño, native of Líma.

Llanéros, inhabitants of the plains of Colombia.

Lómas, downs, or hills.

Matadór, bull-killer.

Măté, infusion of Paraguay herb.

Mendocíno, a native of Mendoza.

Meztízos, mixed casts.

Minístro, a board officer.

Míta, conscription of Indians.

Mitáyo, conscript for the mines.

Montonéros, guerrillas of South America.

Obráge, bridewell, or public workhouse.

Oidór, a judge.

Ojótas, sandals.

Orientál, an inhabitant of the Banda Oriental.

Pampéro, south-west wind, or hurricane of the Pampas.

Peón, out-of-door workman, or attendant.

Piña, pure silver ore.

Pláza, the square which forms the centre of every city, town, and village of Spanish America.

Plazuéla, small square.

Presidénte Vitalício, president chosen for life.

Púna, difficulty of respiration.

Quebráda, a ravine.
Quíchua, language of the ancient Peruvians.

Reál, a Spanish coin of the value of sixpence.
Regidór, a municipal officer.
Réqua, drove, or string of mules.

Sierra, the hills or mountainous districts.
Socabón, adit.

U'sares, hussars.

Vára, a measure somewhat shorter than the English yard.
Véta, lode.
Vitalício, for life.

Xerínga, a surgical instrument.

Yaraví, a plaintive air.

CONTENTS

OF

VOL. I.

CHAPTER I.

CHAPTER II.

CHAPTER III.

CHAPTER IV.

CHAPTER V.

CHAPTER VI.

CHAPTER VII.

CHAPTER VIII.

CHAPTER IX.

CHAPTER X.

CHAPTER XI.

CHAPTER XII.

CHAPTER XIII.

CHAPTER XIV.

CHAPTER XV.

CHAPTER XVI.

APPENDIX.

ERRATA.

Page 59, line 27, *dele* General Elio.
    63, —   1, — Elio.
    320, — 15, *for* being at, *read* on the opposite side of the river.
    ib. — 16, — from the spot, *read* distant.
    326, — 11, — eastern, *read* southern.
    416, head line, *for* Pinchincha, *read* Ica.

MEMOIRS,

&c.

CHAPTER I.

Spanish colonial system.—Tyranny of Spaniards over the aborigines.—Despotism of Spaniards over their own descendants.—
Mita.—Repartimiento.—Obrages.—Tribute.—Ecclesiastical
avarice.—Tupac Amaru; his barbarous execution.—Council
of the Indies.—Prohibitory laws.—Traits of character honourable to Spaniards.

THE unjust and desolating line of policy adopted
by Spain, during three centuries of domination over
her American possessions, may be comprehended
under two heads.

1st. *The tyranny exercised over the aborigines.*

2nd. *The despotism of Spaniards over their own
descendants.*

It is scarcely necessary to assert in this place, because the fact will be admitted by those who take the
trouble to investigate the subject, that not only the
riches derived from Spanish America, but the very
means of subsistence enjoyed by its inhabitants, have
all along been procured by the personal toils of
the aborigines, assisted, it is true, in some of their
laborious tasks, by slaves imported from Africa. But
the latter were too valuable to be expended in the
mines.

as a virtual sentence of death. He carried with him to that dreary abode his wife and children, and made the necessary disposition to provide for the contingency of never again returning. Nor were these forebodings groundless, for, under the most favourable circumstances, scarcely one out of five of these devoted victims survived this odious and most oppressive conscription.

The *mitayo*, or labourer in the mines, received nominally four reales, or about two shillings, a day, which was one half of the wages of the ordinary day-labourer in the fields. Out of this sum, two thirds were supposed to be paid to him; but as this amount did not suffice to meet the expenses of his miserable diet and lodging, which were furnished by the mine proprietor at a most extravagant rate, together with the eight dollars of tribute for which his master was responsible, he found himself, if he outlived the year, still indebted to his employer: in this case he was not allowed to discontinue from work until all arrears were paid. Thus each succeeding year found him more and more deeply involved, and thus was another link added to the galling chain by which he was fettered to his destiny. It generally happened, however, that, before the expiration of the first year, he was released by a welcome death. Languishing under the baneful effects of the transition from the genial air and exercise of his native mountains, to noxious exhalations and exhausting labours; worn out with fatigue, grief, and disease, the wretched mitayo in a few months yielded to his fate, and found a refuge in the grave.

The third part of his wages, which had been reserved to defray the expenses of the return of his
family to their native home, was appropriated to that
purpose.   More than twelve thousand Indians were
annually subject to the mita conscription in Potosi
alone.   It is computed that eight millions two hundred and eighty-five thousand Indians thus perished
in the mines of Peru *.

* The extermination of the aborigines in other parts of America colonized
by Spaniards or Portuguese was even more effectually accomplished.   It is
computed that the Brazilians destroyed in the hostile excursions against the
Spanish possessions of Paraguay and the provinces of the river Plata upwards
of four hundred towns and villages.   These marauders, born of Portuguese,
Dutch, French, and Italians, by Brazilian women, were called *Mamelucos.*
The object of their incursions was to carry off the Guarany and other Indians,
whom the Jesuits had succeeded in converting.   The captives were led to
Brazil, chained or corded in herds like cattle, and there condemned to perpetual
labour.   Infants were torn from the bosoms of their mothers, and cruelly
dashed upon the ground on the way.   Those whom disease or age had rendered
imbecile were either cut down or shot, as being unequal to the daily march.
Many perished from hunger and thirst.   It is asserted (*Lettres Curieuses et
Edifiantes*) that, in the space of one hundred and thirty years, two millions of
Indians were slain or carried into captivity by the *Mamelucos* of Brazil, and
that more than one thousand leagues of country, as far as the river Amazon,
was stripped of inhabitants.   It appears from authentic letters (sent by the
catholic king in the year 1609, September 16) that, in five years, three hundred
thousand Indians of Paraguay were carried into Brazil.   Pedro de Avila, governor of Buenos Ayres, declared that Indians were openly sold in his sight at
Rio Janeiro by the inhabitants of the town of St. Paul; and that six hundred
thousand were so sold at Rio Janeiro alone, from the year 1628 to the year
1630.
     It does not appear that the acts of the *Mamelucos* were authorized.   His
most faithful majesty, Joseph I., confesses, in a decree issued on the 6th of
July, 1755, and inserted in the new code of Portuguese laws, that many millions of Indians were destroyed, and that very few Indian towns remained, and
equally few inhabitants.   He adds, that this was occasioned by the enemies of
their liberty, contrary to the laws of Portugal.   He declares the Indians free,
and orders captives to be set at liberty; and likewise other pious kings of Spain
and Portugal, his predecessors, prohibited all robbery, sale, oppression, and
persecution of the Indians whatsoever, under the same penalties, by repeated
laws.   But these decrees were seldom or never observed, and governors and
other persons who profited from the captivity and sale of the Indians had become too hard-hearted to listen to the feelings of humanity.   The barbarity of
those men towards the Indians was pourtrayed in lively and faithful colours by
the jesuit father Antonio Vieyra, who preached on the subject at the court of
Lisbon in 1662.   For attempting to protect the poor Indians in the province
of Maranham, he had been banished from Brazil.   The royal laws and decrees
in favour of the Indians being disregarded in Brazil, the king found it necessary to have recourse to the threats and penalties of the pope.   Paul III.,
Urban VIII., and Benedict XIV., in consequence threatened to excommunicate
all who should presume, in the words of the Roman court, to reduce the Indians to servitude; to sell, buy, exchange, or give them away.   But the rapacity and cruelty of the *Mamelucos* did not always remain unpunished.   They

The Indians were in like manner pressed into the service of the *corregidores*, or governors of provinces; of the caciques; and of the curates, to serve as *pongos*, or menial servants, who were relieved periodically, but were not allowed to return to their homes until they had procured a certificate stating the due discharge of their services. They received no remuneration except food and miserable clothing. It is computed that upwards of sixty thousand Indians were employed, in Peru alone, in this domestic servitude [*].

For a description of the sufferings to which the Indians were exposed on other properties where the mita prevailed, viz. the cultivated estates, the *estancias*, or grazing farms, and the *obrages*, or public manufactories, the reader is referred to the secret report of Don Jorge Juan and Don Antonio de Ulloa, perhaps the most authentic work upon this subject that has ever appeared in print. For the reproduction of this work, which slept in the archives of Madrid for eighty years, the literary world is now indebted to the indefatigable exertions of Mr. Barry.

2dly. The *repartimiento* [†] was a privilege, originally granted with the best intentions, and most politic views, to the corregidors or governors of pro-

---

were occasionally attacked and overcome by the Guarany Indians, who at length having been permitted by the Spaniards to carry arms for their defence, almost entirely put a stop to the incursions of the Brazilian marauders.—DOBRIZHO-FER's ABIPONES.

[*] It has been impossible to do away entirely with this abuse, and at the present time it exists in many of the villages and towns, notwithstanding that it is prohibited by recent laws.

[†] Tracts of the country, or whole districts of Indians, granted to the early conquerors, were called encomiendas, and sometimes repartimientos. Although the feudal privileges of these grants had been abolished by some decrees of the sovereign, yet they continued to be exercised on a few remaining encomiendas until the final expulsion of the Spaniards.

vinces, to furnish at a fair price articles of necessary consumption to the Indians.   At the period of the conquest, and for a long time afterwards, few if any merchants penetrated into the interior of the conquered countries.   Such governors were therefore necessarily almost the only persons who bartered with subdued or unsubdued Indians, supplied their wants, and received in exchange gold and silver.

This privilege, although regulated by law, was abused, and in the course of a short time converted into a compulsory and disgraceful traffic, as new in the annals of commerce as it was detestable in the eyes of justice and humanity.   Not only were dying mules, damaged goods, and other worthless articles, forced upon the Indians at double or triple the value of the best commodities of the same kind, but razors to men who have no beards; silk stockings, velvets, and other luxuries, of which the barefooted Indian did not even know the use, constituted an important part of the supplies for which the Indians were compelled to pay.

One instance will illustrate the system.   Some foolish speculator in Europe had sent out, amongst other things, a consignment of spectacles, which lay for a long time useless in the stores of a merchant in Lima.   After every hope of disposing of them had failed, for in that country people retain their eyesight unimpaired to a very late period of life, a corregidor was applied to, who, upon issuing an order that no Indian in his district should attend divine service, upon certain festivals, unless ornamented with spec-

tacles, found means to dispose of the whole of them
at an enormous profit.

These abuses originated from the source which
produced all the other grievances of Spanish America,
namely, that the interests of those vast countries
should be made subservient to those of Spain. Needy
Spaniards, who could muster enough money to make
a well-timed present, might, according to the system
so admirably pourtrayed in Gil Blas, ensure an appointment in the Americas, from whence they relied
upon being enabled to return in a very few years with
a competent fortune. Every new viceroy brought
out a shoal of hungry dependents of this class, and
fresh adventurers arrived with every civil, military,
or ecclesiastical appointment, to be applied in succession, so soon as the leeches already in operation
should be gorged and drop off.

Amongst the appointments which were generally
disposed of in this manner was the office of corregidor.

The new dignitary found no difficulty in obtaining,
at a long credit, and at a proportionably high price,
unsaleable or damaged goods, and with these he proceeded to take possession of his district.

The collection of the royal tribute, which was, in
reality, the principal object of the appointment of the
corregidor, afforded him ample means of increasing
and enforcing his exactions. The tribute was an
annual capitation tax of eight dollars, paid by every
Indian between the ages of eighteen and fifty-five.
For the amount of this the corregidor was responsible

to the royal treasury. For the correctness of his conduct, so far as the royal claims were concerned, there
was no deficiency of safeguards; but, the moment that
was secured, there was no further check. If he could
force the Indians to commence the payment of the
tribute at fifteen years of age, and continue it until
seventy, which was often practised, the eighteen years
of surplus became his own. If an unfortunate Indian
was unable to pay, which, owing to innumerable other
exactions to which he was liable, was but too often
the case, he was sent to the *obrage*, or public manufactory, or bridewell. The nature of this punishment
will be best described in the words of the report above
referred to :

 " The Indian in the obrage earns by his labour there
a real (about sixpence) a day. Half of this is stopped
to pay his arrears to the corregidor, and the other half
is allotted for his maintenance. But that is not sufficient for one who is obliged to work unceasingly for
the whole day. Indeed, how can half a real in that
country purchase sufficient food for a man, when it
will barely suffice to pay for his chicha*, without
which an Indian can hardly exist, and which, from
its nourishing and invigorating qualities, he prizes
more than food? Besides, as the Indian is not allowed
to move out, he is obliged to take whatever the keeper
of the obrage chooses to give him for his half real. The
latter, in order to prevent loss to himself, furnishes
him with maize or barley that has been damaged in
the granaries; the carcasses of cattle that have died of

---

* A fermented liquor (in flavour something like sweet wort), made from
Indian corn, from barley, and, in the *sierra* (mountainous parts of the country),
from quinoa (millet).

disease, and have already begun to taint the air; and with other food of a similar nature. The view of the bodies of those persons, when they are brought out dead from such houses, would move the most flinty heart to compassion. They are mere skeletons, fully betraying the cause and manner of their death, and they often expire in the performance of the tasks allotted to them, with the very instruments of labour in their hands; for, notwithstanding the symptoms of their dreadful malady manifested in their looks, the barbarous task-masters do not consider it a sufficient reason to exempt them from labour, or to be at the expense of medical aid *."

It is a lamentable fact, that the general desolation of this hapless race was increased by the very class of men whose duty it was to have mitigated their sufferings, and who were originally placed amongst them as protectors. The priests, to whose spiritual guidance the Indians were assigned, were commonly

* The tribute was collected in the departments of Upper Peru until the end of 1825, a year after they were liberated by the patriots.

The governor of each province was obliged to pay into the departmental treasury a certain sum every quarter, according to the number of tributary Indians his province was computed to contain, by a census made every seven years. It often happened that the population was considerably underrated, in which cases the governors were great gainers. The governor of the province of Porco, in the department of Potosi, was supposed to collect a *surplus* of 10,000 dollars per annum, owing to this circumstance.

When General Bolivar arrived at Potosi, at the latter end of 1825, the tribute was abolished *de facto*. Until then, pretty much the same abuses described by Ulloa existed; and were we at liberty to state the result of some official examinations as to the then actual state of the Indians in those mining districts, it would appear that the unfortunate aborigines were as ill treated by men professing liberal and constitutional principles, as they had been previously by European rulers. The Indians now enjoy by law the same rights and protection as other citizens. Many acts of cruelty and injustice will perhaps continue for a time to be exercised, owing to the undue influence and power of a few of the clergy and unprincipled *employés*. But the laws of the new governments are just and wise on this head, and there is little doubt but that in the course of time they will be observed. Many of the patriot clergy are liberal, enlightened, and enthusiastic in protecting their parishioners. Dr. Calera, one of the curates of Potosi, affords a brilliant example of philanthropic solicitude for the welfare of the Indians.

chosen from amongst the most useless and worthless
of their respective orders, and, instead of enlightening
and protecting the poor, ignorant, and inoffensive
beings committed to their charge, they plundered
them, without mercy, of the little which escaped the
rapacity of the corregidors.

The curate of a moderate living, in the province of
Quito, informed the intelligent travellers before mentioned, that, exclusively of his dues and regular fees,
he received during the year, as presents which he
exacted at certain festivals, 200 sheep, 6,000 head of
poultry, 4,000 guinea pigs, and 50,000 eggs.   Mass
was not said on those days until a due proportion of
the exacted presents were delivered.   Mr. Barry relates that he himself saw a priest's bill for the fees
of interring a person who died in easy circumstances,
which amounted to 134 dollars; by these and other
means, livings of 7 and 800 dollars a year were made
to produce 5 or 6,000.   Many of the livings of Peru
are worth from 10 to 15,000 dollars per annum.

The scandalous example afforded by their licentiousness was still more pernicious than their insa-
tiable avarice.   Religion administered by such men
was calculated rather to do harm than good, because
the Christianity of their precepts was neutralized by
the barbarity of their practices.

The atrocities committed by these wolves in sheep's
clothing would almost surpass belief, were they not
given on the authority of such men as the Ulloas *,

* Had the suggestions of the inestimable and enlightened Ulloas been attended to by the court of Spain, and had the whole of these missions been
transferred, as they recommended, to the Jesuits, to whose character and conduct they bear the highest testimony, as the only agents qualified for the con-

and had we not before us recent facts which confirm
their statement.   All that the Indians have been
taught of religion is to repeat the Pater noster, the
Belief, the Ave Maria, and a few prayers relative to
confession and communion *.   A short time before the
performance of mass on every Sunday morning was
the only time set apart for this sort of superficial instruction.   This weekly attendance on the part of the
Indians was to enable the parish priest to fulfil an
ordinance which at the same time gave him an opportunity of collecting his own fees for the administering
of the sacraments of the Romish church.   The cate-
chism, or the summary mentioned, was taught by the
parish priest, when he understood the language of
the Indians, which was not always the case.   These
priests received a salary from government, but they
extorted casual profits, in the shape of baptismal,
matrimonial, burial, and other fees, which they called
obvenciones.

When the Indians were unable to repeat from
memory prayers they did not understand, they were
often publicly whipped at the church porch.   Hence

version and civilization of the Indians, it is but fair to conclude, judging from
what they so quickly, and under the greatest disadvantages, effected in Paraguay,
that the Indians would have been at this moment a numerous, a civilized, and
a happy people, as well as an assured source of wealth and strength to Spain.

Independently of the many valuable articles of commerce and manufactures
which were produced in the missions of Paraguay, the Jesuits paid annually
into the royal treasury 240,000 dollars, as the tribute of 30,000 men between
the ages of eighteen and fifty-five, at the rate of eight dollars each.

But the court of Madrid had not the inclination, nor perhaps the ability, to
effect the improvements so judiciously pointed out.   Such changes would have
too materially affected the interest of those who were fattening on the abuses
thus denounced.   The Jesuits were expelled, their missions placed on nearly the
same footing as those of other monastic orders, and the same system of general
tyranny and rapacity pursued.   The results are now evident.

* Pope Paul the Third issued a bull, dated 2d June, 1537, pronouncing
the Indians to be really men, and capable of understanding the catholic faith;
their cause being pleaded by Bartolomeo Las Casas, afterwards bishop of
Chiapa.

their aversion to a religion, the benefits of which were
to them unintelligible, but which they felt practically
to be a scourge.

When an Indian lost his wife or his child, he underwent a rigorous examination as to his means of
defraying the fees of interment, which were graduated
at the discretion of the priest. If the Indian refused
to pay, then his mule, his cow, his llama, his sheep,
or other property, was sequestered and publicly sold.
If it were found out that he had concealed any thing
valuable, he was thrown into prison.   In all these
cases, the civil authority lent its aid.   The following
fact is related by an eye-witness now in England:
A poor widow, with a heart full of grief for the loss
of her husband and only support, was summoned to
the presence of the priest, to make a declaration of
the property left by her deceased husband, in order
that the reverend father might fix the scale of his
fees.   In vain the unfortunate woman implored the
priest to forego his demands in favour of her children.
He was inexorable, and would relinquish his claim
only upon condition that she would deliver over her
eldest son, in order that he might reimburse himself
by selling the boy as a slave, or making a present of
him, although the practice was contrary to law.   To
avoid starvation, the afflicted widow gave up her son,
who was eight years old.   The Indian children thus
obtained are highly prized, on account of their value
and fidelity as domestic servants.   This practice was
continued until very lately.   When General Miller
was governor of Potosi, some cases of the same kind
were laid before him.

In 1817, the *cura*, or parish priest, of La Punta de Santa Elena, in the province of Guayaquil, named Ludeña, a native of Cuenca, having occasion to go a long journey, deputed a young priest to officiate in his absence. The first question on his return home was, " Well, what news? who have died?" In giving the list of deaths, the acting cura mentioned the name of a rich cacique. Ludeña rubbed his hands, and exclaimed, " Well, and what did you get for the funeral masses? a thousand dollars, eh?"—" No," replied the other, " the family expressed a wish for the cacique to be buried as a poor Indian, which I permitted, and received the customary fee of six dollars and six reales" (twenty-seven shillings). Having severely reprimanded the novice, Ludeña sent for the sons of the deceased Indian. He told them that they were degenerate children of the best man in the country, and every way unworthy of enjoying the property they inherited; that burying him as a poor man was not only indelicate, undutiful, and unfeeling, but the certain means of prolonging the torments of their good father's soul in the flames of purgatory. The sons expressed the deepest sorrow, but said there was now no remedy. " Yes," says he, " there is: I will compromise the matter: I will have the statue of your late excellent and pious father made in wax: the funeral service shall be read over his effigy, and masses shall be said for the repose of his soul." The sons were glad to pay five or six hundred dollars for the mock funeral, in order to escape from further censures of the enraged and crafty ecclesiastic.

It may be urged by the advocates of the Spanish

government, that the Indians had the power of appealing from such horrible abuses to the viceroys, as representatives of their king. The answer is simple:

A long course of slavery will bend the spirit of the boldest and most independent race; but the Indians were, even in their golden age, under the paternal sway of their splendid Incas, a meek and inoffensive people. The cruelty and tyranny of the first invaders had reduced them, in every moral and philosophical capacity, from the rank of men to a condition little superior to that of the brute creation. The Spaniard despised the Creole, the Creole hated and envied the Spaniard, but both united in maltreating and oppressing the poor Indian. Even the blacks were encouraged to trample upon the aborigines. Up to the present time, the blacks express their contempt for them. Besides, how could the unfortunate being who was shut up for life in a mine, or in a bridewell, escape in order to tell his tale of woe? or how, if he did escape, was he to make his case known to the higher authorities, whom he could rarely approach, or, when this was permitted, could address them only in a language which they did not understand? And even if, from being in a state of momentary freedom, and from the advantage of an accidental proximity to the capital, he did succeed in obtaining an audience, what was the result? Let the answer be given by the two conscientious and virtuous Spaniards already quoted:

A repartimiento had taken place in the year 1743, about forty leagues from Lima. The corregidor had purchased goods for 70,000 dollars; for these goods he exacted from the wretched Indians 300,000 dollars.

" The Indians of this corregimiento," continue our authors, " finding themselves tyrannized over with greater cruelty than they had experienced from the predecessors of the corregidor, determined to com-plain to the viceroy, and produced before him the goods, together with the proofs of the exorbitant prices which they had been obliged to pay for them. We do not state this fact from report, as we happened to be present when the Indians came to make known their grievances. The viceroy heard them, and referred them to the *audiencia;* and the result was, that the Indians were seized and punished as insurgents."

But the bow, however elastic, may be bent until it breaks. The Indians, after enduring the most cruel oppressions for ages, in the hopeless apathy of despair, were roused to vengeance in 1780, by the avarice of the corregidors of Chayanta and Tinta, who, in that single year, ventured to impose three repartimientos, each of which produced about 150,000 dollars.

Don José Gabriel Condorcanqui, cacique of Tun-gasuca, in whom education had awakened the dor-mant feelings of human nature, placed himself at the head of his countrymen. He was a descendant of the inca Tupac Amaru, who in the year 1562 was most unjustly beheaded by order of the viceroy Don Francisco de Toledo.

The cacique of Tungasuca was educated at the college of San Borja at Cuzco, and possessed virtues which in private life render a man amiable and re-spected; but he wanted those essential qualifications

which are requisite to constitute the restorer of an
empire.   His countenance was noble, his manners
prepossessing, his stature lofty, and frame robust; his
disposition intrepid and enterprising; but his passions
were violent, and his knowledge and views in every
respect too confined to realize the grand idea of recovering the lost happiness of his country.   Instead
of uniting and making common cause with the Spanish Americans, who, born on the same soil, and held
in perhaps more galling fetters, were entitled to the
same rights with himself, he directed his hostilities
equally against them as against the Spaniards, the real
tyrants of both; and he met the fate which a policy
so isolated and so unjust could not but ensure.

The popularity of his cause, however, amongst his
own people, soon attracted to his standard a multitude
of undisciplined Indians, whom he had not either
the talent to train in military tactics, or the means
to arm.   He assumed not only the name of his an-
cestor Tupac Amaru, which means, in the *Quechua*
language, *the highly endowed,* but the attributes and
the pomp of the incas.

Some partial successes attended his career.   The
desperate valour of his unarmed followers, in which
even their females partook, seemed to counterbalance
the discipline, the arms, and skill of their opponents;
but, in the end, Tupac Amaru was taken prisoner.
The details of his execution warrant a strong pre-
sumption that civilization which, in every country of
Europe, has alleviated the horrors of war, and mitigated the rage of the victor, had not reached, or at
least not softened, the Spaniard in America.   The

punishment of Tupac Amaru was dictated by the
same ruthless barbarity that had formerly condemned
the young and heroic Guatemozin, the last of the
emperors of Mexico, to expire upon burning coals.
Tupac Amaru beheld from the scaffold the execution
of his wife, of his children, and of many of his faithful
followers; after which his tongue was cut out, and
wild horses, harnessed to his legs and arms, tore his
limbs asunder *.

But this horrible butchery, so far from being of
service to the cause for which it was perpetrated,
may be fairly estimated to have cost the Spaniards
five hundred additional lives for every victim im-
molated upon this occasion. The Indians, barbarous
and ferocious when their passions are strongly excited, as all degraded and debased people become
when once roused against their oppressors, were so
horror-struck at the recital of these enormities, that
many who had until then remained passive joined
in the insurrection. Headed by the Indian chiefs,
among whom was Catari, they kept up a desultory
but destructive warfare, and cut to pieces several
detachments of Spaniards.

Andres, the nephew of Tupac Amaru, laid siege
to Sorata, a town near La Paz, where the Spaniards
of the neighbouring districts had taken refuge with
their families and wealth. The unarmed Indians
were unequal to the storming of fortifications which,
although constructed only of earth, were lined with

* The brother of Tupac Amaru reached Buenos Ayres in 1822, after having
been confined thirty years in Ceuta. The independent government granted him
a house and a pension of thirty dollars per month. An exposition of his sufferings was written by his own hand, and placed in the archives of the state.

artillery. But their leader surmounted this difficulty by the adoption of a measure that would have done credit to any commander. By the construction of a lengthened mound he collected the waters which flow from the neighbouring snowy heights of Ancoma; and turning them against the earthen ramparts, washed them away. The immediate result was the storming of the town, and the massacre of its inhabitants*, with circumstances of horror exceeding the death of Tupac Amaru. Unhappily the vanity of these rude chieftains trifled away, in ridiculous assumptions of royalty, that time which ought to have been spent in warlike operations.

The Spaniards finally succeeded in obtaining by treachery what their cruelty had failed in effecting. The two principal Indian chiefs, in consequence of bribes artfully applied, were delivered up by the treachery of confidential servants; and thus, for a few years longer, was the reign of tyranny upheld by its accustomed associates, fraud and cruelty. This rebellion, however, produced the abolition of the *repartimiento.* In other respects the Indians continued to be as much oppressed as before.

The second head, under which the tyranny of Spain towards her colonies has been classed, relates to the despotism exercised by the Spaniards over their own descendants in America. In order to trace to their proper source the grievances of the creole descendants of the Spaniards, it will be necessary to take a view of the basis of their colonial legislation, a well

---

* Twenty thousand. Excepting the clergy, not a single male was left alive.

intended code, but the abuses of which spread indiscriminate tyranny over whites as well as Indians.

The spirit of a paternal government breathed
through every page of the *Recopilacion de las Leyes
de las Indias*. Amongst other precautions, the kings
of Spain had, with a benignant and sage policy,
rendered America, as it regarded both its aboriginal
inhabitants and the descendants of the Spaniards, a
separate empire, dependent upon the *crown* of Spain,
but independent of the *kingdom* of Spain, and connected with it only through the medium of the sovereign who ruled both *. But unfortunately the kings
of Spain delegated their power over America to a set
of men composing what is called the Council of the
Indies, of which the sovereign was president. It was
placed, as to rank and privileges, upon a footing with
the council of Castile. The council of the Indies
exercised the patronage of the higher appointments
in America, and the members were consequently interested rather in the perpetuation than in the ex-
tinction of abuses. Reform would have narrowed the
usual sources of wealth to their relations, depend-
ants, or protegés, upon whom these appointments
were lavished, and from whom imperative custom
demanded the most expressive tokens of gratitude to
their patrons.

The inevitable result of such a system is readily
conceived. The government of America was virtually vested in the people of Spain, and her interests

---

* Ley. 1, tit. 8. lib. 4. See also the most eminent Spanish commentators,
Soto, Suares, and Zolorzano.

and her happiness were sacrificed to the unjust and short-sighted view of enriching and aggrandizing individuals of the mother country. The beneficent laws of the Indies became a dead letter; regulations, however imperative, were disregarded; and America remained a vast field in which the avarice and cruelty of the Spanish nation might luxuriate with impunity. Some proofs of the accuracy of this conclusion have been brought to light in reviewing the condition of the Indians. A short sketch of the government of the Indies as applied to the descendants of the Spaniards themselves will furnish the remainder.

We have seen a despotic king framing paternal and wise laws for his subjects, but unable to enforce their due observance. Let us now contemplate a nation legislating for the government of its own children, when transplanted to another soil, and we shall find its laws selfish, despotic, unjust, and consequently impolitic in every principle, but enforced with the most jealous exactitude. The monopolising and sordid spirit in which they were framed could be equalled only by the unrelenting severity with which they were carried into effect; and the degrading and demoralising influence of such a government becomes immediately apparent.

By the fundamental laws of the Indies, the natives of Spanish America had been declared to be eligible to its ecclesiastical benefices, and to the offices of trust, importance, and honour in its government*. These, together with the law enacting its total independence of Spain, would, if observed, have been

* Leyes 3. 5. 13. 14. 22. 24. 28.

sufficient to ensure the prosperity and happiness of
Spanish America; but these laws were either superseded or disregarded from the moment that the
kings of Spain, by the appointment of a council of
the Indies, virtually delegated their authority to the
Spanish nation. The spirit of the laws thenceforward
enacted, as well as the observance of the fundamental
laws, were regulated upon principles subversive of
the rights and welfare of America.

These violations of the fundamental laws or Magna
Charta of the Indies may be classed under three heads.

1. *Agricultural and commercial.*
2. *Political and honorary.*
3. *Intellectual and moral.*

In all of these, brevity will confine us to a few
leading points.

1. *Agricultural and commercial.*

The natives of the different governments were prohibited from cultivating, on their own lands, many
valuable fruits and productions to which the soil and
climate were peculiarly adapted. The whole of the
staple commodities of Spain itself were placed under
this edict, in order to secure to the mother country
a certain vent for her own produce*. They were
forbidden to have manufactories of any other kinds
of cloth than those used by the Indians; they were
deprived of every species of traffic, not only with

* Quedando expresamente prohibido pª la Nueva España, Tierra Firme, y
Santa Fé, los vinos, aguardientes, vinagre y azeite de olivas, pasas, y almendras
del Peru y Chile, y privados rigurosamente en todas partes los plantios de olivares y viñas. Gazeta de Mexico, Octubre 6, 1804.

Translation.—Being expressly prohibited in New Spain, Tierra Firme, and
Santa Fé, the wines, brandies, vinegar, oil of olives, raisins, almonds of Peru
and Chile; and the planting of olive-trees and vineyards being every where
strictly forbidden.—Gazette of Mexico, 6 October, 1804.

foreign nations, but even with the other Spanish American states; and orders were transmitted to the different viceroys to prevent, by all possible ways and means, commerce between their respective kingdoms. We give one by way of specimen.

" According to the final resolution of the count of Chinchon, and by the advice of the board of finance, we order and command the viceroys of Peru and New Spain, that they absolutely prohibit and impede all commerce and traffic, between both kingdoms, by all the ways and means in their power *."

Even when foreigners were allowed to prosecute the cod and whale fisheries on the coast of America, the natives were restrained; and they were punished with death if it was proved that they sold an article of commerce to those strangers. They were forbidden to work their mines of quicksilver and iron †. The order to tear up by the roots every forbidden article that had been planted, and to burn and destroy obnoxious implements of agriculture and manufactures, were most rigorously executed.

2nd. *Political and honorary.*

In violation of the fundamental laws, Americans were generally excluded from offices from which either honour or profit could be derived. When a deviation from this system did occur, it was in favour of such as could afford to give enormous bribes, or of those who were most forward in depreciating their

---

* Por ultima resolucion del conde de Chinchon, y acuerdo de hacienda, ordenamos y mamdamos à los virreyes del Peru y Nueva España que infaliblemente prohiban y estorben el comercio y trafico entre ambos reynos por todos los caminos y medios que les fuera posibles. L. 79. tit. 45. lib. 9.

† The quicksilver mine at Guancabelica, in Peru, was allowed to be worked under certain restrictions during the war between England and Spain.

own countrymen, and in tyrannizing over them with
the malignant feelings of renegadoes; and these were
certain of being liberally employed and amply rewarded.   But, carefully as honourable Americans
were excluded *de facto*, still it was, in the last century, seriously debated in the great council of the
Indies, whether they should not be excluded *dé
jure*, and declared incapable of filling any honourable
office.   But this idea was never carried into effect.
It was felt to be superfluous, and was perhaps conceived to be too wanton and flagrant a declaration
of the purpose, to violate those fundamental laws of
the Indies, which enacted, "that in all cases of government, justice, administration of finance, employments, *encomiendas* of Indians, &c. the first dis-
coverers, then the *pacificadores*, and lastly the settlers, and those born in the provinces of America,
are to be preferred."

Another objection to such a measure would have
been the cutting off the most efficient means for procuring the service of recreant natives, who were often
found the fittest tools to be employed in acts of violence and atrocity.   The same motives and ideas influenced the *consulado*, or board of trade, of Mexico,
composed of Spaniards, to represent to the Cortes of
Cadiz, in 1811, "that the Spanish Americans were
a race of monkeys, full of vice and ignorance, and
automata unworthy of representing or being represented *."

The Cortes, which had received their authority

* See debates of Cortes, Sept. 1811. Count Agreda, one of those who signed
the document, has lately been obliged to quit Mexico.

from the Regency, entertained the same animosity against the Americans; and although there were in the Cortes some members chosen from those Americans who happened to be at that time in the Isla de Leon, they were scarcely allowed to speak of their country. " If the Americans," said one of the members of the Cortes, " complain of having been tyrannized over for three hundred years, they shall now experience a similar treatment for three thousand." " I am rejoiced," said another (Count Toreno), after the battle of Albuera, " at the advantage we have gained, because we can now send troops to reduce the insurgents." " I do not know to what class of beasts the Americans belong," said another * (Valiente).

The mode in which the fundamental laws were observed are evinced by the following facts.

Out of one hundred and sixty viceroys who have governed in America, only four have been natives, and out of six hundred and two captains-general and governors, all except fourteen were Spaniards.

The laws of the Indies also provided that the creoles, or descendants of the conquerors and settlers, should have the right of holding the chief ecclesiastical dignities, and that no foreigners, viz. natives of Aragon, Catalonia, Valencia, &c. although they were to be allowed to reside and to traffic in Spanish America, were eligible to any ecclesiastical benefice even if named by the king himself†. And

* See Manifesto of Alvarez Toledo, Deputy of Cortes.
† Ley. 31, tit. 6, lib. 1 ; ley. 32, tit. 2, lib. 2 ; ley. 29, tit. 6, lib. 1. Solorzano, Polit. In. lib. 3, cap. 14.

yet, of five hundred and fifty ecclesiastics who have been advanced to the episcopal dignity in America, only fifty-five were natives.

3rd. *Intellectual and moral.*

A few extracts from the mass of evidence before us will fully illustrate and prove the moral debasement to which the Spaniards endeavoured to reduce their descendants in America. No science was allowed to be studied, the acquirements permitted being the Latin grammar, ancient philosophy, theology, civil and canonical jurisprudence, and the jargon of the schools, which, of whatever equivocal advantage they might be to ecclesiastics, could be of no possible utility to the youth of the laity. Even a nautical school formed at Buenos-Ayres, at the expense of the board of trade, was suppressed by the viceroy, D. Joaquin del Pino, in compliance with orders from Spain. The few schools established for the study of mathematics were ordered to be closed.

Don Juan Francisco, an Opata chief, travelled to Mexico on foot, a distance of five hundred leagues, and then crossed the ocean to Madrid, to solicit a grant for the sole purpose of teaching his fellow Indians the first rudiments of learning; but his request was refused by the council of the Indies in 1798. The cacique, Cirilo de Castella, after soliciting the same favour at Madrid for twenty years, died there without attaining his object.

But the system at last was avowed in all its naked deformity. The city of Merida, in Venezuela, solicited of Charles the Fourth permission to found an university, and his majesty having consulted the council of the Indies, answered in a royal *cedula*, or decree, that he did not conceive it proper for learning to become general in America.

Of all the modes by which Spain so studiously and so effectually contrived to depress and degrade the people of Spanish America, none was so truly disgraceful to itself and galling to its victims, as the state of intellectual and moral abasement, to which it laboured to reduce them. That a short-sighted government, acting upon the base policy that an ignorant people is most easily retained in slavery, should strive to prevent the acquisition of useful knowledge, may be accounted for; but that a government professing Christianity, and knowing that the natural and inevitable results of such a system must be to produce immorality and vice, should for this very reason the more strenuously enforce it, evinces the most unparalleled perverseness and malignity.

That such were the objects of the Spanish government in its colonial legislation, of which some specimens have been produced, it would perhaps be harsh to assert; but that such were the melancholy consequences cannot be concealed. Nothing but the native goodness of disposition, acuteness of intellect, and courage of the natives of Spanish America generally, and the insolent, uncompromising, and infatuated conduct of the Spaniards, could have broken the toils which were wound around them.

A regard for historical truth having drawn forth details discreditable to the Spanish character, candour and justice call for the more agreeable task of

giving some bright exceptions amidst the corruption
and injustice which enveloped Spanish America.

The viceroy Manso retired from the viceregal government of Peru in honourable poverty, and afterwards gained a subsistence in Spain by becoming a
schoolmaster.

Santelices, born in Spain and educated at Salamanca, was governor of Potosi in the reign of Charles
the Third. He soon perceived the abuse of power,
the prostitution of justice, and the general abandon-
ment of duty which pervaded every department. His
upright and strenuous endeavours to correct some of
these evils served only to create enemies in every person interested in perpetuating abuses. Remonstrances
and appeals against his unpalatable reforms were made
to the *real audiencia* of Charcas; which tribunal, sym-
pathising but too feelingly with the complainants, issued repeated royal ordinances against the innovations
of the governor. Finding all endeavours to force him
to swerve from the path of rectitude ineffectual, these
powerful and artful enemies tried the temptation of
wealth and the allurements of beauty to induce him
to commit some act that would compromise or form
a colourable pretext for deposing him. He dexterously avoided the snare, by inviolably adhering to a
resolution never to grant a private audience to any
individual. Worn out, however, at length, by this
unequal struggle, he determined to visit Madrid, and
to expose in person the mal-administration of Peru;
but he died on his passage home, and it has been
strongly suspected that he was poisoned.

The history of Gonzalez Montoya, governor of Puno in 1800, and now living, would be merely a repetition of the same story, with the exception that the result was less tragical.   He not only contrived to return in safety to Spain, but had the firmness to present himself at the bar of the Cortes at Cadiz, and to expose, with energetic eloquence, the whole system; declaring that the acts of the governors in Spanish America were one tissue of *barbaridades*.

Don Antonio Raya, bishop of Cuzco, gave in alms 370,000 dollars in eight years.   Don Gaspar Villaroel, archbishop of Charcas, was a wise and virtuous prelate, whose memory is held in the highest respect. The bishops in Peru were generally virtuous and charitable.   It was seldom that the episcopal bench was disgraced by a character like that of Santa y Ortega, bishop of La Paz, since promoted by Ferdinand to a richer bishopric in Spain.

Amongst the *oidores* were not wanting judges of incorruptible probity, as, for instance, Don Jose Portilla Galves, president of the *real audiencia* of Cuzco, and his contemporary judge Moscoso.   The *oidor* Villota, who quitted the *real audiencia* of Lima so lately as 1821, was a shining example of integrity and love of justice.   The patriots made many unavailing efforts to induce this ornament of the law to remain in Lima.

To the honour of the Spaniard, also, be it remembered, that he is the mildest slave-master in the world; and this redeeming trait has descended to his transatlantic progeny.   In the extensive provinces of the river Plata, and in Chile, few proprietors possess more than a small number of slaves, who, in most cases, in ordinary and peaceful times, were born, lived, and died, without having been transferred to another owner. As children, they were the playmates of the juvenile part of their master's family; and, as adults, placed nearer upon a footing of equality than exists between master and servant in many European countries. The moderate importation of negroes only made this difference, that the creole negro considered himself far superior to his sable brother from Africa.

CHAPTER II.

Loyalty of Spanish Americans contrasted with the conduct of Spaniards.—H. M. S. Acasta.—Agents of King Joseph expelled.—Conduct of Iturrigaray.—Liniers.—Central junta.—Regency.—Cortes.—People of Caracas in 1808.—Marquess Wellesley.—Constitutional measures of the Americans.—Injustice of the Spanish government.—Exterminating character of the war.—Truxillo.—Calleja.—Monteverde.—Boves.—Morillo.—Horrid executions.—States of Spanish America declare their independence.

HAVING in the preceding chapter presented some instances of the system of oppression pursued by the Spaniards in America, it becomes necessary to trace the natural and intimate connexion between the obstinate perseverance in such a system, and its results, as shown in the sequel of this work. Such an explanation is rendered the more necessary, from the partial view that appears to have been generally taken of the origin and motives of the contest, which has terminated in the emancipation of Spanish America.

The Spanish Americans are accused by the king and people of Spain, not only of rebellion, but of an ungrateful and base desertion of the mother country at the moment when she was a prey to foreign invasion. But it will appear upon due investigation that the reverse was the case, and that the charge of disloyalty both to their king and country can, with more truth, be retorted upon the Spaniards themselves. It was in fact the attempts of Spaniards to

betray Spanish America to the Buonapartean dynasty
that first aroused the enthusiastic loyalty of the natives towards their, then in reality, beloved Ferdinand, and it was the cruelty exercised by Spaniards,
which was with unaccountable weakness sanctioned
by Ferdinand himself after his restoration, that converted their loyalty into contempt, and their love into
disgust.

With regard to the mother country and France;
the national antipathy which existed between them;
the insidious means employed by Buonaparte to accomplish his views upon the Peninsula; and, above
all, the fears entertained by the clergy of the introduction of French principles; all concurred in exciting, among the peasantry of Spain, a determined,
simultaneous, and heroic opposition to their invaders.
Many nobles, distinguished officers, men of letters,
and indeed persons of every class, made common
cause with the mass of the people, and displayed a
devotedness, a perseverance, and love of their king,
that reflect the highest honour upon the Spanish
character; but many, very many exceptions must be
made amongst the higher orders of society, who, with
the majority of the public functionaries, joined, or
were evidently disposed to join in betraying their
country, and, with it, the colonies, to the French
dynasty. It would appear that those men considered
themselves as the hereditary proprietors of seventeen
millions of slaves in America; and viewing the power
which the French empire had then attained, as perhaps the only means of ensuring the continued sub-

jection of these slaves, they were content to purchase the assistance of Buonaparte in retaining them, by placing their king and country at his feet.

Alcedo, the governor of Corunna, and Morla, the governor of Cadiz, both highly distinguished for talent and influence, made great efforts to oppose the French when hostilities commenced; but they deserted the cause, and went over to king Joseph. The Spanish authorities, whether of the French party, or whether faithful to their captive sovereign, were alike determined that the Americans should remain in bondage. But the latter, like the peasantry of Spain, resolved not to be the victims of such flagitious conduct. They had, during the first struggles in the Peninsula against the French, contributed by the most generous sacrifices to what they considered the common cause of the monarchy. For this object they levied and forwarded to Spain upwards of ninety millions of dollars. Many of the most distinguished youth crossed the Atlantic, and joined the standard raised in behalf of the imprisoned Ferdinand. Indeed the devoted loyalty of the Americans at this period was carried to a length almost incredible, when the tyranny which had been exercised over them is considered. So fully was the Spanish government impressed with the conviction of their fidelity, that a few hundred men were thought a sufficient garrison for a whole viceroyalty *.

Such was their veneration for the king, which in

* In peaceful times less than two thousand Spanish regulars have garrisoned the line of country extending from Buenos Ayres to Lima and Quito. In a more turbulent period five hundred regulars formed the garrison of all Chile, and of these, three hundred were constantly employed against the Araucanian Indians.

the case of Ferdinand was heightened by his misfortunes, that it was not uncommon with many Americans to touch their hats whenever they mentioned
his name.

On the cession of the crown to Buonaparte, orders
were sent out from Bayonne to every part of Spanish
America, signed by Ferdinand; by the council of the
Indies; and countersigned by the minister Azanza,
for a general transfer of allegiance to Joseph.   It
was provided at the same time, that the Spaniards
in America were to preserve their dignities and employments under the new dynasty.   So perfectly was
this act of the Spanish government in unison with the
feelings and views of the Spanish local authorities in
America, that when Captain Beaver of H. M. S.
Acasta, demanded of the governor of Caracas a
French ship, which had conveyed to La Guayra
agents and printed papers from king Joseph, he
was answered that his ship would be fired upon
from the batteries if he attempted to capture the
imperial flag.   But the Americans, disgusted with
the conduct of their governors, burned the proclamations of Joseph Buonaparte, and expelled his
agents.

Iturrigaray, viceroy of Mexico, was one of the
very few of the Spanish authorities who spurned the
offers of the intrusive king.   He had, in common
with others, received a confirmation of his employment from Joseph, but he refused to compromise his
dignity and loyalty.   On the 5th of August, 1808,
the municipality of Mexico presented to Iturrigaray
an address requesting, in consequence of the imprison-

ment of king Ferdinand, "the convocation of a *junta* of the tribunals and constituted authorities in the capital." Acknowledging that the emergency had occurred which rendered such a measure not only legal and constitutional, but absolutely necessary, the viceroy expressed his determination to comply with the request.   But the other Spanish authorities, united with the merchants, were no sooner apprized of the loyal and patriotic intentions of the viceroy, than they secretly collected a body of troops, arrested him in his palace, and, with many personal indignities, sent him, after a lapse of time, a prisoner to Spain.   Venegas, the viceroy appointed to succeed him, was the bearer of rewards and honours to the principal agents in this act of rebellion.

Liniers, acting as viceroy of Buenos Ayres, in a proclamation to the inhabitants, informed them that "the emperor of the French returned them his thanks for the glorious defence that they had made against the English."   Emparan and Goyeneche, who had both sworn allegiance to king Joseph, were sent out from Cadiz; the first appointed to a command in Venezuela, the second to a command in Peru.

The supreme central junta, on the approach of the French army to the Guadalquivir, retired from Seville to the Isla de Leon.   It was composed of eighty-six individuals, who assuming the entire government of the nation, did not forget, it is said, to serve themselves when distributing honours and other sweets of office.   It was strongly suspected they had made up

their minds to compromise matters with the French;
or, at least, it was evident they wished to possess the
means of doing so. Indeed so barefaced were the disloyal designs of many of the members of the junta,
that they became at last objects of hatred, and they
were afraid, on account of the indignation of the people, to appear in the day-time in the streets of Cadiz.
It was now proved by intercepted correspondence
from Soult, and by other convincing evidence, that
the intentions of the junta in retiring to Cadiz had
been to surrender that place to the French. That
they would have succeeded in this design, little doubt
can be entertained had it not been for the opportune
and unexpected arrival of the duke of Albuquerque
with twelve thousand troops, who by marching to
Cadiz had disobeyed the express orders of the junta,
which had considered one thousand men a sufficient
garrison. Notwithstanding the rapidity of Albuquerque's movement, it was with difficulty he reached
the Isla before the French, who overtook and skirmished with his rear-guard on the march.

The preservation of Cadiz, however, cost the heroic
Albuquerque his life. The disappointed junta soon
afterwards deprived him of his military command, and
he was sent on a mission to England, where he died,
at the age of thirty-seven, of chagrin, caused by what
he considered the traitorous conduct and base ingratitude of the members of the junta. Actuated by
the same principles, they had refused to admit more
than two British regiments into Cadiz, and thwarted
in every possible way the plans and propositions of

sir Arthur and the marquess Wellesley. The people
of Cadiz and of the Isla de Leon would no longer
endure the traitorous junta: it was accordingly dissolved, but not before it had appointed a regency of
five individuals to succeed to the government.

The same unjust, avaricious, and prevaricating
policy towards Spanish America continued. The
ultramarine possessions had been declared by the
junta to be integral parts of the Spanish empire,
and their rights to representation in the general
cortes acknowledged. But these rights, recognised
in theory, were trampled on, or entirely disregarded,
in practice. The Americans had no intervention in
the naming of the regency, for which purpose, according to Spanish laws, a cortes ought to have been
previously assembled.

The council of regency, at the instigation of Mejias,
deputy for Quito, passed a decree, dated May 17th,
permitting the colonies to export to foreign nations
all such articles of their own product, for which there
was not a sufficient vent in old Spain. This decree,
morally just and politically wise, gave offence to the
merchants of Cadiz, on whom the regency were in a
great measure dependent, for the means of continuing
its feeble and slippery government. It was therefore
revoked on the 17th of June, and the regency had
the meanness to declare that it was not authentic, but
an imposition on the public; as if it would have suffered a forgery to have the force of law for a whole
month, in the very place where the regency resided, without protesting against it. Was it possible

that a government so pitifully mean, cunning, and fraudulent could be respected in the colonies?

On the 15th July, 1808, the people of Caracas, in despite of the intrigues and resistance of the Spanish authorities, took by acclamation a solemn oath of allegiance to Ferdinand the Seventh. In giving an account of this proceeding to the government at Cadiz, the captain-general and *audiencia* of Caracas thought it politic to palliate the act by declaring that " they had permitted it in consequence of the clamours and repeated messages of the people and *cabildo*."

A decree of Charles the Fifth in 1530, confirmed by Philip the Second in 1563, authorised, in cases of emergency, the convocation of cortes, or general juntas, in the respective kingdoms of Spanish America. The natives of these kingdoms found themselves at this period placed in one of the emergencies thus provided for. During the temporary suspension of the authority of the crown, by the imprisonment of Ferdinand, they determined to defeat the disloyal machinations of the Spanish authorities, and save themselves from the yoke of France by the exercise of the right legally and constitutionally vested in them. Their motives and views will, perhaps, be best given in their own words, as expressed in the appeal of the junta of Caracas to the king of England, dated June 1, 1810, and presented in July of that year to the British government.

" America remembers well that in the first moments when the irruption of the French troops into Spain and the captivity of her monarch occasioned a dread that the Spanish sections of the new world might be incorporated under the French yoke.

.   .   .   .

" To proclaim the same cause as our brethren in Europe, to swear an endless hatred to France, to invoke the friendship and protection of England, was the impulse of Caracas; this was the lesson she gave to the other provinces of America; and such were the sentiments unanimously manifested by the loyal inhabitants of this city, sentiments which subsequent events have tended only to strengthen and to ratify.

.   .   .   .

" Caracas listened to no other voice than that of honour, she was actuated by no other impulse than that of loyalty, nor did she proclaim allegiance to any other name than that of her unfortunate monarch."

But these noble and generous views did not accord with the policy either of the Spanish government, or of the Spaniards in America. The regency in its proclamation, dated Sept. 6, 1810, manifests its ulterior objects. " No basta," said the regents, " que seais Españoles si no sois de España, y lo sois en qualquiera caso de la fortuna." It is not sufficient that you be Spanish subjects, but that you continue to belong to Spain under every event of fortune.

When a deputy of Mexico proposed to the cortes to mortgage the Mexican mines, in order to raise money to carry on the war against France, on condition that if the French finally prevailed, then, and in that case alone, America should be allowed to establish and defend her independence, his offer was

treated with disdain, and rejected as revolutionary.
By acceding to such proposal, the government at
Cadiz would have restored peace and confidence to
the Americans, by convincing them that it was not
intended to yoke them to the car of Napoleon.

Many more facts might be adduced in proof of
the disloyalty of the Spaniards in America, and of
the government at Cadiz, as well as of the fidelity
and indeed romantic loyalty of Spanish Americans;
but it is presumed, that the proofs which have already
been given are sufficient to satisfy the most incre-
dulous. It may however be due to the cause of truth
to produce one important testimony given at a period
when the executive of Spain had not dared openly
to display its views; but it could not entirely conceal
them from the vigilant and penetrating eye of the
Marquess Wellesley. That able statesman, in a letter
to Mr. Canning, dated September 15th, 1809, says,
" Whether this ill-formed government is sincerely
affected or not to the cause of Spain and her allies,
is certainly dubious."

The justice of the marquess's suspicions became
apparent by the conduct of the Spanish government
in 1810. Its proclamations, and the characters selected as agents to Spanish America, betrayed at once
its ulterior intentions. But the blind loyalty of America baffled equally the views of the Spanish government, and the efforts of its agents in America.

To avoid anarchy, and to preserve inviolate their
allegiance to Ferdinand, the sections had recourse to
the convocation of general juntas, which was the only
constitutional means afforded them. And yet this

step, the only legal measure that a people so circumstanced could have taken to preserve tranquillity, and to demonstrate their devoted attachment, proved to be the signal for the declaration of hostilities by Spain, and the commencement of a war of extermination.

So infatuated was the conduct of the government at Cadiz, that after the French had been allowed to take possession of the whole of Spain, except the Isla de Leon, and another place or two of minor importance, it directed its entire energies against the people of America.   With characteristic virulence it fitted out, not with its own resources, for it possessed none, but with the funds supplied by the devoted loyalty of America, and the arms and clothing afforded for a widely different purpose by England, expeditions exceeding, if possible, in cruelty and injustice those of Cortes and Pizarro.   The nature of the war which, under such circumstances, and with such means, they declared and carried on, could not be adequately described, except in the words of the official despatches of the officers who were employed in conducting it, as published in the official royalist gazettes of Mexico.

The commandant Bustamante, in his despatch to the viceroy, dated Zitaquaro, Oct. 23, 1811, recommends Mariano Ochoa, a dragoon, "who in pursuing the insurgents had a brother who knelt to him to beg his life, which he took with his own hands."

Don Ignacio Garcia Revollo, in his despatch to the viceroy, dated Queretaro, Nov. 23, 1811, recommends serjeant Francisco Montes "as deserving the rank of an officer, for, amongst other gallant actions, he killed one of his own nephews, who, making him-

self known, received for answer, that he knew no
nephew amongst insurgents."

General Truxillo, in another despatch, boasts that
he ordered his men to fire upon a flag of truce
from Hidalgo, accompanied by a banner of the Holy
Virgin, and adds, that he did not expect to be
troubled in that sort of way again. Every person
with the flag of truce was murdered.

General Calleja informs the viceroy that in the
affair of Aculco he had one man killed and two
wounded ; but that he put to the sword 5000 se-
duced Indians, and that their total loss amounted to
double the number. Most of them were killed as
they were kneeling for mercy.

The same general entered Guanaxuato with fire
and sword, where 14,000 old men, women, and children perished, because the insurgent army had taken
up its quarters there, but by a timely retreat had
escaped his fury. Calleja soon after received from
the regency of Cadiz the rank of *mariscal de campo*,
and the viceroy was decorated with the cross of the
order of Charles the Third as a reward for this
distinguished service.

Extracts that have been made from only a few of
the Gazettes published in Mexico in the years 1811
and 1812, boast of 25,344 of the " insurgents" being
killed, 3556 made prisoners, besides 697 shot after
surrendering.

Caracas capitulated to General Monteverde in San
Mateo on the 25th of July, 1812. The basis of this
convention was, that the lives, property, and persons
of every citizen should be held sacred; that no one

should be prosecuted for previous opinions; in short, general oblivion and amnesty were granted. How the faith of this treaty was preserved will perhaps best appear in the words of a respectable English gentleman, who was an eye-witness of the scenes which he describes, and whose statement was transmitted to the Admiralty by one of the English commanders on the West India station.

" Monteverde caused to be arrested nearly every creole of rank throughout the country; he then had them chained in pairs, and conducted to the dungeons of La Guayra and Porto Cabello, where many of them perished by suffocation, or disease." In another part of his statement he says, " Were I to detail all the horrid excesses committed by Boves and Rosette, on the route from the river Oronoco to the valleys of Caracas, it would be scarcely possible to find a reader who could believe such scenes of slaughter and devastation credible. Some idea, however, of the melancholy facts may be conceived, when I assert that these monsters, in traversing a space of more than four hundred miles, left no human being alive of any age or sex, except such as joined their standard."

Boves condemned a patriot to suffer death. A boy under twelve years of age threw himself at the feet of the tyrant, and implored his father's life. Boves said, " Yes; upon condition that you will have an ear cut off without changing countenance." " That I will readily do," said the boy. " But remember," said Boves, "that the smallest flinch will be the death warrant of your father." The ear was

then cut off with a knife. Boves watched the boy,
who bore the mangling operation with astonishing
fortitude. When it was over, instead of performing
his promise, Boves said, " I can see very well that
you will be a more terrible enemy to Spain than
your father has been; therefore you shall be shot
before his eyes." It is needless to add, that both
father and son were instantly executed.

And yet the royalists did not always escape with
impunity. In a battle which the patriots lost near
the Apure, a Frenchman was taken prisoner amongst
other officers. The royalist commander said to him,
" So, monsieur, you are a great patriot." " I am,"
said the Frenchman, " and I hate the Spaniards
most cordially." " Mighty well," rejoined the other;
" now you shall pay for your hatred." " You shall
pay first," said the Frenchman, and drawing his
sword, laid the commander dead at his feet. The
troops around sprang upon the undaunted Frenchman, but did not despatch him until he had slain or
wounded several of his assailants.

It would be disgusting to enter into farther details
of this ferocious warfare. Under all these dreadful
sufferings, the unfortunate Americans, with scarcely
an exception, still preserved their infatuated loyalty,
under the faint hope of the return of Ferdinand, and
under the conviction that his restoration would prove
the harbinger of relief and of redress. Their feelings
may then be easily conceived when they found that,
after all the sacrifices they had made, this eagerly desired event, when it did occur, so far from affording
any alleviation to their miseries or wrongs, proved

only the signal for renewed oppression and still bloodier massacres. So far was he from wishing to reward their long-tried loyalty, or from endeavouring to conciliate, that the commission of atrocities in America formed with him the chief merit and the highest claim. In reward for the violation of the most solemn capitulations, for the boasted murder of the bearers of flags of truce, and for the most cold-blooded and indiscriminate slaughter, they beheld Monteverde, Callejas, Cruz, Truxillo, and other execrable monsters, loaded by Ferdinand with rewards, and covered with decorations.

The Americans recollected that Charles the Fifth, the proudest and most powerful monarch of his time, had, in a case of similar injustice, but not of similar sacrifices on the part of his subjects, listened benignantly to their complaints, and sent out the *Licenciado* Gasca with full powers to redress their grievances, which he effected. The slightest indication of a benevolent inclination towards them would even still have preserved to Ferdinand an empire, and to the Spanish nation brothers and faithful allies, much richer and more powerful than themselves. But Heaven had decreed that justice and right should take their course, and that centuries of misrule, oppression, and cruelty, should at last, through their own instrumentality, meet their merited punishment.

Perhaps nothing will excite more surprise than the circumstance that America did not find in the cortes a few sincere, generous, and powerful advocates, nor amongst those *liberales* who at the same period spoke and wrote with equal freedom and ability upon abuses of power nearer home. The chains of America might indeed have been lightened and burnished by the constitutionalists, but the unanimity of parties on colonial questions forbade the Americans to indulge in the hope that a single link would willingly be removed.

The imbecile Ferdinand did not even vouchsafe to listen to their complaints, although, with the exception of Caracas, they still persisted in their mistaken loyalty to this heartless sovereign for three long years after his restoration. During this period, the feelings and conduct of the Spanish government varied not, nor had its appetite for carnage been satiated.

The following is a list of individuals who suffered death and confiscation of property (without trial, or in violation of amnesties), in New Granada, in consequence of the entrance of the Spanish troops under the command of General Don Pablo Morillo, in the year 1816, taken from official documents transmitted to the court of Madrid:

Carthagena.

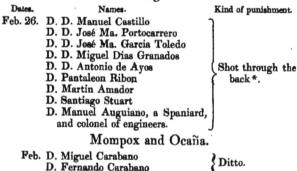

Dates.	Names.	Kind of punishment.
Feb. 26.	D. D. Manuel Castillo	
	D. D. José Ma. Portocarrero	
	D. D. José Ma. Garcia Toledo	
	D. D. Miguel Dias Granados	
	D. D. Antonio de Ayos	Shot through the
	D. Pantaleon Ribon	back *.
	D. Martin Amador	
	D. Santiago Stuart	
	D. Manuel Auguiano, a Spaniard, and colonel of engineers.	

Mompox and Ocaña.

Feb.	D. Miguel Carabano	Ditto.
	D. Fernando Carabano	

* Persons are placed with their backs towards the executioners of their sentence, with the intent of treating them with greater ignominy.

Santa Fé de Bogota.

Dates.	Names.	Kind of punishment.
May 26.	Juan Maria	
June 6.	D. Antonio Villavicencio	
19.	D. D. Ignacio Bargas	Shot through the back.
	D. José Ramon de Leiba, lieu-tenant-colonel and secretary to the viceroyalty	
	D. José Contreras	
	D. José Maria Carbonell	Gibbeted.
July 5.	D. Jorge Lozano	
	D. D. José Gregorio Guiterrez	
	D. D. Emerigildo Benitez	
	D. D. Miguel Pombo	Shot through the back.
	D. D. Fran. Xavier Garcia Hevia	
	D. D. Cristiano Valenzuela	
20.	D. Antonio Baraya	
	D. Pedro Lastra	
Aug. 8.	D. D. Custodio Garcia Ribera	Shot, and placed on a gibbet.
	D. Hermogenes Cespedes	
	D. D. Tomas Antonio Peña	
	D. N. Navas	
13.	D. José Ayala	
29.	D. D. Joaquin Hoyos	
31.	D. D. Joaquin Camacho	
	D. Nicolas Rivas	
Sept. 3.	D. Liborio Megia	
	D. Andres Linares	
	D. Silvestre Hortiz	
	D. Feliz Pelgron	Shot through the back.
	D. Rafael Niño	
	D. Pasqual Andreu	
	D. D. Martin Cortez	
11.	D. Dionisio Tejada	
19.	D. José Cifuentas	
	D. Bernabé Gonzalez	
	D.·José Maria Ordoñez	
	D. José Antonio Valdez	
30.	D. D. Manuel Bernardo Alvarez	
	D. D. José Maria Arrublas	
	D. Joaquim Garcia, escribano	
Oct. 5.	D. D. Manuel Rodriguez Tonces	Shot, placed on a gibbet, their heads cut off, and placed in a cage at the entrance of the city.
	D. D. Camilo Torices	

Dates.	Names.	Kind of punishment.
	The Count de Casa Valencia	
	D. Pedro Felipe Valencia (colonel)	
	D. D. José Maria Davila	
Oct. 12.	D. Salvador Rizo	
	D. Pablo Morillo	
22.	D. Francisco Cabal	
24.	D. Francisco de Paula Aguilar	
	D. Vicente Monzalve	Shot through the
30.	D. D. Francisco de Ulloa	back.
	D. D. Miguel Montalvo	
	D. D. Francisco Caldas	
	D Miguel Buch	
Nov. 8.	D. D. José Maria Chacon	
	Six soldiers	
21.	D. Francisco Morales	
	Two soldiers	
27.	D. Nicolas Nueva Ventura	
	D. Miguel Gomez Plata, aged 80	Shot, after being tortured three times *.
Decem.	D. Antonio Campuzano	
	D. N. Ponce	Ditto.
	A distinguished individual of Ambalema	

Zipaquira.

Aug. 3.	D. Augustin Zapata	Shot, gibbeted, and his head cut off.
	D. Juan Figueroa	
	D. Francisco Zarate	
	D. José Gomez	Shot.
	D. Luis Sanchez	
	D. José Riano Cortez	

Facarativa.

Aug. 31.	D. Mariano Grillo	Ditto.
	D. Joaquin Grillo	

Mesa de Juan Diaz.

Oct. 7.	D. Francisco Olaya	Ditto.
	D. Andres Quijano	

* This individual came to London in 1814, with Colonel Duran, commissioned by the province of Socorro to purchase muskets, and, on his return, he fell into the hands of the Spaniards, and was tortured, for the purpose of forcing him to declare whether the English government, or any mercantile house in London, sold him the arms which he brought with him from Europe, but nothing could be extracted from him.

Villa de Leyba.

Dates.	Names.	Kind of punishment.
Oct. 27.	D. Manuel José Sanchez D. Juan Bautista Gomez D. Joaquin Vinana	} Shot.

Tunja.

Sept. 20.	D. Santiago Abdon Herrera D. Antonio Palacio D. Alberto Montero D. Ignacio Palaza D. Manuel Otero	} Ditto.

Neiba.

26.	D. D. Luis Garcia D. José Dias D. Benito Salas D. Fernando Salas	} Ditto.
	D. Francisco Lopez D. José Maria Lopez D. Miguel Tello	} Shot through the back.

Popayan.

July 8.	D. Augustin Rosas D. José España D. Rafael Lataza	
10.	D. Carlos Montufar (lieut.-colonel)	
Aug.	D. D. Miguel Angulo D. Emerigildo Troyano D. D. José Antonio Ardila D. Pedro Monzalve D. José Monzalve Serjeant Basquez D. José Acuña	
Aug. 22.	D. José Maria Cabal D. José Maria Quijano D. Mariano Matute D. José Maria Guiterrez	Shot through the back.
29.	D. José Maria Ramirez	
Sept. 24.	D. D. Manuel Vallecilla	
Oct.	D. José Pino and D. José Navia D. D. Frutos Guiterrez The officers Salias, Vaez, Olmedilla, and two more	
30.	D. D. Leon Armero	
Nov. 28.	D. D. Juan Nepomuceno Niño D. D. Cayetano Vasquez D. Pedro Manuel Montano D. José Buitrago	
Dec. 12.	D. D. Francisco Antonio Caicedo D. Joaquim Villacella D. José Maria Perlaza	

Another report says, " General Morillo entered Santa Fé de Bogotá in the month of June, 1816, and remained there till the November following. More than six hundred persons, of those who had been in the congress and provincial governments, as well as the chiefs of the independent army, were shot, hanged, or exiled, and the prisons remained full of others who were yet waiting their fate. Amongst those executed were the botanists Don J. Caldas and Don Juan Lozano (who had been ordered by the congress of New Granada to publish the works of Dr. Mutis); Don M. Cabal, an eminent chemist; Don C. Torres, highly distinguished for his learning; Don J. G. Guiterrez Moreno and Don M. R. Torices, both well known for their early devotion to the cause of their country; Don Antonio Palacio-Fajar; Don J. M. Guiterrez; Don Miguel Pombo; Don F. A. Ulloa; and many other learned and estimable characters. The wives of persons executed or exiled by Morillo were themselves exiled." The names mentioned in this account are not included in the preceding official list. The active agent of Ferdinand, General Morillo, in a letter to his master, published in the *Diario Mercantil* of Cadiz, 6th of January 1817, observes, that " his work is to be done in precisely the same manner as the primitive conquest was established;" and boastingly assures his majesty " that he has not left alive, in the kingdom of New Granada, a single individual of sufficient influence or talent to conduct the revolution." On his return to Spain, Morillo was received into special favour, and created Count of Carthagena.

It was not until above one million of Spanish

Americans had been victims; until almost every Spaniard, whom, with a blind generosity, they had retained in situations of trust, had deceived and betrayed them; until they found no hope left, from either prince or people, that the film fell from the eyes of the natives. They at length discovered that the phantom which they had hitherto worshipped was unable to protect and unwilling to serve them, and that they had been, under the king's name, the victims of treachery, avarice, and cruelty.

Upon this discovery, the spirit of enlightened patriotism burst forth. Their duties to their children, and to the land of their nativity, became at once apparent. The kingdoms of a vast continent immediately, and almost simultaneously, declared their independence; and, in the assertion of their rights, placed their whole reliance upon the justice of their cause, and in the goodness of their swords.

The chequered events, and glorious issue, of this sacred contest, are partly sketched in the following chapters.

CHAPTER III.

Buenos Ayres.—Banda Oriental.—Contrabandistas.—Artigas.—
Beresford.—Whitelock.—Princess Carlota.—Cisneros.—Junta
Gubernativa.—Moreno.—Elio.—Obes.—Ocampo.—Balcarce.
—Cotagaita. — Tupiza. — Castelli. — Paraguay.— Francia.—
Goyeneche.—Huaqui.—Saavedra.—Monte Video.—Rondeau.
—Tucuman.—Gobierno Superior.—San Lorenzo.—San Mar-
tin.—Salta.—Tristan.—Belgrano.—Vilcapugio.—Ayoma.—
Supreme Director.—Arenales.—Warnes.—Alvear.—Monte
Video. — Sipe-Sipe. —Viluma.— Congress. — Pueyrredon.—
Pumacagua.—Pezuela.—La Serna.—Gauchos.

As Buenos Ayres may be considered the cradle
of South American independence, a brief historical
sketch of this nursery of freedom, in the Spanish
dominions of the new world, may not prove uninteresting.

Buenos Ayres was a town of little note until the
year 1776, when it received a distinguished rank
among the cities of South America, by its being
erected into the capital of the newly formed viceroyalty of Buenos Ayres.   The false idea of political
economy, which at that time led Spain to value her
colonies only according to their abundance or deficiency in mines of gold or silver, caused the more
solid advantages which Buenos Ayres possessed in
the salubrity of its climate, in the richness of its soil,
and in the superiority of its position for agricultural
and commercial purposes, to be overlooked.   These

advantages, however, in process of time, and in defiance of the ignorance and prejudices of its rulers,
gradually produced their natural results; and Buenos
Ayres, enlarging its trade by extending its connexions, rose to be a place of considerable importance; but this improvement was interrupted by accidental circumstances.

The Spaniards and Portuguese have, by a singular
fatality, been destined to be neighbours and rivals,
not only in the old but in the new world.   The
possession of the neighbouring colony of Brasil
enabled the Portuguese, by means of the immense
and thinly inhabited intervening territory of the
Banda Oriental, to organize a system of contraband
which nearly annihilated regular and legitimate
commerce.

The desperate character of the agents employed in
this illicit trade; their local knowledge of the pathless country and sinuous shores on the eastern side
of the *Plata*, rendered vain every effort of the Spanish
government to check the ruinous progress of the evil.
To such a pitch, indeed, had the insolence of these
daring outlaws arrived, that they negotiated their
bargains sword in hand, and sometimes murdered
the very person with whom they had just had transactions of business.   An evil so desperate in its nature could be cured only by a desperate remedy, and
the means adopted by the Spanish government were
not more extraordinary than efficacious.   The most
noted and resolute of all these smugglers was selected
to subdue his companions, and destroy the system,
and the choice fell upon Don Fernando José de Ar-

54   ARTIGAS.   CHAP. III.

tigas, who afterwards took so conspicuous a lead in
the revolution.

Artigas was a native of Monte Video. His father,
Don Martin Artigas, was an *hacendado*, or gentleman of landed property, in the immediate vicinity of
that town. The deficiency of the means of education
which, owing to the Machiavellian policy of Spain,
then existed throughout all the colonies, confined
the literary acquirements of young Artigas to a knowledge of reading and writing, and restricted his
employments to horsemanship, superintending his
father's herds, and trafficking in hides not only with
the inhabitants of Monte Video, but also with the
contrabandistas. In consequence of these occupations, and his constant intercourse with the lawless
strangers, he acquired a licentiousness of manners,
and an attachment to an independent and unsettled
life, which induced him very soon to emancipate
himself not merely from paternal control, but from
the jurisdiction of the public authorities. In concert
with these bold characters, he commenced by making
predatory excursions, until, at length, associating
entirely with the banditti, he became the terror of
the whole country. Surpassing his companions in
their knowledge of the secret paths, the hiding-
places, and, in short, in the *arcana* of the plains, no
less than he excelled them in bodily strength, horsemanship, daring courage, and superior talents, he
soon acquired that ascendancy which, under such circumstances, those qualities are calculated to command.

The name of Artigas struck terror into the hearts
not only of the people of the country, but of the

Spanish authorities, and afterwards of the whole
body of *contrabandistas*, whether of Spanish or Portuguese origin. These marauders, bold and ferocious
as they were, contemplated, with astonishment and
admiration, the sagacity with which he conceived,
and the unyielding resolution with which he executed,
his various plans when, at the head of his boys ("*mu-
chachos*"), as he styled them, he from time to time
foiled the officers of justice, and scattered the parties
of militia sent to apprehend him. It is reported
that, upon one occasion, when pursued in the plains,
and finding his farther retreat impracticable from the
worn-out state of his horses, he killed a number of
them, and from behind a parapet, constructed of their
dead bodies, maintained so destructive a fire upon
his pursuers, as to compel them to retire with considerable loss. The judicial proceedings of this new
provost-marshal, when employed by the Spanish authorities against his former comrades, were not characterized by the elaborate forms of ordinary courts
of law. The notoriety of the crime was considered
as a sufficient reason for consigning the delinquent
to instant execution, without any other ceremony or
religious preparation than the *credo cimarron*, a sort
of mockery of confession, being the hurried repetition
of prayers which, rather from ignorance than irre-
ligion, formed an unintelligible jargon. But when
the criminals were numerous, and he felt indisposed
to waste powder, he used to bind them in the skins
of cattle newly slain, and leave them with only the
head at liberty, so that in proportion as the hide became dry and shrunk up, the space allotted for the

body contracted until the unfortunate sufferer expired in the extreme of agony and despair. This mode of incarcerating and tormenting criminals was styled *enchipar*, but its extreme barbarity can scarcely be extenuated by the plea, that there existed neither prisons nor guards in those deserts, and that the ferocious and murderous habits of the criminals required such dreadful examples.

Artigas was in person well proportioned and of ordinary stature. His countenance was mild, and expressive of amiability. He was somewhat bald, and of a fair complexion, which constant exposure to sun and weather had not darkened. Dean Funes describes him to be a man who united to extreme sensibility the appearance of coldness; a most insinuating urbanity to decent gravity; a daring frankness to a winning courtesy; an exalted patriotism to a fidelity at times suspicious; the language of peace to a natural inclination to discord; and a lively love of independence to extravagant notions as to the mode of achieving it.

The viceroy of Buenos Ayres offered Artigas an amnesty for the past, and gave him hopes of an honourable promotion, if he would undertake to put an end to the clandestine commerce and depredations of the Portuguese smugglers, and clear the country of banditti. Never did the pardon of a public criminal produce a more signal and immediate benefit. He applied the whole powers of his mind and body so efficaciously to the task of rooting out the numerous bands of vagabonds, robbers, and smugglers, by whom the country had been overrun, that in a short

time the authority of the government became respected, and private property secured to a degree that
had never been attained in the most peaceful and
prosperous period.

Such was the dexterity of Artigas in the management of his horse and in the use of his fire-arms; so
formidable was his strength, and such the impetuosity
of his onset, that the most daring outlaw quailed
under his eye, and surrendered to his appalling shout.
The effects of his exertions claimed and received the
grateful rewards of those whom he had so efficiently
served.. At the instance of the landed proprietors,
he was constituted conservator of the district *(guarda
general de la campaña)*, and the appointment was
accompanied with a salary adequate to its importance, and to his services.   From this period Artigas
became an irreconcilable enemy to the Brasilian *contrabandistas.*

. Relieved by these energetic measures from the ·
evils which had thus impeded its prosperity, Buenos
Ayres advanced so rapidly in population and importance, that, at the period when the ill-starred English
expedition of 1806 arrived in the river *Plata,* the
inhabitants of the city of Buenos Ayres amounted to
60,000 souls.

The native strength, courage, and energy, displayed
on this occasion, and which were so glaringly contrasted with the pusillanimity of the few Spaniards
who had held this great population in blind obedience,
aroused a spirit of military ardour in the mass of the
people, and, at the same time, gave birth, in a few
enlightened minds, to a hope of future independence,

which subsequent events brought to maturity. Nevertheless, when General Beresford offered in the name of the British government to assist the natives in throwing off the Spanish yoke, and to guarantee their independence, and when Sir Samuel Auchmuty sent a flag of truce from Monte Video, in March 1807, to renew the same proposals, they were not listened to—so loyal, at that time, were the Buenos Ayreans. But at length some of the leading characters began to see the necessity of a change, and accordingly Dr. Zuluaga, a highly respectable ecclesiastic, in conjunction with other influential individuals, secretly proposed to General Whitelock, that he should assist the people of Buenos Ayres in establishing their independence of Spain, under the protection of Great Britain, agreeably to the offers made by Generals Beresford and Auchmuty, and in conformity to the declaration made by the British ministry in 1797, to Spanish America, inviting its natives to declare their independence, and promising every sort of support. This proposition was declined by the British commander, under the plea of his having received no instructions to that effect. The fact appears to be, that the policy of the British government, relative to Spain and her colonies, was no longer the same, and the instructions given to Whitelock obliged him to adopt a different line of conduct.

If the British had acquired sufficient local and political knowledge of the country, they would not have attempted the conquest of Buenos Ayres, but would have confined their immediate object to the possession of Monte Video, the key of the river *Plata*.

From its position and strength, it might have been made the Gibraltar of the eastern coast of the Spanish possessions. Buenos Ayres, on the contrary, is an extensive unwalled city, situated on a gentle elevation in a vast plain, and untenable by any power unsupported by the good will of its inhabitants and the *Gauchos*, or natives of the Pampas.

Whilst the public mind at Buenos Ayres was kept in a state of excitement by the aggression of Napoleon in the Peninsula, the transfer of the court of Lisbon to the Brasils inspired the princess regent of Portugal with the ambition of establishing herself in a similar situation at Buenos Ayres. Her father and brother having, at Bayonne, renounced their right to the crown of Spain, she despatched emissaries to Buenos Ayres to assert her contingent claim, and to concert measures for her residence in that capital. Her proposals were received with enthusiasm, and a warm invitation was sent by the most influential characters of the country, amongst whom were Dr. Castelli, Don Manuel Belgrano, D. Ipolito Vietes, and the Señores Peña and Chambo. But when her projects were on the point of being crowned with success, they were rendered abortive by the unexpected arrival, in May, 1809, of the viceroy Cisneros, who, on ascending the river, touched at Monte Video, and concerted measures with the governor, General Elio, and who, like Cisneros, was a stanch supporter of Ferdinand. Cisneros * made every effort to fulfil the

* Cisneros was sent out to supersede Liniers. He was a flag-officer at the battle of Trafalgar, and was one of the very few saved from the *Santisima Trinidad*.

orders of the court of Madrid to close the ports of
the river *Plata* against English trade, which, in spite
of repeated prohibition, continued on the increase.
Dr. Don Mariano Moreno, an enlightened native,
addressed a pamphlet to the viceroy, demonstrating
the necessity of remodelling narrow-minded institutions incompatible with national prosperity. This
representation elevated Moreno in the opinion of his
countrymen, and in the same proportion it attracted
the hatred of the Spaniards, who foresaw, in the admission of strangers, an end to their own monopoly.

The Spanish and Buenos Ayrean merchants assembled, and addressed strong remonstrances, calling upon Cisneros to enforce the colonial laws, and
pointing out the imminent danger *to religion* by
opening commercial channels to the English.   Peremptory decrees were issued almost from day to day,
ordering the English to withdraw within a specified
time, and an *oidor* was appointed to see these decrees
duly executed; but they were evaded under different
pretexts: and such was the effect of Moreno's paper,
that the viceroy was unable to close the ports against
the English.   Nay, he felt compelled to connive at
British merchants carrying on their trade by means
of Spanish consignees; a triumph on the part of
Moreno, which removed or diminished some of the
difficulties which might have obstructed the progress
of the revolution.   An additional reason for the acquiescence of Cisneros was the necessity of replenish-
ing an empty treasury, and which could not be done
without relaxing the prohibitory system.   From this

period the principal supporters of Princess Carlota changed their views, and formed plans of ultimately . setting up the standard of independence.

After some political struggles, they succeeded in deposing the viceroy, and, on the 25th of May, 1810, named a *junta gubernativa*, composed of nine members, with Don Cornelio de Saavedra as their president *, and Don J. J. Passo and Dr. Don Mariano Moreno, as secretaries.

This last-named gentleman was the soul of the new government, and displayed a genius fitted for the times. He saw the facility of overthrowing a weak government, but he also saw the difficulties of eradicating abuses canonized by the habits of ages, and of substituting any system that should introduce liberty unaccompanied by anarchy. Cisneros and the viceregal authorities still retained a dangerous influence in Buenos Ayres, and in the provinces, where a number of individuals possessing identity of interests were of opinion that the *junta gubernativa* ought to be dissolved, and its members punished.

Under these critical circumstances, Moreno conceived it necessary to effect further and more obvious changes, that the new system might continue to progress. Amongst the *oidores* of the city, was the *fiscal* Caspe; he had long foreseen the consequences of the viceroy having permitted the formation of a govern-

---

* About the same time similar feelings had been developed in various and very distant parts of Spanish America. Actuated by the same motives, *Juntas Gubernativas* were formed in Caracas, in Venezuela, 19th April, 1809; La Paz, 15th July, 1809; Quito, 19th August, 1809; Santa Fé de Bogota, 25th May, 1810; Chile, 18th Sept. 1810. On the 16th Sept. 1810, an insurrection took place in the town of Dolores, in Mexico; and so early as the 25th May, 1809, a popular commotion occasioned the deposition of the president Pizarro in Charcas in Upper Peru.

ing junta, under pretence that the government of the mother country was in its dotage.　Caspe publicly expressed his disapprobation of the junta in not reinstating the viceroy, when it became known that the regency was established in the Peninsula.　As a *ministro* of the king, he communicated his opinion to the newly constituted authorities.　It was received as an insult, and as the forerunner of other measures calculated to endanger the existence of the new order of things.　Some patriot officers gave Caspe a severe caning as he quitted an evening party, and assured him that the lesson would be repeated unless he became more guarded in his political conduct.　This assault was considered as the act of the junta, because the perpetrators were its zealous supporters.　It had the desired effect of frightening the adherents of the old form of government.

The hostile feeling arising out of this incident was farther inflamed as the authority of the governing junta became more circumscribed, and which was soon reduced to the limits of Buenos Ayres.　Monte Video did not recognise it.　In the meanwhile the deposed viceroy despatched secret orders to that and other places, not to acknowledge the receipt of his official letter announcing his abdication and the installation of the junta, nor to obey orders emanating from that board.

The port of Monte Video contained a naval depôt; consequently most of the civil and military officers were Spaniards, as were also the greater part of the garrison, who saw all that was ominous to themselves in the changes at Buenos Ayres.　The governor,

Elio, took decisive measures to prevent the extension of the authority of the *junta gubernativa* to Monte Video. He arrested Colonel Murgiondo, commanding the finest regiment in the garrison, and who was supposed to be an advocate for a change of government. Notwithstanding this, the creoles of Monte Video received the news of the installation of the junta with enthusiasm. They assembled at the municipality, and unanimously resolved that it was expedient to unite with the capital. This resolution, the spontaneous expression of public opinion, was rendered fruitless by the precaution of Elio, and by an individual whose ambition was the original cause of the misfortunes which befel the Banda Oriental.

Dr. Obes, an advocate and official legal adviser of Elio the governor, was a young man of considerable talent, who had entered largely into mercantile and other speculations. He supported the pretensions of the Brasils, which he afterwards abandoned. Desirous of playing a conspicuous part in the approaching revolution, he espoused with great warmth the proposal of making common cause with Buenos Ayres, so long as he indulged in the hope of being appointed one of the junta; a post to which he considered his services entitled him. But when he found himself excluded, he changed his plan, and exerted his influence to thwart the views of Buenos Ayres. Without offering direct opposition to the opinions of those assembled at the municipality, he had the art to draw over many of his countrymen in a manner worthy of Machiavel. The assembly having manifested for the

second or third time its willingness to coalesce with
Buenos Ayres, Obes applauded the idea, but suggested that it ought not to be done *unconditionally*.
This was an idea that had not entered the heated
imagination of the people; but falling from the lips
of a popular advocate, it was unhesitatingly adopted
by a few, and presently after by the majority, which
finally resolved that conditions were proper and necessary. But as the meeting knew not what conditions were desirable, nothing was decided upon but
to appoint a committee to consider of the terms, or,
in other words, to discover their unknown wants.
The meeting separated at an early hour in the morning, and was reassembled in the following day. The
interval was dexterously employed by Obes in sowing
the seeds of dissension. He represented the deposition of the viceroy as an act of criminal folly, at a
time when any thing but unfavourable views might
be expected from the Peninsula. Chance favoured
his scheme. A signal was made for a ship in sight
from a transatlantic port; on her arrival a tissue of
European news was forged, which placed peninsular
affairs in so favourable a point of view, as to leave
the royalist party nothing to wish for. The people
taken thus by surprise, and believing the intelligence,
transmitted an answer to Buenos Ayres, signifying
that varying circumstances prevented them from acknowledging an authority not appointed in a legitimate way by the nation. This was the origin of a
schism which has never been closed. Obes went to
Buenos Ayres to invite the viceroy to remove to

Monte Video; but fearful of arrest, he re-embarked before the junta could have an opportunity of giving orders for his apprehension.

Moreno proposed that the viceroy and *oidores* should be banished. A foreign vessel was got ready with the utmost secrecy, to convey them to the Canaries. Such was the want of means, that the master was to be reimbursed by the junta remitting the custom-house duties upon any return cargo of the vessel*. The viceroy and five *oidores* were invited to attend the junta, which they did in full uniform, under the impression that the intention was to re-instate his excellency. On arriving at the saloon, a member signified to the six individuals, that in consequence of mal-administration it had been determined to place them before the majesty of the throne. With this laconic intimation they were sent on board: a *pampero*, or hurricane of the pampas, blew; and when the gazette announced, on the following morning, their departure, the vessel must have been at least twenty leagues at sea.

This measure had the effect of intimidating the royalist party, and shows the decision of Moreno, in whose hands the helm of state never vacillated so long as he retained his influence; he had, too, the happy art of infusing zeal into the subaltern officers of every department; but the severity of his measures differed essentially from the more moderate course which the party of Saavedra proposed to reduce to practice; and it became impossible that the junta, in

* Such was the *morale* of the custom-house, that more goods were passed as the return cargo than could have been stowed away in a line-of-battle ship.

its then divided state, could continue to exist. The result was, the retirement of Moreno's party, and the removal of its leader, who accepted a mission to England. He died on the passage, in the thirty-third year of his age. His best monument is the public library he founded in his native city of Buenos Ayres.

Moreno excelled as an orator and a writer. As a public man, he was honest, enthusiastic, and laborious. His private character was unimpeachable: he was not acquainted with English literature, but was familiar with that of France. Raynal was his favourite author. Had Moreno resided for a time in England, it is probable that the spirit with which the writings of the French philosophers often inspire the American reader would have been corrected, and that practical experience would have given him additional power to become permanently useful to his countrymen.

The Buenos Ayreans having succeeded thus far in establishing their eventual independence, directed their attention to distant points of the viceroyalty. Colonel Ocampo, with a division of patriots, was sent against a formidable faction, which, at Cordova, had declared against the new order of things. Liniers, formerly viceroy, and now the leader of the opposite party, was made prisoner, and shot, with Governor Concha, and Colonels Allende and Rodriguez. These executions took place under the immediate directions of Dr. Castelli, who had been sent from Buenos Ayres for that purpose by the *junta gubernativa*.

Ocampo, successful at Cordova, considerably augmented his forces, but he had incurred the displeasure

of the junta by presuming to represent the risk of
carrying into execution the sentence of death passed
upon Liniers and his followers, was recalled, and his
second in command, Colonel Don Antonio de Balcarce, advanced to liberate the provinces of Upper Peru
(now called Bolivia), composed of the departments
of Charcas, Potosi, Santa Cruz de la Sierra, Cochabamba, and La Paz, and which were formerly comprehended in the viceroyalty of Buenos Ayres.

On the 27th October, the royalist General Nieto
was defeated at Cotagaita, and on the 7th November
following, the royalist Colonel Cordova suffered the
same fate at Tupiza. These successes gave Balcarce
possession of the Upper Peruvian provinces, as far as
the bridge of the Inca across the *Desaguadero*, the
river which forms the outlet of lake Titicaca, where
he augmented his force to about four thousand men.

Castelli was named commissioner, or delegate, as
well as governor of Upper Peru, and was sent to Balcarce's head-quarters, to direct, in the name of the
junta, the operations of the patriot army, which he
joined previous to its arrival at Potosi. Castelli, an
advocate of considerable talent, was shrewd, active,
and decisive, but volatile and fiery; he was perfectly
master of that species of eloquence which captivates
the multitude, but his disposition was stern, and un-
satisfied with half-measures. He proclaimed every
where liberty and hatred to tyranny, condemning, at
the same time, wherever he found them, those who
were opposed to the new order of things. Don
Francisco de Paulo Saens, governor of Potosi, who

had acquired universal respect during a long residence in South America, together with the president of Charcas, General Nieto (an old officer, who had fought under General Blake against the French at Rio Seco in 1808), and a naval officer (the son of Admiral Cordova), were shot in the square at Potosi. These appear to have been acts of unjustifiable cruelty. Castelli alleged that it was necessary to make the patriots commit themselves, and to discourage that sort of neutrality which until then was observed by the bulk of the people, who did not clearly understand the nature of the dispute, or the object in view. The execution of men of high rank and influence struck terror into all, and those in office fancied that in Castelli they saw a second Robespierre, about to immolate as many of them as he thought fit on the shrine of liberty. Castelli was in fact a terrorist, deeply imbued with the maxims of the French revolution, and perfectly familiar with its details.

His violent proceedings produced the effect he intended. The feeble Spaniards, neglectful of their means of defence, abandoned the strongest positions, and were scattered in every rencontre. The retreat of timorous generals, at the head of an insubordinate soldiery, was impeded by their riches. The civil government of the provinces, unable to leave the beaten tracks of slow routine, dissolved on the approach of the patriots without making an effort, and the small division which left the bank of the river Plata celebrated the first anniversary of the revolution amidst the ruins of the palace of the Incas at

Tiaguanaco, on lake Titicaca, the north-west boundary of the viceroyalty, six hundred and ninety leagues from Buenos Ayres.

The *junta gubernativa*, considering all danger removed on the side of Peru, directed its attention to enforce the submission of Paraguay. About two thousand men were raised and equipped at a great expense, and Don Manuel Belgrano was made a general, in order to be appointed to the command. He marched with little interruption to the confines of Paraguay, where he again required the submission of the junta to that of Buenos Ayres. No answer was given, and Belgrano continued to advance unopposed into the heart of the province. Arriving within a day's march of Asumpcion, he halted in the pleasing expectation of making his entry into that capital on the following morning. But, as night closed in, numerous fires were seen to blaze around, and excited considerable alarm. These appearances were the more extraordinary, because in his advance no hostile preparation had been seen or suspected. Indeed an inhabitant had rarely been met with; but when daylight broke upon Belgrano, he perceived his army encircled by countless hordes of armed Paraguayans, evidently resolved to make a determined resistance to the further progress of the invaders, who, upon comparing numbers, anticipated no other result than annihilation. The Buenos Ayreans were attacked and defeated; but Belgrano was agreeably surprised by a flag of truce from Yedros, the general of the Paraguayans, who signified that, although the

Buenos Ayreans were completely in his power, the
government of his province felt no disposition to treat
them as enemies: on the contrary, they considered
Buenos Ayreans as brethren engaged in the same
cause; that Belgrano, having satisfied himself that
the Paraguayans possessed the power and inclination
to maintain themselves independent of Buenos Ayres,
as well as of the regency of Cadiz, was at liberty to
retire unmolested; and that provisions and supplies
of every kind should be furnished to facilitate his
return.   Belgrano, seeing the utter impossibility of
accomplishing the object of the expedition, gladly
accepted the offered terms, and countermarched to
Buenos Ayres.   Dr. Francia, who has since become
celebrated as the dictator of Paraguay, was at this
time secretary to the provincial government, and is
supposed to have been the author of the lesson which
Buenos Ayres will not easily forget, although very
anxious to have it forgotten.

Alarmed at the progress of the Buenos Ayreans
on the Desaguadero, Abascal, viceroy of Peru, made
overtures to Castelli, the representative of those whom
his excellency had, some time before, been pleased to
designate as " men born to vegetate in obscurity and
submission."   Castelli received the proposal for an
armistice with disdainful levity.   His answer was,
that he knew of no other authority than the sovereign
people, of whom the viceroy was an oppressor.   This
arrogant reply cost the patriots dearly.   The viceroy
assembled fresh troops under active generals, whilst
Castelli gave himself up to dissolute pleasures; the

civil-administration of the provinces was neglected; and the military chiefs showing an equal disregard of their duties, the advantages gained in the first campaign were disgracefully thrown away.

General Goyeneche, a native of Arequipa, who had been appointed to the command of the royalist forces, drew four thousand men from Cuzco and Arequipa, and placed himself on the northern side of the Desaguadero, within two days' march of the Buenos Ayreans. Previous to this the patriots had been induced to listen to another proposal for the suspension of hostilities, and an armistice had been adjusted; but Goyeneche, professing that the most solemn engagements, when made with insurgents, might be broken with impunity, attacked and defeated Castelli and Balcarce at Huaqui, on the 20th of June, 1811, six days previous to the time agreed upon for the renewal of hostilities.

The royalists attempted to justify this breach of faith by asserting that Balcarce had, during the armistice, moved forward from La Paz to the Desaguadero. This was the case; but, by so doing, he did not pass the boundaries conceded to him by the terms of the armistice. But Goyeneche had neither delicacy of feeling nor scruples of conscience. He had been brought up to the law, and was, besides, a doctor of theology. When the French entered Spain, he became their partisan, and received instructions from the Grand Duke de Berg, in Madrid, to proceed to South America, to promote the interest of King Joseph. But, upon passing through Seville,

Goyeneche changed his policy, and declared in favour of the central junta. He was raised, in one promotion, from an officer of militia, to the rank of brigadier-general in the army. He embarked with two sets of instructions, namely, those of the Grand Duke de Berg, and those of the central junta. The intrigues and the cringing baseness of this renegade are well known at Monte Video and Buenos Ayres, whence he proceeded to Peru. His servile pliability; great fluency of speech; and a prepossessing address, obtained his appointment to the command.

Balcarce, with a remnant of his force, sought safety in Jujuy, two hundred and thirty-six leagues to the southward of Huaqui. Notwithstanding Balcarce's retreat from Upper Peru, Goyeneche, in his advance, met with great opposition from the patriotic natives of Cochabamba, Santa Cruz de la Sierra, and Chayanta. The cruelties committed under the sanction of Goyeneche are almost incredible, and entitle him not only to the appellation of a denaturalized American, but display the peculiar traits of his own cringing and artful character. The cities of Chuquisaca, La Paz, and many others, will record his infamy. He is now excessively rich, and has been created Count of Huaqui. After the expulsion of the patriots from Upper Peru, Castelli was recalled, and placed under arrest at Buenos Ayres. Anxiety of mind acting upon a broken constitution, the effect of his own irregularities, conducted him to the grave in 1812.

On the 23d of September, 1811, the *junta gubernativa* at Buenos Ayres was dissolved, and Saavedra, the ex-president, compelled to fly; an executive, composed of Don Manuel Sarratea *, of Señor Chiclana, and Dr. Don Juan José Passo, was named.

Saavedra is a native of Buenos Ayres, and of a respectable family. Previously to the revolution he had been elected *alcalde ordinario* for a year; a sign that he had the reputation of integrity, and was esteemed by his fellow-citizens. On the expulsion of Whitelock, the command of a militia corps, which had distinguished itself, was conferred upon Saavedra. This gave him additional importance; and he acted a conspicuous part in suppressing a plot formed by Alzaga, a Spanish merchant, to overthrow the viceroy Liniers, principally because Liniers was a Frenchman. Grown dizzy by his elevation to the presidency, Saavedra wished to exercise a preponderating influence in the junta, but failing in his object, through want of adequate capacity, he intrigued with the deputies from the provinces to exclude the secretary, Dr. Moreno, whose talents and patriotism were insurmountable barriers to the supposed intentions of Saavedra to tread in the footsteps of the viceroy. Moreno contended, that the president was, as to power, only on an equality with the other members of the junta; but Saavedra succeeded in the end in separating Moreno from the executive, and incorporating the provincial deputies with the junta. Saavedra was not long before he abused the ascendancy thus acquired. The first proscriptions of

* This enlightened and talented individual was the envoy from the Argentine republic to the court of London in 1826.

deserving citizens rendered him odious, and caused his downfall.

Saavedra has not since emerged from private life. His administration of the public revenue was unstained by rapacity, and he is now considered an honourable citizen, and a respectable father of a family.

Buenos Ayres had been more successful in her attempt on the Banda Oriental, a province which is bounded on the east by the Brasilian province of Rio Grande, on the south by the river Plata, and on the west and north by the river Uruguay: Monte Video is the capital.   A brilliant little affair took place at Las Piedras in 1811, when nearly a thousand soldiers and sailors sallied from the fortress against a party of two hundred *gauchos*, or mounted peasantry, armed principally with cutlasses and boarding pikes, under the orders of Artigas, who had continued a steady adherent to the Spanish cause until a short time before the action, when he passed over to the patriots, in consequence of a dispute with the governor of Monte Video.   The royalists were driven back into the town with much loss.

On the 31st December, 1812, General Rondeau, at the head of one thousand five hundred newly raised troops, repulsed two thousand Spaniards, who made a second sortie.   This affair took place at el Cerrito, about a league from the fortress, to the very walls of which the royalists were pursued with great slaughter.

Artigas continued to perform prodigies of valour at the head of his brave gauchos, but he had long before displayed symptoms of insubordination, and about this period he withdrew from under the command of Rondeau, and, acting independently, ever after evinced great dislike to the natives of Buenos Ayres.

Balcarce was ordered to Buenos Ayres, and the remnant of his troops, which had escaped from Huaqui, was compelled to retire from Jujuy to Tucuman, one hundred and five leagues farther. After one or two intervening appointments, General Belgrano succeeded to the command; and he had the talent and good fortune, on the 24th September, 1812, to defeat the royalists, three thousand strong, at Tucuman, under General Don Pio Tristan, who had advanced from Potosi, with the intention of penetrating to the city of Buenos Ayres itself. In this affair, Belgrano had only eight hundred soldiers, and some guerillas of ill-armed gauchos. These successful actions gave spirit and confidence to the patriots, who became imboldened in proportion as the royalists were disheartened.

In October, 1812, another change was effected in the government of Buenos Ayres, by military commotion. An executive, styled *el gobierno superior*, was established. It was composed of the Señores Peña, Passo, and Jonte, who were to call together an assembly, representing the people of the viceroyalty. On the 30th of January, 1813, a sovereign constituent assembly was convened at Buenos Ayres. It was not until now that the Spanish flag and cockade were abolished, and replaced by the bi-color (blue and white). The coinage also now bore republican arms. The assembly re-elected the members of the *gobierno superior*, with the exception of Passo, who was replaced by Perez. Don Carlos Alvear was chosen president of the assembly.

In the month of January, 1813, the royalists, still in possession of Monte Video, sent three hundred of the garrison, in some small vessels of war, to make an incursion into the provinces of the river Plata. They disembarked at San Lorenzo, on the right bank of the river Paraná, when Colonel Don José de San Martin, with a hundred and fifty *granaderos à cavallo*, attacked and completely defeated them on the 5th February.

San Martin was wounded in this affair. He is the same officer who, as General San Martin, was afterwards the directing genius of the emancipation of Chile, and who subsequently undertook the bold measure of liberating Peru. He was the first who raised and organized, conformably to the European system, a regiment of cavalry. It was called the *granaderos à caballo*, and was composed of four squadrons. Until this period the importance of disciplined and regular cavalry, and the mode of employing it, was almost unknown in the provinces of the river Plata. The action of San Lorenzo manifested the advantages of the sword over the carbine or pistol.

After the victory of Tucuman, General Belgrano increased his numbers to about two thousand troops, and obtained on the 20th February, 1813, another signal victory over Tristan, who, with two thousand men, had taken refuge in the town of Salta, eighty-seven leagues to the north of Tucuman, around which

they had thrown up some hasty breast-works, and in
the defence of which the Spanish part of the inhabitants assisted the royalist troops with great resolution.

Belgrano gallantly attacked the royalists in their
parapeted hold.   They lost five hundred in killed,
and the patriots three hundred.   The surviving
royalists were all made prisoners.

The brilliant success of Tucuman and Salta were
highly creditable to the patriots, and reflected honour
upon the bravery of the undisciplined supporters of
the infant republic.   But Belgrano marred his prospects by his confiding magnanimity.   He generously
permitted General Tristan to return to Peru, together with his officers and men, upon their engaging,
with the usual solemnities, not to bear arms against
the republic.   Forgetful of his honour, General Tristan violated his parole, and the archbishop of Charcas
profaned the altar of God by pretending to absolve,
with the ceremonies of the Roman catholic church,
Tristan and his soldiers from the performance of
their sacred pledge.   The soldiers followed the example of their more guilty chief, and incorporated
themselves with the royalist army of General Pezuela
(afterwards viceroy of Peru), who, having by these
dishonourable means augmented his force to four
thousand men, attacked and defeated Belgrano, who
commanded about the same number, at Vilcapugio,
between Potosi and Oruro, on the 1st October, 1813,
and again at Ayoma, in the department of Cochabamba, on the 14th November following.   The unfortunate patriot general escaped with a remnant of
his force to Tucuman.

The guerrilla leaders, Warnes, Camargo, and Padilla, remained in the mountains of Upper Peru, and obtained many advantages in rencontres with royalist detachments.

The inhabitants of Cochabamba, and of Santa Cruz de la Sierra, and the Indians of Chayanta and of Yamparaes, lost no opportunity of manifesting their determined hostility to the Spaniards.

On the 31st December, 1813, the *gobierno superior* at Buenos Ayres was abolished, and Señor Posadas was elected supreme director, with a council of seven individuals to assist him.

San Martin was appointed to the command of the remains of the army of Belgrano. San Martin found only five hundred and seventy-seven rank and file at Tucuman, but in March, 1814, he mustered nearly four thousand men of all arms, and a train of fourteen pieces of artillery. He constructed barracks a mile distant from the town of Tucuman, and surrounded them with a ditch and a parapet, in order to serve not only as a *point d'appui*, but also to guard against the desertion of the gaucho soldiery, who, brought up with notions of individual independence, were so predisposed to disunite, and so averse to restraint, that it was no easy matter to establish a discipline incompatible with their roving mode of life.

On the 25th May, 1814, Colonel Arenales obtained some advantage over the royalists in the provinces of Cochabamba. Warnes was equally successful in the *Quebrada* of Santa Barbara on the 9th October of the same year.

The gauchos of Salta, headed by the brave Guemes,

cut off supplies of the royalists in their front. Warnes, Padilla, Muñecas, and other leaders*, distressed the royalist rear, and ultimately obliged Pezuela to fall back upon Cotagaita.

In May, 1814, San Martin was obliged to remove to the Cordovese mountains, on account of ill health. This was unfortunate, as it put an end to a correspondence with Colonel Castro, who commanded the royalist vanguard at Salta, and was afterwards executed by order of General Pezuela, in consequence of its having been discovered that he was about to excite revolt amongst the royalist troops.

On San Martin's recovery he was appointed to the command of the province of Cuyo, which henceforth became an extremely interesting point. The invasion of Chile by sea from Peru, by the Spanish General Osorio, was then threatened. The most fatal effects to the cause of independence were apprehended, and these fears were but too soon realized by the re-establishment of the Spanish dominion throughout Chile about the end of October, 1814.

General Rondeau was succeeded by Colonel Alvear in the command of the patriot force which threatened Monte Video in 1814, the year in which the capture took place (20th June), and which was rendered less difficult by Captain Brown, of the Buenos Ayrean flotilla, having gallantly attacked and destroyed, on the 17th of May, the Spanish naval forces in the harbour, which were very superior in point of numbers to those under his command. Five thousand

* Warnes, Padilla, Muñecas, and Guemes, were successively slain in guerrilla warfare.

five hundred royalist troops, forming the garrison
of Monte Video, capitulated to Colonel Alvear.
Eleven thousand muskets, a complete depôt of ammunition and arms, and magazines of other military
stores, were delivered up to the patriots. Artigas,
as chief of the Banda Oriental, the title he now
assumed, although a stanch patriot, was in open
hostilities with Alvear. He demanded possession
of Monte Video, which was refused. The Buenos
Ayrean General Soler was appointed governor of the
captured town, against whom Artigas carried on an
active war, until he obliged the new governor to
evacuate the place, of which Artigas immediately
took possession.

The extreme folly of Posadas, and of a subsequent
government, in proclaiming Artigas a deserter, and
setting a price upon his head, excited feelings of irre-
concileable hatred; and from this epoch all attempts
made by the Buenos Ayreans, to reduce Artigas to
submission, were vain.

Rondeau, who had succeeded San Martin in the
command of the patriot army at Tucuman, made an
irruption into Upper Peru at the head of three thousand five hundred men, but was totally defeated by
General Pezuela, with equal numbers, on the 28th
of November, 1815, at Sipe-Sipe (between Potosi
and Oruro), and afterwards at Viluma; and Upper
Peru again fell into the possession of the Spaniards.

Posadas having resigned the supreme directorship
(1815), General Alvear was elected in his stead, but
was soon obliged to resign and fly the country. He
was succeeded by Rondeau on the 16th of April,

1816, and a *junta de observacion* was substituted in the place of the sovereign constituent assembly. The first object of the junta of observation and of the new director was to establish a national congress, fairly representing the whole body of the people, and, in order to do away with provincial jealousies against Buenos Ayres, it was ordered to assemble at Tucuman. Accordingly the assembly representative, or general constituent congress, was regularly installed in the city of Tucuman in the month of March, 1816. On the 9th of July it declared the independence of the provinces of the river Plata. General Pueyrredon was on the same day named supreme director of the republic. He had distinguished himself in the defence of Buenos Ayres against the British, and served in Upper Peru against the royalists. Congress was afterwards removed to Buenos Ayres. In the same year Belgrano was re-appointed to the command of the remnant of the army which had escaped from Sipe-Sipe and Viluma. He displayed great activity in re-organizing and augmenting that force.

Several attempts had been made by the house of Braganza to encroach upon the territories of its Argentine* neighbours, but they were frustrated. The dissensions between Artigas and Buenos Ayres appeared to remove every obstacle to the success of an invading force. To place the Brazilian frontier beyond the reach of anarchical contagion was the pretext of the court of Rio Janeiro to take possession of

* The provinces of the river Plata are called the Argentine provinces; and the inhabitants Argentines.

the Banda Oriental, because it was pretended that, in becoming independent of Spain, the province had been the prey of misrule and every species of disorder. About 8000 Portuguese and Brazilian troops, under General Lecor, advanced in three divisions : one by the way of Santa Teresa; the second by the way of Cerro Azul; the third proceeded towards the river Uruguay. After suffering much in repeated skir-mishings with the brave gauchos, General Lecor entered Monte Video on the 19th of January, 1817. Abandoned by Buenos Ayres, the Orientals made an heroic desultory defence. National hatred became more deeply rancorous, and the Portuguese soon found themselves reduced to the fortress occupied by their garrison, and to such parts of the country as were within musket-shot of their encampments.

The Buenos Ayreans, not satisfied with remaining passive spectators of the contest between the Bra-zilians and Artigas, sent two expeditions against the latter, which Artigas defeated or destroyed*.

Within a year after resuming the command, Bel-grano had upwards of 4000 excellently well-equipped troops at Tucuman; but unfortunately a spirit of anarchy extended to the principal officers, who de-posed their general, and spread themselves over the provinces, each with as many soldiers as he could draw over to himself. By such means they usurped the civil and military administration of the provinces, which some have retained to this time. Thus Bel-

* Artigas continued hostile to Buenos Ayres and Brazil several years longer, but having afterwards sustained some reverses in the province of Entre-Rios, he sought an asylum in Paraguay. He was placed under rigid surveillance by Dr. Francia. Artigas died in the sixtieth year of his age at Candalaria, in 1826.

grano saw his troops dispersed and himself made
prisoner, instead of leading them on against the
Spaniards in Upper Peru, agreeably to the combina-
tions of San Martin.

Belgrano was born in Buenos Ayres, of Italian
parents, who acquired and bequeathed to their children a considerable property. Don Manuel was
educated at the university of Salamanca. On his
return from Spain, he was appointed secretary to the
consulado, or chamber of commerce; a situation
which brought him in contact with the commercial
men, at that time the most important class in Buenos
Ayres. The mildness of Belgrano's manners, heightened by something of the Italian polish, his fondness
for music, and his taste for the *belles lettres*, rendered him, in early life, a distinguished member of
society.

He was one of the Buenos Ayrean literati who
wrote in periodical works, subject to a censorship,
the object of which was to prepare the way to independence, by calling forth a proper spirit in the
minds of the Argentine youth. The only print-
ing press in Buenos Ayres was an indifferent one,
formerly belonging to the Jesuits of Cordova, sold
in 1809 by auction, and bought by a patriotic club
formed by Moreno, and of which Belgrano was a member. He was at one time a partisan of the Princess
Carlota of Portugal; but, dubious of the policy of
supporting the pretensions of the sister of Ferdinand,
he altered his plan, and dedicated his efforts to bring
about the independence of his country, with a degree

G 2

of disinterestedness seldom equalled. His relative
Castelli; his friend Vietes; and Don Julian Espinosa,
who were likewise favourable to the claims of the
Bourbon princess, also veered about.   Belgrano displayed considerable ardour, but not much military
capacity.   He was deficient in coolness, and he had
not the robustness of frame necessary to undergo the
fatigue of a harassing campaign.   Nevertheless he
applied himself closely to the study of tactics, and
established strict discipline.   He was temperate at
table, and indefatigable in his duties, but he had
neither the experience, nor all the military tact necessary to success in a general officer.   He gave to
his country two days of glory in the actions of Tucuman and Salta, and many of mourning for those
of Vilcapugio and Ayoma.

His popularity did not shield him from persecution,
which was sometimes carried to an unjust extreme,
but his mind was never depressed.   He continued
to labour for the welfare of his country with unwearied zeal, being persuaded that, unless the people
were enlightened by a more general diffusion of
knowledge, liberty would remain an empty sound.
Belgrano was one of the most liberal, the most humane, the most honourable, and the most disinterested men that South America has produced.   His
death, in 1820, was justly deplored by every class.

The civil dissensions which afflicted Buenos Ayres
after this period are endless and uninteresting.

The intrigues of France and Austria to impose
upon the Buenos Ayreans a Bourbon or an Austrian

prince were defeated by the good sense and patriotism of that people, notwithstanding the anarchy which had reduced them to the brink of destruction.

In Peru, the attention of the viceroy Abascal had been diverted by the simultaneous rising of the Indians in the provinces of Cuzco, Huamanga, and Arequipa. As the declared object of their leader, Pumacagua, was to establish the independence of the whole country, many Creoles flocked to his standard; but the activity of General Ramirez soon crushed the efforts of these unarmed multitudes. Amongst the patriots who suffered death was Melgar, a youth of twenty, and a native of Arequipa. He was the Moore of Peru, and composed some *Yaravi* melodies of which the author of Lallah Rookh might have been proud. The fate of Melgar excited universal commiseration, and his memory is cherished with affectionate respect. His life, though short, was tinged with the romance of ardent but hapless love. A beautiful girl refused his proposals of marriage, and this severe disappointment drew from his muse those plaintive *tristes* which are still sung all over the country. The priest appointed to attend Melgar at the place of execution appeared to be earnestly exhorting him, when the prisoner exclaimed aloud, "Holy father, this is not the moment to talk of politics, or of the things of this world. I came here prepared, but you have disturbed the calm of my mind." He then asked the officer of the escort for a cigar. This was given, and having smoked about half of it, he regained his composure; and

coolly announcing that he was ready, he met his
death manfully.

The severity of the numerous punishments * which
followed produced a calm which lasted until the
arrival of San Martin at Pisco, in 1820.

Abascal was superseded in the viceroyalty of Peru
by General Pezuela, who made his public entry into
Lima on the 7th of July, 1816. The king of Spain,
at the same time, appointed General La Serna to
relieve Pezuela in the command of the army of Upper
Peru. La Serna arrived from Spain in the Venganza,
at Arica, on the 7th of September, 1816. Two thousand Spanish troops arrived also about the same time,
by the way of Panama, and round Cape Horn.

La Serna, and many other officers who had also
served in the peninsular war, affected a superiority
over those who had been many years in Peru, and
spoke with contempt of every other system of warfare
except that which had been so successfully practised
in the mother country. La Serna introduced so
many innovations† quite inapplicable to Peru, and
his correspondence with the viceroy betrayed such
an anxiety to show his attainments as a tactician,
that Pezuela, as well as the generality of old officers,
were disgusted with the pedantry of pretensions which
soon became ridiculous by his total failure, and retreat, before a few irregularly-armed gauchos.

La Serna seems to have formed his opinion of the

---

* Pumacagua was one of those who suffered death.
† One, however, must be recorded to his honour. He issued an order that
thenceforwards no officer should inflict the punishment of death on account of
political opinions, without obtaining his previous sanction.

practicability of marching over land to Buenos Ayres
by studying the map; for, in a letter dated Arica,
12th of September, 1816, he gravely tells the viceroy
that he purposed to take Buenos Ayres in the month
of May in the following year; but wisely adds, " if
topographical and political difficulties do not prevent it."

 La Serna, with four or five thousand men, penetrated as far as Salta, but deemed it prudent to fall
back upon Jujuy, fourteen leagues to the northward
on the Potosi road. Jujuy is a straggling place,
about half a league in extent, and contained at that
time a population of about three thousand souls. The
town is beautifully situated on the bank of a river,
which flows through a finely-wooded valley. It is
at the debouchement of the valley of Jujuy that the
town is situated, and is the first on the Pampas which
the traveller comes to on his way southward from
Potosi.

 La Serna could penetrate no farther. The Spaniards occupied no more of the country than the
ground they stood upon; or, at any rate, none beyond the range of their musketry. They were
hemmed in by about as many hundred gauchos, as
La Serna counted thousands of regular troops. Some
of the gauchos were armed with muskets; others
with swords, carbines, or pistols; but many were
only provided with a long knife, *bolas*, and the *lasso*.

 A small round hat, a shirt, a poncho, breeches
open at the knees, and boots made of raw hide, were
the only articles of dress commonly worn by the peasantry. These gauchos concealed themselves in the

depth of forests in the day-time, and often made an
attack in the night upon the royalist quarters, or
outposts.   The gauchos outside the town were in
constant communication with the inhabitants; many
of the latter would join in nocturnal surprises, and
be found at home by daylight next morning.   It
was useless for La Serna to send out strong piquets.
The royalists lost so many men in this way, without
ever gaining a single advantage, that they were
obliged to give over every attempt to move beyond
the outskirts of the suburbs in pursuit.   ·

The manner in which the gauchos carried on their
operations was as follows : They kept men constantly
on the highest trees, to watch every movement of
the royalists, or to receive communications from
friends in the town.   Royalists who straggled to a
small distance were invariably cut off.   On some of
the trees bells were hung ; and, tolling them, the
gauchos would call out to the Spaniards, " Come,
Goths, and hear mass."   From other trees, drums
were suspended, and the call to arms beaten ever
and anon ; whilst, in others, men would be sounding
bugles, at intervals, both day and night.   If the
royalists approached, the gaucho on the look-out
would glide from the branches like a squirrel, vault
into the saddle, and, watching a favourable opportunity, level his musket or pistol, fire, and probably
bring down a royalist, before he galloped off and
dived into the recesses of the forest.   All this served
to intimidate and harass the Spaniards to an amazing
degree.   Numerous desertions took place ; supplies
were cut off; and even fuel became so scarce, that

the rafters and other wood-work of untenanted houses were made use of for the purpose of cooking.

La Serna himself was driven to desperation. Foiled at the very entrance of the Pampas, by a handful of undisciplined but well-mounted gauchos, he had the additional mortification of finding all his vaunted plans of conducting the war *en regle* inapplicable to the country into which he had, with so much pompous parade, endeavoured to introduce them. He was finally compelled to abandon Jujuy and retire to Cotagaita, in order to avoid starvation.

CHAPTER IV.

Army of the Andes.—Royalist forces in Chile.—Palaver with
the Pehuenche Indians.—Ninconyancu.—Father Julian.—
Millyagin.—Savage life.—Passage of the Andes.

IT has already been stated, that General San Martin had been appointed governor of Cuyo, where he
laboured incessantly to raise an army. This force,
which assumed the denomination of the army of the
Andes, had for its nucleus a detachment of one hundred and eighty recruits of the Buenos Ayrean battalion No. 8, which followed San Martin to Mendoza,
soon after his appointment to the governorship in
the month of September, 1814. The slender resources of the provincial government, and the thinly
sprinkled population of fifty thousand souls over a
vast extent of pampa, prevented the governor forming an army, strong enough to threaten Chile, in a
shorter space of time than two years. Its organization reflects the highest credit upon the tact, talent,
and industry of San Martin. The discipline which
he established showed that the experience he acquired
in the peninsular war had given system and efficacy
to those natural qualifications which fitted him so
well for the task. His popularity is evident from
the alacrity with which his exertions were seconded
by the inhabitants of the province, whose patriotism
and cheerful submission to great sacrifices were

beyond praise. The confidence of British merchants at Buenos Ayres was also conspicuous in the readiness with which they gave credit to the government for supplies intended for San Martin. He was beloved by the provincials, and he enjoyed the confidence of his officers and men to a degree never shown to any preceding commander in that part of the world.

San Martin having received from Buenos Ayres a reinforcement of four hundred and fifty men of the battalion No. 7, and two hundred of the regiment of *granaderos à caballo*, was enabled, in the middle of the year 1816, to form at Mendoza about four thousand regular troops, tolerably well clothed and armed, besides a considerable number of unarmed militia. According to the original official returns for December, 1816, still in the possession of a patriot general, the royalist force in Chile under the president, Captain-General Marco, consisted of seven thousand six hundred and thirteen regulars, and eight hundred militia. The latter were armed and paid, which was not uniformly the case with the militia. Notwithstanding this disparity of force, San Martin determined upon making the attempt to liberate Chile, and he was the more anxious to commence at once offensive operations, as some symptoms of party spirit had been shown by two or three chiefs of the army.

The patriot general hoped to be enabled by *ruse de guerre* to cause Marco to divide his forces. For this purpose, when every preparation to march was nearly completed, San Martin caused a conference to be held with the Indians of Pehuenche, for the ostensible object of soliciting leave to march unmolested through their territories, for the purpose of attacking the Spaniards from the pass of *el Planchon*. On the day before that fixed upon for an interview with the Indians, San Martin caused to be sent to the fort of San Carlos, on the river Aguanda, one hundred and twenty goat-skins of *aguardiente* or grape brandy, three hundred skins of wine, a great number of bridles, spurs, all the old embroidered or laced dresses, that could, with great diligence, be collected in the province, hats, handkerchiefs of an ordinary kind, glass beads, dried fruits, &c. &c. &c. for presents; an indispensable preliminary to success in any Indian negotiation.

At eight o'clock on the morning of the —— of September, 1816, the *caciques* approached the esplanade in front of the fort, with all the pomp of savage life, each at the head of his warriors; their wives and children bringing up the rear. Polygamy being practised, the wives were very numerous. The men wore their hair unconfined and long; their bodies, naked from the waist upwards, were painted with different colours. Their horses were also stained precisely in the same manner as when they go to war. In fact, it was the fighting costume of man and horse. Each cacique was preceded by a small party of patriot cavalry, sent by the general for the purpose of keeping up an irregular fire of blank cartridges from their pistols as the tribe advanced. This mode of ushering the Indians to the presence of Christians is a compliment with which they never dispense. As the tribes arrived on the esplanade, the women and children filed off, and took their station on one side, without dismounting. When all the tribes had arrived, the warriors of one tribe commenced a sham fight, during which they kept the horses at full speed, or made them turn on their hind legs, curvet, caper, and prance about in the most extraordinary manner. During the exhibition, a gun was fired every six minutes from the fort. The Indians answered the salute by slapping their mouths, and making the most frightful noises, in token of satisfaction. This sort of tournament lasted about a quarter of an hour for each tribe, which afterwards retired towards the spot occupied by the women, and remained on horseback, spectators of the performance of the other tribes, which exhibited in turn. These martial exercises lasted till noon, and San Martin's escort of a troop of cavalry and two hundred militia remained formed on the parade during the whole time.

The prelude to business being over, the palaver commenced in the place d'armes, where the governor of the fort had provided a table covered with the cloth of the chapel pulpit, and benches for the cáciques, and war-captains, who were the only persons admitted to conference with the general. The Indians outside remained formed and mounted, keeping themselves on the alert, until the result should be made known.

Upon arriving at the place d'armes, the chiefs took their seats according to seniority; the caciques first, and then the war-captains. San Martin, the governor of the fort, and the interpreter, placed themselves on a bench at the head of the table. The general, as a matter of courtesy, proposed a friendly glass previous to proceeding to business; but all declined, assigning as a reason, that if they drank, their heads could not be firm to give proper consideration to the matter they had assembled to discuss. The interpreter, father Julian, a Franciscan friar, an Araucanian by birth, and brought up by a Creole family from the age of ten, then commenced an harangue. He reminded them of the good understanding which had subsisted between the Pehuenche Indians and the general in chief, who relied with confidence upon a continuation of the harmony so happily established, and who had convened them in solemn PALAVER to compliment them with drink-offerings and gifts, and to request that the patriot army might be permitted to pass through the Pehuenche territory, in order to attack the Spaniards, who were strangers in the land, and whose views and intentions were to dispossess them of their pastures, rob them of their cattle, carry off their wives and children, &c. &c.

A dead silence followed: these painted savages, wrapped up in profound meditation for a quarter of an hour, presented a picture truly striking. At length the senior cacique, named Ninconyancu, broke silence. He was nearly eighty years of age, his hair was snow-white, and his appearance venerable in the extreme. Directing his discourse to his brother chiefs, he calmly asked if they were of opinion that the proposals just made by the Christians ought or ought not to be accepted. The debate which followed was carried on in a manner exceedingly interesting. Each chief in his proper turn declared

his sentiments with the utmost tranquillity, and without the slightest interruption, or sign of impatience,
from the rest.   Having agreed upon the answer proper to be given, Ninconyancu addressed himself to
the general, and informed him that the Pehuenches,
with the exception of three caciques, whom the rest
knew how to restrain, accepted his proposals.   All
then rose from their seats, except the three caciques,
who did not concur in opinion with the majority,
and, in testimony of their sincerity, embraced the
general.   Without losing a moment, the cacique Millyagin stepped out, and communicated to the Indians
on the esplanade, that the proposals of the Christians
were such as could be accepted.   They instantly un-
saddled, and delivered their horses to the militia to
turn them out to feed.   They next proceeded to deposit their lances, hatchets, and knives (the arms of
the Pehuenches), in a barrack-room, not to be returned till after the conclusion of the revels which
invariably follow a palaver.

The voluntary surrender of their arms into the
hands of their natural enemies is an extraordinary
trait in the Indian character.   The motive is to avoid
bloodshed amongst themselves during the dreadful
intoxication which forms an essential part of the
ceremony of every palaver.   The blind confidence
with which they disarm themselves shows the elevated notions they entertain of the sacred rites of
hospitality, and a consciousness of the necessity of
rendering themselves comparatively harmless during
the maddening influence of excessive drinking.   The

solicitude of the women to remove weapons at such times is highly interesting.

Having lodged their arms in the fort, they proceeded to the corral, or cattle-pen, where some mares had been shut up for slaughter. They trip up the animal by means of the *lasso;* tie its feet together, as butchers in England do those of sheep; and then open a vein in the neck, whence they sometimes suck the blood, in which operation the women and children take precedence. The carcass is cut up and roasted, which is done very quickly. The skins are carefully preserved, and formed into reservoirs in the following manner. An excavation, two feet deep and four or five in circumference, is made in the ground; the fresh skin is then placed, with the hair, undermost, in the concavity, and fastened round the brim by wooden pegs. Into this skin-lined cistern wine and brandy are indiscriminately poured. Sixteen or eighteen men squat themselves around these wells, the number which are of course in proportion to the number of people. The women did not commence *their* carousings, which were held apart, until sunset, when they seated themselves around similar reservoirs filled with the same mixture. From motives of delicacy, which cannot but be admired, four or five females of each tribe abstained from drink altogether, in order to keep watch over their companions when reason had taken its flight.

The scene which next presented itself was singularly novel. Two thousand persons, including women and children, were seated in circles upon

the esplanade.   One of the first subjects of conversation was their own feats, or the deeds of their
ancestors.   Some were affected to weeping in re-
lating family history.   As soon as the liquor exercised its influence all talked together, and shouted,
and yelled with deafening din.   Quarrels ensued,
as a matter of course, and many fought, when, in
the absence of weapons, they bit and kicked each
other, and tore out hair by handfuls.   The uproar
amongst the men, the vociferation, the laughing, and
the shrieks of the women, and the squalling of infant children, formed altogether a combination of
discords that · must · be left for the imagination to
conceive.   Small parties of the patriot militia, placed
on duty for that purpose, were kept in full employ
in separating combatants.   Towards midnight the
revels subsided into the silence of the grave.   Men
and women were stretched upon the ground as if in
a lethargy, or in the arms of death, except a very
few who still retained the power to crawl or roll a
few paces; but the greater part were perfectly motionless.   The horrid carousal was kept up in the
same style for three successive days, that is, until the
last drop of liquor was exhausted.   In consequence
of the precautions of San Martin, the casualties were
unusually few.   Only two men and one woman were
killed in the course of the *entertainment*; a very
trifling loss of life, when it is considered that for
such occasions it is the custom to treasure up the
memory of old quarrels, and endeavour to take ample
vengeance.   In negotiations with Indians it is impossible to avoid contributing to excesses, because a

stinted supply of liquor is construed into an insult never to be forgiven.

A day was set apart for the exchange of gifts. Each cacique presented the general with a *poncho,* the manufacture of his wives. The poncho is an upper garment in universal use amongst the men of all ranks throughout South America. It is an oblong piece of woollen or cotton; a sort of scarf with a slit in the centre, through which the head passes, and the drapery falls from the shoulders behind and before near to the ankle, and on each side to the elbow, leaving the arms in perfect liberty. A short poncho which reaches below the waist is equally common, and is usually worn in-doors. Some of the ponchos accepted by the general were by no means contemptible as specimens of native manufacture, particularly in the liveliness of the pattern, and the permanence of the colours. What the Indians appeared to prize most highly of the gifts they received were the hats, and the embroidered or lace dresses, which were put on and worn the instant they came into their possession.

The distribution of presents was made on the fourth day, and rendered it the most fatiguing of the whole period. Those who know the unscrupulous and harassing importunity of the Indian character can alone form an idea of the manner in which the general was besieged without the respite of a moment.

On the sixth day, San Martin received despatches from General Pueyrredon, who was marching from Salta to Cordova, where San Martin proceeded to meet him.

The commandant of the fort of San Carlos was charged to do the honours of the palaver until it should be over. The Pehuenches remained at San Carlos eight days longer, on account of some dealers having appeared from Mendoza with spirits, and bartered them away for most of the presents which the Indians had received from San Martin. The Pehuenches departed at the end of a fortnight, so highly gratified by the entertainment, that they declared that such a splendid palaver was not known in the annals of tradition.

A circumstance occurred which proved the existence of the custom of bathing immediately after child-birth, which had been spoken of, but doubted. The accouchement of an Indian woman took place two days after her arrival. Accompanied by two women of her tribe, she immediately took a bath in the river, and, with her new-born son, remained in the water for a considerable time. A few days after her delivery she set out with the party upon their return to their own country, in the full enjoyment of health and strength. The zealous friar, Father Julian, did not lose this opportunity of rescuing, by a pious stratagem, the soul of the babe from the "talons of Satan." Under pretence of exhibiting the child to his companions, he baptized it in the general's apartment, and prevailed upon his excellency to become godfather.

The Pehuenches are separated from the Araucanians by the cordillera of the Andes. The men are of lofty stature, of muscular frame, and have a lively expressive countenance. Their population is esti-

mated at from twelve to fourteen thousand, which is
far below what it used to be, before the small-pox
and a more loathsome disease made such dreadful
ravages amongst them. They do not appear to have
any object of adoration, or to observe any form of
worship. They occupy the territory which lies at
the foot of the eastern side of the Andes, and extends one hundred and twenty leagues from the right
or south bank of the river Diamante, which forms
the southern boundary of the province of Cuyo.
They are accounted the most courageous people of
the pampas, and are often engaged in warfare with
the neighbouring Indian nations. They never give
quarter excepting to women and children, who are
carried into captivity. It is remarkable that kid-
napped whites or Creoles do not always avail themselves of opportunities to return to civilized society.
There seem to be pleasures in savage life, which
those who have once tasted seldom wish to exchange
for the charms of more polished intercourse. For
example, a Creole boy was carried off at the age of
thirteen; at twenty-six he returned to Buenos Ayres
on some speculation of barter. He said, that whoever had lived upon horse-flesh would never eat beef,
unless driven by necessity or hunger; he described
the flesh of a colt to be the most delicately flavoured
of all viands. Having transacted the business which
led him to Buenos Ayres, he voluntarily returned to
his favourite haunts, and is probably living amongst
the Indians to this day.

In the year 1784, a rich landed proprietor of Cordova repaired with his family to one of his most di-

stant *haciendas* for the purpose of superintending the
marking of his cattle. The peasantry, far and near,
had collected to assist him. Whilst he was one day
occupied in this important operation at a considerable distance from the house, a horde of Indians suddenly pounced upon his family and domestics, who
had remained at home; killed all the males; plundered
the house; and carried off the females. Amongst
these were two lovely girls, daughters of the proprietor, one of thirteen, the other of fifteen years of
age. After a lapse of three years a truce was concluded with these Indians, one of the stipulations
being, that the captured females should be ransomed.
The father set out with stores of bridles, spurs, and
other articles, to redeem his daughters. One of them
had become the mother of an only daughter, and the
other of three sons. The Indians felt themselves
bound to restore the women, but it was considered
a point of honour not to give up the children. They
were accordingly left; the daughters accompanied
their father home, and nothing that wealth could
procure was spared to render them happy. Three
years subsequent to this transaction the family re-
visited the estate which had been the scene of their
misfortune. Whether this awakened maternal and
conjugal affection, or that an attachment to savage
life once indulged becomes uncontrollable, the very
first night of their arrival at the *hacienda*, the ladies,
instead of retiring to their apartments, persuaded a
servant to saddle a couple of their father's horses, and
to attend them to the Indian frontier. The horses
were missed at daybreak, but it excited no particular

alarm, in consequence of its being attributed to robbery. But the ladies being sought for at the hour
of breakfast, it was discovered that their beds had
been unoccupied the previous night. The truth instantly darted upon the father's mind; his fleetest
horses were immediately prepared, and an ample relay
driven before the pursuers; but notwithstanding the
speed with which they travelled, they did not over-
take the fair fugitives until the third day. The distracted father compelled them to return, and they
have since passed their days at Cordova, vainly sighing
to rejoin their husbands and children, and regretting
the enjoyments of what civilized people haughtily de-
nominate savage life. This anecdote was recounted
to the author by General San Martin, who was personally acquainted with the ladies.

Hospitality is the virtue in highest repute amongst
the Pehuenches. Revenge their cherished and pre-
dominating vice. Their indolence is such, that they
pass the greater part of their lives stretched out on
the ground drinking a fermented liquor made from
wild fruits. Agriculture is not known amongst them;
they subsist upon horse-flesh and wild fruits*. Their
wives, in addition to domestic labours, attend to the
horses, take and fetch them to and from pasture, and
saddle them for their husbands. Their intervals of
leisure are occupied in spinning and weaving ponchos,
which their husbands convey to Mendoza, and barter
for liquor, dried fruits, &c. They lead a wandering
life, and change of abode is regulated by the suf-

---

* The kernel of the araucaria is called pehuen, or peguen, and gives its name
to the tribe.

ficiency of pasturage for their numerous *cavalladas*, or droves of horses.   They are bold, skilful riders, and they move individually, or in a body, with incredible rapidity.   An Indian drives ten or a dozen spare horses before him, and changes on the road as occasion may require: the horses are so docile and so well trained, that oftentimes, when called by name, one will come from pasture at the sound of his master's voice, and quietly suffer the *lasso* to be thrown over his head.

During the revolution the Pehuenches observed a strict neutrality, notwithstanding the efforts of the Spanish authorities to seduce them to act against the patriots, who, on their part, took care to encourage this pacific conduct by seasonable presents to the most influential of the caciques.   It cannot, however, be supposed that they were well inclined towards either party; and, as San Martin foresaw, they soon sold the secret (that the patriots intended to invade Chile by the southern passes) to Captain-General Marco, who instantly divided his forces by transferring the greater part from the north to Talca and San Fernando, in the full conviction that Chile would receive the first blow from one of the southern passes of the Andes.   He was strengthened in this opinion by knowing, that these passes are less difficult of access, and that they occasionally furnish pasturage, of which the passes more to the north are totally destitute.   To keep up the illusion, San Martin sent guerrillas to make demonstrations towards the south on the eastern side of the Cordillera.

The known practicable passes, in a length of a

hundred and forty leagues of the ridge of mountains which *wall in* Chile, on the eastern side, are six. Beginning with the northern, they are as follows:

La Rioja, which debouches into the province of Coquimbo; Los Patos, which debouches into the valley of Putaendo; Uspallata into the valley of Aconcagua; El Portillo * into the valley of San Gabriel, near to the capital; Las Damas into the valley of Colchagua; and El Planchon into the valley of Talca.

The obstructions which nature has raised to impede the passage of a numerous body of men over the mighty barrier of the Andes, are not easily conceived but by those who have crossed these stupendous ridges. A novel kind of warfare might be carried on by means of a few men, who could be made to defy the utmost efforts of a numerous army. Supported by a few rude field-works, they might prevent the strongest division from advancing; and, taking a circuitous route, might gain the rear, and, by similar works, hem in an invading column amongst horrid defiles and mountainous wildernesses, whence not a man could escape.

At length the patriot army broke up its cantonments, and marched from Mendoza on the 17th January, 1817. As it defiled into the gorges of the Andes, the sedate but warm-hearted Mendozinos took a most affectionate farewell of the departing warriors. It consisted of the following corps:

---

* Whilst the army of the Andes was at Mendoza, Captain, now Colonel O'Brien was stationed at the Portillo with thirty men: eleven died in consequence of the severity of the weather. The colonel remained there for six months.

Battalion No. 7, Lieutenant-Colonel Conde.

Battalion No. 8, Lieutenant-Colonel Cramner.

Battalion No. 11, Lieutenant-Colonel Las Heras.

Cazadores, Lieutenant-Colonel Alvarado.

Regiment of *granaderos à caballo*, Lieutenant-Colonel Sapiola.

TRANSLATION OF A RETURN,

Showing the number of men, of horses, and of saddle and baggage mules, which composed the army of the Andes, that marched from Mendoza to Chile in 1817.

	Horses.	Mules. Saddle.	Baggage.
2800 infantry, one mule to each man, and one extra mule to every fifth man		3360	150
200 chiefs and officers of infantry, three saddle mules for every two officers, one baggage mule for every two officers, two baggage mules for every chief - -		300	140
900 cavalry and artillery, three saddle mules for every two men, including five baggage mules per company - -		1350	60
60 chiefs and officers of cavalry and artillery in the same proportion as that allowed to infantry - - - -		90	40
Staff - - - - - -		71	46
Hospital and hospital-attendants -		47	75
Company of artificers with their tools		74	30
120 workmen with implements to render the mountain tracks passable -		180	10
1200 militia in charge of spare mules and the transport of artillery - -		1800	
Provisions for fifteen days for five thousand two hundred men - -			510
113 loads of wine, the rations being a bottle per day each man - - -			113
Train conducting a cable bridge, grapples, &c. - - - - -			65

	Horses.	Mules.	
		Saddle.	Baggage.
Field-train of artillery, one hundred and ten rounds per gun, 500,000 musket-ball-cartridges, 180 loads of spare arms		87	683
Spare horses for cavalry and artillery - - - - - -	1600		
	1600	7359	1922

This does not include the division of Lieutenant-Colonel Freyre of three hundred and eighty men, or of Lieutenant-Colonel Lemus of one hundred and thirty men, who crossed the Andes by the pass of the Portillo, taking with them a thousand and twenty mules.

The provisions consisted of jerked beef, highly seasoned with capsicum, &c. &c. toasted Indian corn, biscuit, cheese, and a great quantity of onions and garlic. The latter was indispensable to provide against the *puna* or *soroche*. [Note by the translator. When animals are affected with the *soroche*, their nostrils are rubbed with garlic.]

The most serious difficulties encountered consisted in the time and labour expended in making mountain paths transitable; in the want of fuel; and in the nature of the climate. Out of nine thousand two hundred and eighty-one mules and one thousand six hundred horses, which left Mendoza with the troops, not more than four thousand three hundred mules and five hundred horses arrived in Chile, in spite of every precaution that the keenest ingenuity could devise. Five hundred of the militia were told off to convey the howitzers and field-pieces of artillery, under the superintendence of the praiseworthy and indefatigable Friar Beltran, who, abandoning his cell, became an officer of artillery. Where the ground was comparatively good, each piece of ordnance was carried between two mules, by means of a pole or bar fastened "fore and aft" to a pack-saddle on each mule; the gun was suspended from the pole, and hung in an horizontal position, about two feet from the ground, between the tail of the foremost and nose of the hindmost mule.   Sometimes it was carried on the shoulders, and sometimes in the arms of the militia-men; at other times dragged up and lowered down declivities by means of ropes.   The *cabrestante* (a sort of portable capstan) was also occasionally used to assist in raising the gun, or to steady it in the descent.   *Sorras,* a sort of narrow sledges constructed of dried bull-hides, were frequently made to serve as carriages.   Seven hundred oxen formed a part of the provision for fifteen days.   To provide against starvation, in the event of defeat, provisions were left in depôt at about every twelfth league, in charge of a small militia guard.

Between the town of Mendoza and Chile five principal ridges run north and south, besides innumerable colossal ramifications.   The intense cold on the summits killed many men; nearly the whole army was affected in the course of the march with the *puna,* or a difficulty of respiration, and numbers died in consequence.   Every step the patriots took convinced the least reflecting, that the obstacles already overcome were of a nature that left not a ray of hope that a retreat would be practicable, if they were beaten in the field; but, instead of despondency, a spirit of union pervaded all, and they marched full of confidence, each corps emulating the rest in enduring submission to hardships of no common severity.   Hence the successful day of Chacabuco, that placed nearly all Chile in the hands of the patriot party.   But before entering into the details of that decisive affair, we will give some account of the events which characterized the revolution of Chile.

CHAPTER V.

Chile in 1810.—Figueroa.—Carreras.—Pareja.—Yerbas-Bu-
enas.—Chillan.—Sanchez.—O'Higgins.—Mackenna,—Membrillar.—Gainza.—Talca.—Dissensions.—Breach of faith of
the royalists.—Desperate defence of Rancagua.—Patriots
emigrate.—Sambruno.—Osorio.—Exiles of Juan Fernandez.
—Rodriguez.—Freyre.—Army of the Andes.—Soler.—Martinez.—Necochea.—Chacabuco.— Supreme director.—San
Martin. —Talcahuano. — Las Heras.— Quintana, — Patriot
army.—Commodore Bowles.

CHILE continued tranquil under Spanish misrule
until the 18th of July, 1810.   On that day the Captain-General Carrasco was displaced, and the Count
de la Conquista appointed in his stead.   During the
administration of the latter, the plan of the revolution
was formed.   The Señor Alvarez de Jonte, highly
distinguished for talent and patriotism, was powerfully instrumental in bringing about this change, to
promote which he was sent expressly from Buenos
Ayres by the *junta gubernativa* *.

On the 18th of September, 1810, a junta of government, composed of seven of the most distinguished
citizens of the capital, was established in Santiago de
Chile.   Its authority was instantly acknowledged by
the provinces with every demonstration of joy.   To

* Alvares de Jonte resided some time in London. He accompanied Lord
Cochrane to Chile, and was employed as secretary in one of the cruises to the
coast of Peru. He afterwards sailed from Valparaiso as judge-advocate to the
liberating army. He died at Pisco. The government of Peru granted a pension
to his children.

the general causes which gave birth to the revolution
of Spanish America, may be added some incidental
events which distinguished the early efforts for emancipation in Chile from those of every other state.
One of the most striking peculiarities was the perfect unanimity which pervaded all classes. Here the
highest ranks of society stood foremost in promoting
a change. In other states, numbers of the corresponding rank either hesitated, or were so much interested
in the preservation of the old régime, that they did
not, as a body, join the people until the cause was
pretty firmly established, and it became comparatively
safe for them to change sides. In Chile, the humbler
classes retained their habits of passive obedience
longest, and *followed* instead of taking the lead; but
unanimity was the grand characteristic of the blood-
less revolution of 1810.

The sovereignty of Ferdinand VII. was acknowledged by the junta. The coinage continued to bear
his effigy, and, notwithstanding a very general desire
to declare for independence, the communication with
the viceroy of Lima was preserved according to the
forms of the old routine.

The tribunal of the *real audiencia* remained in
full exercise of its functions; and justice was administered, as before, in the royal name. No Spaniard was removed from the employment, or divested
of the dignity, to which he had been previously appointed, or of which he was in the actual enjoyment
at the date of the revolution. It is probable that less
alarm was felt, on account of the Spaniards being
fewer than in other sections of Spanish America.

The great political change was unstained by crime
or severity, and nothing occurred to disturb the tranquillity and satisfaction of the people at large, until
the 1st of April, 1811, when the capital heard, for
the first time, the sound of hostile musketry, and saw
the blood of some of its citizens flow. The Spanish
colonel, Figueroa, having gained over a part of the
garrison, attempted to overthrow the newly established government. Fortunately the junta was able
to bring an opposing force, which defeated the hostile
faction: fifty-six lives only were lost. The Spanish
leader was taken, brought to trial, and shot. The
indignation of the people was satisfied by this act of
justice, though the Spanish residents in general were
loudly accused of being implicated. It was also
known that the *real audiencia* had encouraged, and
secretly assisted, the conspirators. That tribunal was
therefore dissolved, but its members were permitted
to remain in the capital, in the undisturbed possession
of their liberty; and a tribunal called " *camera de
apelacion*" (court of appeal) was substituted in its
room.

At the time Figueroa attempted to carry his plot
into execution, the Chilenos were occupied in the
choice of members of the first congress, which assembled in June, 1811. Its measures were distinguished by liberality. It reformed many abuses;
proclaimed unrestricted commerce, with an exception
in favour of coarse cloths and flannels; decreed that
the office of *regidor*, hitherto hereditary or purchase-
able, should thenceforth be filled up by annual pa-
rochial elections; useless places were abolished, and

salaries reduced. The clergy were to be paid by the treasury, and they were forbidden to take fees from their parishioners. A manufactory of arms; a school for artillery; and other useful establishments, were ordered. It had the honour to be the first legislative body in Spanish America which took effectual steps to bring about the gradual, but total, abolition of slavery within the republic. Children born of slaves after the date of its first meeting were declared to be free, and all slaves brought into the country were to receive manumission after residing there a specified period. The liberty of the press was established, and a happy futurity seemed to dawn upon the infant republic. But the unprincipled ambition of three young men arrested the beneficent march of events, and introduced into the bosom of the state intestine commotions. The three Carreras were descended from a highly respectable family, and held commissions in the army. They, particularly the eldest, were gifted with talents which gave them some claims to consideration, in spite of licentious habits, until they brought their country to the brink of ruin, for the sake of personal aggrandizement. Their sister, called the Anna Boleyn of Chile, was a powerful instrument in forwarding their designs; and although some forty summers have now passed over her head, she still retains the bloom of beauty. She is a woman of splendid natural abilities, but, it is said, too much addicted to the artful intrigues of political parties.

The disproportionate number of deputies chosen for the city and province of Santiago, and the illegality of some elections, according to the provisions of an act made by the first junta, produced much disquietude, and some heated remonstrances from the provinces. Congress, seeing the necessity of an alteration, reduced the number of deputies representing Santiago to one half, and countenanced the re-election of an increased number for Concepcion. Tranquillity was restored, but reform was the pretext of the Carreras. Possessed of manners which rendered them favourites with the troops, and with many of the people, they formed a party; seized the helm of government; and, on the 2nd of December, 1811, dissolved the congress.

A junta was formed, at the head of which the elder brother placed himself. Public affairs were conducted in a manner which could not produce any other result than divisions and discontent in every class of society. Dissensions, which afterwards arose between the brothers, occasioned the momentary retirement of the elder; but a reconciliation having been brought about, he re-assumed his post at the head of the junta. Meanwhile, Abascal, viceroy of Peru, who had always affected a desire to maintain a good understanding with the democratical government, watched the progress of anarchy, and was not slow to avail himself of the opportunity, which the general dissatisfaction arising out of the misrule of the Carreras gave, to make their usurpation subservient to his own sinister views. Accordingly he despatched a force from Lima, under General Pareja, who disembarked at San Vicente, near Talcahuano, in the beginning of the year 1813.

It appears throughout the revolution, that the

Chilenos have almost invariably erred on the side of extreme moderation. Neither the conspiracy of Figueroa, nor some disturbances which were caused by the Spaniards at Aconcagua and other points, nor the unequivocal signs of enmity daily manifested by the Spanish residents to the new establishment, were sufficient to induce the incautious Chilenos to displace those Europeans who had been appointed to responsible situations by the king's government. One of the natural consequences of this misplaced confidence was, the instant surrender of Concepcion by the governor, a Spaniard, who had thoughtlessly been permitted to retain his command. At Talcahuano, a Creole officer and a priest made some resistance, but these two Chilenos having no other support than the enthusiasm of an unarmed population, were speedily reduced to submission, and Talcahuano, like the neighbouring city of Concepcion, became a royalist station.

The intelligence of the landing of Pareja, and of his uninterrupted march towards the river Maule, at length awakened the Chilenos from their slumber. The manner in which they met the threatening danger did honour to their spirit and patriotism. Party feeling disappeared; just causes of complaint against the Carreras were consigned to oblivion; and rival factions were lost sight of in a noble emulation to make every sacrifice to preserve their country from the yoke so lately shaken off. The provinces resounded with expressions of corresponding feelings, and unanimity once more pervaded the public mind. A military chest, with ample funds, was instantly

formed, and a force of six thousand men sent into
the field as if by magic. The command was intrusted to Don José Miguel Carrera, who, upon
quitting Santiago, delegated the civil power to his
brother, Don Juan José, one of the three to whose
unbridled ambition Chile traces her heaviest misfortunes.

The campaign was opened, on the 31st of March,
1813, by a bold and skilful movement with a division
of the Chileno troops, which fell by surprise upon the
whole royalist army at a place called Yerbas Buenas.
Had the first success been immediately followed by
repeated blows skilfully directed, the contest might
have been decided at once; but the undisciplined
levies of the patriots scattered themselves to indulge
in pillage, instead of pursuing the affrighted royalists,
who, left to recover themselves, rallied, and took up
an advantageous position. The specimen which General Pareja had of the valour of the Chilenos induced
him to retire to San Carlos (about thirty-five leagues
from Yerbas Buenas), in front of which town he
posted his troops, on ground favourable for defence,
and awaited a second attack. In a severe action,
which lasted several hours, Carrera was unable to
break the squares of the royalists; nor was it till the
following morning that the patriots were aware they
had obtained a victory. They then discovered that
the royalists had retreated, leaving the field covered
with dead and wounded. The royalist garrisons,
hastily withdrawn from Concepcion and Talcahuano,
concentrated at Chillan, whither General Pareja fled
for shelter, and where he died, in old age it is true,

but, as is generally supposed, of chagrin at his un-
looked-for reverses.

Colonel Sanchez succeeded to the command, and
displayed extraordinary activity in strengthening,
by field-works, every point around the town of
Chillan.

The siege which followed was long and harassing.
The patriots obtained signal successes in various
assaults, and penetrated at last to the great square in
the centre of the city; but the Spaniards, retiring
to a convent which served as a sort of citadel, maintained themselves there against all the efforts of a
force but poorly provided with means of attack. The
severity of the weather, from rain and cold, at length
obliged the patriots to raise the siege, which had
been signalized by many brilliant proofs of personal
courage, and in which not a few of the gallant Chilenos met an honourable death.

From that time the fortune of war inclined alternately to either side. A series of minor affairs took
place, in which, on the part of the patriots, the names
of O'Higgins and of Mackenna shine with distinguished lustre. But the Spaniards had better officers
than the Chilenos, and the tactics of their general
frequently rendered indecisive the undisciplined
valour of the patriot forces. The royalist general,
fruitful in resources, had the address to bring over
the Araucanian Indians to his support. He also
availed himself so well of the ancient habits of the
Chilenos, and of their blind submission to the orders
of the king, that he found little difficulty in swelling
his ranks with recruits from the brave but misguided

peasantry within the limits of the country occupied by the royalists.

In this undertaking Sanchez was ably seconded by the efforts of Spanish missionaries, who employed those engines which are likely to succeed with the ignorant and superstitious. Unfortunately many of the peasantry were, at that time, further confirmed in their hostility to the cause of independence by the absence of all discretion and common morality in the conduct of the Carreras, whose excesses rendered their dismissal a measure of indispensable necessity, because their example led the patriot troops into the greatest irregularities.

José Miguel Carrera had shown his military incapacity by not making the most of the advantages gained by the brave Chilenos under his orders at Yerbas Buenas. He next converted his command into a sort of dictatorship in the districts occupied by his troops. At length the government of Santiago mustered up sufficient energy to suspend the Carreras from rank and employment. They were ordered to Santiago, but they were taken on the road by the royalists, and sent to Chillan as prisoners of war.

Colonel Don Bernardo O'Higgins, who, on the 24th of November, 1813, succeeded Carrera in the command of the army, had distinguished himself for personal courage and rectitude of conduct; whilst the prudence and talents of Mackenna made up in some measure for the deficiency of discipline and want of organization in the patriot forces.

The independents were formed into two brigades:

one under O'Higgins, in Concepcion; the other under Mackenna, at Membrillar, near Chillan.

About this time the royalist cause was strengthened by a reinforcement from Lima, under the command of General Gainza, whose personal and professional qualities rendered him a formidable enemy; but, in spite of these changes, almost a year passed without producing any important occurrence.

On the 19th March, 1814, Mackenna repulsed, at Membrillar, a sharp attack of General Gainza, who, on the following day, was again worsted by the corps of O'Higgins, hastening from Concepcion to the support of Mackenna *. Discouraged by these rencontres, Gainza left the patriot brigades behind him, and marched towards the capital, an open city without a garrison. The movement was made under the supposition that O'Higgins would be unable to follow for want of horses. Gainza crossed the river Maule eighty leagues south of Santiago, and took the city of Talca, but not without an heroic though unavailing opposition from a party of the inhabitants, who, unprovided with means of defence, perished in the vain attempt to preserve the town.

The people of Santiago ascribed the loss of Talca to the negligence of the executive. It was therefore considered opportune to dissolve the governing junta of three persons, and to nominate a supreme director. Don Francisco Lastra was the first invested with that dignity. He hastily collected a small division, and

* This officer, a native of Ireland, was killed by one of the Carreras, in a duel fought at Buenos Ayres in 1814.

sent it, under Don Manuel Blanco Ciceron, against
the enemy; but that officer was totally defeated at
Cancharayada by the vanguard of the royalists.

In the meanwhile O'Higgins prepared to follow
Gainza; and, by forced marches, made under great
difficulties, arrived on the left bank of the river. He
immediately bivouacked, as if it had been his intention to remain there for the purpose of watching the
enemy's motions; but as soon as it became dark he
crossed the rapid Maule at several points, a few miles
above the Spanish posts, and when morning broke,
the astonished enemy beheld the patriot army in a
strong position, which commanded the road to Santiago, as well as that to Chillan, the centre of the
royalist resources. The masterly passage of the
Maule may be considered as equivalent to a victory.
General Gainza, cut off from retreating either way,
was compelled to shut himself up in Talca.

It was during this state of affairs that Captain
Hillyar, of His Britannic Majesty's ship Phœbe, arrived from Callao at Valparaiso with overtures from
the viceroy of Peru. The supreme director appointed
commissioners to negotiate, and Captain Hillyar accompanied them to Talca, where, under his mediation,
a treaty was concluded, on the 5th of May, 1814.
General Gainza bound himself to re-embark for Peru,
with all his troops, within the space of two months,
and to leave the fortifications of every place, then
occupied, in the same state he found them. It was
also stipulated that the viceroy should acknowledge
the new order of things, whilst Chile engaged on her
part to send deputies to the Spanish cortes, and to

acknowledge the government established in the Peninsula during the captivity of Ferdinand the Seventh. Hostages were given on both sides.

The Chilenos in general expressed their dissatisfaction at a convention which they considered disadvantageous, under circumstances which gave just grounds for hope that a single blow would have terminated the campaign gloriously, and rendered the country completely independent of Spain. Nevertheless peace was considered so firmly established, that the militia were permitted to return to their homes; the troops of the line were indiscreetly reduced; and the directorial government hastened to fulfil, with scrupulous fidelity, such articles of the treaty as could be carried into immediate execution.

Don José Miguel and Don Luis Carrera had been set at liberty by the royalists, in virtue of the treaty of Talca. Don Juan José had been banished across the Andes, but had returned. In May, 1814, a court martial was ordered to assemble, for the purpose of exhibiting (as was stated to the public) the bad conduct of the three brothers. Don Luis was arrested, but Don José Miguel and Don Juan José succeeded in concealing themselves. The present juncture was considered by them to be favourable to a new usurpation of the reins of government. They secretly organized in the capital a party with which they had never ceased to correspond, and which now assisted in carrying into execution their criminal designs. A part of the garrison having been gained over, the Carreras showed themselves on the 23rd of August, 1814, and deposed the supreme director Lastra.

A junta was formed, and the elder Carrera placed himself at the head of it, as in the first usurpation. The indignant citizens, although much dissatisfied with Lastra, immediately assembled, and signified their extreme displeasure to the Carreras; but finding the latter deaf to remonstrances, unsupported by the bayonet, they appealed for protection to O'Higgins, who lost no time in obeying the call. He marched from Talca, and a partial rencontre took place in the vicinity of Santiago. The rival parties were on the eve of a general action, when a messenger appeared from the royalist general, and a suspension of arms was agreed upon, to receive his despatches.

The messenger was the bearer of an official letter, intimating that the viceroy had refused to ratify the treaty of Talca; that the only measure left for the insurgent authorities to secure the royal clemency was by surrendering at discretion. The despatch concluded by the assurance that the sword was unsheathed, in order not to leave one stone upon another in case of resistance.

It also appeared that Gainza had been recalled to Peru, although he had some claims upon the consideration of a viceroy remarkable for his disregard of public faith towards the patriots, but who in other respects bore an honourable character. Gainza had violated the treaty by remaining, under various pretexts, in Concepcion, until General Osorio arrived with fresh troops, and a supply of military stores of every kind; and events ultimately proved that he had signed the treaty for no other purpose than that time might be gained for these reinforcements to arrive. The plan of the Spaniards was so well formed, that 4000 troops were already within fifty leagues of the capital when the summons for unconditional submission was received.

Agitated by conflicting feelings, O'Higgins magnanimously sacrificed his just resentments to save his country. He acceded to the demands of his rival, and nobly turned his arms against the common enemy. Carrera followed O'Higgins with a strong division; but discipline no longer gave efficiency to soldiers who had often fought gloriously: desertion to an alarming extent prevailed. To consolidate his ill-acquired power, Carrera had weakened the army by removing some deserving officers, and had banished from the capital many distinguished citizens, for no other reason than their discountenance of his arbitrary proceedings.

O'Higgins encountered the royalist force on the bank of the river Cachapoal; but, having only 900 men, was defeated, and he took shelter in the town of Rancagua, twenty-three leagues from Santiago. He caused the entrances of the streets to be blocked up, and made the place as difficult of access as his very slender means permitted.

On the 1st of October, 1814, the royalists commenced an attack which lasted for thirty-six hours, during which time the fire on both sides was kept up with unremitting vigour. Each party hoisted the black flag, and no quarter was given. In the hottest of the action the magazine of the patriots exploded, and produced the most destructive effects; but, undismayed by the heavy misfortune, their

efforts seemed to redouble, and the Spanish general
determined to abandon the enterprise.   He had actually given orders to retreat, under the impression
that Carrera, who had remained an unmoved spec-
tator, would cut off his retreat, and that his exhausted
royalists would be attacked in a disadvantageous position by that chief with fresh troops.   But General
Ordoñez, the second in command, perceiving the in-
action of Carrera, who evidently exhibited no intention to effect a diversion, or to send to O'Higgins
the smallest succour, determined upon making another grand effort.   By means of the hatchet and
the flames the royalists penetrated through the walls
of the houses, and at length fought their way, inch
by inch, to the square in the centre of the town.
Here O'Higgins made his last stand with two hundred survivors, worn out with fatigue, tormented
with raging thirst, and surrounded by heaps of slain;
till observing all was lost, he, although wounded in
the leg, headed the brave relics of his party, and
gallantly cut his way through the royalists.   Such
was the impression produced by this desperate act
of valour, that none ventured to pursue the patriots,
who continued their retreat without further molesta-
tion to the capital.   The royalists remained in Rancagua to despatch the wounded; to butcher the few
remaining inhabitants; and to destroy what had
escaped the flames.

The Carreras had still under their command one
thousand five hundred men; but they abandoned the
capital without a struggle.   The depredations committed by the troops of the Carreras irritated the

citizens to such a degree, that a deputation was sent
to Osorio, to request him to enter Santiago and re-
establish order.   Six hundred troops crossed the
Andes with Carrera.   General O'Higgins emigrated
with about one thousand four hundred persons, many
of whom were ladies of rank, who passed the snowy
ridges of the Andes on foot.   All were received at
Mendoza with generous hospitality by General San
Martin, and few returned home until after the battle
of Chacabuco in 1817.

In Santiago, Osorio assumed the rank and exercised the powers of captain-general.   His first
measure was to proclaim an amnesty; and some of
the wealthy citizens, who had fled to their estates, or
to distant parts of the country, returned to the bosom
of their families: but so soon as Osorio felt himself
secure, he threw off the mask, and imitated the rest
of his countrymen in their violation of the most
solemn engagements with Americans.   In less than
a month after the disaster of Rancagua, the principal
citizens of the capital were arrested.   Confiscation,
prosecution, and imprisonment were the order of the
day; but, fearful of exasperating too far a people who
bore the yoke with extreme impatience, the captain-
general had not the courage to shed the blood of his
victims.

Forty-six fathers of families were sentenced to be
transported to the island of Juan Fernandez.   Their
wives and daughters, clad in deep mourning, besought
with tears and prayers for permission to share the
exile of their husbands and fathers; but the tyrant
not only turned a deaf ear to their piteous entreaties,

but forbade all communication under the severest
penalties.   One lady only overcame the difficulties
thrown in the way.   By the kind interposition of
Sir Thomas Staines of H. M. S. Briton, with the
captain of the corvette, the amiable and accomplished
Doña Rosario de Rosales was permitted to follow her
father, who was between seventy and eighty years of
age. Most of the exiles were in the decline of life; some
of very advanced age; two of them paralytic; and all
of them, accustomed to the comforts and conveniences
of affluence, were crowded into a Spanish corvette of
war, and sentinels were placed at the hatchways, with
orders to fire upon any who might put their heads
out to breathe a less impure atmosphere.   None were
permitted to retire for a moment, even upon the most
urgent occasion; and pestiferous air, engendered by
the congregation of so many persons, and the accumulation of filth, might have caused the death of all,
or the greater part, and thus, had the voyage been
tedious, have produced the effect probably intended
by Osorio; but luckily the passage was made in a
single week.   The patriots were left on shore with
no other allowance than the rations of a soldier.

Until 1813 Juan Fernandez had been the island
to which criminals were banished.   Since that period
it had been uninhabited, and rats had multiplied to
an incredible extent.   They soon devoured a fourth
part of the provisions sent from Chile; and although
millions of the vermin were soon destroyed, there was
no perceptible diminution in their numbers.   The
situation of the unfortunate exiles was aggravated by
the extortions of successive governors, who, under

pain of death, prohibited the introduction of the
smallest supply from their families or friends, unless
it passed previously through their own hands.　Five
hundred per cent. was considered a conscientious
profit, and it was seldom that the cruel orders of government were evaded.　Sometimes the governor permitted the owners to take a small proportion of what
had not been plundered on the passage; and, countenanced by higher authority, sold the rest at enormous prices by auction; the right owners being generally the only purchasers.　By such nefarious means
one of the governors realized in less than a year
upwards of 20,000 dollars.

The jail of Santiago was filled with persons of
condition suspected of *infidencia,* or a political bias
towards independence.　Many of them became the
victims of a plot, which seems to have been got up for
no other purpose than to gratify the pleasure which
some of the vilest of Spaniards felt in the shedding
of blood.

The two battalions of the regiment of Talavera
were composed of the worst characters from the Peninsula.　It was the terror of Chile, on account of the
systematic perpetration of enormities which it pursued, and which caused females to secrete themselves,
if they could, wherever the regiment appeared.　The
officers not only set a frightful example, but openly
encouraged their men; and it is difficult to decide
which party exceeded the other in deeds which must
not be particularized, but which frequently occasioned
death.

Captain Sambruno, pre-eminent in atrocity amongst

the atrocious *Talaverinos*, had been selected by Osorio to fill the office of chief *del tribunal de vigilancia*, a police appointment, which gave to Sambruno ample opportunities to indulge in passions at once malignant and licentious. Gentlemen were sometimes thrown into prison with threats of immediate execution, in order that a beautiful daughter or sister might become the intercessor. The sequel need not be told.

Not content with the commission or encouragement of such outrages, Sambruno formed a plan for the destruction of the immured citizens. A serjeant and a few other *Talaverinos* were employed to represent to the prisoners, that their incarceration had excited the sympathy of the royalist troops, who were stated to be in readiness to rise to overthrow Osorio, and to establish a government independent of Spain. Improbable as was the tale, the unhappy men fell into the snare, and, at an appointed hour of the second or third night, suffered themselves to be let out of their dormitories by the pretended conspirators, and conducted to the *salon*, or great room, to deliberate upon the measures expedient to be adopted to secure their offered freedom. When a number were assembled, Sambruno, at the head of a party of *Talaverinos*, burst into the *salon*, and carried on the work of butchery with an unrelenting ferocity, worthy the times of Robespierre. Osorio, who was not always able to restrain the *Talaverinos*, sent his *fiscal* Rodriguez to put a stop to the massacre; but when this law officer arrived, murder had already finished its task, and the assassins were in the act of throwing the lifeless bodies from a gallery into the court below*.

To detail every other act of tyranny committed by Osorio, and his still more cruel successor Marco, would fill a volume. Suffice it to say, that, in two years and four months, the barbarity of these despots caused more mourning to be worn by the principal families around, more oppression in every class of the people, and spread more ruin over the country in general, than all the misfortunes of every other period of the war of independence in Chile.

The domination of the tyrants was not, however, altogether free from alarms. The captain-general was, from time to time, made uneasy by intelligence of the warlike preparations of San Martin at Mendoza. Accordingly, cruel edicts were published and enforced to augment the royalist army, not merely for the defence of Chile against the threatened invasion, but also under the pretence to act on the offensive, by seeking the patriots on their own ground, in the Pampas, and ultimately to open the way to Buenos Ayres. But the extraordinary activity and boldness of a patriot guerrilla party soon obliged Osorio to confine his views to Chile.

Don Manuel Rodriguez, a barrister, was the son of a distinguished Chileno family, and had latterly been employed with remarkable success as an emissary of San Martin. A price was set upon the head

* Sambruno was taken prisoner by Captain Alvarez Condarco, aide-de-camp to General San Martin, at the battle of Chacabuco; tried for murder, and suffered death in front of the prison of Santiago, amidst the execrations of the populace.

.of Rodriguez; but he, without arms, undertook to supply himself by taking them from his enemies, and to produce the necessity of separating the royal army into detachments, and of dispersing them over the country. At the head of a few guerrillas, he entered various towns; proclaimed their independence; took horses from the royalists; and harassed them by every species of hostility in his power.

The captain-general was obliged to send strong divisions to distant points, to prevent a general rising. Whenever one of these approached the spot where Rodriguez chanced to be, the roads were lined, and ambuscades planted by the royalists at every known outlet to prevent escape; but, well acquainted with the localities, he would order his guerrillas to disperse, and rendezvous at some point distant from any royalist garrison, where he would again hoist the standard of independence; again draw upon himself a superior force; and again elude their vigilance. This was the less difficult, as the people every where clamoured for a deliverer. Rodriguez could easily awaken their enthusiasm, and, when overpowered, could safely rely upon their assistance in making his escape. Although the people sometimes suffered severely for these proofs of their attachment, nothing could keep down the spirit of patriotism whenever an incident brought it into play. Thus supported, Rodriguez, with all the resources of his ready genius, and with a valour bordering upon rashness, occupied the attention of the royalists, and certainly contributed in a great measure to pave the way to the subsequent successes of the army of the Andes.

A division was also effected in the south by Com-. mandant Freyre and the intrepid Neira, a guerrilla chief, who took possession of Talca with a small force, raised in the province of Concepcion, and composed partly of men who had been expelled from their homes, either by the edicts of the captain-general, or by an apprehension of sooner or later becoming his victims.

To arrest the progress of the Spanish arms, in the first instance; to recover the ground that had been lost, in the second; and, finally, to elevate Chile to the rank of an independent state, were the objects of assembling an army at Mendoza. San Martin formed that army into two brigades, and placed them under the respective command of Generals Soler and O'Higgins. The passage of that wondrous barrier the Andes has already been described.

On the 7th of February, 1817, Major Don En-- rique Martinez, commanding the advance of the army of the Andes, drove in the Spanish piquet at La Guardia, which suffered some loss. On the 8th, Lieutenant-Colonel Necochea routed, with inferior forces, a body of royalist hussars. Having overcome the first difficulties, in defiles, where the natural de- fences had been strengthened by hastily constructed field-works, the patriots issued from the mountains, and debouching into the valley of Putaendo, took possession of the towns of Aconcagua and Santa Rosa.

The royalists retained for the protection of the northern provinces of Chile, under the command of Brigadier Maroto, consisted of the regiments of Tala-- vera, Chiloe, Valdivia, two squadrons of hussars, one of dragoons, eight pieces of artillery; altogether about four thousand men, which were concentrated in the vicinity of Chacabuco. The *cuesta*, or mountain of Chacabuco, which is very difficult of ascent, was occupied by a strong royalist detachment that enfiladed the high road leading from Santa Rosa to Santiago.

The hostile parties bivouacked on the 10th of February, not far from each other. San Martin intended to postpone the attack till the arrival of his artillery and spare horses, which were expected to join on the 14th; but having ascertained that the royalist forces, detached to the south, were rapidly countermarching, he decided upon immediate action. On the 12th of February he directed the brigade, composed of battalions No. 7 and 8, and three squadrons of the *granaderos à caballo*, to advance. Whilst this brigade moved to the front, General Soler, with the battalion No. 11, the battalion of *casadores*, and some cavalry, made an oblique movement half a league to the right. The commanding officer of the Spanish advanced detachment on the cuesta perceiving his retreat endangered, fell back a league and a half towards the estate of Chacabuco, where he joined the rest of the royal army, which Maroto had formed on the side of a hill, with a deep ravine in front. This position was advantageous to repel an attack along the high road, but it was ill calculated to resist the brigade of Soler, of whose movement the Spanish general was ignorant until it was too late to vary his position. San Martin had continued his front movement, and arrived within.

K 2

range of the enemy at the moment Soler was half a
league distant. San Martin, aware of the advantages
to be obtained by leading young and enthusiastic
troops boldly on, and the danger of procrastination
in the presence of well-disciplined foes, had determined, on forming his plan of operations for the
campaign, to become the assailant wherever, or whenever, he came up with his enemy. An immediate
attack was therefore ordered, and O'Higgins placed
himself at the head of the infantry. The first effort
was unsuccessful, the battalion No. 8 being repulsed
with severe loss. San Martin then charged the
enemy's right with two squadrons of cavalry, and
the battalions Nos. 7 and 8 perceiving this, returned
to the attack at the same time. At this moment the
head of Soler's columns appeared in sight, and his
cavalry came on in time to take part in the last
charges, which led to complete success. The Spaniards attempted to rally in a vineyard, but they were
overthrown by a brilliant charge of cavalry, led by
Necochea, whose gallant brother, Don Eugenio, was
badly wounded. Six hundred Spaniards were left
dead on the field. The rest dispersed, and the patriots
entered Santiago in triumph on the 14th of February.
On the 18th, President Captain-General Marco and
three thousand six hundred royalists had been taken
prisoners at various points: five hundred escaped by
embarking at Valparaiso, and sailing to Lima; the
rest who escaped retired to Talcahuano.

Captain O'Brien, aide-de-camp to San Martin,
was sent with a detachment of cavalry in pursuit of
the fugitives towards Valparaiso. He made some

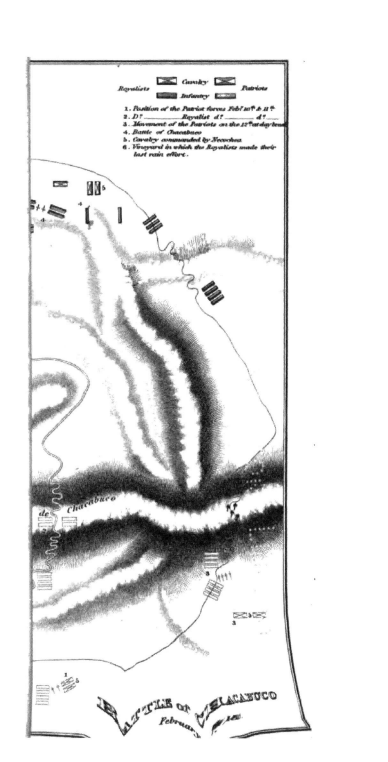

Royalists ▭ Cavalry ▭ Patriots
          ▬ Infantry ▬

1. Position of the Patriot forces Feb! 10ᵗʰ & 11ᵗʰ
2. Dᵒ _____ Royalist dᵒ _____ dᵒ _____
3. Movement of the Patriots on the 12ᵗʰ at day break
4. Battle of Chacabuco
5. Cavalry commanded by Necochea
6. Vineyard in which the Royalists made their
   last vain effort.

de Chacabuco

BATTLE OF CHACABUCO
February 1817

prisoners at the Cuesta del Prado, and amongst the baggage also taken there, the captain found two *alforjas*, or wallets, containing one thousand seven hundred doubloons; which treasure he sent to San Martin, who caused them to be placed in the public treasury.   The gallant and disinterested O'Brien received a letter of thanks from the supreme government.

. The grateful Chilenos elected San Martin supreme director, but he declined the office; upon which the brave and meritorious O'Higgins became the object of their choice.

 . Lieutenant-Colonel Las Heras was then ordered with a division to follow up the royalists; but he suffered himself to be detained at Rancagua, Talca, and other towns on the march, as if the work of liberation had been entirely accomplished at Chacabuco. Delay, originating rather from the inexperience of young chiefs, grown giddy with success, than from a worse motive, enabled the royalists, under the judicious and able Brigadier Ordoñez, to retire without further losses; to collect scattered garrisons; and to fortify Talcahuano on the bay of Concepcion, where they made a successful stand.

While these events were going on in the province of Concepcion, or rather a few days after the victory of Chacabuco, San Martin proceeded to Buenos Ayres for the purpose of soliciting such reinforcement as might enable him to extend his operations to Peru, and to represent to the Buenos Ayrean government the impossibility of carrying into execution its orders to raise, by means of forced contribution, a million of dollars in Chile, as well as the impolicy of attempting it.

During San Martin's absence from Chile, the supreme director, O'Higgins, left the capital of Santiago, and took the command of the patriot forces in the province of Concepcion; two Chileno regiments having been raised during the investment of Talcahuano, which still continued.

The intrenchments thrown up at Talcahuano by the royalists were formidable, when the feeble means of attack are taken into consideration. The ditch on the land side of the town was ten feet deep, and fourteen wide at the top, with a parapet, and here and there a small battery of heavy ordnance. On the 1st of December, 1817, the patriots, led by the brave Las Heras, advanced boldly to the assault; behaved nobly; and suffered severely; but they were repulsed: for the Spaniards, who fight well behind walls, were better disciplined than their opponents, amongst whom most of the officers were killed or wounded. Amongst the latter were the gallant Major Correa, a Buenos Ayrean, and Major Beauchef, a Frenchman, Captain Dias, a Chileno, and Lieutenants Carson and Manning, North Americans. Lieutenant Eldridge, also, a very brave young North American, was killed. Although the assault was a complete failure, it speaks volumes in favour of the patriot soldiers, who were animated with the finest spirit of union, firmness, and enterprise. General Brayer*, who formerly commanded a brigade of the French imperial guard, had joined the patriot army

* General Brayer quitted the patriot army in 1818.

after the battle of Chacabuco, and was employed as chief of the staff at the investment of Talcahuano.

In the absence of O'Higgins from Santiago, the seat of the Chileno government, Colonel Don Hilarion de la Quintana had been named supreme delegate, and was afterwards superseded by Don Luis Cruz.

San Martin, who had returned from Buenos Ayres to Chile, in the month of April, established his head-quarters at Las Tablas, near Valparaiso. The troops, amounting to about 5000, with San Martin, were composed of the following corps:—Battalion of *cazadores de los Andes;* battalion No. 8; battalion No. 2, of Coquimbo; two squadrons of *granaderos à caballo;* two ditto of *cazadores à caballo;* twenty-five pieces of artillery.

The division with O'Higgins in the south, now reduced to about three thousand men, was composed as follows:—Nos. 1 and 3, battalions of Chile; No. 7, and No. 11, of Buenos Ayres; two squadrons of *granaderos à caballo;* one squadron of cavalry of Chile; ten pieces of artillery.

At one of the reviews which occurred at Las Tablas, Commodore Bowles, who commanded the British naval force on the South American station, was present, and expressed his opinion of the efficiency and appearance of the troops in terms highly favourable; which was a source of great gratification to the officers of the army, who did not fail to give full value to the compliment of a British officer universally respected on that station.

It was known that Pezuela, the viceroy of Peru,

was preparing an expedition against Chile. Indeed,
it was hourly expected on the coast. The best spirit
pervaded the independent army, and the troops were
in a good state of discipline.

This was the posture of affairs when the subject of
these memoirs arrived in Chile.

CHAPTER VI.

Miller—enters the service of Buenos Ayres.—Tour towards Patagonia.—Pampas.—Republican encroachments.—Chascomus. —Los dos Talos.—Spanish prisoners of war.—Las Bruscas.— Tigers.—Lions.—Emigration.—Gauchos.—Ostriches.—Viscachas.—Zorrinos.—Deer.—Indians.—Horsemanship.—Horses. —Return to Buenos Ayres.

WILLIAM MILLER was born on the 2nd of December, 1795, at Wingham, in the county of Kent. He served, in the field-train department of the royal artillery, with the British army, from the 1st of January, 1811, until the peace of 1815. In August, 1811, he landed at Lisbon, and was present at the subsequent sieges of Ciudad Rodrigo, Badajoz, and San Sebastian; at the battle of Vitoria, and at the investment of Bayonne. In 1812, he made an excursion, upon leave, from Badajoz to Seville, Cadiz, and Gibraltar. A movement of the French interfering with his return by the way of the Sierra Morena, he embarked at Cadiz, with his horses and servant, in an open craft, for Algarve, but was cast away at Lepe, near the mouth of the Guadiana. In June, 1814, he left Bourdeaux, and sailed from the Gironde, in his majesty's ship Madagascar, Captain (now Sir Bentick) Doyle, to the Bermudas, whence he proceeded to the Chesapeake, and joined the expedition against Washington and Baltimore, where he witnessed the fall of General Ross. On the 27th

of November, in the same year, he sailed from Jamaica with the British forces destined to act against
New Orleans. After quitting the Mississippi, he
was shipwrecked in *The Ranger*, ordnance transport,
off Mobile.   He subsequently sailed from Isle Dau-
phine for the Havannah, and reached England in the
summer of 1815.

The years 1816 and 1817 were mostly spent upon
the continent of Europe. During his residence there,
an opportunity offered by which he might have become the partner in a French mercantile house; but,
after a very short trial, he relinquished the intention
of advancing his fortunes in that way.   Returning
to England, he soon grew tired of inactivity; and
turning his attention to the state of the struggle
between Spanish America and the mother country,
considered, after due inquiry, that the river Plata
was the most eligible point to which he could direct
his course.   Few English candidates for military
fame had proceeded to that country; and this was
one reason why he preferred it to Colombia, already
overrun with adventurers of all descriptions.   After
dedicating a few months to the study of those military
acquirements in which he was deficient, he sailed from
the Downs in August, 1817, and landed at Buenos
Ayres in the following month of September.

A very few letters of introduction paved the way
to that welcome which is so cheering to an aspirant
at the commencement of his career.   Upon his
arrival, he was presented by his excellent friend,
Mr. Dickson, to the supreme director, Pueyrredon,

who, on learning the object of his visit to Buenos
Ayres, desired an application to be made in writing.
Miller drew up a memorial, shortly stating how and
where he had served, and requesting employment in
the army of the Andes, which was then in Chile,
under the orders of San Martin.   A month after this
application was made, a captain's commission was delivered to him.   In the meantime, the hospitality of
his countrymen, and of some Buenos Ayrean families,
ripened into friendship.   Some tempting prospects
of a lucrative nature were placed before his view;
and although he internally adhered with firmness to
his original plan of inlisting in the cause of freedom,
he could hardly make up his mind to give a decided
negative to such flattering proposals.

Whilst in this state, his own resolves were fortified
by the opinion of an English lady, who, after some
preliminary conversation, observed, " I find that
there exists a wish to prevail upon you to devote
yourself to money-making pursuits.   Now, I dissent
from this well-intentioned advice.   Were I a young
man, I would never abandon the career of glory for
the sake of gain."   In eight and forty hours from the
time of that conversation, he took an affectionate leave
of the lady, of her husband (Mr. Mackinlay), and
of their numerous family, from all of whom he had
received the kindest attentions during his stay in
Buenos Ayres.   But before we relate his journey
across the continent, we will describe a tour which
he made, in a direction, little frequented, towards
Patagonia.

At ten o'clock, A.M., on the 28th of October, 1817,

he set out, in company with four Buenos Ayrean
gentlemen, whose object was to visit their *estancias*,
or grazing farms. They were attended by two *peones*,
or out-of-door servants. Twenty horses formed the
cavalcade, the spare ones being driven on before as
a sort of moving relay. This is the general mode
of making long journeys on the Pampas, if not
travelling post. At noon, the party halted at the
estancia of Don Francisco Masiel. Milk and *mate*
were presented on alighting. *Mate* is the infusion
of the leaf of a plant, said to be a species of *ilex*, the
growth of Paraguay, and is in universal use over a
vast extent of South America. It is usually sipped
the first thing in the morning, and several times in
the course of the day. It is served in an egg-shaped
cup, commonly the shell of a small gourd. Sugar
and a little lemon-peel are sometimes added, to im-
prove the flavour. It is sucked, very hot, through a
bombilla, or little tube, generally made of silver. It
was the common practice to pass the same tube from
mouth to mouth; but the custom is growing unfa-
shionable. Novices frequently burn their lips, or
scald the tongue. At other places, in the course of
the excursion, ostrich and other eggs were put upon
table. The mutton of this country is poor; and
pork, on account of its being fed upon the flesh and
offal of oxen and horses, is execrable. The *iguana*,
or large lizard, and the ostrich, are also eaten. On
the following day, the 29th, the party proceeded for
twenty-three leagues, over one continued plain, covered with coarse luxuriant grass, growing in tufts
partially mixed with wild oats and trefoil. The

thistle grows in great abundance ; and when it sheds its down, the wind sometimes blows it into heaps, and balls are formed, which are driven along the bowling-green-like Pampas, until they acquire a dia- meter above six feet. The general appearance of the Pampas in every direction is flat and uninteresting.

The estancias are at considerable distances from each other. People living within half a dozen miles consider themselves as next door neighbours, whilst those who reside within twenty miles form only one circle of acquaintance. To people invariably well mounted, twenty or thirty miles are only a gallop to make a friendly visit or a morning call. The sight of a *hombu* is a certain indication of a human habita- tion, for one of these trees is always planted when- ever a hut is constructed. It grows to a considerable size, but is serviceable only as a landmark and for shade *.

It is, however, the only sort of tree, excepting fruit trees, which grows within fifty leagues south of Buenos Ayres. Herds of oxen, flocks of sheep, droves of horses, asses, and mules, numbers of deer, and clouds of birds, were continually within view.

One hundred years ago, when the plains were co- vered with cattle, travellers were accustomed to send people on before to clear the road. The Spaniards finding the trade in hides † extremely lucrative, em-

---

* Wood was formerly so scarce, and cattle so plentiful, that sheep were driven into the furnace of limekilns, in order to answer the purposes of fuel. We should not have dared to repeat this fact, however undoubted, if a decree of the king of Spain, prohibiting this barbarous custom, were not still preserved in the archives of Buenos Ayres.

† Hides have not only become valuable on account of the immense number of them exported to Europe, but also because the consumption is so great in South America. Incredible quantities are expended in the manufacture of *lassos*,

ployed troops of gaucho horsemen for the purpose
of slaughtering the cattle.   Each party had separate
tasks assigned to it: some, particularly well mounted,
attacked a herd of oxen, and with a crescent-shaped
knife fixed to the end of a long handle, hamstrung
the cattle as they fled; a second party threw down
other oxen by means of the *lasso;* a third brought
up and drew a knife across the throat of the prostrate
animals.   A fourth party was employed in stripping
off the hides, and in conveying them to an appointed
place; fixing them to the ground with pegs; and
taking out, and carrying away, the tongues and fat.
The flesh, which would have sufficed to feed a numerous army in Europe, was left on the plain to be
devoured by tigers, wild dogs, and ravens.   In an
expedition of this sort, which generally lasted for
some weeks, the person at whose expense it was undertaken obtained several thousands of hides, each
of which, when dried, was worth four times as much
as a live bullock, in consequence of the expense
necessarily incurred in killing the oxen, and the
labour of drying the hides in the sun.   This custom
of hunting and slaughtering cattle having been practised for a whole century, almost exhausted the plains
of unowned cattle.   The herds now seen are the
property of individuals.

Oxen seldom wander far from their native pastures,
and are easily prevented from straying into adjoining
estates by a little attention on the part of the *peones.*
Every proprietor knows his own stock by a particular

in the fastenings of houses, fences, and cattle-pens, and in the making of trunks
and bags to convey the herb of Paraguay, tobacco, sugar, wheat, cotton, and
other goods.

mark which is branded at the castrating season. The young bull is caught with the *lasso*, thrown down, and the horns fixed into the ground whilst he undergoes the operation. The time of performing this is made an annual scene of jollity; neighbours assembling at different estates in turn, and ending their daily labours with carousings. *Carne con cuero*, or meat in the skin, is a favourite dish on occasions of festivity. The moment a bullock is killed for this purpose, the flesh on each side of the spine, beginning at the rump, is cut out with enough of the hide to lap over and meet, so as to be sewed together, to prevent the juices from escaping. It is then covered with embers, and roasted like an onion or potato.

The travellers took up their quarters for the night at the estancia of Don Miguel Rodriguez, situated on the border of the lake Bitel, which abounds in two sorts of fish, namely, the *liza* and the *pex el rey* (king fish): the last is not very unlike the smelt. Both sorts are sometimes taken to market at Buenos Ayres. The previous rains had laid a great part of the level under water, and it was very irksome to wade through extensive pools, formed by shallow concavities, which retain the water until it evaporates in the dry season. This is the case with many of the pools large enough to be called lakes. Hence fresh and rich pasturage is, during every season of the year, abundant on the plains. Estancias are generally established on the margin of a lake, or upon the bank of some running stream. But water is to be got at no great depth by digging wells.

On the 30th the travellers advanced three leagues

and a half to Chascomus, where they partook of an
early dinner with Dr. Campana. Chascomus is a
miserable looking village, situated on the side of a
lake eight leagues in circumference, producing the
same sorts of fish as lake Bitel. It consists of about
a hundred and fifty mud huts, containing six or seven
hundred souls, exclusive of two hundred militia then
in cantonments there, preparatory to the establishment of a line of posts about to be formed by order of
the Buenos Ayrean government. This was a direct
encroachment upon the territory of the uncivilized
Indians, who had been elbowed off in order that the
republican territory might be properly rounded. It
is not a little curious that the Creole bayonet, which
expelled the Spaniards, should be unscrupulously employed to drive the Indians from as much territory as
it suited the convenience of the Buenos Ayreans to
take possession of. The latter have with reason com-
plained of colonial oppressions : but had the Indians
an equal means of publishing *their* grievances, not a
slender catalogue of wrongs might make the newly
emancipated people blush for their own inconsist-
encies. Fifty years ago Chascomus had constantly in
its immediate vicinity some of the Indian moveable villages, which consist of tents made of untanned hides
sewed together, and fixed upon a frame-work of poles
made fast by thongs. The Indian occupants served
for a long time as a barrier, preventing all, excepting
their own hordes, from penetrating the country towards Patagonia. Chascomus is thirty leagues south
of Buenos Ayres, and as many north from what the
Buenos Ayreans had considered their own frontier,

although their outposts were not extended so far to the south.

At two P. M. the travellers again set out, and at six, arrived at the estancia of Don Antonio Servieta, a Spaniard, whose house is close to the lake del Burro. On this day's ride they waded through several inundations, and more than once the lower part of the saddle-flaps were under water for above a mile of the road.

On the 30th of October the party set out as usual at dawn of day. At noon they were ferried across the river Salado, twelve leagues from its mouth. The horses were made to swim over after the ferry-boat, the river being there about two hundred yards in width. The water, as the name denotes, is salt, from its source being in a saline soil, which is the case with many streams flowing through the Pampas.

At five P. M. they reached Los dos Talos. At a *pulperia*, or shop and public house, they procured a supper. The only other habitations in the place were three miserable hovels, occupied by thirty-eight Spanish officers, who had been made prisoners of war at Monte Video in 1814. They left Cadiz so lately as 1813, having served during the greater part of the peninsular war. Mr. Miller visited them, and they were highly delighted to see an European; for, excepting a few Creoles and Indians, they seldom saw a stranger. What added to the interest of the meeting was the circumstance that he, when in Spain, had formed an acquaintance with several of the friends of some of the prisoners. He was therefore made doubly welcome; for they could speak of their native

country, and tell their tale of sorrows in a wilderness,
to a person capable of sympathizing with them.

The government of Buenos Ayres kept these unfortunate gentlemen upon rations of beef and salt,
without any other allowance.   The little game they
caught was an occasional luxury, and if they got a
bason of milk, it was a rare act of charity. In a scope
of a hundred miles around Los dos Talos, there were
not more than twenty estancias, and those were occupied by gauchos, whose antipathy to Spaniards was
most violent, and they often considered them fit
objects of revenge.   Rendered desperate by such a
distressing seclusion from the civilized world, ten of
the prisoners, headed by Major Livinia, made their
escape two years before. They took shelter amongst
the savage Indians, intending to make the best of
their way to Chile, then in possession of the royalists:
but, after undergoing dreadful privations, in wandering about for above a thousand miles, and seven
of them having died of hunger and fatigue, the three
survivors, despairing of accomplishing their object,
delivered themselves up to a patriot outpost towards
the Pehuenche territory, preferring even their hard
lot as prisoners to the life they were obliged to lead
amongst savages, whose manners and customs, as
described by the major, were disgusting in the extreme.   He and his companions were conveyed to
their old abode in bullock cars, being too weak to
walk, for above twelve hundred miles, unsupplied
with sufficient raiment to cover their persons.   The
major still remained in a pitiable state. His ghastly
countenance, long beard, and squalid figure, rendered

him the picture of wretchedness; stretched out upon
a sort of truckle bed, composed of two or three rugs
placed upon cross sticks, run into the mud wall at
one end, and fastened at the other to upright sticks
driven into the earthen floor. His eyes had become
diseased; and an old sack was hung up as a curtain
to shield them from the glare of day. A three-legged
stool, ten inches high, covered with a woollen rag,
was the only seat for the invalid, who reclined against
a wall, the dampness of which was kept off by a piece
of canvas battened upon sticks. A long plank, with
the extremities between the horns of two bullock
skulls, served as a bench for the rest of the company.
Some clasp and case knives and forks, some horn
spoons, a kettle or two, a frying-pan, a ramrod (for
a spit), a couple of gridirons, an earthen dish, and
about a dozen shattered cups and saucers, formed the
whole of their household utensils. Some *lassos* and
bolas hung upon the walls, but they were seldom
used; because permission for one or two of the prisoners at a time to get on horseback was only occasionally granted, and the favour depended entirely on
the caprice of the officer on guard, who, being of the
gaucho militia, thought such an indulgence would
be a breach of trust. The beards of the prisoners
were the growth of years. They said soap was an
article too expensive for their pockets. If a pleasura-
ble sensation could be felt in the abode of wretchedness, it could only arise from the power of making
its unfortunate inmates forgetful, for a few hours, of
their situation.

The major received a trifling present of tea with

more grateful acknowledgments than, under other
circumstances, he would have made for the most
costly gifts, and insisted upon Mr. Miller placing
his blanket on the bench already described. This
courtesy was gladly accepted; for the night was chilly,
and there was no getting under cover elsewhere.

An impressive silence preceded the separation on
the following morning. The major, too weak to
stand, sat upon his bed, and stretching out his thin
hands, embraced Miller with a fervency that may
be readily imagined. The other unfortunate gentlemen followed his example, and also added to their
embraces their most earnest benedictions. It was a
melancholy parting; for every eye was dim, and even
the gauchos were moved. Not a word was exchanged
by the travellers after their departure till they had
proceeded many miles. The major died in captivity;
the rest, profiting by the dissensions which arose
amongst the Buenos Ayrean factions of 1819, dispersed, and severally escaped to Monte Video, Talcahuano, or Potosi.

The principal dépôt for prisoners of war was at
Las Bruscas, about three leagues from Los dos Talos.
Five hundred officers and non-commissioned officers
were in confinement there; the private soldiers having
been permitted to settle as servants in the houses, or
as *peones* on the estates of Creoles *.

A ride of fifteen leagues brought the travellers, on

---

* Amongst the South Americans confined at Las Bruscas for their adhesion
to the cause of the mother country was Captain Santa Cruz, who, having escaped
to Peru in 1819, served with the royalists again until 1820, when the Spanish
general O'Reilly was defeated at Pasco; upon which Santa Cruz, with a party
of royalists, passed over into the service of the patriots. Santa Cruz was placed
at the head of the Peruvian government by Bolivar in 1826.

the evening of the 1st of November, to Monsalvo,
which contains two or three mud dwellings. At four
leagues from Los dos Talos they entered the Monte
de Tordillo, a slip of country thinly sprinkled with
one species of small tree, which is used in the construction of huts and cattle-pens, and for fuel.

  The Monte de Tordillo is, at the part now traversed, eight leagues in breadth. It extends from
the sea-coast to Patagonia in a south-west direction, and is infested with a few tigers, which are
not very ferocious, on account of the facility with
which they obtain their prey on the plains.   They
are not equal in size or in ferocity to the Bengal
tiger. They run fast, but soon tire. They commit great havock amongst the oxen, sheep, mules,
and asses. A great many tigers are caught with the
lasso by the Indian and Creole inhabitants for the
sake of their skins. They are also sometimes entrapped in the following manner: a large chest, or
wooden frame, is made, supported upon four wheels,
and is dragged by oxen to a place where the traces of
tigers have been discovered.   In the furthest corner
of the chest is put a putrid piece of flesh, by way of
bait, which is no sooner laid hold of by the tiger than
the door of the trap falls; he is killed by a musket
ball, or a spear thrust through the crevices of the
planks.   There are also some lions, but they are
unlike those of Africa in form, size, and disposition.
They seldom attack any thing but calves, foals, and
sheep. The colour of their skin is tawny, with whitish
spots. Their head is large and round, eyes sparkling,
and nose flattish.

In this day's journey the travellers rode through several extensive inundations, and swam their horses across some *arroyos*, or rivers, the beds of which are dry gullies in summer. Some Indians pursuing deer were spoken to in the morning. They use no dogs, but gallop after the animal until they approach within thirty yards of it, when they twirl the *bolas* in their right hand over their head, and lanch them with great dexterity, seldom missing their mark : they generally entangle the animal by its leg. Deer are caught for the sake of their skins, which are bartered away with the gauchos for *mate*, tobacco, and biscuit. The *bolas* are three stones, or more commonly balls of lead, tied to the ends of three slips of ox-hide about two feet long, joined in the centre, and may be spread into the figure of the arms of the Isle of Man. One of the amusements of children is to trip up lambs, dogs, poultry, cats, or tame young ostriches, with bolas suited to their strength.

At noon, on the 2nd of November, the travellers arrived at the estancia of Don Andres Hidalgo, who formed one of the party from Buenos Ayres. His mud-walled house is pleasantly situated on a rising ground, overlooking the lake of Mariancul, eighty-five leagues from Buenos Ayres, and about fifteen from the sea-coast. Hidalgo's farm was the termination of the journey.

Throughout the tour the land appeared to be of excellent quality, but it improved perceptibly on the two last days: not a stone was to be seen. The soil, for about the depth of a foot, is of a black mould; under that is a stratum of clay, then sand, and below

a gravelly bed, until water is found. Some of the
lakes deposit a white slime, which is used as a substitute for lime. The travellers rode for many leagues
through grass, trefoil, and wild oats, growing as high
as the horses' heads. It no longer appeared surprising
that settlers should penetrate two or three hundred
miles to form a grazing farm where good land might
be had by the outlay of a trifling sum on title deeds,
and in throwing up a few mounds of earth to mark
the boundary. The inducements are, that the land
here is better than the best land near Buenos Ayres,
and stock is much less exposed to depredations, because the chance of detection increases in proportion
to the distance from a market to dispose of stolen
cattle.

A feeling of regret arises involuntarily in the mind
of an Englishman, as he contemplates the fertile
tracts chiefly tenanted by beasts and birds, whilst his
own country swarms with industrious poor, willing
to work, but reduced to misery for want of steady
employment. No man should be advised to leave
his home, so long as he can get an honest livelihood;
but when he must starve or steal, emigration to proper spots in these savannahs would be a salutary
change. The sober and industrious would, in a few
years, become persons of property *in land* and *in
cattle*, though without much ready money. Many
sorts of produce would be raised which are now
almost unknown. Bread is not to be procured in
the part of the Pampas now spoken of; and such is
the listlessness of the inhabitants in this respect, that

they are contented to subsist upon beef and salt, with
a little *mate* and the solace of a cigar, rather than undergo the toil of cultivation.   The bounties of nature
are disregarded, and the gauchos live wretchedly, if we
measure their enjoyments by the factitious European
standard: whereas, if they laboured three days out of
the seven, it would be sufficient to procure them bread
and vegetables in as great abundance as they now
obtain meat.   The axiom that idleness is the parent
of vice does not hold good to the same degree in the
interior of the Pampas.   In Europe, a lazy penny-
less man resorts to illegal means for subsistence; but
in the Pampas meat is so plentiful, that it is never
given or received as a favour.   A stranger has only
to seat himself in any house he chooses to enter, and
he is sure to be made welcome to family fare.   The
usual courtesies are exchanged, but no invitation is
necessary or expected.   Indeed, to give one would
be to break through the understood customs of the
country.

The gauchos are a well grown race of people,
and handsome faces are frequently seen amongst the
women.   The men are bold, sociable, and unembarrassed in their deportment.   They are good-natured
and obliging; but so high spirited, that the infliction
of a blow on a gaucho is perilous to the aggressor,
be he who he may; for the knife is instantly drawn
to avenge the indignity.   The children of intermar-
riages between white and Indian parents possess an
interesting cast of countenance.

The gauchos have enjoyed from time immemorial

a degree of individual liberty not to be seen perhaps amongst any other people. Thinly sprinkled over immeasurable plains, they were scarcely within the control of a local magistracy, and they set at open defiance the viceregal authority whenever it trenched upon personal freedom.   In an unadvanced state of civilization, they retain more of the noble traits of the Spanish character, in the brightest era of the monarchy, than is to be found in the mother country, or in any part of what were once her colonial possessions.   Inheriting the abstemiousness of their forefathers, they are surrounded by an abundance more than sufficient for their wants, and they pass their days in cheerful indolence, or in roaming over their treeless savannahs in the pursuit of business or pleasure.   Hence dishonesty was rare, and highway robbery unknown.

Robberies and murders have indeed been committed during the unhappy period of civil broils; but the perpetrators have been deserters from the army, and seldom or never gauchos, or sons of the Pampas.

Silver and gold were conveyed regularly from Upper Peru and Chile to Buenos Ayres in large quantities, unescorted, in charge of a single conductor, without the smallest risk of loss.   This mode of conveying treasure across the Pampas was resumed in 1825.

It is a generally received opinion, that mountainous countries produce a people animated by an attachment to liberty, and endowed with courage to preserve it; while the inhabitants of flat lands are considered to be more pliant to the fetters of despotism.   But this order of things will be found to be inverted, if we compare the wandering gaucho, who has always virtually enjoyed individual independence, to the abject mountaineer of Peru, who was treated infinitely worse than the negro slave in any part of the world.   Hence it appears that political institutions have sometimes more influence upon the formation of national character than can be ascribed to mountains or plains.

The buildings on the farm of Don Andres Hidalgo were three dwellings: the principal consisted of a single apartment, without a window or chimney, forty-two feet by eighteen.   All three huts were made of reed walls, covered outside and in with clay.   The few spars are brought from the Monte del Tordillo, eighteen leagues distant: the rafters, like those of every house in the Pampas, are fastened by strips of hide; a nail is never used: the doors are frequently made of a bullock's skin stretched out upon a frame.   Don Andres had as much land as he chose to allow three thousand two hundred oxen and three hundred horses to range over.   This was considered a small establishment: it was formed only the year before.   Some estancias have twenty thousand head of oxen, with horses, asses, and mules in proportion.   One *peon* is equal to the care of one thousand head.   His duty is to count them morning and evening, and to fetch back such as may have strayed.

On a clear day the high ridge, called the Sierra de Volcan, twenty leagues to the south, can be discerned with the naked eye.   Thither it was wished

to extend the ride, but it was not then practicable,
nor would it become so until the waters in the *arroyos*
should subside sufficiently to render them fordable.

The government intended to take from the Indians
such another slice of the Pampas as would place the
Sierra within the Buenos Ayrean frontier; and it
may be fairly inferred, that these intentions proceeded
from motives equally laudable as those of the Emperor
Pedro, who, by way of rounding *his* territories, was
very desirous of adding the Banda Oriental to the
Brazilian empire. If crowned heads are fond of aggrandizement, republicans are not quite so far behind them as they profess to be, in playing the same
game. The Buenos Ayrean outposts were then
twelve leagues south of the estancia before mentioned, which, together with two or three estates,
still more in advance, were consequently exposed to
the visits, and sometimes depredations, of the Indians, whose huts, or awnings of skin, are often less
than four leagues distant, and within the line of
scattered outposts.

Don Andres entertained his fellow-travellers for
six days. They amused themselves in chasing deer,
running down ostriches, and shooting wild ducks,
pigeons, and quails, of which there are immense numbers. Partridges were so tame, or rather stupid, that
the usual mode of killing them was to knock them
down with a long stick. Several were despatched
in that way by one person on horseback, within the
space of a very few minutes. They are so plentiful
every where that, in the market of Buenos Ayres,
the price is sometimes below tenpence the dozen.

Ostriches impart a lively interest to a ride in the Pampas. They are seen sometimes in coveys of twenty or thirty, gliding elegantly along the gentle undulations of the plain, at half pistol shot distance from each other, like skirmishers. The young are easily domesticated, and soon become attached to those who caress them, but they are troublesome in-mates; for, stalking about the house, they will, when full grown, swallow coin, shirt-pins, and every small article of metal within reach. Their usual food, in a wild state, is seeds, herbage, and insects: the flesh is a reddish brown, and, if young, not of bad flavour. A great many eggs are laid in the same nest, which is lined with dry grass. Some accounts were given which exonerate the ostrich from the charge of being the most stupid bird in the creation. For example, the hen counts her eggs every day. This has been proved by the experiment of taking an egg away, or by putting one in addition. In either case she de-stroys the whole by smashing them with her feet. Although she does not attend to secrecy, in selecting a situation for her nest, she will forsake it if the eggs have been handled. It is also said that she rolls a few eggs, thirty yards distant from the nest, and cracks the shells, which, by the time her young come forth, being filled with maggots, and covered with in-sects, form the first repast of her infant brood. The male bird is said to take upon himself the rearing of the young, and to attach more importance to paternal authority than to the favours of his mate. If two cock-birds meet, each with a family, they fight for the supremacy over both; for which reason an ostrich has sometimes under his tutelage broods of different ages.

In running down ostriches, there is some danger of the horse stepping in holes burrowed by the *viscacha*. This animal resembles what might be expected between a rabbit and a cat, but is larger than either. In the plains, particularly on the hillocks, these animals scratch burrows so skilfully, as to be safe from inundation. They are divided into several compartments, and several families usually inhabit the same warren. On the surface many holes are opened, near which numbers of them are seen at sunset gazing at the passer by: if all be quiet, they go out to seek for food, and make great havock if they be near fields, for they will not eat grass when they can get wheat or Indian corn. They are also very fond of a sort of pumpkins. In order to hunt viscachas, water is forced into the subterraneous dwellings, and they are knocked down as they bolt out. Their flesh is not bad eating. A diminutive owl is in the daytime to be seen at the entrance of the burrows, as if standing sentry.

The *zorrino* is very common on the plains. It is equal in size to a small rabbit, of a very dark chestnut colour, marked on each side by two broad white lines, which are a continuation of the fur on the belly part. Its shape is elegant, but it emits an intolerable odour; and if annoyed or frightened, it squirts, with unerring aim, a liquor so pestilent, that dogs, when sprinkled with it, will howl and roll themselves on the ground as if scalded. This fluid shines in the night like phosphorus. Although this animal is small and weak, it may be considered the terror of the plains, for it is dreaded by tigers, lions, mastiffs, and every animal, as well as human beings. It sometimes enters houses, in which case the family caress it until some one has an opportunity of seizing it by the tail, when, holding it with the head downwards, they kill it, without danger to themselves; for by this means it loses the use of the muscles which enable it to emit its pestiferous defence. The fur is very soft and pretty.

Few rabbits are to be seen southward of Buenos Ayres, but they are more common in the provinces bordering on Peru. Roebucks are numerous, but the red deer is seldom to be met with, except near the banks of the larger rivers.

One day the party dined with Don José Pita, who was another fellow-traveller from Buenos Ayres, and whose estancia, four leagues from Hidalgo's, was the most advanced of any in a southerly direction. There they met a cacique promenading, with his wives, his children, and a few attendants: some of them spoke Spanish tolerably. They appeared to be of a race superior to the Creek Indians employed with the British against New Orleans. Their faces were stained with the blood of horses, and they wore feathers. Their complexion is a dull copper colour, hair long, lank, and of a shining black. The men look upon the women as beings of a less noble species, and accordingly treat them with indifference.

Trafficking with the aborigines must yield a large profit, because a tiger's skin, worth eight dollars in Buenos Ayres, was purchased on the road for a dollar and a quarter. For the eighth of a dollar's worth of

Paraguay tea, six viscacha skins were bought: at Buenos Ayres the same articles would sell for three quarters of a dollar.

One day was devoted to a visit to an Indian village, or encampment, with the inhabitants of which Don Andres was very popular. These, like all other Indians, have an inveterate custom of begging for every thing they see and fancy in the possession of a stranger; pocket-handkerchiefs, gloves, whips, pen-knives, pencils, and metal buttons were eagerly grasped at. They all took a childish fancy to Mr. Miller's pelisse, and it was with evident mortification they suffered themselves to be dissuaded from taking it off his back; a foraging cap was preserved with almost as much difficulty: but, notwithstanding this disappointment, the Indians ultimately took leave of their guests in a very friendly manner.

As we do not profess to adhere to strict chronological order, some observations, made at subsequent periods, are here introduced, because they are deemed illustrative of gaucho manners.

Amongst other exhibitions for the entertainment of his guests, skill in horsemanship is a favourite display by an *estanciero*. He will order a few young horses to be "gentled." A number, never crossed before, are driven into a *corral*, or cattle-pen, which is a circular enclosure, formed of strong stakes driven like palisades into the ground, and tied crosswise with strong slips of hide: it is sometimes made of a mud or stone wall. A bar is placed at a proper height across the only entrance, which is narrowed so as to permit the egress of a single horse at a time. A *peon*

perches himself upon the bar, and drops adroitly upon
the back of one as it passes out at a gallop; he holds
on without bridle or saddle, by sticking his long spurs
into the side of the wild colt, which bounds away,
kicks, plunges, rears, jumps, and uses every effort to
throw his rider, until, frightened and wearied, he becomes perfectly manageable.   If the peon wishes to
dismount before the horse grows tired, he trips it
up by putting his spurs between its fore legs, close
under the chest, and, preserving an upright seat,
comes down himself unhurt upon his feet.   The
breaking-in of colts is afterwards easily effected, but
it is not well done, for the horses have generally very
hard mouths.   In Chile and Peru the art is better
understood.

The horses on the plains of Buenos Ayres are
from fourteen to sixteen hands high, plenty of bone,
and swift.   Although their food is pasturage alone,
they are often ridden a distance almost incredible.
Thirty-five leagues in fourteen or fifteen hours is not
an uncommon thing for one horse to perform.   The
equality of the stoneless plain, and the easy gait of the
unshod horse, do not a little concur to render the performance of long journeys easy.   In summer, the horses
are exposed to the stings of musquitoes and scorching
suns; to heavy rains and hoar-frosts in winter, when
the south wind blows bitingly cold; all which render
them extremely hardy: whilst the liberty they enjoy
in wandering up and down the plains, plunging in
running streams, or large pools of water, at pleasure,
added to the invigorating effects of pure air, render
them less subject to disease than the horses of Europe,

confined in hot and unwholesome stables, and where the hardness of the roads subjects the hoof to the torments of the smith.

Mares were not used for the saddle until some Englishmen, in spite of the ridicule of the natives, introduced the custom, which, however, is not even yet general. Tails of horses were never cut; but our countrymen have likewise introduced that cruel fashion.

Horses, mules, and cattle bred on some higher parts of the Pampas, which abound in stone or rock, as in the neighbourhood of Cordova, are preferred, and sell for more than those bred on estates having a soft and clayey bottom.

The gaucho can get more work out of a horse than an European. An Englishman, who had been accustomed to ride from infancy, states that it has often happened that, when he has not been able to get a jaded horse out of a walk, he has changed horses with a gaucho postillion, who has immediately started off at a full gallop. The horse of the postillion has proved as dull as the first under the European rider, and upon exchanging the same horses a second time the same thing has again occurred. It appears that they have the art of keeping them going until they drop; and as ordinary horses are low priced, the loss and the cruelty are equally matters of no consideration.

The gauchos regard with a sort of pitying disdain the timid or unskilful horseman. Their remarks upon a new-comer from Europe are irresistibly ludicrous. The contempt they entertain towards foreigners unable to manage a restive horse is more

than a counterpart of a John Bull's sneers and scorn
for countries which have not the comforts or accom-
modations of England.   When Miller travelled from
Buenos Ayres to Chile, ⬤ second postillion eagerly
inquired of the first, upon stopping to change horses,
what sort of a young man he had brought with him.
The first shrugged up his shoulders, and answered,
No sabe nada, ni pitar siquiera, " He knows absolutely nothing; why, he cannot even smoke." This
was because an offered cigar had been declined on
the road.

On the 10th of November the tourists set out upon
their return, and arrived, at dusk on the second day,
at lake Ligonel, where they fared badly, and where
the musquitoes were so annoying as to render it impossible to sleep.   Upon rolling up their blankets
next morning, they disturbed numbers of frogs which
had crept underneath them in the course of the night.

On the 12th of November they re-crossed the river
Salado.   On the 13th they made a late start from
Chascomus, on account of their horses being nearly
knocked up.   On reaching the estancia of Don
Miguel Rodriguez, he unhesitatingly lent Miller
two of his best horses for the rest of the journey,
although Rodriguez had never seen Miller before,
excepting when he passed on his way from Buenos
Ayres.   The party put up for the night at the house
of an *estanciero* who possessed a mill, the rude ma-
chinery of which was set in motion by a mule.

On the 14th of November the tourists arrived at
Buenos Ayres, having ridden about a thousand miles
in nine days, not including six spent at the *estancia*
of Don Andres Hidálgo.

CHAPTER VII.

Journey to Mendoza.—Andes.—Chile.—Santiago. —Roads.—
Army at Las Tablas.—Mess.—Artillery.—Appointments.—
Rapidity of movement.—March.—Lasso bridge.—Quechere-
guas.—Cancharayada.—Consternation in the capital.—Rodri-
guez.—Maypo.—The Lautaro.—Blockade of Valparaiso.—The
Esmeralda.

On the 6th of January, 1818, Captain Miller set
out from Buenos Ayres, provided with a passport and
fifty dollars, as outfit, from the government. Travelling post, he took a horse for himself, another for
his baggage, and a third for the postillion, who was
relieved at every stage. The passport was an authority to pay *with certificates,* supposed to be afterwards liquidated by the treasury at the rate of a quarter of a real, or about three halfpence per league for
each horse, being half the sum paid *in cash* by travellers not upon the public service. The military now
pay in coin, and at the same rate as other travellers.
Post-houses are situated at from four to seven or eight
leagues distance from each other. A postillion does
not expect to be "remembered," but he receives with
satisfaction the compliment of half a real (threepence). It is not usually given, and never asked
for. Although persons posting across the Pampas
often meet with delay in obtaining fresh horses, forty
or fifty leagues is a common day's journey. At the

M 2

different relays a detached house, of one large room, is
appropriated for the use of travellers.   No charge is
made for lodgings.   The climate is so fine that a dry
bullock hide, spread in the open air, and covered with
saddle-cloths, cloak, or *poncho*, is preferred, when it
does not rain, to sleeping under cover.   The saddle answers the purposes of a pillow.   Those who have been
reared in the lap of luxury may listen with a smile of
disdain to the mention of these humble accommoda-
tions.   Such persons can have no idea of the pleasure
with which the weary traveller eyes the lowly couch
where delicious slumber is not broken until the gray
of morning rouses him refreshed, and prepared for
renewed exertion.   They cannot imagine with what
eagerness he alights again in the evening at some
distant post-house; nor the relish which hunger gives
to the plain but wholesome supper; nor the complacency with which he listens to the rude guitar,
the simple song, and the conversation of gauchos
drawn together by the arrival of a stranger.   These
are pleasures known only to those who have been
content to take things as they find them.   Persons
of fastidious taste, and unconforming mind, pre-
determined to pronounce every thing wrong, and
who feel in romantic novelty no compensation for
fatigues, and the absence of accustomed comforts,
might find causes of complaint at every step, and
relief only in the publication of their miseries.

After a ride of three hundred leagues, Miller
reached Mendoza on the ninth day.   It is a large
town, in an extensive and well-cultivated plain at the
foot of the Andes, and is the capital of the province

of Cuyo.   Its most remarkable feature is a .fine
alameda, or public promenade, of great length and
beauty, formed by four rows of poplars of extraordinary height and regularity.   The introduction of this
tree by a Spaniard is deserving of notice, because it is
honourable to patriot liberality.   The poplar was found
to thrive exceedingly by the side of the *azequias*
(small shallow canals), by which the cultivated spots
are irrigated.   Within ten years from their first introduction, half a million of poplars were planted.
When the revolution broke out, this worthy Spaniard,
Don Juan ——, was, by an express decree, excepted
from the hostility shown to his countrymen; exempted
from the payment of all direct taxes; and taken
under the protection of government.

The manners of the people of Mendoza are mild,
and, in simplicity, pre-eminently republican.   None
have much money, although many possess large
estates.   On the other hand, very few are in destitute circumstances.   Ardent spirits are abundant
and cheap, but notwithstanding this, great crimes
are rare.   Of seventy-two offenders brought to trial in
one year, three only were *Cuyanos*, or natives of the
province.

In the country a great deal of social visiting takes
place, particularly on a Sunday.   Good horses shorten
distances, and large parties assemble at farm-houses,
where playing at forfeits, dancing, and singing, are
amongst the usual amusements.   A lady, sometimes
in a riding-habit, perhaps with a long whip in her
hand, and gentlemen variously attired, walk a minuet by day-light, with infinite grace, on an earthen

floor. Waltzes are also danced in these gay and good-humoured parties; but the heat of the weather makes the minuet more common.

The goître is prevalent at Mendoza, and still more so at the large and populous village of San Vicente, a league distant; but it is not accompanied by idiotcy, as in some of the cantons of Switzerland.

Miller crossed the Andes by the pass of Uspallata, and reached Santiago, a distance of ninety leagues from Mendoza, in three days and a half.

It is impossible to convey an adequate idea of the solitary grandeur of those immeasurable ridges, whose peaky summits seem to pierce the firmament.   The wearisome, and almost never-ending, ascents and descents along the course of rumbling torrents, so far beneath as to be, though within *hearing*, not always within *sight*, impart a character of loneliness not common to mountain barriers, when enlivened by a few scattered human habitations.   In the Cordillera it is a pleasure to meet even the stag-like gaze of the *guanaco*, and equally a relief to look at the condor, as, with unfluttering wing, it floats almost movelessly above, bearing the same relative proportion to the eagle of Europe that his native Andes do to the Alps. The snow in some of the highest table-lands is difficult to pass, because it dissolves in such a manner as to leave an irregular surface like fields of sugar-loaves of different sizes.   Mules frequently sink to the girth, and surmount these obstructions with great toil.   The strange noises made by gusts of wind in the reverberating valleys sound to the ear of the timorous guide like moans; and he does not fail to recount long

stories of travellers that have perished, and whose
souls he supposes still haunt the vicinity of their un-
buried remains.   He also *enlivens* the journey by
strange tales of witchcraft and of mountain demons.

On entering Chile, the scene changes from the
sublime to the beautiful.   Wherever water is to be
found, the fertility of the soil is incomparably greater
than in almost any other country of the world. Fruit
used to be so cheap that it was the custom for a man
to load his mule from a garden with whatever sorts
he chose to select, for a real (sixpence).   One of the
consequences of the revolution has been to enhance
the value of the products of the earth, and a dollar
is now demanded for the same privilege.   In 1818,
as much bread as would suffice six men, for a day, cost
a real.   At the houses of entertainment by the road-
side, a real and a half was the charge for a chicken
with an unstinted accompaniment of vegetables.

Miller crossed the heights of Chacabuco, and
arrived at Santiago on the 24th of January, 1818.
This city is the capital of Chile.   Perhaps it covers
nearly four square miles, although its population does
not exceed forty thousand souls.   The houses are of
a single story, roofed with pantiles.   The principal
residences have lofty and ornamental gateways. The
street front is sometimes built into shops, without
any outlet into the court-yard behind.

Water is conveyed from the river Mapocho in
axequias, which run through the principal streets,
and feed smaller ones, which supply the houses and
carry off impurities.   The water of other *axequias*
is expended in the irrigation of fields.   Wherever

this can be done, perpetual verdure clothes the face
of the country, but every where else barrenness prevails, excepting in the rainy season.

The north side of the great square of Santiago is
occupied by the Directorial Palace, a fine building,
having the city prison under the same roof. The
unfinished cathedral, and mean-looking palace of the
bishop, form the west side. The mint, a very fine
building, is situated in an obscure part of the city.
The *alameda*, the *tajamar*, or wall to guard against
occasional overflowings of the Mapocho, and, in fact,
every other great and useful public work, were suggested and carried into execution by Captain-General
O'Higgins, the father of the late supreme director.
His road from Santiago to Valparaiso is the Simplon
of the New World.   He also planned and executed
several great works in Lima whilst viceroy of Peru.

On the morning of the 26th of January, Miller
quitted Santiago, and, after a ride of twenty-five
leagues, joined the division of the army bivouacked
at Las Tablas, near Valparaiso. The officers and
men were comfortably hutted. The encampment
extended over above a league of ground, being intersected by ravines, formed by mountain torrents
gushing, in the rainy season, through the bottoms
of little vales. The different corps, in order to their
being conveniently supplied with water, were stationed on the borders of the ravines, at the distance
of about a mile from each other. Each corps possessed
six or eight tents, which were used by the guard, and
as magazines for stores when halting at the end of a
day's march.

Miller reported his arrival to General San Martin, whose head-quarters were at the *hacienda* of Dorego, three or four leagues from Las Tablas. He was then ordered to his regiment, the Buenos Ayrean artillery. On his presenting himself to the commandant, Lieutenant-Colonel Plaza, the latter, without inviting him to be seated, sent an orderly to show him an unoccupied tent. As his baggage had not come up, Miller threw himself on the ground, and slept soundly till morning, when he received visits from the officers of the regiment, whose politeness effaced the unfavourable impression made by the lieutenant-colonel's uncourteous reception. Each grade had a separate mess, and Miller gladly accepted the invitation to join that of the captains.

Amongst them was Don Francisco Dias, a Spaniard, and formerly in the navy. He was a proficient in the mathematics, understood fortification, spoke English fluently, was familiar with French literature, and extremely sociable with those to whom he was attached. His wife, a native of Monte Video, was an amiable woman, and an honorary member of the mess. She had accompanied her husband in all his campaigns, and underwent extraordinary privations and fatigues with unchangeable gaiety.

Don Juan Apostol Martinez, a captain in the regiment, when a mere youth, distinguished himself in the defence of Buenos Ayres against the British; he was a brave officer and a cheerful companion, but of a very eccentric character. His antipathy to Spaniards was unconquerable. He would never call Captain Dias by any other name than " Gallego Dias," until three duels, in which each received wounds,

produced a tacit agreement, that Juan Apostol was
never to mention Dias by the name of "Gallego" in
his presence.

On the march, Don Juan Apostol was accustomed
to play his tricks upon the priesthood, if Spaniards
or of the royalist party. He has been known to
send for a monk, and, pretending to be dangerously
ill, would, with groans forced by apparent bodily
sufferings, confess himself guilty of all the deadly
sins. When he had obtained the full attention of
the confessor, Don Juan Apostol concluded by re-
lating a pretended dream, in which he stated that he
had kicked a priest out of the house; " and now,"
said he, " behold the dream of John the Apostle
come to pass." More than one holy friar carried,
for days, the marks of Juan's anti-apostolical feet.
For these and other practical jokes Captain Martinez
was sometimes placed under arrest; but, as he judiciously confined the exercise of his wit to disreputable
friars, and as his character was held in deserved
esteem, he always got off with a slight admonition.

. Beltran, who has been mentioned as superintending the passing of the artillery across the Andes from
Mendoza, was now captain in the regiment, and placed
in charge of the *maestranza*, or field depôt, to which
about fifty artificers were attached. The revolution
found Beltran in the cloister of a convent, but throwing aside the cowl, he became an active, intelligent,
and useful officer*.

* This officer afterwards served with distinction throughout the campaigns
of Chile and Peru. The war concluded, he retired to Buenos Ayres, and, re-
signing his commission of lieutenant-colonel, to which rank he had attained with
so much honour and credit, he became a clergyman. It is a matter of regret that
this truly meritorious man died, neglected and in penury, in 1827.

Captain Giroust, who had been educated at *l'école polytechnique* at Paris, and who was afterwards page to King Jerome Bonaparte, was another officer in the corps, but was at this time detached at Valparaiso *, under the orders of Major Arcos† of the engineers.

The adjutant, Talmayancu, was an Araucanian Indian, who had been brought up and educated by Father Julian, mentioned in the account of the Indian palaver. The adjutant was stout and squat; his complexion sallow and shining: from under a low forehead peered out two twinkling eyes, which, from their good-humoured vivacity, relieved the expression of a countenance that was often compared to the full moon. He was fond of creating false alarms in the encampment, by answering the challenge of sentinels at night, as if enemies were at hand. The day after his arrival Miller mounted guard: Talmayancu attempted to play his usual pranks upon the new comer; but being overheard by an officer who knew his voice, he was detected, and placed under a short arrest.

There were some very fine young men amongst the other officers of the corps, and all were extremely obliging. Most of them played on the guitar, or

* Captain Giroust was made prisoner by the royalists in Peru. He obtained his liberty, and resigned his commission in the patriot service. He has since married a lady of the country, and is established at Lima.

† Arcos, a native of Galicia, served on the staff of Marshal Jourdan at the battle of Vitoria. Being obliged to quit the patriot army after the retreat from Cancharayada, he became a contractor. A little before the downfall of O'Higgins, and his minister Rodriguez Aldea, Arcos was compelled to make a precipitate retreat from Chile, not before, however, he had realized a considerable fortune, which he has since greatly augmented in Europe. He is now living at Paris, with the ostentation of a prince, and the meanness of a Jew. His beautiful wife is the daughter of a distinguished Chileno family, and her unimpeachable conduct forms an amiable contrast to her husband's

" Meanness that soars, and pride that licks the dust."

sang, and good fellowship reigned throughout the camp.

The style of living was simple but substantial. A benign climate permitted persons to sleep and to live in the open air, excepting in the heat of the day. *Mate*, served by a lame invalid, retained for that purpose, was taken from hut to hut before the occupant arose from his mattrass. Breakfast *à la fourchette* was served at nine. The dinner, between two and three o'clock, consisted of excellent soup, roasted strips of flesh, brought to table on a stick or ramrod, which answered the purpose of a spit, poultry, vegetables, and fruit in great abundance. The prices in the camp market were, for poultry one shilling a couple; vegetables for six or eight people threepence; apples and pears a shilling per bushel; water-melons three halfpence each; bread and other articles of food were proportionably cheap.

The rations, which consisted of meat and salt, and sometimes vegetables, for the whole corps, four hundred and eighty men, cost the government less than 1000 dollars per month. The pay of a private soldier was four dollars per month; the half was stopped on account of rations, &c. The net pay of a captain of artillery was sixty-five dollars per month.

Mate was again served round at sunset, and a supper followed for those who chose to partake of it.

Sudden changes of temperature were felt at Las Tablas in the course of twenty-four hours. At noon Fahrenheit's thermometer would stand at 85°; at sunset a breeze arose, and the mercury sunk to 65°. Before this, black clouds appeared to rise up directly

out of the ocean, and were seen flying towards the
summits of the Andes, which attracted and intercepted them.   Perhaps in no other country is the
sun seen to set in so much glory. For a long time
after he has sunk below the horizon, he still gilds
the summits of the mighty wall of the Cordillera;
broken masses of clouds, magnificently tinged, impart to the scene a degree of splendour absolutely
inconceivable.

The corps of Buenos Ayrean artillery consisted of
ten six-pounders and one howitzer, and four companies
of one hundred and twenty men each.   The first
company was attached to the guns.   Each gun was
drawn by four horses, and each horse ridden by a gunner, there being no corps of drivers in the service. A
non-commissioned officer and seven gunners mounted,
were, besides the four already mentioned, attached to
each piece of artillery. The carriage and limber differ
but little from what are used in the English service,
excepting that a pole is substituted for shafts.   The
horses are put to the carriages by a thong of hide,
one end of which is strapped to a ring at the end of
the girth, high up under the flap of the saddle ; the
other end of the thong is strapped in like manner to
another ring at the end of the pole.   The thong
traces of the leaders differ from those of the wheel
horses in nothing but being longer.   The saddle
girth is about four inches broad, and is made of
strips of hide plaited.   At each end is an iron ring,
by which the girth is fastened to the saddle by laces
of hide.   It is to one of these rings that the thong
trace is fixed. Buckles, collars, cruppers, and breast-

plates are not in use. Every gunner is competent
to repair, or even to make a harness. The only im-
plement required is a clasp knife, and the only material a piece of hide. This *lasso* harness, if so it may
be termed, possesses the advantages of strength and
simplicity, and is at the same time free from many
inconveniences attending harnesses more pleasing to
the eye. To protect the wheel from the action of
the sun, strips of hide an inch broad are bound round
every spoke and every felloe. This is done with
green hide, and as the strips harden and tighten
gradually as they dry, they add very much to the
strength of the wheel. Even that part of the overlay
which covers the tire lasts a long time upon the South
American carriage roads, and when it wears out it is
easily renewed; but this species of clothing gives
clumsiness to the wheels, and therefore upon going
into action it is all cut away.

Each gunner of the first company wore a dragoon
sabre. Those of the second company acted as cavalry,
and were armed with sabres and pistols. The third
and fourth companies had muskets, and acted as infantry. All however were taught the horse-artillery,
cavalry, and infantry exercises; and being all equally
good horsemen, no difficulty or confusion arose out of
this complexity of arms. Every man was skilful in
breaking in a colt, and was accustomed to catch wild
horses with the *lasso*.

Upwards of six hundred horses were attached to the
corps. When wanted they were driven into a circle,
where each man would unerringly throw the *lasso*
over the head of the horse he had fixed his eye upon.

The saddles were put on; the horses hooked to the carriages; all was done, and the regiment formed, in less than twelve minutes.   Every movement was made with surprising celerity.   The exercise of the patriot artillery does not differ materially from the European system.

.   If a horse knocks up on the march, one of the gunners rides up with a fresh one, and, with it, takes the place of the jaded animal without the party slackening its march to effect the change.   Several hundred spare horses follow in the rear.

The South American artillery can with ease perform a march of fifty or sixty miles a day for many days successively.   If necessary, it could march from Mendoza, across the level Pampas, to Buenos Ayres, at the rate of even ninety miles per day; supposing always the spare horses to be sufficiently numerous to allow of fresh ones being put to the carriage after it had been drawn at a gallop for two or three leagues.

The carriages have no drags.   To supply this deficiency, two gunners fasten one end of their *lassos* to the washers, and the other end to the ring of their saddle-girths.   By making their horses hold back, the purpose of a drag is answered.   On ascending a hill, on crossing rivers, on passing over swampy ground, as well as in bad roads, additional horses are hooked on to the washers.   All this can be done without halting for a moment.

.   To hear Creole officers speak of their cavalry as comparable with the finest in Europe was calculated to excite a smile in a newly arrived European, who, at first sight, would consider the comparison preposterous; but when his eye had become accustomed to the *poncho* and the slovenly appearance of the men, and he had seen them in action, he would then readily acknowledge that no European cavalry could cope with gaucho lancers, throughout a campaign, on South American ground.

The appearance of the troops in general, at the time we are speaking of, was not calculated to produce a very favourable impression upon the mind of. a superficial observer. A man on guard without a stock, and perhaps without a button to his coat, was a strange sight to one accustomed to see well-dressed soldiers. Yet the composition of the army of the Andes was good, and although the dress of the soldiers was unsightly, they were well armed, tolerably well disciplined, and very enthusiastic. National airs and hymns to liberty, accompanied by the sound of guitars, were heard throughout the encampment every evening till a late hour.

A week or ten days after Miller's arrival at Las Tablas, he rode to Valparaiso to see the port, and to deliver a letter of introduction, which Captain Sharpe, of the British navy, had been kind enough to give him at Buenos Ayres, for Commodore Bowles. On reaching the table-land, which rises immediately behind Valparaiso, the vast Pacific Ocean suddenly appeared in view. The sun shone upon the unruffled expanse, and altogether the effect was startingly interesting. It revived feelings which had been excited in boyhood, by the perusal of that part of the history of the conquest of Mexico which describes Balbao as leaving his companions, and advancing alone to the brow of a ridge on the Isthmus of Panama, whence he caught the first glance of the magnificent great South Sea. The English flag, which Miller had not seen for some months, now appeared at the mast-head of two vessels at anchor in the port, and created in his mind a sensation of intense pleasure.

With feelings of gratified curiosity, Miller continued his ride along the table-land, and descended the zigzag road which leads to the *Almendral,* a sort of suburb of Valparaiso. Upon his arrival at the port, he proceeded on board H. M. S. Amphion, where he was most cordially received by Commodore Bowles, at whose table he met Captain Biddle of the U. S. Ship Ontario, and Judge Prevost. To the two latter gentlemen Miller is indebted for much subsequent kind attention.

The arrival at Lima from Spain of the first battalion of the regiment of Burgos, a squadron of *Lanzeros del Rey,* and a troop of horse-artillery, enabled Pezuela to complete the equipment of an expedition destined to reconquer Chile. General Osorio, son-in-law to the viceroy, sailed from Callao on the 9th of Dec. 1817, and disembarked at Talcahuano with three regiments of infantry, one of cavalry, and twelve pieces of artillery, in all about three thousand six hundred men. To these were added the garrison of Talcahuano under Ordoñez, and some recruits obtained by Sanchez in the province of Concepcion.

Osorio having completed his force to six thousand effective men, advanced towards the capital of Chile. Previous to this, O'Higgins and Las Heras had fallen back towards Talca. The division at Las Tablas under San Martin marched to form a junction with that of O'Higgins, in order to give battle to Osorio.

The first little incident that occurred was in crossing the river Maypo, six leagues south of Santiago. The Maypo is a torrent which rushes from a gorge of the Andes. The only bridge over it is made of what may be called hide cables. It is about two hundred and fifty feet long, and just wide enough to admit a carriage. It is upon the principle of suspension, and constructed where the banks of the river are so bold as to furnish natural piers. The figure of the bridge is nearly that of an inverted arch. Formed of elastic materials, it rocks a good deal when passengers go over it. The infantry, however, passed upon the present occasion without the smallest difficulty. The cavalry also passed without any accident by going a few at a time, and each man leading his horse. When the artillery came up, doubts were entertained of the possibility of getting it over. The general had placed himself on an eminence to see his army file to the opposite side of the river. A consultation was held upon the practicability of passing the artillery. Miller volunteered to conduct the first gun. The limber was taken off, and drag ropes were fastened to the washers, to prevent the gun from descending too rapidly. The trail, carried foremost, was held up by two gunners, but, notwithstanding every precaution, the bridge swung from side to side, and the carriage acquired so much velocity, that the gunners who held up the trail, assisted by Miller, lost their equilibrium, and the gun upset. The carriage, becoming entangled in the thong balustrade, was prevented from falling into the river, but the platform of the bridge acquired an inclination almost perpendicular, and all upon it were obliged to cling to whatever they could catch hold of to save themselves from being precipitated into the torrent, which rolled and foamed sixty feet below. For some little time none dared go to the relief of the party thus suspended, because it was supposed that the bridge would snap asunder, and it was expected that in a few moments all would drop into the abyss beneath. However, as nothing material gave way, the alarm on shore subsided, and two or three men ventured on the bridge to give assistance. The gun was dismounted with great difficulty, the carriage dismantled, and conveyed piecemeal to the opposite shore. The rest of the artillery then made a detour, and crossed at a ford four or five leagues lower down the river. Notwithstanding this accident, Miller lost no credit by the attempt.

On the 15th of March, San Martin formed a junction with the supreme director O'Higgins and Colonel Las Heras at San Fernando. The patriot army now counted seven thousand infantry, fifteen hundred cavalry, thirty-three field-pieces, and two howitzers.

Ignorant of the numbers and movements of his opponents, the royalist general crossed the river Maule, and was proceeding on to Santiago, when, on the 18th of March, the vanguard of each army came in contact at Quechereguas. In the affair which took place the royalist advance was worsted. Osorio, having ascertained the superiority of the patriots, countermarched with evident precipitation. San Martin obliqued to his own left for the purpose of interposing between the royalists and the ford of the Maule. On the morning of the 19th, the two armies crossed the river Lircay at the same time, at the distance of four miles from each other, and continued to march in almost parallel but gradually approximating columns over five leagues of open country. The patriots advanced in the finest order, and with the utmost regularity. The Spaniards quickened their march in some slight confusion, and were the first to reach the town of Talca, in front of which they took up a position an hour before sunset amongst enclosed fields. The patriot columns approached, and, whilst they drew up in line on the plain of Cancharayada, some sharp skirmishing took place. A regiment of Chileno cavalry charged; but having committed the error of getting into a gallop at too great a distance from the enemy, formed behind a ravine which had not been perceived, it was repulsed, but retired in good order, under cover of the Chileno artillery commanded by Lieutenant-Colonel Blanco Ciceron, and particularly well served. On this occasion Lieutenant Gerrard, a brave young Scotchman, who had distinguished himself the day before at Quechereguas, was killed. He formerly belonged to the British rifle corps.

San Martin purposed to delay attacking till the morning of the 20th. The situation of the royal army had become extremely critical. The able manner in which San Martin manœuvred on the preceding day gave the royalists little room to hope for success in risking a battle; whilst to retire to the difficult ford of the Maule, still five leagues off, in the presence of a superior enemy, threatened to expose their army to destruction.   In this extremity the incompetent Osorio is said to have retired to a church in Talca, and to have spent that time in prayer to an effigy of the Virgin Mary, which his second in command, General Ordoñez and Colonel Beza, devoted to action. Disgusted with the pusillanimity of their commander, they took upon themselves to plan and direct an immediate attack.   Accordingly, two or three Spanish corps in column, and favoured by the darkness of night, fell unexpectedly upon the patriots at a moment when some battalions and the Buenos Ayrean artillery were moving from the left to the right of the line.   The advanced posts of the patriots placed in the open country were dispersed or made prisoners. An ill-directed volley was fired from the line, which became panic-struck, and, upon General O'Higgins being wounded, all fled in irremediable confusion, with the exception of the right wing.

The commanding officer of the Buenos Ayrean artillery participating in the general alarm, took the road to Santiago, and the guns were abandoned. The dispersion of the left and centre of the line was complete.

This affair has been called a surprise, but it does not appear to have been so.   The patriot soldiers were allowed to sit down it is true, but not out of their formation.   They were not even permitted to ground or pile their arms.   The attack was unexpected, but not unprepared for, and might have been

repelled with ease.   But the effect of an attack in
the dark upon the minds of raw troops accounts naturally enough for the total rout, without its being
at all necessary to inculpate the generals who commanded.   Nor was it possible for them to counteract,
by any conduct of their own, at the moment, the effect
of the panic which, originating in a few, spread from
rank to rank like wildfire.

Three thousand infantry, under Colonel Las Heras,
on the right, partook of the general disorder, but not
to the same extent.   The presence of mind and
bravery of Las Heras enabled him to keep two-thirds
of his numbers together, and, under a heavy fire, to
rally and form most of the remainder before he left
the field.   To his courage and conduct upon this
occasion Chile is deeply indebted.   He retired in excellent order, with his division, and with the Chileno
artillery under Blanco Ciceron.

Miller was fortunate enough to save two guns of
the Buenos Ayrean artillery.   Ensign Moreno of
that corps remained by him.   He was a boy of sixteen, and behaved with perfect heroism.   He cheered
and encouraged the gunners, and kept together a few
infantry, until a severe wound made it necessary for
Miller to send him to the rear, with one of the guns
which could no longer be worked, on account of most
of the gunners having been killed or wounded.   In
the confusion, the patriots on the right began to fire
upon the only remaining field-piece, on which Miller
sent it also to the rear.   He then attached himself
to Las Heras, and acted as his adjutant during the
arduous retreat.

Lieutenant Don Juan de Larrain, a fine and promising youth of nineteen years of age, was shot through the heart, whilst attempting to rally a dispersed battalion, at the side of San Martin, to whom he was aide-de-camp. This youth was the son of Don Martin de Larrain, whose family ranks amongst the richest and most respectable of Chile. Juan was one of twenty-seven children by the same parents, of whom twenty-two were then living. His appearance was extremely prepossessing, and he was beloved by all, not less for his amiable qualities than for the military ardour and noble patriotism which marked his short but glorious career.

San Martin halted at San Fernando until Las Heras came up. Having reviewed the division, San Martin set out for the capital.

Some of the fugitives from Cancharayada rode eighty leagues in twenty-six hours, and, on the morning of the 21st, spread the disastrous news in Santiago. At such times, facts are not merely distorted, but lost in fearful rumours. It was believed that not so many as fifty patriots remained together in a body, and that Osorio might be expected almost hourly. The recollections of his tyranny and cruelty on a former occasion gave rise to anticipations, made the more dreadful by the knowledge that the former companions of the infamous Sambruno accompanied him. The capital became a scene of confusion that baffles description. People, with dismay and terror depicted on their countenances, were seen conveying valuables to nunneries and convents for safety. Others were loaded with household furniture, to be deposited in the houses of friends connected with the royalists, or supposed to be likely to be respected in the event of partial pillage.   Sights still more distressing were groups of wives, mothers, and young women, who gathered together, and bewailed with wild cries the supposed loss of husbands, sons, brothers, or lovers. Several sunk insensible on the pavement.   Despair seemed to have taken possession of every mind.   Many of the inhabitants, ill provided with means for crossing the snowy Cordillera, fled, whilst those who were obliged to remain became almost frantic.   Don Luis Cruz, the supreme delegado, did not preserve his presence of mind, and every public department was in a state of utter confusion, until the gallant Rodriguez placed himself at the head of affairs, and restored a degree of order.   He obliged the functionaries who had left Santiago with the public treasure to return.   He put a stop to further emigration; provided quarters for the fugitives; raised recruits; and took a public and solemn oath not to abandon his country under any circumstances.   Many followed his example, and a ray of hope beamed upon the prospect.   The arrival of O'Higgins and San Martin increased the confidence which Rodriguez * had inspired, and vigorous measures were adopted to make a stand on the plains of Maypo.   ·

The royalists, instead of continuing in pursuit towards Santiago, returned on the night of the 19th, having proceeded a mile or two, and occupied them-

* This brave, amiable, and highly endowed patriot was, about a month afterwards, imprisoned on suspicion of having planned a conspiracy to overthrow the government.   The officer of an escort belonging to a Buenos Ayrean regiment, whilst conducting Rodriguez to Quillota, barbarously assassinated him, on the plea that he attempted to make his escape.

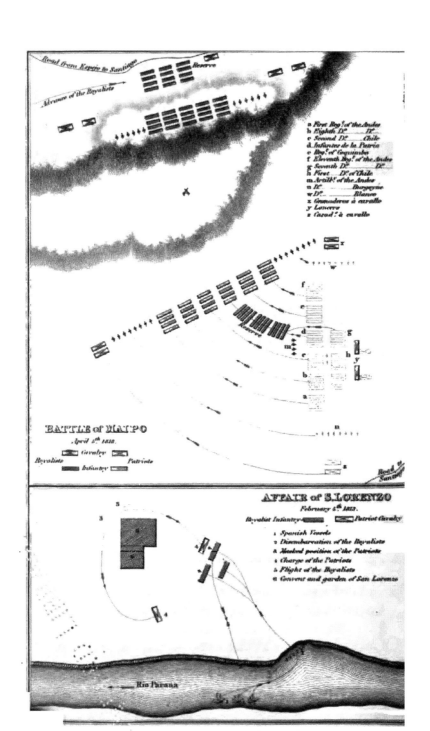

Road from Kexin to Santiago

Reserve

Advance of the Royalists

a First Reg.t of the Andes
b Eighth D.o   D.o
c Second D.o .... Chile
d Infantes de la Patria
e Reg.t of Coquimbo
f Eleventh Reg.t of the Andes
g Seventh D.o   D.o
m First   D.o of Chile
m Artill.a of the Andes
n D.o   .... Burgoyne
w D.o   .... Blanco
x Granaderos à cavallo
y Lanceros
z Cazad.e à cavallo

BATTLE of MAIPO

April 5th 1818.

Royalists   Cavalry   Patriots

Infantry

AFFAIR of S. LORENZO

February 3th 1813.

Royalist Infantry ▬▬◄   ▭▭▭► Patriot Cavalry

1 Spanish Vessels
2 Disembarcation of the Royalists
3 Masked position of the Patriots
4 Charge of the Patriots
5 Flight of the Royalists
6 Convent and garden of San Lorenzo

Rio Parana

selves in plundering the baggage found in the patriot
position, and then re-entered Talca.   The feeble
Osorio, who knew not how to profit by the unhoped-
for advantages gained by his second in command, and
Colonel Beza, marched northwards so slowly, that he
did not again come in contact with the patriots until
seventeen days afterwards.

This valuable interval was actively employed by
the supreme director, and San Martin, in re-assem-
bling the fugitives, and in re-organizing the army,
now encamped about two leagues from the capital.
Its numbers might be 6500, including 1000 militia.

On the morning of the 5th of April, 1818, the
royalist army, 6000 strong, was discovered at the
distance of six miles, approaching by the road which
leads from the ford of the Maypo to Santiago.   San
Martin moved a mile or two to his right, to preserve
his communication with Valparaiso.

About 11 A. M. the royalists formed nearly parallel
with the patriot line.   A brisk cannonade opened on
both sides.   Shortly afterwards, two patriot battalions
charged the Spanish right, but were repulsed with
considerable slaughter.   Two battalions of the Spaniards pressed forward in column; but whilst de-
ploying, they were charged and broken by the patriot
reserve under General Don Hilarion de la Quintana,
who, supported by the two battalions which had given
way, interposed between the Spanish line and its reserve, placed in the rear of the centre of their line.
At the same time, some charges of the patriot cavalry,
directed against the Spanish left, made an impression;
and in less than an hour from the commencement of

the action, the Spaniards gave way at every point.
The brave Ordoñez rallied and made a desperate
though fruitless struggle at the *hacienda* of Espejo,
about a league in the rear.   Osorio, and about one
hundred men, had previously made their escape, and
with great difficulty reached Talcahuano through by-
roads.   About two thousand royalists were slain, and
three thousand five hundred were made prisoners of
war.   The activity of the zealous Captain Don Juan
Apostol Martinez, and Lieutenant Olavarria, who
with a party operated on the enemy's rear, was very
conspicuous, and they, together with the followers
of Rodriguez, contributed to render the victory complete.   The patriots lost upwards of one thousand
in killed or wounded.   Amongst the former were
the brave Lieutenant-Colonel Bueras, and Lieutenant
Don Juan Gana, a very enterprising youth.

During the cannonade, the feelings of the inhabitants of Santiago were wound up to breathless in-
tensity, which, on the news of victory, found vent
in wild expressions of ungovernable ecstasy.   People
embraced each other, laughed, wept, and shrieked as
if deprived of their senses.   Some went literally mad,
and one or two of them have never recovered their
reason.   One man dropped down and expired instan-
taneously.   The glorious intelligence of the victory
overtook a large party of emigrants, principally ladies,
on the elevated pass of Uspallata.   They were so
overjoyed, that they hardly knew whether to proceed
to Mendoza or to return to Santiago.   Several were
so overcome, that they were left on the mountain
with a few attendants until they found themselves

sufficiently composed to resume their journey towards home. The young lady, whose filial piety made her the companion of her father's exile in Juan Fernandez, fell from her mule, and received an injury, from which she has never perfectly recovered.

Five days after this great event, which fixed the destinies of Chile, the victorious San Martin repaired a second time to Buenos Ayres, where he was received with something approaching to idolatrous admiration. His object was to lay before the government there his plan for the invasion of Peru by sea from Valparaiso; to solicit reinforcements to enable him to carry his plan into early execution; and to prevail upon General Belgrano to act in concert, by marching with the army at Tucuman, to attack the Spaniards in Peru, on the side of Potosi, whilst San Martin effected a descent near Lima.

Upon the return of San Martin he remained at Mendoza. From thence he directed a battalion of *cazadores*, and piquets of two cavalry regiments (in all nine hundred men) to join him from Chile. These orders were given at the desire of the Buenos Ayrean government, anxious to augment its forces, to be prepared for the event of the threatened expedition from Cadiz making a descent upon their territory. In three months San Martin increased those detachments to the number of two thousand six hundred men.

Previous to the battle of Maypo, Miller was detached with a company of infantry to take possession of the Lautaro * frigate, and to secure the shipping

---

* The Wyndham, an old East-Indiaman of 800 tons, purchased the day before the battle of Maypo.

in the port of Valparaiso, to provide, in case of further reverses, the means of conveying the retiring patriots to Coquimbo. He embarked with his detachment on board the newly-purchased frigate of forty-four guns, commanded by Captain O'Brien, formerly a lieutenant of the British navy, and who had distinguished himself in the capture of the United States frigate the Essex.

Valparaiso was blockaded by the Spanish frigate, Esmeralda, of forty-four guns, and by the brig Pezuela, of eighteen guns. The Lautaro was suddenly equipped, manned, and ordered out to raise the blockade. She was officered principally by Englishmen. Her ship's company was composed of one hundred foreign seamen, two hundred and fifty Chilenos, most of whom had never before been afloat, besides the above-mentioned marines. The Chilenos were so eager to go upon the service, that several swam off to the frigate. As soon as the motley but enthusiastic crew was hurried on board, the ship got under weigh in a state ill calculated for immediate action. The Europeans had just before received bounty money, and, of all the ship's company, were, from inebriety, the least efficient, whilst hardly a naval officer could give an order in the Spanish language. Nevertheless, in ten hours after weighing anchor, the Lautaro was engaged.

The Esmeralda seeing a frigate-built vessel approach, mistook it for his H. M. S. Amphion, Commodore Bowles, who had before communicated occasionally upon subjects relative to the blockade with the Esmeralda, which last therefore lay-to with her topsails to the mast to speak the supposed Amphion. In that situation the Lautaro ranged upon the weather quarter of the enemy, when, having hauled down British colours, and hoisted the Chileno, she discharged her foremost guns. It was Captain O'Brien's first intention to have laid the Lautaro alongside, but having altered his mind, he ran upon the Esmeralda's quarter. The Lautaro's bowsprit caught the enemy's mizen rigging, and hung her in a way so inconvenient for boarding, that O'Brien jumped on board with only thirty followers. The marines kept up a steady fire from the forecastle of the Lautaro, which caused a heavy loss to the Esmeralda's crew, who, panic-struck by the appearance of the boarding party, ran below, and the Spanish ensign was hauled down by the assailants. Unfortunately it did not occur to any one to prevent the two ships from separating by lashing them together, or to disable the prize by cutting her wheel-ropes and topsail haulyards. A jerk of the sea canted the ships clear of each other, upon which the Lautaro lowered her boats to send a reinforcement; but before that could be accomplished, the Esmeralda's men, seeing but a handful of patriots upon deck, rallied, fired from below, and shot the gallant O'Brien, whose last words were, " Never leave her, my boys : the ship is ours." Meanwhile the Lautaro had incautiously left the main object to take possession of the Pezuela, which had struck, but was stealing away.

Upon perceiving the change of fortune on board the Esmeralda, the Lautaro gave over chasing the brig, and steered for the frigate; but before she could

approach, the boarders were overpowered, and both
the Spanish ships having rehoisted their own colours,
escaped by superior sailing.   Lieut. Walker, of the
H. E. I. company's service, distinguished himself
considerably; and before the Lautaro returned to
port, captured a vessel having on board as passengers
a number of rich Spaniards, who had fled from Concepcion to take refuge in Lima.   Upon them the
Chileno government levied a contribution, in the
shape of ransom, which more than reimbursed the
original purchase-money of the Lautaro.

CHAPTER VIII.

Chileno squadron sails.—How equipped.—Cholos.—Capture of
the Spanish frigate, Reyna Maria Isabel.—Harsh treatment
of Major Miller, the bearer of a flag of truce.—General San-
ches.—Difficulties of getting off the prize.—New danger.—
Spanish transports captured.—Chileno squadron returns.—
Rejoicings.—Chileno manners.

ALTHOUGH this first naval essay was not completely successful, yet it had the effect of raising the
blockade of Valparaiso, and Chile may be considered
to have acquired, from that moment, the superiority
over Spain in the Chileno seas.

The supreme director seeing the importance of
creating a marine force, purchased the Cumberland
of twelve hundred tons, and some smaller vessels.
For the payment of the ships, and to defray the expenses of arming and fitting them for sea, the Chilenos made the most generous sacrifices. Not only
was family plate sent to the mint, but the productions
of estates were contributed in kind by those proprietors whose means did not enable them to place
on the altar of freedom a more splendid donation.

It was known that part of the expedition preparing
at Cadiz was destined for Chile. The patriots, aware
that the struggle for freedom had become a struggle
for existence, strained every nerve to meet manfully
the threatening danger.

The shipping were soon manned, victualled, and
got ready for sea; but a delay arose from the dif-

ficulty of naming a commander. Foreigners, who
were candidates for the command, were so exorbitant
in their conditions, and so much divided amongst
themselves, that the government was unable to select
a proper person from amongst those in Chile.   The
supreme director at length appointed as commodore
Lieut.-Colonel Don Manuel Blanco Ciceron, who
had served, as a midshipman, and *alferez de navio,*
in the Spanish navy.

Miller having been a second time strongly recommended, was now promoted to the rank of brevet
major; and re-embarked as senior officer of the troops
distributed in the squadron, consisting of

	Guns.	
The San Martin	56	{ Commodore Blanco, Captain Wilkinson.
The Lautaro .	44	Captain Worster.
The Chacabuco	20	Captain Dias *.
The Araucano .	16	Captain Morris.

It put to sea at noon on the 9th of October, 1818.
A feeling of anxious solicitude pervaded the whole
country.   The salute returned by the forts announced
the departure of the expedition.   A steady southerly
breeze enabled the ships to preserve exact order,
sailing in line.   The highest points of the hills, for
many miles along the coast, were occupied by clusters
of men, women, and children, who had relations embarked, and towards whom they seemed determined
to gaze as long as a sail remained in sight.

A few months before, Valparaiso was blockaded,

* This deserving officer has been mentioned as commanding a company of
Buenos Ayrean artillery at Las Tablas.   An intimate and uninterrupted friend-
ship subsisted between him and the subject of these memoirs, until the death of
Dias in 1822.

the country kept in a state of continual alarm, and
its rising commerce crippled.   The supreme director
had left the seat of government to superintend the
outfit of the equipment, and through his personal
exertions, the object was accomplished under difficulties of no ordinary magnitude.   The anticipations
of public opinion were various, and generally unfavourable.   Some foretold a mutiny; others that
the ships would founder in the first gale of wind, on
account of the insufficiency of seamen to work them;
whilst many considered that a single Spanish frigate
would be able to capture the whole squadron.   Nor
were these forebodings altogether without the appearance of being well grounded.   The crews were, for
the most part, made up from *cholos*, or native peasants, many of whom had never before *seen* the sea.
The naval officers were nearly all English or North
American, who spoke the Spanish language imper-
fectly, or not at all.   With a very few exceptions,
they affected a prejudice against every thing that
differed from the rules of the service in which they
had been brought up, and they were too full of pre-
conceived notions to be willing to do justice to the
capacity of the unassuming people placed under their
orders.   But the commodore was a young man who,
in spite of a manner which displeases on first acquaintance, fortunately possessed the qualities requisite to
establish union, harmony, and good order; qualities
more valuable, under those circumstances, than great
practical skill.

Being out of sight of land, on the first evening
Commodore Blanco opened his sealed instructions,

and as Major Miller had to make their purport known by interpreting to the respective captains, he learned, that their destination was to proceed to the island of La Mocha, in search of the Spanish frigate Reyna Maria Isabel, daily expected round Cape Horn, with eight or ten transports, conveying two thousand eight hundred troops from Cadiz. This information had been acquired in the following manner. The troops on board one of the Spanish transports, headed by a serjeant, having mutinied on reaching the latitude of the river Plata, they proceeded to Buenos Ayres, and placed themselves at the disposal of that government, which lost no time in transmitting over-land the instructions given at Cadiz, by which means every rendezvous was ascertained.

During a long passage of the Chileno squadron, the crews were brought into something like a state of efficiency. The marines and *cholos* being continually exercised, were found to possess the valuable qualities which constitute good soldiers or sailors. They were subordinate, and soon afterwards proved themselves to be brave. They evinced an eagerness to be taught, and a quickness to learn. They were grateful for any small attention to their comforts, and always showed an earnest desire to please, for even an approving word or look seemed to be to them an object of ambition. In short, they only required common pains to be taken by their officers, in order to be rendered equal to any undertaking. When off duty they sang national airs; and when the officers danced on the quarter-deck, the *cholos* danced with the sailors in the waist and on the forecastle. They always behaved well; and during a heavy gale, which lasted two days, they were made more useful in assisting to work the ship than could have been reasonably expected from men who had hardly found their *sea legs.* Whilst beating against the prevailing winds, the Chacabuco parted company.

On the 26th of October, at day-break, they made the island of Santa Maria, near the southern side of the great bay of Concepcion; but in consequence of light airs, the squadron could not near it until the evening, when three boats were lowered and manned, to board a vessel discovered at the distance of five miles on the southern side of the island; but the boats were in such a leaky state, that it was deemed unsafe to send them. The Araucano was detached to look into the port of Talcahuano, situated twelve leagues off on the southern side of the bay.

Early on the 27th, the sail seen on the night before was boarded. She proved to be the *Shakespeare,* an English whaler, and gave information that the Spanish frigate, having parted company with her convoy, had touched at Santa Maria; crew sickly; in want of provisions; and that she had sailed five days before for Talcahuano, whither two Spanish transports had followed.

This information was confirmed by a boat from the shore, which was decoyed by the Spanish flag being kept flying in the Chileno squadron, and unsuspectingly delivered up the sealed instructions left by the captain of the Maria Isabel, for the respective masters of transports, ordering them to rendezvous at Talcahuano. For that port the San Martin and

the Lautaro immediately crowded all sail.   At night
they were becalmed off Concepcion; but a fine north-
erly breeze, very uncommon in those latitudes, brought
them, at noon on the 28th, in sight of the Spanish
frigate lying at anchor within pistol-shot of Talcahuano.   The commodore, under English colours,
steered directly towards the enemy, but, on coming
within musket range, hoisted the Chileno ensign.
An ill-directed broadside was given from the Spanish
frigate, and the compliment was returned with as
many guns as could be brought to bear from the San
Martin, which dropped anchor within pistol-shot of
her opponent, upon which the Spaniards cut their
cable and ran their ship on shore.   Many of the
crew escaped in boats, whilst numbers jumped overboard and swam to the beach.   Immediate possession
was taken of the prize, and an attempt made to get
her off; but the wind blowing fresh upon the land,
every effort was then ineffectual.   At this crisis the
commodore sent Miller with a flag of truce, to offer
generous treatment to the fugitives, if they chose to
surrender rather than prolong their miseries in a
country inimical to the royalist cause.   Upon approaching within fifteen or twenty yards of the beach,
a number of *guasos*, or Chileno yeomanry, levelled
their muskets; and it was with no small difficulty
that Major Miller made them comprehend the mean-
ing of the white flag, and prevented them from firing
a volley.   Having waited a considerable time in the
boat for an officer to come down, and receive him,
agreeably to custom in such cases, he jumped ashore,
rather because retreat would have hazarded the lives

of his boat's crew, than from any hope of being able
to succeed in the object of his mission. He found himself awkwardly circumstanced.   The *guasos* formed
themselves into groups, to decide whether he should
at once be despatched.   Some of them, on the contrary, showed a disposition to treat him civilly.   Disputes ran high; hard words were exchanged; but at
last Miller had the good fortune to allay a ferment
of which he expected every moment to become the
victim.

Two militia officers now appeared in sight. They
would not come down to the beach, but beckoned
Miller to go to them, which he did with some re-
luctance. On his way, a musket-ball, fired by a *guaso*,
lodged in the shoulder of one of the men escorting
Miller. The militia officers received him with great
incivility, and affected a mysterious style of conversation, evidently with an intention to give importance to themselves, and to create alarm. They
compelled their prisoner, for the major was now
treated as such, to accompany them on the road to
Concepcion; but before they had walked two miles,
they met General Sanchez at the head of sixteen
hundred men, part of these being troops left behind by
Osorio, when he blew up the fortifications about six
weeks previous to Blanco's arrival, and the remainder
had been landed from the Maria Isabel and two
transports, which had afterwards proceeded to Lima.
Sanchez passed on without deigning to speak to Miller, but ordered him to be blindfolded.   The militia
officers, encouraged by this appearance of harshness,
increased their former incivility, and became brutally

insulting. One of them poured forth an uninterrupted torrent of abuse for nearly two hours, and
then desired two men to tighten the handkerchief.
over the major's eyes, which they did with all their
strength. Sanchez at length ordered the prisoner to
be brought into his presence, to communicate the
commodore's proposals. The general listened to them
with the utmost contempt, and, with a roughness of
manner which showed he was a stranger to the com-
monest forms of good breeding, gave for answer that
the bearer should be *despatched* in the way he
deserved.

In the early contest between Spain and her colonies, the laws of war were frequently violated without scruple or compunction, and a lenient sentence
could hardly be expected from a ferocious man, whose
feelings had been worked up to exasperation by recent losses and disappointments. Although a war
of extermination had never been openly declared in
Chile, it often happened that quarter was refused in
action, and many were frequently sacrificed in cold
blood.

The royalist armed *guasos* in Talcahuano still kept
up such an annoying fire from behind walls upon the
patriots on board the captured frigate, that it was
judged necessary by Blanco to land the marines, for
the purpose of dislodging them, which was soon effected. Upon the arrival, however, of Sanchez, with
his party from Concepcion, the marines were obliged
to withdraw to the ships, with some loss in killed and
in prisoners.

Miller having been taken from the beach under

circumstances calculated to excite suspicion, and the
commodore perceiving that he did not return within
the half hour prescribed, sent Captain Warnes, who
threw upon the beach an official letter, signifying,
that if the bearer of the flag of truce were not immediately sent on board, and if he were not treated
according to the laws of war, he (Blanco) would order
all the Spanish prisoners of war, then in his power,
to be hung up at the yard-arm, and that the same
fate should await all such as might thenceforward
fall into his hands.   Sanchez told his prisoner that
the commodore had sacrificed him, by having landed
troops, and that he might prepare for death.   The
uncompromising tone with which Miller argued his
own cause greatly irritated the general, who appeared
to be still determined to carry his threats into execution.   He ordered the prisoner to be conveyed to
a shed, within range of the guns of the patriot squadron, and in the precise direction that they were then
firing.   It seemed as if Sanchez wished his captive
to be disposed of by a chance shot.   Several fell near
the shed, and some passed through the roof.   His
guard, fearful for their own lives, deserted their
charge for a short time.   In this situation, fatigued,
hungry, and thirsty, without being able to procure
refreshment of any kind, he passed the night.   The
firmness with which he had disputed the right and
questioned the policy of sacrificing him had produced
no good effect upon Sanchez, but it had made a very
different impression on the minds of some of the
chiefs who were present.   Two of them, Colonel
Loriga (of the artillery), and Colonel Cabañas, who

had served in the *Guardias Wallones*, both visited him in the course of the night, evidently with a view that their occasional presence might prove a check against personal violence.   The interest of these interviews was increased by discovering, in conversation, that Miller was intimately acquainted with some of Loriga's friends in the Peninsula.

Meanwhile, the royalists erected a battery of four guns, which played upon the Maria Isabel with such effect, that it was contemplated, at one time, so set fire to her.   But the unwearied exertions of the officers and good conduct of the men finally surmounted every difficulty.   At seven A. M. on the 29th, the wind veered round to the southward: every effort was redoubled, and Miller had the gratification to hear the Spaniards lament their own misfortune. The frigate was again afloat, and sailing out of the bay.

The interval of time had been employed by Loriga and Cabañas to make a magnanimous effort in behalf of the prisoner.   At first Sanchez refused to listen to them, and it was not until the colonels had given some intelligible hints, comparing the number and quality of the bayonets in their respective battalions with the other force of the general, that he reluctantly gave way to their generous importunities.   At eight A. M. Miller was led to the beach, accompanied by Loriga *, and suffered to remove the bandage from his eyes.   An hour elapsed before the San Martin

---

* From the chivalrous part which Loriga acted on this occasion, a warm friendship arose between him and Miller, which was afterwards kept up in Peru, by a correspondence, whenever a flag of truce furnished an opportunity to transmit open letters, and by an interchange of kind offices, when circumstances permitted.

answered the signal for a boat, and sent for him.
The major's reception on board was of a kind which
more than made amends for the villanous treatment
he had experienced. All thought that he had fallen
a sacrifice, and his unexpected return was hailed with
hearty cheers.   He found that his marines and *cholos*, upon hearing of his detention, went aft, in a
body, and requested the commodore to permit them
to land and rescue their commandant.

Soon afterwards the San Martin weighed anchor
with the utmost difficulty, for Captain Wilkinson,
most of the officers, and a great part of the ship's
company, were on board the prize; those that remained were almost exhausted from excessive fatigue
and want of rest during the preceding eight-and-forty
hours.   To add to their embarrassment, the ship
struck on a sand-bank in two fathoms and a half.
The ship was lightened by starting the water; they
set more sail, and she floated into deeper water, but
had hardly cleared one danger before she ran into another.   The breeze died away, and the man at the
helm, being completely worn out, dropped down upon
the deck before he could be relieved.   The ship
broached to, and was swept by a strong current and
heavy swell to within half a cable's length of the
rocky coast.   The anchor was let go, but the confusion was indescribable.   The only naval officer on
board, excepting the commodore, was the first lieutenant, Ramsay, who, on the day before, had become
deaf from the effects of the firing, and now became
dumb, or at least so hoarse as to be unable to make
himself heard; and the commodore, being ignorant

of the English language, could not himself give orders to the foreign seamen. Miller, the surgeon, Mr. Green, and the purser, were therefore the only three officers capable of communicating an order: but as none of them understood any thing of seamanship, the scene became truly distressing. There were above eighty prisoners to watch over, and only fifteen seamen on board, exclusive of the marines and *cholos*, who exerted themselves to the utmost. Two hours before day-break on the 30th, the cable of the San Martin was cut, in the expectation that a land breeze, then felt, would carry her clear of the rock-bound coast; but a heavy swell prevented her from shooting ahead, and in a few minutes she was taken aback, and drifted rapidly towards the rocks. The last anchor was let go, and the ship swung with her stern within a few yards of the breakers. Their situation was now rendered desperate from the exhausted state of the crew, and the great deficiency of nautical skill. The aggravating idea, of losing the largest ship of the state, filled their minds with feelings of mortified disappointment. At nine A. M. a welcome breeze sprung up, and carried the ship clear off the shore. The time had now arrived for repose, but Miller, noting the effects of this harassing service upon himself, has this remark in his journal: " During three days and three nights I did not get two hours of sleep; but, notwithstanding, I found it impossible to close my eyes for several hours after retiring to my cot."

On the 1st of November the squadron anchored with the prize between the island of Santa Maria and

the main land.   The Chacabuco, which had rejoined,
was detached to cruise off Talcahuano.   The Galvarino of 18 guns, Captain Spry, joined at the same
time from Valparaiso.   This vessel, formerly the He-
cate of the British navy, was exceedingly well manned,
officered, and equipped.   She was sold to the Chileno
government by Captain Guise.

In the course of a week seven transports arrived
separately.   Seeing Spanish colours flying at every
mast-head, the transports, in succession, obeyed the
telegraphic signal to anchor astern of the Maria
Isabel.   As they approached, the military officers, in
uniform, were seen eager to pay their respects to their
commanding officer, who they supposed on board the
frigate.   Crowds of soldiers, women, and children,
were looking over the sides of the vessel, rejoicing
and apparently congratulating each other on the
termination of a tedious and disastrous passage of six
months.   On dropping anchor, a musket was fired
ahead from the commodore's ship, and the patriot
ensign substituted for that of Spain.   On the discovery of their error, a wild cry burst forth, and their
confusion was evidently extreme: they had all been
taught to believe that the patriots gave no quarter.

The Spanish expedition had sailed from Cadiz on
the 21st of May, 1818.   It consisted of two battalions
of the regiment of Cantabria, a squadron of *cazadores
dragones*, and one troop of horse-artillery, in all
about two thousand eight hundred men.   One sixth
died on the passage, and at least one half of those that
still lived were *hors de combat* from the effects of

scurvy. The state of the vessels was filthy in the extreme, and the decks were so greasy that it was difficult to preserve firm foot-hold. The misery of the scene was greatly aggravated by the sight of several unfortunate men, who, eaten up by scurvy, were stretched out at the gangways in the agonies of death. Colonel Hoyos commanded the expedition. He, with about eight hundred men, including the greater part of the crew of the Maria Isabel, had landed at Talcahuano, and the two transports already alluded to, after disembarking the men, sailed for Callao. A third transport, with two companies of the Cantabria regiment, had also escaped to Callao. All the rest were captured.

The Maria Isabel was a very fine ship of fifty guns, and one of the four which Spain had bought of Russia. The filthy state in which she was found was a disgrace even to the Spanish navy *.

The return of the squadron to Valparaiso on the 7th of November gave rise to the most pleasing sensations. Thirteen sail entered the bay in line, and were welcomed by cheers from multitudes on the beach and upon the hills, amongst whom were many who had predicted a very different result.

The capture of the convoy was an event of the greatest importance: it prevented the junction of upwards of two thousand Spanish troops, with one

---

* Captain Capaz, who commanded the Maria Isabel, was, upon his return to Spain, most clamorous against Spanish America. He contended, that a few ships-of-war would be quite sufficient to put down the insurrection. His violence afterwards formed a strange contrast with the tameness of his behaviour at Talcahuano. He became minister of marine.

thousand six hundred under the command of Sanchez. These might soon have been augmented, by forced levies, to above five thousand, a force of sufficient strength to again threaten Santiago, whence a considerable portion of the army of the Andes had been detached across the Cordillera to the assistance of the Argentine republic.

Soon after arriving at Valparaiso, Commodore Blanco went to Santiago, accompanied by Miller. They were met a few leagues from the capital by the state-carriage of the supreme director, sent for their conveyance. The approach was rendered inexpressibly delightful by the cheering welcome of those who came to meet them on the road. Even a party of recruits, tied hand to hand, halted and uttered their *vivas* as heartily as did their escort. On reaching the suburbs, the entry became, *as far as feelings went,* a perfect triumph. A warm-hearted people, recently escaped from the most galling vassalage, felt and naturally expressed their boundless satisfaction that their first naval triumph should have been so complete. They dwelt with honest pride on the reflection that this victory had been achieved by a Chileno commander. They, at the same time, gave their due meed of praise to the foreigners employed on the occasion. Their imagination sketched fresh triumphs, and banished from every mind the idea of subjection to any foreign power. A countenance unmarked with an expression of exultation was not to be seen. This hearty welcome of the people was followed by dinners and balls, given to

Blanco during the eight or nine days he remained at
Santiago.

The society of that city is highly agreeable, and
foreigners and natives associate together perhaps more
than in any other great town of South America. This
renders Santiago a gay and delightful residence.

CHAPTER IX.

TOWARDS the end of November, 1818, Lord
Cochrane arrived at Valparaiso, and, in conformity
to stipulations agreed upon in London, was named
commander-in-chief of the naval forces of Chile. He
was received by the authorities with the distinction
due to his rank, and by the people with the enthusiasm excited by the brilliancy of his naval career.
The rejoicings which already pervaded the country
were greatly heightened by the accession of so distinguished an officer. The governor of Valparaiso
gave a grand dinner on the occasion. The compliment was returned on St. Andrew's day by Cochrane,
who presided in the full costume of a Scottish chief.
Extraordinary good cheer was followed by toasts
drank with uncommon enthusiasm in extraordinary
good wine. No one escaped its enlivening influence.
St. Andrew was voted the patron saint of champaign,
and many curious adventures of that night have furnished the subject of some still remembered anecdotes.
A succession of diversions rendered Valparaiso

more than usually gay. Captain Shirreff and the
officers of H. M. S. Andromache, who had made
themselves highly popular with all parties, contributed largely to vary the general stock of amusement. A match at cricket between the officers of
the Andromache and those of H. M. S. Blossom led
to the establishment of a club, the members of which
met twice a week, and dined under canvas. The
play-ground was a level on a hill, jutting into the
Pacific, so that passengers in ships entering the bay
of Valparaiso witnessed, from the deck, sports not
to be looked for round Cape Horn. The same pro-
montory was frequently used as a race-course. Pic-
nic parties were occasionally got up, and pleasant
jaunts were made to Quillota and other places in the
neighbourhood.

The intercourse between Valparaiso and the capital was incessant. A grand ball at one place drew
numbers of the *beau monde* from the other. *Ter-
tulias,* or routs, and dances were given nearly every
evening at Valparaiso. The two presiding *belles*
were Lady Cochrane and Mrs. Commodore Blanco,
both young, fascinating, and highly gifted. The first
was a flattering specimen of the beauty of England,
and the second was perhaps the most beautiful and
engaging woman of Chile. To these stars of the first
magnitude might be added Miss Cochrane (now Mrs.
Forster), who, if she yielded somewhat in personal
charms, remained uneclipsed in amiability.

In the bright galaxy of Chilena enchantresses are
to be recorded the names of Dias-Cajigas, Cotapos,
Vicuña, Perez, Caldera, Gana, Barra, with a hundred

more, all calculated to produce ineffaceable impressions. There was not a single foreign officer that frequented those happy parties who was not more or less smitten by charms and manners absolutely irresistible.

In the midst of these gay scenes the outfit of the squadron was completed.

On the 14th of January, 1819, the under-mentioned ships put to sea:

	Guns.	
O'Higgins	50	{ Vice-Admiral Lord Cochrane. Captain Forster. }
San Martin	56	Captain Wilkinson.
Lautaro	48	Captain Guise.
Chacabuco	20	Captain Carter.

The object of the Chileno government was to destroy the Spanish shipping at Callao; to blockade the principal ports; and to endeavour to dispose the Peruvians to co-operate with the troops, intended to be embarked at Valparaiso, for the purpose of liberating Peru.

Miller was re-appointed to the command of the troops serving as marines. His journal expresses the deep-felt regret with which he separated from his numerous friends in Chile, where it appears that both natives and foreigners had, by boundless attentions, established the strongest claims upon his best feelings. The hope that Lord Cochrane would, before he returned to port, attempt something worthy of his naval renown, reconciled the officers embarked to the change from a life of pleasure on shore to the tedious monotony of a seafaring existence.

The vessels of the squadron were not in a very efficient state when they left Valparaiso, and during the voyage the rigging underwent a refit. For this reason the squadron proceeded under easy sail, and did not arrive in the latitude of Callao until the 16th of February, when it fell in with H. M. ships Andromache and Blossom, the latter freighted with treasure to a great amount.

For some years after the great Spanish American struggle had commenced, the policy of Europe towards the belligerents was so obscure and conjectural, that it required no ordinary degree of tact to avoid unpleasant collision on the high seas; each naval commander being ignorant of the instructions or intended line of conduct of the other. On the present occasion Captain Shirreff seems to have acquitted himself with great discretion. Reports had been circulated at Valparaiso, that the first meeting of the British and Chileno squadron was likely to be any thing but cordial. Similar impressions appeared to have been made at Callao, for the ships' companies of the Andromache and Blossom were at quarters, as well as those of the San Martin and Lautaro, when the ships approached each other. The Andromache hailed the O'Higgins, and after a friendly interchange of the usual civilities, Captain Shirreff went on board the Chileno flag-ship, waving, as he expressed himself to Lord Cochrane, all consideration of etiquette, for the purpose of establishing, in a frank manner, a clear understanding as to the manner in which British commerce was to be treated by the Chileno flag. This important interview produced a harmony between the two services;

and, during the period that Captain Shirreff commanded the British naval force in the Pacific, not a single vessel of his nation was subjected to seizure.

The first plan of the admiral was to cut out the Spanish frigates Esmeralda and Venganza from under the castles of Callao. The O'Higgins was to assume the name of the Macedonian, and the Lautaro that of the John Adams, two United States' frigates then daily looked for in the Pacific. A packet was made up and addressed, in due form, to the viceroy, as if containing despatches from the Spanish ambassador at Washington, and which was to be delivered to the first government boat that hailed. The O'Higgins was to board the Esmeralda, and the Lautaro the Venganza, and the boats of both were afterwards to take a corvette reported to have sixty thousand dollars on board. The San Martin was to anchor outside of the island of San Lorenzo, which was to be taken possession of the day after the Spanish frigates and corvette were captured. The Spanish force consisted of the two frigates already mentioned, two brigs of war, twenty-six gun-boats, and some merchantmen armed to assist in the defence, all supported by one hundred and sixty-five guns from the fortifications.

It was intended that the attack should have been made on the 23d of February, on account of its being the last day of the carnival, when it was usual for most of the officers and some of the men of the garrison, as well as many belonging to the vessels at Callao, to be absent on leave in Lima; but a variety of causes concurred to prevent its execution on that day. On the 22d, Captain Guise went on board the flag-ship for final orders. Before he could return to his own ship (the Lautaro) the weather became so hazy that she parted company, and although signals were instantly made, and muskets* discharged during the night, she did not rejoin until the fourth day, during which interval the weather was so hazy that the land could not be made.

The Chacabuco, which had been sent back to Valparaiso on the 15th of January, rejoined on the 26th of February. On her way out a second time, the crew mutinied. The officers were kept in close confinement for several days, but, instigated by the gallant Lieutenant Morgell, they regained, with the assistance of the marines, possession of the ship. Morgell and the boatswain who headed the mutineers wrestled together for upwards of ten minutes. At last the boatswain disengaged himself; ran to the forecastle, and was in the act of firing off a carronade pointed towards the quarter-deck when he was shot through the head by a marine. Two other mutineers were killed in the scuffle, several were wounded, and six of the ringleaders were afterwards tried and shot at Coquimbo.

A good deal of fever prevailed in the squadron upon approaching Peru, where very heavy dews fall at night, and where the weather is hazy for weeks together. It happened that a vessel bound to Europe met a cruiser, and hailed to ask if the latter had any commands. " Remember us to the sun when you see him," was the answer.

---

* Guns were not fired, lest the report should be heard on shore.

....nading
....hers en-
....ntinued
.... dense that
.... ahead. Ac-
.... Higgins, she
.... withstanding
.... at the rate of
.... San Lorenzo
.... seen from the
.... so close that it
.... p on shore before
...... the surf along shore
...... those on board was
...... rigate could be placed
...... he fog suddenly cleared
...... extended to the main-land,
...... found themselves almost
...... her. A Spanish gun-boat
...... scovered within musket-shot, and
...... e prisoners stated, that the viceroy
...... the morning to review the garrison,
...... shipping. The crews of the vessels
...... men on shore had been exercised at
...... ham fight had taken place, and hence
...... firing which attracted the patriot ships to
...... point.

...... nish brig, with every sail set, was observed
...... ard. It afterwards appeared that the viceroy,
...... bout sixty persons of his court, were on board.
...... had embarked for a trip of pleasure in the bay,
...... Cochrane had known the circumstance, all

might have been taken; but the admiral being determined to attack the vessels at anchor, paid no attention to the brig, little suspecting that the principal
military and civil personages of Lima were on board.
The O'Higgins, followed by the Lautaro, stood direct
for the Spanish shipping.   On nearing them, the
wind unfortunately decreased so much, that it was
not considered advisable or even practicable to lay
the O'Higgins and Lautaro alongside, as intended;
but the former came to an anchor at the distance of
a thousand yards, with springs on her cable.   The
Spaniards paid no respect to the colours of the
United States, which were kept flying, but opened a
tremendous fire, which was briskly returned for about
an hour, during which time a thick fog occasionally
hid the combatants from a view of each other; which
circumstance may account for the trifling damage
sustained by the O'Higgins from the fire of upwards
of two hundred pieces of ordnance.   Very few men
were killed or wounded, but the running rigging was
much cut, and the boom shot away.   Guise was
dangerously wounded in the early part of the action.
His first lieutenant managed so badly that the Lautaro sheered off, and did not come within range again.
The San Martin and Chacabuco lagged astern for
want of wind, and never got under fire.   In the
evening the patriot vessels anchored under the lee of
the island of San Lorenzo.   The ship's company of
the O'Higgins, Chilenos as well as foreigners, behaved
exceedingly well. A fine example of skill and bravery
was before their eyes in the person of Cochrane, who
is never seen to such shining advantage as in the heat

of battle.   He is remarkable for the quickness with which he can discern a shot coming, and the accuracy with which he can tell its direction.

In a subsequent affair at the same place, he was sitting astride upon the hammocks according to his usual custom.   Miller was standing on a carronade upon the quarter-deck, close to the admiral, who said, " There comes a shot straight for us, but don't move, for it will strike below us;" and it entered just underneath, at the lower part of the very port above which both had placed themselves.   The shot struck off the head of a marine who had dodged to avoid it, and wounded four seamen.   One, named José de San Martin, had been a chieftain of banditti in Chile, and had been sent on board from the condemned cell. His leg was carried away, and the bone shattered so much that he afterwards suffered amputation above the knee, which he bore with astonishing fortitude, exclaiming " *Viva la patria!*" repeatedly during the operation *.

Tom Cochrane, a son of the admiral, only ten years of age, was walking about on the quarter-deck, when the shot scattered the brains of the marine in the child's face.   He ran up to his father, and, with an air of hereditary self-possession and unconcern, called out, " Indeed, papa, the shot did not touch me; indeed I am not hurt."

On the 2d of March, Captain Forster and Miller

---

* In February, 1824, Miller met the same man, begging alms *on horseback* in the streets of Santiago.   Upon asking if he received a pension from government, he answered with gaiety, that he obtained so much in charity that he never thought it worth while to apply for a pension.

took possession of the barren island of San Lorenzo,
about fifteen miles in circumference, situated in the
bay of Callao.   The highest point is about six hundred feet above the level of the sea, and commands
a fine view of the domes of Lima, situated in a plain
six miles from the shore, and precisely at the same
height above the ocean as the top of San Lorenzo.
The city appeared to be immediately at the foot of
the majestic Andes, and forms a picturesque object.

Cochrane finding his original plan of attack impracticable with his slender means, resolved to fit out
fire-ships.   A laboratory was formed upon San Lorenzo, under the superintendence of Miller. On the
19th of March, an accidental explosion took place,
which scorched the major and ten men in a dreadful
manner.   The former lost the nails from both hands,
and the injury was so severe that his face was swelled
to twice its natural dimensions.   Scarcely a feature
was discernible, and he was obliged to be fed through
a sort of plaster mask.   He was blind and delirious
for some days, and was confined to his cabin for six
weeks.   His fellow sufferers on the occasion evinced
an extraordinary and heroic degree of attachment;
for in the midst of their sufferings they refused to
have their own burns dressed until they were assured by the surgeon that their officer had been
attended to.

At 10 P. M. on the 22nd of March the squadron
got under weigh.   The O'Higgins stood close in,
and received a heavy fire from the forts and shipping.
The explosion-vessel unfortunately grounded within

musket-shot of them, knocked a hole in her bottom, and filled *. This circumstance, together with the wind dying away, and the Lautaro and San Martin keeping far astern, induced his lordship to relinquish the attack for that night. The squadron therefore returned to its anchorage, leaving the fire-ship to go to pieces.

At day-break on the 25th, the Spanish gun-boats and some armed launches came out, and, under cover of a thick fog, approached within pistol-shot, but did not attempt to board. The O'Higgins gave some well directed broadsides, and a breeze springing up at the end of an hour's firing, she got under weigh. The gun-boats made their escape with some difficulty, and took refuge under the batteries.

Want of water and provisions compelled the ships to go to Huacho. The Chacabuco was left at San Lorenzo to cruise off and on. The people of Huacho assisted the watering party; for which two were after-wards shot, and others severely punished, by the royalist Colonel Cevallos. A party of marines and some seamen, under the orders of Captain Forster, marched to Haura, and the garrison of the town was soon put to flight. The governor had a few hours before sent an impertinent letter of defiance to the admiral.

On the 1st of April, Rear-Admiral Blanco in the Galvarino, of twenty-two guns, and the Pueyrredon, of sixteen guns, arrived at Huacho, when Blanco shifted his flag to the San Martin. The O'Higgins

* On the following day the viceroy promoted some officers employed in the batteries, for *having sunk the explosion-vessel.*

and Galvarino sailed to Supe, where a party of marines landed on the 5th, and took seventy thousand
dollars, Spanish property, going from Lima to be
embarked at the port of Guambacho. The squadron
touched at Guarmey, where sixty thousand dollars,
Spanish property, were taken from the French brig
Griselle.

On the 13th, the squadron arrived in the port of
Payta, which formerly obtained the name of "little
Jamaica" when a thriving trade was carried on with
the West Indies across the Isthmus of Panama, and
when it was the grand entrepôt for contraband. It
is situated in a noble bay, but the town is eight or
nine miles from the nearest drop of fresh water, which,
brought in barrels on the backs of asses, is sold at about
ninepence the load in the morning market. It is fourteen leagues from Piura, the first town that Pizarro
founded in Peru, and of which Payta is the port.
The best mules of Peru come from Piura. Payta
contained four thousand inhabitants, who deserted
the town, when the garrison of one hundred men
fled, on Captain Forster's landing with one hundred
and twenty men, and the place was given up to plunder. A schooner taken in the bay was loaded with
captured ordnance, cocoa, and spirits.

On the 5th of May, the O'Higgins sailed for her
former cruising ground off Callao. Having reconnoitred, she proceeded to leeward again, and on the
8th arrived off Supe. An attempt made to land the
marines failed, on account of a heavy surf; but a
second effort, after dark, succeeded. Captain Forster
disembarked with some seamen, and was the senior

officer. The detachment advanced to an estate called
el Conventillo, where it arrived at dawn of day.
While the troops were dispersed at breakfast, they
were attacked by thirty-six cavalry and forty infantry
of the Spaniards, who sprang up from an ambuscade.
The marines under Miller formed quickly, and soon
put the royalists to flight, killing and wounding several, and taking some prisoners, with a stand of colours
and some arms.

On the 13th, three hundred of the enemy advanced
upon the marines; but the latter having taken up a
good position, the royalists declined attacking them.
Having embarked one hundred and fifty slaves, some
sugar, and a few oxen from the estate of Don Manuel
Garcia, a royalist, the marines withdrew, and the squadron sailed to the southward. Major (afterwards General) Garcia Camba, who commanded the royalist
detachment sent from Lima, and who did not venture
to attack the patriots, wrote such a bombastic despatch
to the viceroy about driving the insurgents into the
sea, that he was immediately promoted. The only
trophies which fell into the power of Camba were five
great-coats left behind through negligence *.

At Huarmey, the marines landed, and took off a
quantity of saltpetre. Young Vidal, a lad not seventeen years of age, who had emigrated from Lima,
and attached himself to the squadron, acted as a volunteer, and here first displayed that prowess for which

---

* General Garcia Camba was notorious for the virulence of his writings, and
for being the suggester of cruel measures. But when he became a prisoner at
Ayacucho his manner formed a disgusting contrast to his previous haughtiness.
With trembling anxiety, he sought out General La Mar, and cringed to the
chief, who had been one of those most abused by his malignant pen.

he became remarkable. Having strayed to some distance from the party on shore, he was suddenly attacked by two royalist dragoons. After a short conflict, one fled, and the other was wounded and taken prisoner by Vidal, who received a sabre wound on the head. The marines landed again at Guambacho to protect a party sent for water; the procuring of which along the coast is generally a work of time and labour, on account of the difficulty of getting barrels afloat through the tremendous surf, for which purpose *balsas* are often used. They are of several kinds. The largest sort is formed of seven or nine trunks of trees lashed together, then three or four cross-pieces, and then a second flooring of the same number of logs as the bottom tier. These rafts are run aground, and the surf, in moderate weather, does not break over the upper tier so as to spoil goods or to wet passengers. A pole is stuck up in the middle, to which a sail is rigged. The rudder is a plank run into the water between the logs, rather abaft the centre. The whole is so unwieldy that wind and tide must be in its favour to work it with effect. When these rafts are wanted to windward they are taken to pieces, the logs carried the proper distance by land, and then put together at low water. In this way merchant-vessels are commonly unloaded on many parts of the coast. In some places a long bundle of rushes, tapering at each extremity, is used, particularly by fishermen, who seat themselves astride and paddle through the swell.

Near Guambacho are the remains of an extensive line of fortification, constructed previous to the conquest. The wall in many parts is still entire, and has saliant angles, somewhat resembling rude bastions. The wall runs along the side of a lofty mountain, close to the sea. A great battle was gained here by the Inca over Chimu, the last king of the province now called Truxillo. An immense quantity of human bones is scattered over the ground. Some of the skulls retain all the hair. The *guacas* or tumuli scattered over Peru are ransacked for the sake of the gold and silver ornaments sometimes found placed in the mouth, ears, under the nape of the neck, and on the navel of the persons buried in them. Earthen jars, of curious shape and workmanship, are often dug up, together with household utensils, wearing apparel, and grains of Indian corn, which last have been known to vegetate on being sown in an irrigated spot, after lying in the desert above three hundred years. The jars were filled with *chicha,* all supposed to be needful to the deceased; the quantity or value of the supply being proportioned to his rank in life. Phosphoric exhalations are seen sometimes as large as the flame of a bonfire. This is considered by the country people an indication that gold is to be found, and they fall to work to ransack the tumulus, which had probably been pillaged twenty times before.

The squadron having completed the watering, and taken in sea stock, sailed to windward, and cast anchor in the bay of Valparaiso on the 17th of June, 1819.

: Blanco, in the San Martin, together with the Lautaro, had previously arrived, having been obliged to raise the blockade of Callao for want of provisions.

For this Blanco incurred the displeasure of government. He was put under an arrest, but honourably acquitted by a court of inquiry.

To avoid an interruption in the narrative, we have deferred until now the mention that a Spanish serjeant and ten men were taken on the island of San Lorenzo. They formed the guard over thirty-seven unfortunate patriot soldiers, who had been made prisoners of war at the battles of Ayoma and Huaqui in 1811. The prisoners were loaded with chains like convicts, and kept to hard labour in the stone quarries of the island. At night they were linked by one leg to an iron bar under a miserable shed, scarcely roomy enough to lodge them. The poor fellows were overpowered with joy upon finding themselves unexpectedly set free, and once more under the protection of the patriot flag. Their unshaken fidelity had drawn down the barbarous treatment, which had been fatal to the greater part of their companions in misfortune. Cochrane carried to Chile the shackles found upon the persons of these unfortunate soldiers, whose fate gave rise to a very spirited correspondence between his lordship and the viceroy, relative to the maltreatment of patriot prisoners of war.

His excellency answered in courteous terms, but denied that the patriot prisoners were treated ill, and he declined to exchange those taken in the privateer (Maypo brig), after a very severe action with a superior force, on the plea that they were pirates. The surviving officers of the Maypo were kept in irons for sixteen months, and the fetters round their ankles laid the bones bare. The commander, Captain Brown,

had the sentence of death hanging over him for above
a year, when, by the assistance of Alomi, a corporal
of the guard, he escaped, and took refuge on board
H. M. S. Tyne. Captain Falcon refused to give him
up to the viceroy, who, in an angry and voluminous
correspondence, proved by precedents commencing
in the year of our Lord 1499, and ending Anno
Domini 1808, that the British commander had over-
stepped the boundaries marked out by international
law. But Captain Falcon, more alive to the dictates
of an humane mind, took upon himself the respon-
sibility of rescuing a brave countryman, exposed to a
lingering, if not a violent, death in a horrid dungeon.
The corporal, Alomi, had been an officer in the
patriot service. Falling a prisoner in Colombia, he
was compelled to serve in the regiment of Numancia, and intended to pass over to the patriot standard;
but the officer of the watch did not consider himself
justified in extending protection to a Peruvian subject, and he was not received on board the Tyne.
He was taken by the royalists, and condemned to be
shot; and it speaks much for the humanity of the
viceroy's personal character that the sentence was not
carried into execution.

   Amongst the other patriot prisoners was the amiable, the gallant, and unfortunate Captain Esmonde,
brother to Sir Thomas Esmonde, Baronet. The
circumstances attending his captivity and release are
the more interesting as they afford an instance of re-
tributive justice, in which savage cruelty is punished
through the immediate agency of the sufferer, in a

more summary and obvious mode than usually occurs in the history of human transactions.

One of the authorities at Pisco, to whose charge the patriot prisoners had been consigned, was Don Francisco Algorte, who, in addition to the brutal tyranny which he exercised over the unfortunate prisoners, descended frequently to the cowardly violence of striking Esmonde upon the head with a cane. From this situation, more horrible than death to the mind of a gentlemanly and high-spirited officer, Esmonde was removed to the casemates of Callao, whence he was liberated by the kind interposition of Captain Shirreff, with whom, in compliance with the terms of his release, he returned to England.

On the capture of Pisco in 1821 by the patriots, under the command of Miller, an estate of Algorte was, as belonging to a violent and uncompromising Spaniard, taken possession of, and subsequently confiscated.

Algorte repaired to Lima, and, in the course of a few months, by well directed presents, secured the support of some powerful friends, whose influence had nearly obtained from the protector the restoration of his estate. Nothing was wanting to complete his success but the report of Miller, upon a reference made to him, and which was necessary to legalize the restoration. To ensure his acquiescence, Algorte had recourse to a mutual friend, a rich Spanish merchant of the highest character. This gentleman, without venturing to enter into particulars, intimated that he was authorised to subscribe to *any* terms.   An intimate friend of Miller's, an English merchant, was also employed, and who, in a jocose manner, hinted that, in the event of a favourable report, five or six thousand dollars might be accidentally found at the door of the colonel's apartments.

Esmonde, who had fulfilled the conditions of his release, and returned to Peru, happened at this moment to be in Lima.   To him, therefore, Miller, who had heard some reports of Algorte's treatment of the prisoners, referred for their correctness, without mentioning either then or afterwards the motive for his inquiries.   Esmonde simply recounted the conduct of Algorte towards himself and his fellow-prisoners.   The result may be anticipated.   Miller's report was immediately forwarded, and Algorte's estate irrecoverably lost.

Captain Esmonde was afterwards employed by the Peruvian government to examine and report upon the possibility of making canals near Tarapacá.   The vessel on board of which he embarked having never been heard of, is supposed to have foundered at sea,

CHAPTER X.

Balcarce.—Concepcion.—Benavides.—His barbarities.—Araucanian Indians.—Chileno squadron sails.—Unsuccessful against Callao.—Sails to Pisco.—Lieutenant-Colonel Charles killed.—His character.—Major Miller wounded.—Squadron sails to Guayaquil.—Returns.

Osorio having escaped from Maypo to Talcahuano, remained there until September following, when, blinded by his fears, he destroyed the fortifications and sailed for Callao. General Sanchez, then in the interior, was left in command of the province of Concepcion.

Early in 1819, General Balcarce with three thousand patriot troops marched against Sanchez, who had augmented his force to two thousand men. The royalists were driven with loss from the inland island of Laja, and from Nacimiento, both of which places were rudely fortified.

The former city of Concepcion, or Penco, was pleasantly situated on the right bank of the river Bio-Bio, and contained a population of above thirty thousand souls, but was overthrown by an earthquake. The new town, built upon nearly the same site, had been ruined by the alternate occupation of royalists, patriots, and Araucanians. The country around is also subject to the incursions of these Indians, whose custom is to massacre all males and to carry off all females. Several hundred women were in captivity at the time now referred to.

Upon the advance of the independents, Sanchez collected his forces from Concepcion, Chillan, and Laja, and fell back upon the Araucanian territory. He had already gained over several caciques, and had the address to obtain the unprecedented favour of permission to march with Spanish troops through Arauco to Valdivia, about sixty leagues to the southward of Talcahuano.

In crossing the Bio-Bio, Sanchez was overtaken by Balcarce, and after losing six hundred men in an unsuccessful stand, the royalists were compelled to make a precipitate flight. Lieutenant-Colonels Viel and Don M. Escalada, and Major Caxaravilla, signalized themselves greatly about this period. Balcarce * returned to Santiago, leaving Colonel Freyre in the military and civil command of the province of Concepcion.

The persevering Sanchez reached Valdivia with about nine hundred followers, but not without great difficulties; for the caciques on the line of march extorted presents, and it cost much to preserve a good understanding. The very soldiers parted with every small article of metal, and arrived at Valdivia without a button on their clothes.

In order to keep alive a hostile feeling towards the patriots, the celebrated leader Benavides was, with a few desperado volunteers, left amongst the Araucanian tribes. These destructive bands of free-

---

* Don Antonio de Balcarce had served with credit in Spain. He was taken prisoner by the British at Monte Video in 1807. He was amongst the first to embrace the cause of independence, and gained for Buenos Ayres her first laurels at Cotagaita. He died on the 15th of August, 1819. He was an active, upright, and zealous patriot.

Q 2

booters, strengthened by numbers of deserters from
the independents, became so formidable that Colonel
Freyre, with two thousand men, was scarcely able to
keep them in check.   Several strong patriot parties
crossed the Bio-Bio, to extirpate the depredators;
but after some fighting, and sustaining considerable
losses, they always returned without having effected
their object.

The acts of barbarity committed by Benavides are
almost incredible. Captain Quitospi, a Russian officer
in the patriot service, Colonel O'Carrol, who had
served in Spain, Lieutenant Bayley, with many other
officers, were wounded and taken in action at different
periods, and, amongst other horrid mutilations, had
their tongues cut out.   General Don Andres Alca-
zar, who bore the character of extraordinary virtue
and bravery, and who from his advanced age was considered to be the patriarch of the province, fell into
the hands of the Indians, and suffered similar mutilations.   Such were the effects of revengeful recollections ; for the Araucanians had not forgotten the
impalings of their ancestors, and the cruel wrongs
done them by the Spaniards in their vain attempts
for three hundred years to subjugate them.   These
feelings were continually excited by their traditions
and their war songs, which record the victories their
forefathers obtained over the barbarous whites. They
cared not on which side they fought, provided they
were instrumental to the destruction of either, as
they considered both parties their natural enemies.
Perhaps Benavides himself is indebted for a part of
his popularity with the Indians to his hatred of the

very Spaniards he served, as evinced by his shooting or hanging, under different pretexts, every respectable Spanish officer sent from Valdivia to assist him.

Three months were busily employed by Cochrane in the manufacture of rockets, and making other preparations for a renewed attack upon the shipping under the walls of Callao.

On the 12th of September, 1819, the undermentioned men-of-war sailed from Valparaiso :

	Guns.	
O'Higgins	48	Vice-Admiral Lord Cochrane.
San Martin	60	{ Rear-Admiral Blanco. Captain Wilkinson.
Lautaro	46	Captain Guise.
Independencia	28	Forster.
Pueyrredon	14	Prunier.

Vitoria and Xerezana to be fitted up as fire-ships.

Galvarino	18	Captain Spry	} joined
Araucano	16	Crosbie	afterwards.

Four hundred soldiers were embarked to act as marines. The proportion distributed in the Chileno vessels was above double the usual complement of marines employed in ships of the same class in the British navy. The Chileno soldiers so embarked did the duty of seamen as well as of marines. Lieutenant-Colonel Charles, who had the superintendence of the rocket department, was the commanding officer. Major Miller re-embarked as second in command of the troops.

On the 25th September, the squadron entered the bay of Coquimbo, and received some marines on board. Coquimbo is the principal city of the pro-

vince of the same name, which is fertile, and contains
rich copper mines.   The town is situated twenty
miles from the port, and contains a population of ten
thousand souls.   It is remarkable for the salubrity of
its climate, and for the hospitality of its inhabitants,
who, with a few foreign merchants, showed how
highly they appreciated the services of the marines,
by raising in a few hours a subscription of four hundred dollars, to be laid out by Miller in the purchase
of what he considered they stood most in need of.
On the 17th, the squadron sailed for Callao.   On
the 28th, the respective captains repaired on board
the flag-ship, to learn the plan of attack.

The O'Higgins was to lead ; the San Martin and
Lautaro were to follow; and all three were to anchor
in a line parallel with the enemy's shipping.   Miller,
on a raft with one mortar, was to take his station in
advance on the extreme left, towards Boca Negra,
the mouth of the Rimac.   Captain Hind, on a raft
with rockets, was to place himself between the mortar-raft and the O'Higgins.   Charles, on another
raft, with rockets, was to place himself on the right
of the Lautaro.   The Galvarino and Araucano, with
the two fire-ships, were to anchor off the N. E. point
of San Lorenzo.   The brigs were to weigh anchor
on the attack commencing, and, with the Independencia, to remove to the outside of the patriot line,
in order to be in readiness to intercept any vessels
that might attempt to escape.

On the 30th, the squadron stood into the bay of
Callao.   The O'Higgins hoisted a flag of truce, and
Cochrane sent a boat ashore with a letter to the

viceroy, challenging him to send out as many ships as he chose, and the admiral would fight them ship for ship, and gun for gun. This proposal, of very questionable propriety, met with the laconic answer which might have been expected. The equally use-less measure of sending a rocket in the boat to ex-hibit to the royalists made an impression very different from what was intended.

The squadron manœuvred for several hours in the bay, and then came to anchor off San Lorenzo, with the exception of the Independencia, which continued to cruise off the bay.

On the first and following day of October the rafts were put together. Charles reconnoitred in a boat, and tried some rockets, which were not found to answer expectation.

A partial attack took place on the night of the 2d. The Galvarino led the van, towing Miller's mortar-raft, and, under a heavy fire, placed it within eight hundred yards of the enemy's batteries. The Pueyr-redon followed with the shells and magazine upon another raft. The Araucano, having Hind's rocket-raft in tow, followed next. Charles, in the last raft, was towed by the Independencia. The rest of the squadron remained at anchor.

The persons employed upon the rafts were provided with life-preservers made of tin, in the shape of the front-piece of a cuirass, and filled with air. The rafts were formed of two tiers of large logs of timber, of the dimensions of sleepers used in laying down platforms in batteries. The upper tier was about a foot above the surface of the water. Not more than one rocket in six went off properly. Some burst, from the badness of the cylinders; some took a wrong direction, in consequence of the sticks being made of knotty wood; and most of them fell short. The shells sunk a gun-boat, and did some execution in the forts and amongst the shipping; but the lashings of the mortar-bed gave way, and it was with difficulty that the logs of which the raft was composed could be kept together. A great deal of time was lost in repairing the defective state of the fastenings. Daylight began to appear, and the rockets having completely failed, the rafts were ordered to retire, and were towed off by boats left in attendance for that purpose, to their respective protecting vessels, which again took them in charge and towed them out of range. Thus failed an attack from which so much had been expected. The disappointment was extreme; but the loss of only about twenty in killed and wounded was considered small under such a heavy fire. About forty shot struck the Galvarino. Red-hot shot were fired from the batteries, but without much effect. These red balls had an alarming appearance, for they were distinctly visible from the moment they issued from the gun until they hissed in the water. All the men employed were volunteers; yet such was the effect of the heavy fire, that one man jumped from a raft into the water two or three times from fear. Lieutenant Bayley, a very brave young man, and a most active officer, was cut in two by a twenty-four-pounder shot, which also took off the head of a marine, on the same mortar-raft. Twelve men were much burnt by the bursting of some rockets. Hind and several of the men were thrown into the sea, but were prevented from sinking by the life-preservers.

In the night of the 4th, much amusement was excited in the patriot squadron by the alarm on shore caused by a tar barrel being set on fire and carried by the tide towards the Spanish shipping. A tremendous fire opened upon it, which was kept up for above an hour.

Disappointed by the total failure of the rocket attack, the admiral determined to try what could be done by means of fire-ships. Accordingly one of the explosion-vessels being completed, Lieutenant Morgell and a few men got her under weigh at eight P. M. on the 5th, and stood, in gallant style, towards the Spanish shipping; but the wind dying away, the vessel was shot through and through like a sieve. The water gaining fast, the train was fired, and the vessel abandoned. She exploded at too great a distance from the shipping to do any serious mischief. The rocket-raft was again employed; but the rockets did as little execution as on the previous occasion. The other fire-ship, in charge of Lieutenant Cobbett, was kept in reserve for a future service.

The Araucano, which had been sent on the 4th to cruise outside of the bay, returned on the 6th, and reported that she had seen a strange sail six miles to windward off Chorillos, which Captain Crosbie had no doubt was a frigate. The squadron got under weigh, and soon caught sight of the stranger; but Cochrane, mistaking her for a North American whaler, returned to his former anchorage on the 7th. It was afterwards ascertained that the strange ship was the Prueba, Spanish frigate, of fifty guns, from Cadiz, bound to Lima; but seeing the patriot squadron, she made off and escaped to Guayaquil. In the almost momentary absence of the blockading squadron, a Spanish ship, with a cargo valued at half a million of dollars, entered Callao in safety.

The admiral, considering that the Spanish shipping could not be destroyed without risking the existence of the patriot squadron, decided upon a different plan of operations. On the evening of the 7th October, the squadron weighed, with the intention of going to Arica; but some of the ships were such dull sailers, that, after beating for three weeks to windward, and against the current, Cochrane determined upon landing the marines at Pisco, for the purpose of procuring brandy for the use of the squadron. Three hundred and fifty soldiers were distributed on board the Lautaro, Galvarino, and a transport (late fire-ship). Cochrane then proceeded to the northward with the O'Higgins, San Martin, Araucano and Pueyrredon, leaving Captain Guise in command to proceed to Pisco.

Pisco is situated a mile from the sea-shore, on the spacious bay of Pararca, and is fourteen leagues to the northward and westward of the town of Ica. It is the great entrepôt for the brandy (called Pisco) distilled in great quantities from the grape in the valleys of Palpa, Nasca, Chincha, Cañete, and Ica. Sugar is another article of export. The town contains a population of nearly two thousand inhabitants; the adjoining valley of Chunchanga five thousand, two-thirds of whom are negro slaves.

It was known that a strong detachment of regular troops had been stationed in Pisco, at the request of the royalist merchants and landowners, to protect their property in depôt there. The patriots intended to land in the night and take the garrison by surprise; but the wind failing, the ships could not get near enough to disembark the troops until broad day-light on the 7th November, 1819. On landing, information was given that the Spanish garrison amounted to one thousand men. It might therefore have been prudent for the patriots to have re-embarked, especially as two-thirds of the marines were mere recruits, who had not even been taught the platoon exercise; but the remembrance of the disappointments before Callao produced an unanimous desire to attack.

The Spanish force, consisting of six hundred infantry, one hundred and sixty cavalry, and four field-pieces, under the command of Lieutenant-General Gonzalez, were drawn up to receive the assailants. The field-artillery, supported by their cavalry, occupied on their left a piece of rising ground, which commanded the entrance of the town, in the square of which their infantry was formed. Their right was supported by a fort on the sea-shore.

Charles, with twenty-five men, filed off to his right to reconnoitre the enemy's left, whilst Miller pushed on to the town with the rest of the marines. Hind, with a rocket party, composed of seamen, occupied the attention of the fort. The Spaniards kept up a brisk fire from the field-pieces, and from the artillery in the fort, as well as from the infantry posted behind walls, on the tops of houses, and on the tower of the church.   Not a musket was fired, or a word spoken, in the patriot column, which marched with the cool-ness and steadiness of veterans, in spite of the loss it sustained at every step.   The silence, rapidity, and good order with which they advanced struck a panic into the Spaniards, who fled when the patriots ap-proached within fifteen yards of the bayonets.   The royalists were completely routed.   The gallant Charles was mortally wounded whilst charging four times his own numbers outside the town.   The last volley of the Spaniards in the square brought down Miller. A musket-ball wounded him in the right arm; an-other permanently disabled his left hand; a third ball entered his chest, and, fracturing a rib, passed out at the back.   His recovery was despaired of.   Charles and Miller were conveyed on board the Lautaro. The two friends, both apparently on the brink of the grave, took leave of each other in the most affectionate manner, as Charles was conveyed aft through the fore cabin, in which Miller was already placed by the kind-ness of Captain Guise.   In a few hours Charles ex-pired.   Cool and collected to the last moment, the manner in which he died would have done honour to any hero of ancient or modern times.   He was brave and talented; and his gentleness and suavity of manners had acquired for him universal love and respect.   Charles was educated at the Royal Military Academy at Woolwich.   Having obtained a lieute-nancy in the royal regiment, he went out to Portugal in the year 1808 with a detachment of artillery, appointed to serve with the *Lusitanian Legion*, then raising under the orders of Sir Robert Wilson, who, perceiving the excellent qualities of Charles, appointed him his aide-de-camp; and throughout the service in the Peninsula he distinguished himself on every occasion by his talents, activity, and intrepidity. When Sir Robert Wilson was sent to Constantinople to assist in the negotiations for peace between the Turks and Russians, Charles was again put on his staff, but his junction with Sir Robert was delayed till that general had been appointed as military commissioner with the Russian army. Charles, during the whole of the campaign in Germany and in Italy, continued to do the duty of aide-de-camp to Sir Robert Wilson, and gained the affection and esteem of all the allied commanders. The sovereigns particularly distinguished him, conferring on him the Cross of St. George of Russia, of Merit of Prussia, and of Maria Theresa of Austria. There never perhaps was an officer, serving in foreign armies, who was more universally a favourite, and who displayed qualities which more entitled him, professionally and personally, to estimation.

Captain Sowersby, who succeeded to the command of the marines, remained on shore for four days unmolested, in which time all that was required for the ships was embarked. Two hundred thousand dollars' worth of brandy, private property, lying upon the beach, was wantonly destroyed by a party of seamen.

Amongst the officers who distinguished themselves, besides those already mentioned, were Captain Don

Manuel Urquisa (severely wounded), a Buenos
Ayrean; Captain Guitica, a German; Lieutenant
Rivera, a Chileno; Lieutenant Carson, a North
American; and Monsieur Soyer, a Frenchman
(purser of the Lautaro), who acted as a volunteer.
No despatch of the affair of Pisco was ever published.
This was an act of injustice towards the marines,
especially as room was found in the gazettes for the
elaborate correspondence between Cochrane and Pezuela, relative to prisoners of war, and for very minute details of naval operations before Callao.

On the 16th, the Lautaro and her consort, with
the transport, joined Lord Cochrane off Santa, in
south lat. 8° 48″. Ensign Vidal, who had remained
on board the admiral's ship with the marines not employed at Pisco, had taken possession of Santa, after
defeating three times his own number of Spaniards.

The whole squadron having procured water and
provisions, now put to sea. On the 21st, the O'Higgins, Lautaro, Galvarino, and Pueyrredon stood to
the northward. A sort of brain fever, called the
chavalonga, broke out, and carried off five or six
men daily. The San Martin and Independencia,
being in the most sickly state, were ordered to make
the best of their way to Valparaiso. Rear-Admiral
Blanco went on board the Lautaro to offer Miller a
passage to Chile; but, in his then precarious condition, it was considered dangerous to attempt to
remove him.

On the 27th November, Cochrane entered the
river Guayaquil, and, notwithstanding the danger of
the navigation, on account of shifting sand-banks,

he continued to crowd all sail during the night, and captured next morning, before the crews had time to run them ashore, two ships, the Aguila and Begoña, of eight hundred tons and twenty-eight guns each, laden with planks. The Spanish frigate Prueba, which so narrowly escaped from Callao, had been hauled up the river five days before, and, being lightened of her guns, was moored into shallow water, under the protection of the batteries.

On the 30th, sixty marines, under the command of Lieutenant Carson, were landed to procure fresh meat, vegetables, and fruit, with which the country abounds. The fruit, particularly the pine-apple, is delicious. The banks of the river are flat, swampy, and covered with wood; the river swarms with alligators; the climate is intolerably hot; the earth teems with reptiles, and the air with insects. The mosquitoes are so numerous that it is said they sometimes extinguish a candle. The houses are built upon piles, so that the lower floor is elevated a few feet above the ground.

On the 13th December, Miller was removed in his cot from the Lautaro to the flag-ship O'Higgins, which sailed from the river with the Lautaro and the two prizes in company. Each ship was ordered to make the best of her way to Valparaiso. The Galvarino and Pueyrredon were left behind to cruise.

CHAPTER XI.

The O'Higgins makes Valdivia.—Captures the brig of war
Potrillo.—Interesting meeting.—Concepcion.—Reinforcement.
—The O'Higgins strikes on a rock.—Dismay on board.—Lord
Cochrane's sang froid.—Valdivia taken.

LORD COCHRANE having made the wide offing
necessary in sailing upon these coasts from north to
south, and finding himself in 110° west longitude,
about equi-distant from Valdivia and Valparaiso, decided upon looking into the former port.

On the 18th January, 1820, he approached under
Spanish colours. On this occasion Miller was brought
upon deck for the first time since receiving his wounds
at Pisco, eleven weeks before. A signal was made
for a pilot, who, with an officer of the garrison and
four soldiers to row the boat, was sent from the
shore to point out a safe anchorage. They were of
course detained, and some useful information procured.

Whilst the O'Higgins was standing close in to
reconnoitre, a strange sail hove in sight, and after
three hours' chase, the Spanish brig of war Potrillo,
of sixteen guns, became an unresisting prize. She
was two days from Chiloe, bound to Valdivia with
despatches, and twenty thousand dollars for the payment of the garrison.

One of those highly interesting meetings which
rarely occur now took place. The admiral's secretary,

Captain Benet, who by some chance had been left in the Araucanian territory seventeen years before, re-cognised among the prisoners a family, named del Rio, the heads of which had rescued him from the Araucanians, and adopted him. He was treated as a son, and remained with them until the jealous policy of the Spanish colonial system compelled the governor of Concepcion to send him to Lima, on account of his being a British subject; so that, after an interval of sixteen years, accident again brought them together. The parental and filial ardour with which they rushed into each other's arms at the moment of mutual re-cognition excited the sympathy of every witness to the affecting scene. The secretary had the additional gratification of finding himself in a situation that enabled him to repay, in some measure, the kind-nesses he had experienced when, as a youth and a prisoner, he was in need of protection.

On entering the bay of Talcahuano, in the night of the 20th January, the O'Higgins grounded on a bank near the island of Quiriquina, but soon got off. She unexpectedly found the brig Intrepido, Captain Carter, and the schooner Montezuma at anchor there. Miller went ashore, and rode to Concepcion, but was too weak either to get on horseback or to dismount without assistance. The next morning Cochrane rode to the city, and was received a league in ad-vance by the governor, Colonel Freyre, who gave a dinner on the occasion. About forty persons sat down, and, to exemplify the hospitality of the coun-try, it may be worth while to mention that enough was brought upon table to feed six hundred.

Miller crossed the river Bio Bio to inspect the fort
of San Pedro, which mounted four nine-pounders,
surrounded by a ditch, palisades, and a musket-proof
casemate round the ramparts.   It was garrisoned by
fifty men, who were so often attacked that they invariably slept upon their arms.   The bridge was kept
drawn up night and day, because there was not a
moment in the year in which the Indians were not
lying in ambush near it.   The Araucanians had attacked this fort two days before, and were repulsed,
after losing their leader, a brother of Benavides.
Notwithstanding this success, the garrison could not
venture to make a sortie; and the audacious Indians
still kept possession of the adjoining heights.

Cochrane having conceived the daring plan of
carrying Valdivia by a coup-de-main, employed all
his eloquence to induce Freyre to grant a small reinforcement.   The governor gave two hundred and
fifty men, commanded by Major Beauchef.   They
embarked in the frigate O'Higgins, the Montezuma
schooner, and the brig of war Intrepido belonging
to Buenos Ayres.   All got under weigh on the 25th
January, at five P. M., with a light contrary wind; at
night it fell calm.   The officer of the watch, leaving
the deck, gave the O'Higgins in charge to a midshipman, who, falling asleep, neglected to report
when a breeze sprung up.   Upon passing the island
of Quiriquina the ship struck upon the sharp edge
of a rock, and was suspended amidship on her keel.
She shook in a manner to produce the greatest alarm;
for had the swell increased she must have gone to
pieces.   Cochrane preserved his customary *sang*

froid; ordered out the kedges; superintended every thing himself; and, at length, got the ship off. His skill and presence of mind on this trying occasion made a deep impression on all who beheld it. When the ship was out of danger, some of the officers suggested that she should be examined: a stern negative was the answer of the admiral, who, turning round to Miller, said, "Well, Major, Valdivia we must take. Sooner than put back, it would be better that we all went to the bottom." In fact, his lordship felt keenly his disappointments before Callao. He was aware that his enemies in Chile would raise a clamour if he returned without doing something decisive, and he had made up his mind to run every risk in order to grasp a redeeming laurel. "Cool calculation," he observed to Miller, "would make it appear that the attempt to take Valdivia is madness. This is one reason why the Spaniards will hardly believe us in earnest, even when we commence; and you will see that a bold onset, and a little perseverance afterwards, will give a complete triumph; for operations, unexpected by the enemy, are, when well executed, almost certain to succeed, whatever may be the odds; and success will preserve the enterprise from the imputation of rashness."

The officers participated in the same adventurous spirit, and hailed with eager satisfaction a determination likely to retrieve the credit of the navy and make former discomfitures forgotten. The admiral was so resolutely bent upon pursuing his course that it was not until sunset on the 26th that he would receive the first report of "*five feet water in the hold.*" The ship was then thirty miles from land. The pumps were found to be so much out of order that they could not be worked. At eight o'clock seven feet was reported. The carpenter, who was a very indifferent mechanic, failed in his efforts to put the pumps in order. The water, though bailed out with buckets, still continued to gain upon them. The powder magazine was inundated, and the ammunition of every description rendered totally unserviceable, excepting the cartridges in the cartouch boxes of the soldiers.

Notwithstanding it was a dead calm, the swell was considerable, and the brig and schooner were out of sight. Of six hundred men on board the frigate, not more than one hundred and sixty could have escaped in the boats. The inhospitable coast of Arauco was forty miles distant, and to land there would have been worse than death. The vindictive character of the Araucanians was well known, and to those who saw no hope of keeping the ship afloat till morning the alternative was terrific. Alarm and despair were depicted in the countenances of most on board. But Cochrane, still undismayed, pulled off his coat, tucked up his shirt-sleeves, and succeeded by midnight in putting two of the pumps into a serviceable state. By his indefatigable activity and skill the frigate was prevented from sinking, and by the serenity and firmness of his conduct he checked a general disposition to abandon the ship. The leak was happily prevented from gaining. The schooner and brig rejoined in the morning, and the vessels arrived in the latitude of Valdivia on the 2d of February. When about thirty miles from land, the troops in the frigate were removed to the schooner Montezuma and brig Intrepido in a high sea.   Miller attempted to climb up the schooner's side, and caught hold of the main chains, but not possessing sufficient strength to lift himself, or, when the boat sunk into a trough of the sea, to sustain himself, he was on the point of letting go his hold, when Lord Cochrane caught him, and prevented his falling under the counter of the vessel.   The admiral having shifted his flag to the schooner, left the frigate to stand off and on, out of sight of land, to avoid exciting the suspicions of the Spaniards on shore.   There was, however, so little wind, that all hopes of effecting a landing that night vanished.   The brig and the schooner made what way they could for the port, in the hope of taking the royalists by surprise.

The noble harbour of Valdivia, situated in 39° 50′ south lat. and 73° 28′ west lon. forms a capacious basin, bordered by a lofty and impenetrable forest advancing to the water's edge.   It is encircled by a chain of forts, which are so placed as not only to defend the entrance, but to enfilade every part of the harbour.

These forts are Niebla on the east, and Amargos on the west, completely commanding the entrance, which is only three-fourths of a mile in width.   Corral, Chorocomayo, San Carlos, and el Yngles, on the west side; Manzanera, on an island near the southern extremity or bottom of the harbour; and el Piojo and Carbonero are on the east side.   These different forts were mounted with one hundred and eighteen pieces

of ordnance, eighteen and twenty-four pounders, each
fort with a deep ditch and a rampart where they were
not washed by the sea, excepting el Yngles, which
had merely a rampart faced with palisades.   They
were manned by a force which, according to the
muster-rolls of the preceding month, consisted of
seven hundred and eighty regulars, and eight hundred and twenty-nine militia.   The greater part of
the latter were stationed at Osorno, thirty leagues
towards the straits of Magellan, and the remainder
at the town of Valdivia, fourteen miles up the river.
So impervious is the forest, from the ravines by which
it is intersected, and from its entangled underwood,
that there is no land communication between the
forts, excepting by a narrow rugged path, which,
winding between the rocky beach and the forest,
scarcely at any point admits of the passage of more
than one man at a time.   Even this path, in crossing
a deep ravine between fort Chorocomayo and Corral,
was enfiladed by three guns, situated on the crest of
the opposite acclivity.

About a quarter of a mile beyond the fort of San
Carlos, and outside of the harbour, is situated the
exterior fort of Yngles, and half a mile westward
of the fort is the *caleta*, or inlet which forms a
landing-place, both of which communicate with each
other, and with San Carlos, by a path equally narrow,
rugged, and serpentine as that between the other
forts.

The schooner and the brig, having hoisted Spanish
colours, anchored on the 3d of February, at three
P. M., under the guns of the fort of Yngles, opposite

the *caleta*, the only landing-place, and between the two. When hailed from the shore, Captain Basques, a Spaniard by birth, who had embarked at Tal-cahuano as a volunteer, was directed to answer that they had sailed from Cadiz under convoy of the St. Elmo of seventy-four guns; that they had parted company in a gale of wind off Cape Horn; and to request a pilot might be sent off. At this time the swell was so great as to render an immediate dis-embarkation impracticable, as the launches would have drifted under the fort. Cochrane's object, therefore, was to wait until the evening, when the wind would have abated, and the swell have subsided. The Spaniards, who had already begun to entertain suspicions, ordered the vessels to send a boat ashore, to which it was answered, they had lost them in the severe gales they had encountered. This however did not satisfy the garrison, which immediately fired alarm guns, and expresses were despatched to the governor at Valdivia. The garrisons of all the western forts united at fort Yngles. Fifty or sixty men were posted on the rampart commanding the approach from the *caleta*. The rest, about three hundred, formed on a small esplanade in the rear of the fort.

Whilst this was passing, the vessels remained un-molested; but at four o'clock one of the launches, which had been carefully concealed from the view of those on shore, by being kept close under the off-side of the vessel, unfortunately drifted astern. Before it could be hauled out of sight again, it was perceived by the garrison, which, having no longer any doubts as to the hostile nature of the visit, immediately

opened a fire upon the vessels, and sent a party of
seventy-five men to defend the landing-place.   This
detachment was accurately counted by those on board,
as it proceeded one by one along the narrow and difficult path to the *caleta*.   The first shots fired from
the fort having passed through the sides of the brig,
and killed two men, the troops were ordered up from
below, and to land without further delay.   But the
two launches, which constituted the only means of
disembarkation, appeared very inadequate to the effectual performance of such an attempt.   Miller, with
forty-four marines, pushed off in the first launch.
After overcoming the difficulties of the heavy swell,
an accumulation of sea-weed, in comparatively smooth
water, loaded the oars at every stroke, and impeded
the progress of the assailants, who now began to
suffer from the effects of a brisk fire from the party
stationed at the landing-place.   The launch was per-
forated with musket-balls, and the water rushed in
through the holes.   Four or five men were wounded.
Two of the foreign seamen were daunted, and ceased
to row, under pretence that it was impossible to make
way through the sea-weed.   One of the soldiers previously named to keep a watch upon them, in an-
ticipation of some such occurrence, knocked one of
these fellows off his seat with the but-end of a musket.   No further difficulty was made.   Quarter-master
Thompson of the O'Higgins, who acted as coxswain,
was shot through the shoulder, upon which Miller
took the helm.   He seated himself on a spare oar,
finding the seat inconvenient, he had the oar removed, by which he somewhat lowered his position.

He had scarcely done so, when a ball passed through
his hat, and grazed the crown of his head. He
ordered a few of his party to fire, and soon after
jumped on shore with his marines; dislodged the
royalists at the inlet; and made good his footing:
but he was still so feeble that he was unable to
clamber over the rough rocks without assistance. So
soon as the landing was perceived to have been
effected, the party in the second launch pushed off
from the brig, and in less than an hour three hundred and fifty patriot soldiers were disembarked.
Shortly after sunset they advanced in single files
along the rocky track, leading to fort Yngles,
rendered slippery by the spray of the surf, which
dashed, with deafening noise, upon the shore, which
was rather favourable than otherwise to the adventurous party. The royalist detachment, after being
driven from the landing-place, retreated along this
path, and entered fort Yngles by a ladder, which
was drawn up, and consequently the patriots found
nobody on the *outside* to oppose their approach. The
men advanced gallantly to the attack; but, from the
nature of the track, in very extended order. The
leading files were soldiers, whose courage had been
before proved, and who, enjoying amongst their comrades a degree of deference and respect, claimed the
foremost post in danger. They advanced with firm
but noiseless step, and while those who next followed
cheered with cries of "*adelante!*" (onwards!) others
still farther behind raised clamorous shouts of "*Viva
la patria!*" and many of them fired in the air. The
path led to the salient angle of the fort, which on one

side was washed by the sea, and on the other side
flanked by the forest, the boughs and branches of
which overhung a considerable space of the rampart.
Favoured by the darkness of the night, by the in-
termingling roar of artillery and musketry, by the
lashings of the surge, and by the clamour of the garrison itself, a few men, under the gallant Ensign
Vidal, crept under the inland flank of the fort, and
whilst the fire of the garrison was solely directed to
the vociferous patriots in the rear, those in advance
contrived, without being heard or perceived, to tear
up some loosened palisades, with which they constructed a rude scaling ladder, one end of which
they placed against the rampart, and the other upon
a mound of earth which favoured the design.   By
the assistance of this ladder Ensign Vidal and his
party mounted the rampart; got unperceived into the
fort; and formed under cover of the branches of the
trees which overhung that flank.   The fifty or sixty
men who composed the garrison were occupied in
firing upon those of the assailants still approaching
in single files.   A volley from Vidal's party, which
had thus taken the Spaniards in flank, followed by a
rush, and accompanied by the terrific Indian yell,
echoed by the reverberating valleys of the mountains
around, produced terror and immediate flight.   The
panic was communicated to the column of three
hundred men, formed on an arena behind the fort,
and the whole body, with the exception of those who
were bayoneted, made the best of their way along the
path that led to the other forts, but which, in their
confusion, they did not attempt to occupy or defend.

Upon arriving at the gorge of a ravine, between Fort Chorocomayo and the castle of Corral, about one hundred men escaped in boats lying there, and rowed to Valdivia. The remainder, about two hundred men, neglecting the three guns on the height, which, if properly defended, would have effectually checked the advance of their pursuers, retreated into the Corral. This castle, however, was almost immediately stormed by the victorious patriots, who, favoured by a part of the rampart, which had crumbled down and partly filled up the ditch, rushed forward, and thus obtained possession of all the western side of the harbour. The royalists could retreat no farther, for there the land communication ended. One hundred Spaniards were bayoneted, and about the same number, exclusive of officers, were made prisoners. Miller was unable to climb the ladder placed against fort Yngles without assistance, and became so exhausted in the subsequent pursuit, that he could not keep pace with the troops until he made two of his men carry him in their arms. Such was the rapidity with which the patriots followed up their success, that the royalists had not time to destroy their military stores, or even to spike a gun. Daylight of the 4th found the independents in possession of the five forts, el Yngles, San Carlos, Amargos, Chorocomayo, and Corral. So completely was attention absorbed during the night by the rapid succession of exciting events, that till an officer remarked the next morning that Miller's hair was clotted with blood, he did not recollect the scratch he had received previous to landing.

Amongst the prisoners taken in the castle of Corral

was Colonel Hoyos, commanding the regiment of
Cantabria, who, in an agony of mind, produced by
reflecting on the loss of the forts, had drunk a quantity of rum, and, when Miller appeared, broke out
into terms of outrageous abuse.   It was with the
utmost difficulty that the victorious soldiers could
be restrained from killing the colonel.   The next
morning Hoyos said to Miller, " I thank you for
having preserved my life; but, after what has happened, death would have been a mercy."   He added,
" It is singular that I should owe my life to you,
whom I was in some measure instrumental in saving,
by supporting the efforts of Loriga in your favour
at Talcahuano."   About the time fort Yngles was
carried, Cochrane left the Montezuma, and caused
himself to be rowed as near the scene of action as
the surf would permit a boat to approach.   The
patriot troops mistaking the boat for an enemy's,
fired upon it from fort San Carlos, and obliged it
to sheer off.

On the morning of the 4th, the schooner and brig
entered the harbour, and anchored under the castle
of Corral, after receiving a few shots from the forts
on the eastern side, still in the possession of the
Spaniards.   In order to dislodge them, two hundred men embarked in the brig and schooner: the
latter ran aground in crossing the harbour, but soon
got off again.   The Spaniards, however, alarmed at
the movement, abandoned the castle of Niebla, fort
Carbonero, Piojo, and Manzanera.   The patriots,
not less surprised than pleased, found themselves,
without further opposition, masters of what may

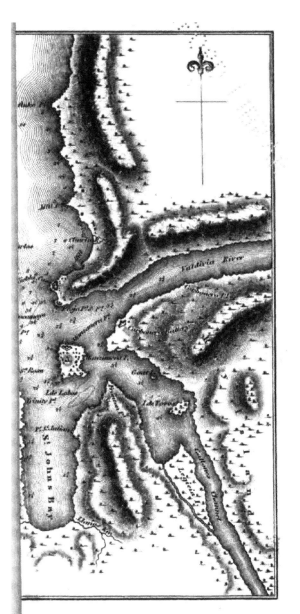

Published Jan.ʸ 1ˢᵗ 1823 by Longman and Co.

be called the Gibraltar of South America.   In the
evening the O'Higgins entered the port almost
water-logged, and, to keep her from sinking, she
was run aground on a muddy bottom, for the purpose of undergoing a repair.

The following are extracts from Major Miller's
official report to the admiral, written at the castle of
Corral on the morning of the 4th : " Having disembarked with little opposition, at the Aguada Yngles,
on the N. W. shore of the bay, with the marines
under my command, I continued my march, united
to the detachment of infantry under the orders of
Major Beauchef, to attack the enemy on that side.
In his formidable position he considered himself perfectly secure from any attack that could be made;
and, indeed, if due weight be given to the obstacles
we had to contend with through narrow and almost
impenetrable tracks, it is not surprising that such
confidence should have existed on his part.   But
the valour and intrepidity of our officers and soldiers were irresistible, and the most complete success crowned, if not one of the most arduous under-
takings ever attempted by such a handful of men,
one at least that will add new laurels to the gallant
sons of South America."

*   *   *   *

" It is impossible for me to give your lordship
an adequate idea of the valour and determined perseverance of our small but enthusiastic force.   No
veterans could have surpassed them : few could have
done so much."

On the 5th, Majors Beauchef and Miller proceeded

up the river with Lord Cochrane, who took possession of the town of Valdivia, at the head of two hundred of the troops.   The enemy, five hundred in
number, had abandoned it in the morning, and had
fled towards Osorno to cross the water to Chiloe.
On deserting the town, the Spaniards plundered and
committed great disorders.   The governor, Colonel
Montoya, was the first to make his escape.   His age
and infirmities must have incapacitated him for command, or he ought to have made a stand against such
an inferior force.   The admiral issued a proclamation,
which induced many of the inhabitants, who had fled
from the town on the approach of the patriots, to
return to their homes.

Amongst the public property taken at Valdivia,
were some silver ornaments and vessels, of which
Sanchez had stripped the churches of Concepcion.
This booty was valued at the time at from twelve
to sixteen thousand dollars.   There was, besides, a
custodia inlaid with gold and set with gems.   A
ship, called the *Dolores*, anchored off the Corral,
and taken by the soldiers in the night of the 3d,
was sold by the prize agent at Valparaiso for about
twenty thousand dollars.   A quantity of sugar,
spirits, and other articles were taken and disposed
of in like manner, for nearly the same sum.   The
foregoing statement does not include a claim made
by Cochrane on account of captured ordnance.   The
el dorado views, however, founded on the capture of
Valdivia, all fell to the ground.   Neither Miller,
nor any officer or soldier of his corps, ever received
prize money on that account.

The town of Valdivia, on the left bank of the river, contained about fifteen hundred souls. The houses are built of wood, and the streets intersect each other at right angles. The river is now navigable for boats only, but it is supposed that formerly large vessels anchored near to the town. Where the Dutch line-of-battle ships are said to have anchored in 1598 and 1603, there are now only six feet water. The river, like many others which empty themselves into the Pacific, is gradually filling up or becoming more shallow as time rolls on. The banks of the river are bold, and covered with majestic cedars, and other forest trees. The country is beautiful, and clothed in perpetual verdure, rains being frequent and heavy ten months out of the twelve. The soil is rich, and produces potatoes of a superior quality. Apples are also very abundant, and great quantities of cider are made there. The Chilenos, accustomed to a serene sky, consider the climate of Valdivia as insupportably humid. It was a place of banishment for delinquents, who acquired the rights of citizens after serving a given time, regulated by the nature of their offence.

Osorno is a colony settled some fifty years ago, by the illustrious father of General O'Higgins, and contains three thousand inhabitants. Its plains are extremely fertile, and the ground having been partially cleared of wood, produces wheat; and it rains less there than at Valdivia. The country is surrounded by Indians, who are occasionally troublesome. The Spanish governor granted pensions to certain caciques, and the admiral promised that their allowances should be doubled by the Patriots.

CHAPTER XII.

Benavides.—His marvellous escape.—Unsuccessful attack upon Chiloe.—Gallantry of the patriot soldiers.—Major Miller wounded.—Fanaticism.—Major Beauchef.—Royalists in Osorno annihilated.—Santalla.—Captain Bobadilla.—Squadron arrives at Valparaiso.—Humane character of the Chilenos.—Misunderstanding between San Martin and the Buenos Ayrean government.—La Logia, or club.—Colonel Martinez.—Battalion No. 8.—Preparations to liberate Peru.—Obstacles.—Royalist forces in Peru.

THE acquisition of Valdivia enabled General San Martin to bestow his undivided attention upon the liberation of Peru. It at the same time afforded a great advantage to the patriots, by dispossessing Spain of her best harbour and strongest hold in the Pacific, and by depriving the royalist ruffian Benavides of the depôt from which he drew the *matériel* to carry on his desolating inroads at the head of free-booters and Indians, over whom he, although an uneducated man, had obtained unbounded influence. That chieftain had become so formidable that, had he not been deprived of an important *point d'appui*, and of his usual resources, an expedition must have been fitted out, in order to preserve the southern provinces of Chile from his daring and bloody incursions. On taking the port, a small vessel fell into the hands of the patriots. It was about to sail to Arauco with two or three officers, and four non-com-

missioned officers, together with arms and ammunition for Benavides.   There is something so extraordinary in the character and career of this desperado,
that a short account of both may not be unseasonable.

Benavides was born in the province of Concepcion,
and, together with one of his brothers, had served in
the Buenos Ayrean battalion No. 11; the first as a
serjeant, the second as a corporal.   In 1814, both
were sentenced to death for some crime, but escaped
from their condemned cell, and passed over to the
royalists, having, as was strongly suspected, set fire
to the field depôt, which was burnt on the night they
absconded.   Both were made prisoners of war at the
battle of Maypo, but were not recognised until after
the government of Chile had published a general
pardon to all military offenders, in celebration of the
victory.   The supreme director could not then except the brothers from the amnesty; but he ordered
them to be sent out of the country, as dangerous and
enterprising criminals, and to be placed at the disposal of the government of the united provinces of
La Plata.   On the march, the commandant of the
escort was informed by two of his soldiers that the
men in custody had offered bribes to connive at their
evasion.   The officer stated that, upon charging them
with this proceeding, the prisoners acknowledged the
truth of the accusation; that seventeen doubloons and
a dagger were found about the person of the elder
brother.   Upon which the officer, acting, as he said,
in conformity to his instructions in the event of his
prisoners' attempting to escape, ordered them to be
shot, and they were executed accordingly.

On San Martin's return from Mendoza to Santiago, a stanch patriot, nearly related to the wife of
Benavides, apprised the general that the unfortunate
man was still living, and that he felt an unconquerable desire to have an interview with his excellency,
not only to communicate upon subjects of high importance, but also to manifest the sincerity of his
wishes to re-attach himself to the cause of independence.   He, however, stipulated for a guarantee in
writing, and the concealment of the fact of his existence, particularly from the knowledge of the supreme
director.   These conditions were acceded to, and the
first meeting took place at midnight, in the chapel
porch of the *Conventillo*, a country-seat about a mile
from Santiago.   San Martin went with a pocket pistol
in each hand, and was otherwise well armed, to be
provided against sinister intentions.

The following is the account which Benavides
himself gave of the transaction to San Martin.   He
said that, upon leaving Santiago, neither he nor his
brother entertained any suspicion they were to be
executed on the road; that if they had apprehended
any such design, it would have been easy for them
to have absconded before they left the capital : but
feeling satisfied on the score of personal safety, they
postponed the attempt until a favourable opportunity
should occur in the course of their march, and more
particularly as they wished to avoid compromising
their friends of the royalist party then resident at
Santiago ; that on the evening of the second day the
officer of the escort ordered a halt for the brothers
to be searched, and seventeen doubloons being found

in the lining of the boots of the elder, the officer
asked if they had attempted to bribe the soldiers,
which was answered in the negative; that the party
then left the road, and having arrived at a lonely
spot at nightfall, the officer ordered them (the two
brothers) to prepare for instant death.   They were
made to kneel, with eyes unbound, and a volley was
fired.   Benavides received two balls, one of which
passed through his right shoulder, the other through
his left side.   He fell, but, preserving his presence
of mind, he feigned himself dead, in the hope of
ultimately effecting his escape.   The serjeant of the
escort, as he supposed, drew his sword, and gave him
a heavy cut across the throat*, saying at the same
time, "Take that, villain, for the murder of my family!"   The soldiers then threw a quantity of earth
and stones over the two bodies, and withdrew.   Benavides remained motionless for some minutes, when,
finding that his executioners had finally left him, he
immediately set to work to disengage himself from
the load of earth with which he was encumbered; he
then with great difficulty untied the cords with which
he was bound, and having stripped off the jacket and
shirt of his deceased brother, to bind up his own
wounds, he quitted the fatal spot.   He walked the
greater part of the night, suffering acutely from the
pain of his wounds, and from the still less supportable
agonies of thirst.   Having reached the hovel of a
good old man and woman, they took pity upon him;
and although poverty confined their means of cure
to the constant washing of his wounds with water

* Benavides carried his head awry ever afterwards.

from a neighbouring rill, Benavides found himself sufficiently recovered, at the end of sixteen days, to. creep unperceived into Santiago, where he remained concealed.

San Martin and Benavides had several subsequent meetings, which were held at night near the fountain, in the great square of the city.   Benavides revealed the names of those who were still inimical to the patriot cause, and also the means they employed to carry on their correspondence with the royalists, and to remit subscriptions to promote the restoration of the ancient order of things.   He reiterated the offer of his services to the republic : they were accepted, and a plan of operations for the ensuing campaign in the south of Chile was determined upon.   He was soon afterwards sent, in charge of an officer, who was kept in ignorance of the name of the person he escorted, to General Balcarce, at that time command-. ing the troops in the province of Concepcion, and who was minutely informed of the character and conduct of Benavides, and of the circumstances which rendered it expedient to place such a person upon his staff.   Balcarce was instructed to observe the utmost circumspection in carrying into execution plans suggested by Benavides; and, taking care not to betray any signs of mistrust, to keep a watchful eye over that extraordinary man, whose local know- ledge and prior connexions with the royalist chiefs, as well as his influence over the Araucanians, gave value and weight to his opinions, and rendered him a desirable instrument in the prosecution of the war. There can be no doubt that to his counsel was owing the conquest of the inland island of Lajas and of the fort Nacimiento, and the successful issue of that campaign.   Indeed, Balcarce distinctly attributed it to the advice of Benavides, whose adhesion to the cause of the country became undoubted.

Unhappily Balcarce imparted his secret to Freyre, governor of Concepcion, who, in a conference at which all three were present, had the indiscretion to tell Benavides, in a moment of warm discussion, that a man of his *species* was not to be trusted.   Fired at the insult, the stern Benavides disappeared within eight-and-forty hours, and speedily commenced a de-solating war with fire and sword, committing un-heard-of barbarities upon the helpless and unoffend-ing inhabitants.

Cochrane having made the necessary arrangements for the security of Valdivia, turned his views to other objects.   His next attempt was to wrest the important island of Chiloe from the dominion of Spain.   Al-though it was known to be defended by one thousand regulars, besides a hardy militia, yet the garrison was supposed to be in a discontented state, and it was hoped that a majority of it would gladly avail themselves of an opportunity of joining the patriot cause.

Chiloe is the largest of an archipelago of seventy-two islands, stretching along the dreary and inhos-pitable coast between the straits of Magellan and Valdivia.   The navigation is very intricate and dan-gerous, on account of eddies, currents, and whirlpools; moreover, the tremendous surf of the Pacific Ocean breaking with fury on the iron-bound coast, renders

it almost every where unapproachable. The temperature is moderate ; the soil is generally rich, and
the islands produce fine timber. Some species of
larch, cleft into deals, is one of the few articles of
export for the supply of the coasts of Chile and Peru.
The humidity of the climate prevents the cultivation
of wheat. The potatoes are perhaps the finest in the
world. Chiloe abounds with swine, fed upon the
abundant shell-fish. The hams are so highly esteemed
that it may be called the Westphalia of the New
World. The manufacture of *ponchos* is carried on
to a considerable extent. The population is loosely
estimated at thirty-four thousand. But, in point of
civilization, the Chilotes are but one remove from
the Araucanians.

On the 10th of February, the Governor Quintanilla, an active officer, was apprised of Cochrane's
intention, and instantly made his arrangements for
an obstinate defence. On the morning of the 17th
the admiral approached the west point of the island,
which forms the south side of the bay in which San
Carlos, the seat of government, is situated, and at
sunset anchored off a little inlet in the bay of Hue-
chucucay. Sixty infantry and thirty cavalry, with
a field-piece, were sent to dispute the landing ; but
their attention was divided between the real place
of intended disembarkation, and another inlet farther
up the bay, whither for that purpose a boat had been
sent with a few rockets. Meanwhile Miller effected
a landing; and the royalist detachment, divided into
two parties, was put to flight, and their field-piece
abandoned. At eight P. M. the patriots, one hun-

dred and seventy in number, advanced; but the
night was so dark that no object could be distinguished at the distance of three paces.   The surf
ran very high, and broke upon the beach with.a roar
that drowned the voice of command.   The guide
soon lost his way, and, either through ignorance or
treachery, could not or would not recover it.   The
party wandered about all night, making unavailing
efforts.   At dawn of day the track was again found,
and the party moved on.   Fort Corona, and a
detached battery, were carried without loss.   Having
halted for an hour, the patriots pushed forward to
storm the principal defence, Fort Aguy, which
mounted twelve eighteen-pounders, and was raised
on a commanding eminence, washed on one side by
the sea, and having on the opposite side an impenetrable wood.   The only access to the fort was by
a narrow path on the beach, enfiladed by some
pieces of ordnance, and flanked by two gun-boats
anchored just out of musket range.   The path forms
a zigzag from the foot of the rising ground to the
crest upon which the fort is situated.   At each angle
was a small parapet for infantry.   The garrison of
Aguy consisted of three companies of regulars, two
companies of militia, and a proportion of artillerymen,
in all about five hundred men *.   Two friars upon the
rampart were seen to excite them during the assault,
each with a lance in one hand and a crucifix in the
other.   To the violence of these infuriated bigots
might be advantageously contrasted the calm advance

---

* According to a despatch from Quintanilla to the viceroy of Peru, published
in a Lima Gazette.

credit on his military skill and on his enthusiastic
bravery, routed the royalists. Seventeen officers and
two hundred and twenty men were taken prisoners.
The rest were killed in action, excepting a few who
escaped, with the two commanding officers, to Chiloe.
Quintanilla was so much ashamed of the whole party
that he sent off Santalla and Bobadilla * in deserved
disgrace to Lima.

Captain Labé, of the Chileno service, highly distinguished himself on this occasion, as he had done
during the assault of Valdivia.

On the 20th of February, Cochrane, Miller, and
the wounded, sailed for Valparaiso in the Montezuma, the O'Higgins not having completed the re-
pairs necessary to make her sea-worthy. Three miles
west of the westernmost point of the island of Santa
Maria are sunken rocks not laid down in any chart.
The Montezuma passed safely between them and the
island. She was abreast of them, and going at the
rate of eight knots, before the breakers were seen.

Miller experienced a long and severe illness, the
result of so many wounds; of so much fatigue; and
of privations incidental to such a service. It was
fortunate that he arrived at that period in Chile,
where the national character does not perhaps display
a more amiable trait than the unceasing care with
which people of every class watch over the stranger
whom sickness overtakes and places at their threshold.
Without distinction of rank or party, the palace or
the hut is alike open to the invalid, for whom the

---

* Both these officers survived the dangers of the campaigns of Peru, and
returned to Spain. Captain *Bobadil* was amongst those who capitulated at
Ayacucho.

liveliest sympathy is evinced by every individual of
the family. At Santiago, Miller occupied apartments
in Cochrane's mansion; but the whole family being
at Valparaiso, a Chileno officer of distinction, with
his amiable and accomplished wife, visited him daily,
and at length prevailed upon him to remove to their
own house, where he was watched night and day
with unremitting solicitude, till returning health and
strength enabled him to take the field once more.
This kindness of the Chilenos fixes upon the heart
of the recovered stranger ineffaceable impressions of
the most grateful and pleasing remembrance.

After the battle of Maypo, ladies of the highest
rank visited the hospitals, as a matter of course, each
undertaking the care of as many of the wounded as
her means would allow.   They administered medicines, and brought refreshments, prepared at their
own houses; and all exerted themselves to soothe the
suffering, in a way which seemed to proclaim that
every wounded patriot was their brother.   He whose
task it is historically to portray the features of desolating warfare cannot but dwell with pleasure on
traits which soften and illuminate the dark melancholy picture.

The repeated delay in the sailing of the grand expedition from Cadiz was now ascertained to have
arisen from a disinclination of the troops to embark,
and which ended in the revolution under Quiroga of
the Isla de Leon, and the establishment of the cortes.
It was therefore no longer apprehended that an invasion would take place.   Spain was rendered inca-

pable of attempting the re-conquest of America in consequence of her own intestine divisions.

General San Martin set out from Mendoza in the beginning of January, 1820, for Chile; and, apprehensive that the spirit of disunion, which then agitated the provinces of the Rio de la Plata, would extend itself to the recruits raised in the province of Cuyo, he directed that the whole of the troops should march for Chile. The two cavalry regiments obeyed orders, and, after losing some men from desertion on the march, they arrived at Rancagua in February, 1820. The light-infantry battalion, one thousand and seventy strong, under the command of Colonel Alvarado, mutinied at San Juan, and dispersed; many to return to their homes, and others to attach themselves to some favourite leader.

A misunderstanding now arose between the Buenos Ayrean government and San Martin, who was ordered, with the troops of that state, to re-cross the Andes, to quell some disturbances which had broken out in several of the provinces. The general, supported by the unanimous decision of a council of war, declined to obey the order, upon the ground, that to take any part in the civil dissensions which distracted the provinces of Tucuman, Cordova, Santa Fé, Entre-Rios, and Buenos Ayres, would be to set aside the projected expedition to subvert the Spanish authority in Peru; and that it would expose the whole of his army to the contagion of those anarchical principles which had already proved so fatal to the battalion of Cazadores at San Juan.

This refusal gave great offence. The Buenos Ayreans accused San Martin of having, by that act, withdrawn his allegiance from the general government of the United Provinces of the River Plata, as the executive in Buenos Ayres styled itself. Every effort was made to lower San Martin in public opinion. Some lawyers and other civilians, jealous of the natural influence which services in the field gave to the general, were amongst the most active underminers of his reputation. These detractors, never having exposed their own persons in action, were the declared enemies of the military. It may be politic to prevent successful generals from retaining an undue preponderance, but the littleness of mind by which many of San Martin's enemies were actuated is too manifest to exempt them from feelings of contempt.

From that time all co-operation on the part of Buenos Ayres was withheld. A club, called the *Logia*, an institution of Spanish origin, and introduced at Buenos Ayres for the ostensible object of promoting the emancipation of Spanish America, lent its aid to bring San Martin into disrepute, although he himself was a principal member. The Logia, in a noiseless manner, gradually monopolized the patronage of the principal civil and military appointments, and arrogated to themselves the privilege of secretly selecting the commanding officers of regiments, or of ratifying appointments made by the general; and they disputed the right of any general-in-chief to remove such officers, for any cause, without the previous concurrence of the club. Such members as were chiefs in the army of the Andes, and had be-

come more or less inimical to San Martin, were supposed to receive proportionate support and countenance from the Logia. The members also took upon
themselves to influence, if not to direct, military
operations. If General Belgrano had paid less deference to the plans of a mischievous knot of incompetent directors, he would have marched to Upper
Peru, instead of waiting in Tucuman, where he saw
his army of four thousand fine troops waste away by
desertion. The result of his blind obedience to the
Logia * was, that he was made prisoner by his own
men.

To the charge of withdrawing his allegiance, San
Martin is reported to have answered, that, besides
the weighty reasons which influenced the unanimous
decision of the council of war, there did not, in point
of fact, exist any legitimate government at all; and
that Buenos Ayres was ruled by successive factions,
which displaced each other once a month, and sometimes oftener; an assertion which will be borne out
by the history of Buenos Ayres at that period. From
Santiago San Martin sent a sealed packet to the chief
of the staff, and second in command, Colonel Las
Heras, whose head-quarters were then at Rancagua.
The packet, opened in the presence of the whole of
the officers of the army, convened for that purpose,
contained a letter, which intimated that, as the government, whence San Martin's commission as commander-in-chief emanated, was dissolved, he felt it to

---

* Clubs in South America have, like the Comuneros of Spain, and Carbonari
of Italy, proved, in the end, to be highly prejudicial to the cause they were
intended to uphold. Many of the petty revolutions in South America are at
this time ascribable to their mischievous influence.

be his duty to tender his resignation to the officers
of the army at large, and to authorise them to elect,
by ballot, a successor to the chief command. On the
same day San Martin was unanimously re-elected.

The above details appear to be necessary to account
for the tardy progress of the independent cause, after
the decisive advantages obtained by the victory of
Maypo.

On the 11th of June, 1820, Miller was promoted
by General San Martin to the lieutenant-colonelcy of
the eighth or black battalion of Buenos Ayres, eight
hundred strong. Don Enrique Martinez, the colonel
commanding, received Miller with as much kindness
and consideration as if the appointment had taken
place upon his own recommendation. The friendly
hospitality, which he received on joining, was continued during nearly two years that he served in the
battalion. Nor did this promotion produce any symptoms of an ungracious feeling on the part of the
major and other officers thus passed over. The
officers of the eighth had commenced their career
at the dawn of the revolution, and had served with
distinction. One and all uniformly, and with the
greatest cordiality, lent their willing assistance to
supply the deficiencies which arose partly from Miller's
not speaking the language perfectly, and from his
not being thoroughly versed in the duties of his new
appointment.

The privates of the battalion No. 8 were Creole
negroes, and had been for the most part in-door slaves
previously to the commencement of the revolution,
when, by becoming soldiers, they obtained their free-

dom. They were distinguished throughout the war
for their valour, constancy, and patriotism. They
were docile, easy to instruct, and devotedly attached
to their officers. Many were remarkable for their
intelligence, cleanliness, and good conduct. They
went through their evolutions exceedingly well, and
it was generally allowed that they marched better
than the corps formed of whites. Many of them
rose to be good non-commissioned officers; some had
taught themselves to read and write, while others
had been instructed by a kind owner, or by some
part of his family. The band was composed of twenty-
seven, and, with the exception of three, all played by
ear, and exceedingly well. The master of the band,
named Sarmiento, was the son of a mulatto woman
by an African. He could both read and write, and
was a tolerable composer of music.

In the provinces of the Rio de la Plata and Chile
few proprietors possess more than a very small number of slaves, who, being kindly treated, are superior
to the mass of those in Peru, where, on the great
sugar or vine estates, hundreds are herded in *galpones*, or slave huts, surrounded by a high wall.
Cooped up in this small enclosure, except when they
sally forth to work, they become debased and vile.
Subjected to the caprice and cruelty of their drivers,
the lash of the whip, and the cries of the flogged, are
often heard; and even instruments of torture were
sometimes used. It is not therefore surprising that
these miserable beings should imbibe all the vices attendant upon such cruel treatment, and that they
should sink to a state of debasement which furnishes

matter for enemies to their freedom, to represent them as irrational and unfit to enjoy the rights of men. Such cruelty is enough to change their very nature. The governor of Mala, a Peruvian town, as he was shivering with an ague fit, once said to the author of these memoirs, " Here am I quite neglected, although I have fourteen slave rascals in nominal attendance, but those who are not thieves are drunkards."

San Martin, having wisely declined to interfere in the dissensions of the Buenos Ayrean provinces, and finding himself placed again at the head of the army of the Andes by the unanimous vote of its officers, directed his attention to his favourite project of liberating Peru; a measure which had now become indispensable, if only to employ his army, which, in the absence of a foreign enemy, was fast mouldering away by desertion.

The obstacles to the equipment of the expedition were almost insurmountable. The Chileno treasury had been drained for the support of the army, which was kept together with some difficulty; and by the formation of the navy. Without money and without credit, the attention of the government was repeatedly diverted from the object of emancipating Peru, in order to counteract the continued machinations of the remnant of the Carrera party.

The squadron was divided and agitated by the conflicting parties of Cochrane and Guise *.

* These originated in bickerings on some unimportant points of etiquette, and were carried to a length which proved highly detrimental to the service. But as these disputes do not, it would appear, reflect credit upon either of the principal parties, the subject will pass without further remark.

In the south, Benavides*, although deprived of
the resources of Valdivia, was formidable enough to
render the measures for the security of the province
of Concepcion a source of very great expense and
alarm.   Buenos Ayres, a prey to successive anar-
chies, had neither the power nor the will to lend her
assistance.

The army of General Belgrano having dissolved in
Tucuman, the royalist army, under General Ramirez,
was at full liberty to march from Upper Peru, to
any part of the coast, to the assistance of the viceroy
Pezuela.

The government of Chile, hopeless of farther co-
operation from Buenos Ayres, and suffering from
intestine divisions, managed, with great difficulty, to
assemble a force of four thousand five hundred men.
Under other circumstances, this number might have
been more than doubled.   But notwithstanding the
disunion of the patriots, it was evident that the Spanish yoke was equally dreaded by all; and that the
desire of independence was so ardent as not to be
suppressed by partial dissensions.

On the present occasion, the merchants came forward with a liberality which proved them to be animated by a zealous patriotism.   To their confidence

* Benavides remained with the Araucanians until, finding himself cut off from
most of his followers, he embarked at the end of two years in an open launch,
and sailed for Arica, intending to join the royalist party in Peru. Being in
want of water on the passage, the launch put into a small cove near Valparaiso.
One of his men betrayed him, and Benavides closed his blood-stained career on
the scaffold, at Santiago, on the 23d February, 1823, amidst the execrations of
the populace. On leaving his cell the manhood of Benavides failed him, and
he was borne along, or rather dragged, to the place of execution, and underwent
the sentence of the law, with a degree of cowardice worthy of a Robespierre.

and timely assistance the final equipment of the expedition must, in a great measure, be ascribed; for if it had failed, the terms of their contracts with the government would most probably never have been fulfilled.

It may not be amiss now to give a statement of the strength and distribution of the royalist forces in Peru, on the authority of the viceroy Pezuela, as stated in his Manifesto, published at Madrid in 1821; according to which, the grand total of his force in 1820 was twenty-three thousand regulars.

There were in Callao and Lima . 7815
In Pisco, Cañete, and Chancay . . 700
The rest might have been distributed as follows:
Upper Peru 6000
Arequipa and province, Truxillo, Guayaquil, Guamanga, Cuzco, Xauxa, &c. . } 8485

—————
23,000

The above comparative statement will furnish perhaps the best answer to the Spanish *constitutionalists*, and others, who have contended that the Peruvians did not generally wish for independence; for, without the support of public opinion, could General San Martin have maintained himself in Peru? It will also justify the cautious measures of that commander, in abstaining from risking the existence of his army in a general action.

CHAPTER XIII.

Liberating army.—Sails from Valparaiso.—Disembarks at Pisco.
—Arenales.—Affair at Nasca.—Army re-embarks.—Ancon.
—Guayaquil.—Esmeralda.—Army disembarks at Huacho.—
Chancay.—Colonel Campino.—Exchange of prisoners of war.
—Battalion of Numancia.—Action of Cerro de Pasco.—
Dissensions of the royalists.—Pezuela deposed.—La Serna
made viceroy.—Lady Cochrane.—The admiral sails to Callao.
—Returns to Huacho.—Proceeds to Pisco.—Armistice of
Punchauca.

THE unceasing exertions and determined perseverance of the supreme director, and of General San
Martin, seconded by the commendable spirit of adventure and zealous patriotism of the merchants,
overcame, at last, those obstacles which had for so
long a period delayed the sailing of the expedition.

The liberating force assembled at Valparaiso on
the 19th of August, 1820. On the 19th and 20th
the following corps embarked:

Infantry, . Battalions No. 7,
                           8,
                          11, Division of the
Cavalry, Granaderos à Caballo,   Andes*;
          Cazadores à Caballo,
Artillery, two troops,

---

* One-third of the soldiers of the division of the Andes were Chilenos; but
the officers were Buenos Ayreans: many other Buenos Ayreans were also in the
division of Chile.

Infantry, . Battalions No. 2,
4,
(in skeleton)   5, } Division of Chile:
Artillery, one troop,

and sailed on the 21st, under convoy of the Chileno ships of war: the total number not exceeding four thousand five hundred soldiers (including the men afterwards taken on board at Coquimbo), with twelve pieces of artillery.

Lieutenant-Colonel Miller embarked in the Santa Rosa transport, with two companies of his own battalion (No. 8 of Buenos Ayres), and two companies of his former corps, the Buenos Ayrean artillery*. The arrangements for the embarkation of the troops were highly creditable to Colonel Las Heras and the naval officers who superintended this operation.

Notwithstanding the numerical weakness of the expedition, the effort now made to liberate Peru will be regarded as one of no inconsiderable importance, especially when the unsettled state of Chile and the exhausted condition of its resources are considered. Three years had hardly elapsed since Chile herself lay prostrate at the feet of that paralyzing despotism

* It is remarkable that Miller was the only field-officer who sailed with the expeditionary army from Valparaiso, who was also present at the great final victory of Ayacucho. Thus it was his singular fortune to have been the first patriot officer to land on the coast (1819), and to have heard the first and last shots fired during the Peruvian war of independence. Of nearly five thousand that sailed from Valparaiso in 1820, not more than ten officers and ninety privates continued in active service in Peru, to be present at the last victory. Besides the proportion which fell by the usual casualties of the war, many of the higher ranks were displaced by faction; numbers were swept off by the prevailing diseases of the country; and not a few for want of medical attendance. The hospitals were in a state of wretchedness beyond imagination; there was scarcely a regimental surgeon in the army, and the medical staff was composed of so very few, that the lives of the sick or wounded soldiers may be said to have been trusted almost solely to nature. The want of medicines was sometimes even greater than the want of medical men.

which had enthralled her for ages. Although enfeebled by the struggle with her oppressor, as well as
by civil dissensions, she now put forth her remaining
strength to liberate a neighbouring state. It was in
truth an imposing and an exciting spectacle to behold that bay crowded with shipping, under patriot
banners, which formerly received only one merchant
vessel annually. As the several corps, marching from
cantonments, with music playing, through cheering
multitudes, severally arrived upon the beach, they
were taken off to their respective transports in the
greatest order, and without the occurrence of a single
accident.

The population of the capital and of the country
had poured into Valparaiso, and every avenue was
crowded with spectators. Many females who had
shared the fortunes of other campaigns were now
unavoidably left behind, and their farewell ejaculations, accompanied by the weeping of children, gave
a deep and distressing interest to the busy scene.

Miller, on his leaving Valparaiso, received from
numerous friends those hearty expressions of good
wishes which, at such a time, relieve the heart from
that heaviness which approaching separation always
produces. A scene not devoid of affecting interest
awaited him upon the strand. Some twenty or thirty
marines who happened to be on shore from the different men of war, and who had served with him in
his former expeditions, had spontaneously assembled
at the water's edge to witness his embarkation. These
faithful comrades continued to shout their parting
vivas until the receding boat was out of hearing.

On the 25th of August, 1820, the liberating expedition hove to off Coquimbo.   Lord Cochrane, in
the O'Higgins, stood into the bay to order out the
brig-of-war Araucano, and a transport having on
board the Chileno battalion No. 2.   On the 26th,
the convoy again made sail.   On the 27th, the Aguila
transport, with seven hundred men of the battalion
No. 4, parted company.   In the night of the 30th,
the Santa Rosa, with Miller on board, also parted
company, in consequence of the carelessness of the
mate of the watch,   The Santa Rosa continued her
voyage to the second rendezvous, and stood off and
on for two days, without catching sight of a vessel.
She then made sail for the third rendezvous, Punta
de Caballo.   On her arrival there, the supply of
water taken in at Valparaiso was nearly expended,
and it was therefore determined to proceed to the
bay of Pararca, in latitude 13° south.   On making
the bay, the greater part of the expedition was discovered at anchor there.   The Santa Rosa narrowly
escaped being captured by two Spanish frigates, which
were seen in the offing the evening before.   Had she
been twelve hours earlier, she must have fallen into
their hands.   The patriot ships of war had given chase,
but the Spanish frigates outsailed them.

The convoy had reached an anchorage in Pararca
bay at six P.M. on the 7th of September, having
made the passage from Valparaiso, a distance of
about fifteen hundred miles, in sixteen days.   Las
Heras, chief of the staff, with three battalions (Nos.
2, 7, and 11), two pieces of mountain artillery, and
fifty cavalry, landed, on the 8th, two leagues south

of the town of Pisco, but did not approach within
musket-shot until seven P. M., when a halt was
ordered, and a careful reconnoissance made. About
eighty Spanish cavalry were seen to retire from the
town in the course of the day. A few long shots
were uselessly fired at them from the Montezuma,
but the troops on shore did not molest their retreat.
Having ascertained that the town was abandoned,
the patriot division entered and bivouacked for the
night in the Plaza. The disembarkation of the rest
of the troops was not completed until the 12th.

The first object of San Martin was, after having
taken Pisco, to occupy the surrounding country, for
the purpose of adding to his numbers by taking able-
bodied slaves from the vineyards and sugar estates
situated at great and irregular distances; but the
disembarkation of the troops having been so leisurely
performed, and the men under Las Heras having advanced with such extraordinary caution, the owners
had time to remove the principal part of their negro
property.

The reason assigned for this delay was the tardy
arrival of a heavy-sailing transport, bringing horses
for the cavalry, staff, and field officers.

San Martin had given up the Santa Rosa for lost,
and was so delighted upon her arrival, that he ordered the band of every corps in Pisco to welcome
the troops, by playing the *diana* (reveillé). The
Aguila had previously arrived.

On the 13th, San Martin established his head-
quarters at Pisco. On the 22d, Colonel Alvarado,
with the regiment of Granaderos à Caballo, took pos-

session of the two villages of Upper and Lower Chincha. On the 23d, San Martin reconnoitred the valley
of the same name, and was received with enthusiasm
by the inhabitants. The Marquess of San Miguel,
who possessed large estates in that neighbourhood,
joined the patriots. He received the rank of colonel,
and was appointed aide-de-camp to the general-in-
chief. On the 26th of September a suspension of
arms, for eight days, was agreed upon between the
commissioners of San Martin and those of the viceroy, at Miraflores, near Lima, for the purpose of
adjusting a pacification, on the basis of the entire
independence of Peru; but. as the viceroy would not
accede to this point, hostilities recommenced, on the
expiration of the truce.

On the 5th of October, General Arenales marched
from Pisco with battalions No. 2 and 11, eighty cavalry, and two field-pieces, and entered Ica on the
6th, where they were received by the inhabitants
with every expression of satisfaction. The royalist
Colonel Quimper and the Count de Montemar abandoned Ica with eight hundred regulars and militia.
Two companies of the latter, with their officers, passed
over to Arenales. On the 12th, Lieutenant-Colonel
Roxas, second in command under Arenales, was detached with eighty infantry, and the same number of
cavalry, in pursuit; and on the 15th reached Changuilla, four leagues north of Nasca, where the royalists
had halted.

The small party of patriot cavalry, led by Captains
Lavalle and Brandsen, and Lieutenant Don Vicente
Suares, galloped into the town; surprised the royal-

ists; put them to flight; pursued them for above a
league; and killed and wounded upwards of sixty.
Six officers and eighty soldiers were made prisoners,
besides a number of militia. Three hundred muskets,
with a quantity of swords and lances, fell into the
hands of the patriots. The Spanish force, consisting
the day before of six hundred men, was totally dispersed. The inhabitants of Nasca hailed the party
of Roxas as deliverers, and gave information that
one hundred mules, laden with military stores and
effects, carried away from Ica, were still at Acari,
thirty leagues south of Nasca. Roxas sent Lieutenant Don Vicente Suares forward with a party of
cavalry, and, in spite of the difficulty of the desert
they had to pass, and length of the march, this indefatigable officer reached Acari at two P. M. on the
16th, and captured the whole royalist convoy. On
the 19th, Roxas and Suares returned to Ica.

On the 20th of October, Arenales marched from
Ica for the interior, leaving a detachment under Lieutenant-Colonel Bermudes and Major Aldao to retain
possession of that province. On the 25th, the remainder of the liberating force re-embarked at Pisco,
and sailed northward on the 26th.

On the 29th the squadron anchored in the bay of
Callao. On the 30th the transports, under convoy
of the San Martin, sailed to the little bay of Ancon,
six or eight leagues north of Lima. Ancon consists
of a few fishermen's huts, half buried in the drifted
sand : there is no fresh water within several miles.
On the 31st, fifty cavalry and twenty infantry, under
Lieutenant Raulet, a French officer, were landed.

A detachment of royalist cavalry appeared in the
sandy plain to reconnoitre. On the 1st of November,
Raulet advanced to Copacabana, within five leagues
of Lima, where he remained in observation. On
the 3d, two hundred infantry and forty cavalry were
disembarked at Ancon, and sent under the command
of Major Reyes to Chancay.

On the 5th, a battalion of royalist infantry and
two squadrons of cavalry made a reconnoissance upon
Ancon. Corporal Alomi, who was instrumental in
saving Captain Brown of the Maypo, passed over
from the royalist regiment of Numancia, and was
made a serjeant of No. 8.

On the 4th, the *Alcance* schooner arrived at Ancon
with despatches from the municipality of Guayaquil,
announcing that that province had declared itself independent of Spain, and offering to place its resources
at the disposal of San Martin, in furtherance of his
object of emancipating Peru. This change was
brought about by Lieutenant-Colonel Don Gregorio
Escovedo, who, with the assistance of the troops of
the garrison, established a provisional government,
of which Escovedo was appointed president.

The Chileno squadron remained at anchor in the
bay of Callao, blockading the Spanish shipping. Lord
Cochrane having planned the cutting out of the
Esmeralda, four days were actively devoted to preparations. The Spanish frigate was protected by the
castles, a corvette, two brigs of war, several armed
merchant-men, and above twenty gun-boats.

At 11 o'clock at night of the 5th November, one
hundred and eighty seamen, and one hundred ma-

rines, in two divisions, commanded by Captains
Guise and Crosbie, put off in the launches of the
squadron, led by Cochrane in person. They approached the Esmeralda unperceived, until hailed by
a sentry in a gun-boat astern of the frigate. Cochrane answered, "Silence or death." In half a minute
the boats were alongside the Esmeralda, and boarded
starboard and larboard at the same moment. The
Spaniards made a spirited resistance with small arms,
but before one o'clock of the 6th the Esmeralda was
in possession of the admiral. Her cables were cut,
her sails set, and she, with two gun-boats, at half-
past one, was transferred to another anchorage. The
British frigate Hyperion, and the United States ship
Macedonian, which happened to be in the port during
this operation, got under weigh, and hoisted lights
as signals, as had been previously agreed upon with
the governor, to prevent being fired upon, in the
event of a night attack. Cochrane, with admirable
adroitness, ordered similar lights to be hoisted, so
that the Spaniards could not distinguish neutral from
enemy. In the whole naval career of Cochrane there
will not be found perhaps any thing to exceed this
ably planned and brilliantly executed exploit. His
lordship was wounded in the thigh by a musket-ball.
Lord Cochrane and Captain Guise boarded the opposite quarters of the frigate at the same time. They
met on the quarter-deck, and supported each other
in the thickest of the fight. This circumstance produced a short-lived reconciliation. The brave Lieutenant Grenfell, now admiral in the service of the
Brazils, and who has since lost an arm, was wounded.

The Spaniards lost a hundred and fifty men, in killed and wounded, on board the Esmeralda. Amongst the latter was Captain Coy, the late commander, who, after capture, received a severe contusion from a splinter caused by a shot from the castles, or a gun-boat. The patriots had fifty killed and wounded. The Esmeralda was ready for sea; she had provisions for three months, and stores for two years on board.

The garrison of Callao was so much exasperated by the result of the daring enterprise, that they massacred an officer and boat's crew sent on shore, soon after day-break, from the United States frigate Macedonian, under the pretext that the "Devil" Cochrane would never have succeeded unless he had been assisted by the neutral men-of-war.

A short time after this event, two officers of H. M. S. Conway happening to go on shore in plain clothes, they were rudely arrested and thrown into prison as spies of Cochrane. Captain Hall made repeated applications for their release, and, finding them unavailing, went on shore to claim in person his officers; but the Spanish authorities affected to be so satisfied in their own minds that the two gentlemen were spies, that they uncourteously refused to take the word of Captain Hall, and the incarcerated officers were not set free until some days afterwards.

At ten o'clock on the morning of the 6th, the admiral sent a flag of truce to propose an exchange of prisoners, upon principles to which, until then, the viceroy would never accede.

Huánuco, shortly after this time, signified its ad-

herence to the cause of independence.   To show
that the cry of *" Viva la patria !"* had also been
heard beyond the Andes, a young man arrived in
seventeen days from the banks of the Marañon, or
river of the Amazons, with five horses as a present
from his mother to the commander-in-chief of the
liberating army, wherever he might be found.   The
youth, having embraced the general, and seen the
patriot troops, returned to his widowed mother with
intelligence calculated to strengthen her hopes that
the hour of emancipation was at hand.

The viceroy, being informed that Major Reyes
had taken possession of Chancay, ordered Colonel
Don Geronimo Valdez to march to that place with
400 infantry and 200 cavalry.   He passed Ancon
on the night of the 7th November.   Reyes prepared to retire to Supe, a few leagues to the north
of Haura.   On perceiving the royalist force halt,
and form upon the road, which winds down a lofty
sand-hill at the entrance of the valley, a mile or
two from Chancay, the patriot infantry fell in; the
dragoons saddled their horses; and all retired whilst
Valdez sent a party to reconnoitre, instead of advancing with all his men; but so soon as he saw the
patriot infantry emerge from the cultivated valley
into the desert on the opposite side, Valdez pushed
on.   Reyes continued his retreat with the infantry.
Captain Brandsen remained with forty dragoons in
the rear, and, watching a favourable opportunity,
charged the royalist cavalry as they advanced by a
narrow road, walled on both sides, and drove them,

with the loss of three officers and many men, back
on their infantry.   Brandsen then rejoined his own
party.   The further retreat of the patriots was unmolested.   Valdez followed them at a cautious distance for three leagues, and then returned to Chancay.   On the morning of that day, San Martin set
sail for Callao.   On the following day he returned
to Ancon bay with Cochrane and the whole of the
squadron, including the Esmeralda, which was afterwards named the Valdivia.   In the evening of the
8th, the squadron and convoy again left Ancon.
They arrived on the 9th off Huacho, where, in the
course of the two following days, all the troops were
disembarked.   Huacho is twenty-eight leagues north
of Lima, and is the port of Haura.   The valley of
that name is two leagues in width at the end nearest
the sea, and ten leagues in length from west to east.
The surrounding country is a sandy waste.   San
Martin placed his troops on the right bank of a river,
fordable at only a few places.   This position cut off
the usual communication between Lima and Truxillo,
Lambayeque and Payta, by the roads on the coast.

On the 14th, Colonels Guido and Lusuriaga sailed
for Guayaquil, to compliment the provisional government on the recent changes; and to establish a good
understanding between it and the liberating forces.

On the 17th, the patriot infantry moved to Supe.
In the battalions Nos. 7 and 8 were above a hundred
blacks, who had been taken as recruits, the year before, from estates in the neighbourhood.   Upon this
occasion they were permitted to leave the ranks to
converse with their parents, brothers, or friends, who

came forth from their huts to welcome those who, so recently, had been their fellow-slaves. The account which the black soldiers gave of the service induced many slaves to inlist. Many royalists also passed over daily to the patriot troops.

Vidal, whose prowess materially contributed towards the reduction of Valdivia, was now here, having been promoted to a lieutenancy with the rank of brevet-captain. He had been sent, in a small vessel, from Valparaiso, by San Martin, a little time previous to the sailing of the liberating forces from that port. He was the bearer of proclamations and overtures addressed to the favourably disposed part of the Peruvian population. On attempting to land near Haura, the boat was swamped in a heavy surf; two men were drowned; and two others fell into the power of the royalists. Vidal alone escaped to his native town of Supe, where he remained. concealed, but not idle. He held frequent meetings with some of his young friends. A plan to surprise a royalist detachment of thirty-eight cavalry was agreed upon, and carried one night into triumphant execution by Vidal and fifteen of his townsmen. Thus supplied with arms and horses, he found no difficulty in forming a guerrilla, with which he commenced offensive operations by marching towards Lima, along the foot of the Andes, increasing his number and his means by the results of well-timed attacks; while, by dividing the attention of the royalists, he produced an important diversion.

On the 21st of November, the battalion No. 5 marched for Huaras, twenty-eight leagues to the

north-east. On the same day, the royalists advanced
from Chancay to Chancaíllo. In the expectation
that they were proceeding to Sayan, Alvarado fell
back from that place to Supe, where he arrived on the
24th. On the 25th, San Martin went from Supe to
Huacho, and directed Alvarado to reconnoitre the
next day. The only party which came in contact with
the royalists, was Lieutenant Pringuel and twenty
granaderos à caballo, whose retreat was cut off by
eighty royalist cavalry. The twenty patriots did not
surrender until three were killed and eleven wounded.
These small affairs, although not always successful,
produced an impression upon the royalists, which
perhaps accounts for the viceroy not employing his
superior numbers in a more decisive manner. On
the 27th, San Martin returned to Supe. On the
29th, the patriot Colonel Campino, having rapidly advanced with a small detachment of his battalion, took
Huaras by surprise, and made prisoners Lieutenant-
Colonel Lantaño, two other officers, and sixty-seven
rank and file.

The 2d December was an interesting day at
Supe. Twenty-two officers and eighty-five non-commissioned officers and privates were landed from a
lugger. These unfortunate men had been released,
in pursuance of the agreement between the viceroy
and San Martin for an exchange of prisoners. They
were the only survivors of upwards of a thousand
patriots, who had been made prisoners in the early
part of the revolution, on the plains of Buenos Ayres,
or in Upper Peru. Shackled together, they had been
forced to march from four to six hundred leagues,

and were afterwards immured in the dismal casemates of the castles of Callao.

In order to induce the prisoners to become apo-
states to the cause they had espoused, specious offers
were made to them by the viceroy: when these
allurements proved unavailing, he threatened them
with the death due to rebels, and the priesthood refused the consolations of religion to the sick at their
dying hour. To a man they adhered firmly to the
principles for which they had fought, but not more
than one out of ten outlived the horrors of nine
years of such imprisonment. .

It was an affecting sight to witness the arrival
of these heroic survivors, whose wan sallow countenances, meagre forms, and tottering gait, bespoke
the fatal inroads which prolonged captivity, under
ferocious gaolers, had made in their constitutions.
They were, of course, received with open arms by the
officers and soldiers of San Martin, amongst whom
they recognised many an old companion in arms.

San Martin gave these devoted soldiers the option
of returning to their homes; but such was their enthusiasm, that all volunteered to serve in the liberating army, to promote the cause of their country,
and avenge their own individual wrongs. Several of
them died in a short time, in consequence of the
sudden change from imprisonment to a life of liberty,
and others were afterwards killed in action. Of the
whole number, perhaps there are not twenty alive
at this day.

It would be well for the republican governments
to seek out the remnant of these brave unfortunates,

and to make the remainder of their days glide on
in ease and comfort.   The South American governments, *if they sought for them,* might easily trace
other deserving veterans, pinched by want, enfeebled
by disease, and scattered about in obscurity.   It
would well become them to pension invalids, and to
see that such pensions were actually paid; for it is to
the constancy and devotion of such men that they
owe their existence as *governments.*   They would do
themselves more honour by providing for veterans,
pining in poverty, than by sending forth proclamations
and decrees full of high sounding words and pompous
declamation.   Those " *doctores,*" who are so fond of
displaying their eloquence and fine writing, ought to
cite the examples of these veterans, instead of over-
loading their speeches and productions, with those
eternal pedantic allusions to the heroes of Greece
and Rome, which often make their language unintelligible to the mass of the people.   Liberty is their
constant theme; but it is to be regretted that the
practical illustration of it should be so little understood amongst them.   Independence has indeed been
attained, but Liberty has only hovered along the coast,
where she has been kept in strict quarantine.   Hitherto
her *name* is all that has been smuggled ashore.

   On the 3d December the Spanish battalion of Numancia, six hundred and fifty in number, passed over
in a body to the service of the patriots, with Captains
Don Tomas Heres and Don Ramon Herrera at their
head.   This battalion formed the rear-guard of a
royalist division, which had advanced from Copaca-

u 2

bana, to make a reconnoissance, as it was in the act of retiring from Palpa. It had marched all day, and halted about two leagues in the rear, when, suddenly countermarching, it carried into effect a plan conceived by Lieutenants Guas, Izquierdo, and other subalterns, who had the address to gain over not only the non-commissioned officers and men, but also the captains. The only persons who opposed the measure were Colonel Delgado and two officers, who were delivered up as prisoners to the patriots at Retes. The battalion was conveyed in two transports from Chancay to Huacho, where they arrived on the following day. The Numancia regiment was originally sent out from Spain to Venezuela, under General Morillo. At the time of their joining the patriot standard, the men were nearly all Colombians, who had been pressed into the service to fill up the vacancies occasioned by casualties. The Numancia was at this time in a state of discipline not inferior to any corps in any European service.

On the 8th of December, thirty-eight officers and several cadets absconded from Lima, and passed over to the patriot service, joining the advanced post at Chancay. Among them was Salaverri, a boy only twelve years of age, who had left his father's house, and who, on the party being closely pursued, displayed an extraordinary spirit of perseverance.

On the 5th of December, San Martin directed the infantry to resume its position on the right bank of the river Haura, which was now strengthened by field-works. The right of this extended line rested upon the sea, having Huacho in front, and the left at Sayan, seven or eight leagues up the valley of Haura. The royalists withdrew their advance to Asnapugio, two leagues north of Lima, in order to render desertion to the patriots more difficult.

It has been already stated that General Arenales, with about a thousand patriots, marched from Ica on the 21st of October, 1820. He entered Guamanga on the 31st, Guanta on the 6th of November, Xauxa on the 21st, and Tarma on the 23d. Here it was his intention to remain, in order to favour the rising of the Indians in support of the cause of independence; but having ascertained that the royalist General O'Reilly had arrived at Canta, on his way to Pasco, with one thousand infantry, one hundred and eighty cavalry, and a company of artillery, Arenales marched for the same point, with seven hundred and forty infantry, one hundred and twenty cavalry, and four field-pieces. On the 6th of December, he arrived at the Cerro de Pasco, where he found the royalists drawn up in line behind a deep ravine. On their right was swampy ground, and on their left a small lake. The patriot battalion No. 2, commanded by the gallant Lieutenant-Colonel Aldunate, made a detour of the lake, and threatened the royalists in flank, at the moment the No. 11, under the brave Lieutenant-Colonel Deza, attacked in front. The royalists gave way: one officer and fifty-eight rank and file were killed, one officer and nineteen rank and file wounded; twenty-eight officers and three hundred and fifteen rank and file, two pieces of artillery, and three hundred and sixty muskets, were taken on the field. The patriot cavalry, under Major Lavalle, followed up General O'Reilly * so closely, that he was taken prisoner by Lieutenant Don Vincente Suarez, and hardly a man of his division escaped. Lieutenant-Colonel Don Andres Santa Cruz delivered himself up to Major Lavalle, and from that period served with the independents.

This complete and brilliant affair was the close of Arenales's expedition. It had been attended with a degree of success which could not have been reasonably anticipated. Having accomplished so much, it was natural to expect that Arenales would have maintained his ground. But it happened, unfortunately, that Alvarado, who commanded the advance of San Martin's forces at Palpa, near Chancay, was misled by false intelligence, and wrote to Arenales in a way which induced the latter to re-cross the Andes. So soon as San Martin was informed of this mistake, he ordered Arenales to countermarch to Pasco; but he had already passed the Cordillera, and he was permitted to continue his march to Retes, where his division arrived on the 8th of January, in a deplorable state, in consequence of the sufferings, fatigue, and privations they had undergone in repassing the mountains.

The Indians who had been induced by Arenales to rise against the royalists made a gallant stand at Huancáyo and other points; but, unsupported, they were routed with merciless slaughter by the royalist General Ricaforte.

---

* O'Reilly was an Irishman. He was permitted to return to Spain, but this reverse preyed so much on his mind, that on the passage he threw himself overboard, in a state of delirium, and was drowned.

Pasco, and a considerable line of country to the south of it, was however held by a party which had been left at Ica, and which had been obliged to abandon that province and follow the movement of Arenales. Major Aldao, who commanded this detachment, distinguished himself on several occasions, and particularly in the affair at Huancáyo. He reached Pasco after Arenales had quitted that place.

On the 9th of January, 1821, the Araucano, Captain Carter, captured, after a gallant resistance, the Aranzazu, a Spanish schooner, of six guns and one long eighteen pounder on a traverse. On the 17th, the patriot transports arrived at Huacho, from the port of Chancay, and on the 18th, the O'Higgins and Valdivia arrived from the bay of Callao.

Dissensions broke out amongst the royalist chiefs about this time; which having considerable influence upon the progress of events, we shall now give a short account of them. General La Serna having been foiled by the *gauchos* in all his boasted plans of carrying on the war *en règle*, obtained the king's leave to return to Spain. In 1819 he arrived in Lima to embark; but in consequence of the expectation of an invasion from Chile, the viceroy promoted him to the rank of lieutenant-general, and prevailed upon him to remain. Soon after San Martin landed at Huacho, La Serna was ordered to march against him; but he refused to have any thing to do with military operations, unless the viceroy would consent to the establishment of a sort of aulic council, to be composed of generals, and to be called the *junta directiva*, in which the viceroy was to have only his individual vote. The directive junta was to decide upon all measures relative to carrying on the war; to have the power of applying the public funds to the payment of the army, in preference to the claims of other departments; to have the removal and nomination of governors and intendants of provinces, and other similar appointments. The majority of the junta being well disposed towards La Serna, the latter became, in point of fact, supreme in military matters. Colonel Loriga was named secretary to the junta.

Notwithstanding these arrangements, La Serna and the junta displayed but little spirit or ability. A very moderate degree of both would have enabled them to have driven the inferior forces of San Martin into the sea; but the measures of the junta appear to have been confined to encamping their army in the unhealthy position of Asnapugio, and to a demonstration of attack, which induced San Martin, on the 18th of January, to fall back from Retes to the right bank of the river Haura, where he reoccupied his former position, threw up additional redoubts to command the few fordable passages of the river, and fixed his head-quarters within a league of Haura, determined to make a stand should the royalists attack him.

The division Valdez moved upon Chancay, where Captain Raulet had an affair with its advance, in which he displayed his usual intrepidity, but was forced to retire with some loss. Before Valdez could advance any farther, he received an order from the vacillating directive junta which compelled him to return to Lima; in doing which he lost above a hundred men by desertion, most of whom passed over to the patriots.

Whatever might have been the faults of Pezuela, it is evident that the junta, which soon managed to invest itself with vice-regal authority, as to military matters, showed neither energy, local knowledge, nor information as to the numbers and quality of the invading forces. Had San Martin been attacked upon his first landing at Huacho, he would have been compelled to re-embark and make for Truxillo. Why the royalist army at Asnapugio, upwards of eight thousand in number, did not instantly march against San Martin, is a question which La Serna, Canterac, Valdez, and Loriga, are best able to answer. It may fairly be presumed that the victory of Pasco; the cutting out of the Esmeralda; and the rencontres of Nasca and Chancay, had impressed the minds of the royalist leaders with a considerable degree of diffidence. Certain it was that the sight of the patriot troops at this time inspired respect. The revolutions of Guayaquil and Truxillo, and the defection of the Numancia regiment, appeared to paralyze the *junta directiva*. Divisions arose between the Spanish chiefs; and Pezuela, who was loudly accused of being the cause of the desponding aspect of affairs, was deposed by military commotion on the 29th of January, 1821, when La Serna was appointed viceroy in his stead.

On the 24th January, one hundred individuals of various classes passed over to the patriots from Lima. Amongst the military were Colonel Gamarra and Lieutenant-Colonels Velasco and Elespuru. Of the

civilians, the most distinguished were Doctor Lopez
Aldana, Don Miguel Otero, and Don Joaquin Campino.

About this time a battalion of Peruvians was raised,
by order of San Martin.

On the 25th six hundred infantry and sixty cavalry, all picked men, were placed under the command of Miller, who received directions to embark
on a secret service, under the orders of Lord Cochrane. He proceeded to Huacho. On the day after
his arrival there, and whilst he was inspecting the detachments in the *Plaza*, Lady Cochrane galloped on
to the parade to speak to him. The sudden appearance of youth and beauty, on a fiery horse, managed
with skill and elegance, absolutely electrified the men,
who had never before seen an English lady : *que her-
mosa! que graciosa! que linda! que guapa! que
airosa! es un angel del cielo!* were exclamations
that escaped from one end of the line to the other.
The lieutenant-colonel, not displeased at this in-
voluntary homage, paid to the beauty of a country-
woman, said to the men, "This is our *generala.*"
Her ladyship turned her sparkling eyes towards the
line, and bowed graciously. The troops could no
longer confine their expressions of admiration to
half-suppressed interjections; loud *vivas* burst from
officers as well as men. Lady Cochrane smiled her
acknowledgments, and cantered off the ground with
the grace of a fairy.

On the 30th of January, the detachments embarked, and the squadron sailed. The object of the
expedition was to get possession of the castles of Cal-

lao. Some of the royalist officers there, having been gained over by San Martin, had engaged to hoist the independent flag, provided they were supported by the disembarkation of a respectable body of patriots; but on the day before the sailing of the troops from Huacho, Pezuela was deposed, and the garrison of Callao relieved, by troops in the interest of the new viceroy; the expedition consequently returned to Huacho on the 19th of February, without attempting a landing. The troops were disembarked, but kept in readiness to be sent afloat upon some other service.

On the 24th of February, Colonel Gamarra marched to the interior to take the command of the patriots in the sierra south of Pasco. Lieutenant-Colonel Don Leon Febres Cordero accompanied him as second in command.

The patriot advanced posts were at Chancay, eighteen leagues south of the position of their army, on the Haura. On the 6th March, Captain Roxas retired from Chancay before very superior numbers; but when he reached Torre Blanco, three leagues from Chancay, he turned round upon two hundred of his pursuers, made a brilliant charge, and, killing many, totally dispersed the remainder. The gallant Roxas was then permitted to continue his retreat unmolested. On the following morning the royalists evacuated Chancay, and retired to their encampment at Asnapugio. Chancay was re-occupied by the patriots. About this time, Vidal, now promoted to the rank of captain, with a *montonero* party defeated a detachment of the royalists at Quilcachamay. Two captains, one subaltern, seven rank and file were killed, and seven made prisoners.

On the 12th of March, Captain Quiros, with another montonero party, defeated another detachment of royalists at San Geronimo, in the vicinity of which the royalists had burned six villages.

On the 23d of March, Captain Vidal advanced to the *hacienda* of Pedreros, within three leagues of Lima, and carried off without opposition two hundred and forty horses and mules, and one hundred and fifty head of oxen. These and other operations have been detailed with minute precision, because it is considered that they illustrate the manner in which the war was carried on.

On the 13th of March, Cochrane sailed again from Huacho, on board the San Martin, with five hundred infantry and eighty dismounted cavalry, commanded by Miller. In the night of the 21st of March, this detachment, together with the marines of the squadron, landed at Pisco. At sunset on the 22d, their advanced post was at Chincha, eight leagues from the place of disembarkation, having forded the rapid river of Pisco with much difficulty and danger.

At six A. M. on the 26th, Captain Videla, with a company of infantry and a few cavalry, was attacked at Chincha by Colonel Loriga, who was repulsed, leaving four killed in the town.

On the 25th of March, the *Capitan de fragata* Don Manuel Abreu, commissioner from the King of Spain, arrived by the way of Panama at General San Martin's head-quarters. On the 29th April he proceeded to Lima, where the respectful manner in which he (Abreu) spoke of the patriot officers and army, gave umbrage to the ultra-royalists. This officer was ·sent out on the recommendation of the *liberal* party in the cortes to ascertain the precise nature of the demands of the Americans; but the same *liberales* did not scruple to avow, in conversation, that the real object of the mission was to gain time, and that their real determination was, *never to acknowledge the independence of America.*

At the beginning of April, Colonels Lusuriaga and Guido returned from Guayaquil, the provisional government of which place was firmly established. Considerable supplies of arms and ammunition had been sent there from Colombia.

On the 2d of April, orders were issued for the patriot army to be in readiness to advance from its position on the Haura.   The battalion No. 5 joined from Supe.   On the 12th of April, Captain Raulet surprised, and made prisoners, the royalist advanced post at Tambo Inca, five leagues from Lima.

About this time Arenales marched with three bat- · talions and the regiment of granaderos à caballo, towards the Cerro de Pasco, which was threatened by a royalist division under Colonel Carratalà.

On the 27th the patriot infantry broke up their encampment on the Haura; embarked in the transports at Salinas (three leagues south of Huacho); and sailed with the commander-in-chief to windward. The sick and baggage were sent to Supe.   The cavalry remained at Huacho.

On the 2d of May the royalist division under General Ricaforte was repulsed by the montoneros of the indefatigable Captains Vidal, Quiros, Elguerra, and Navajas, at Quiapata, near Canta. Ricaforte was severely wounded. The royalists left one officer and nineteen rank and file killed; two officers, forty-three rank and file, prisoners; many also were drowned in retreating across a river.

On the 12th of May the viceroy La Serna, as president of a *junta pacificadora*, proposed an armistice. San Martin appointed Colonel Guido, Don Juan Garcia del Rio, Don Ignacio de la Rosa, as commissioners, and Doctor Lopez Aldana, secretary to the deputation. They met the royalist commissioners, who were the sub-inspector of artillery, Don Manuel Llano y Najera, and the *alcalde de segundo voto*, Don Mariana Galdiano y Mendoza, at Punchauca, five leagues north of Lima.

On the same day the division of Arenales entered Pasco, and but for a dreadful snow-storm would have prevented the retreat of Carratalà and his division, which had taken possession of the town a few days previously. The subsequent notification of the armistice prevented Arenales from taking advantage of his position. Had it been delayed, Carratalà's division must have been taken near Huancayo.

San Martin had in the meantime arrived in the bay of Ancon, and had pushed his advanced posts to within two leagues of the capital. On the 23d of May, 1821, an armistice for twenty days was concluded. San Martin and the viceroy had an interview at Punchauca. The convoy, with the infantry, then returned from Ancon to Huacho.

The armistice being agreed upon, San Martin next

proposed the following terms as the basis of a treaty of peace.   Firstly, the recognition of the independence of Peru: secondly, that a *junta gubernativa* should be formed, composed of three individuals; one to be named by the viceroy, another by San Martin, and a third, on the part of the Peruvians, by a *junta electoral*, consisting of a member from each province. The *junta gubernativa* was to establish a provisional constitution, which was to be acted upon until the assembling of a general congress.   Thirdly, that two commissioners (one named by the viceroy, the other by San Martin) should be sent to Spain, to notify to the king the declaration of independence, and to invite his majesty to place a prince of his family on the throne of Peru, upon condition that the new sovereign should first swear to accept and maintain the constitution.   The other articles were relative to the position which each army was to occupy in the meanwhile.

The viceroy gave his personal assent to the proposals; but in two days after his return to Lima he wrote to San Martin, to acquaint him that he had consulted the chiefs of the royalist army, and that the proposals were pronounced to be inadmissible.

San Martin was well aware that the cabinet of Madrid would never be induced to ratify the treaty; but his secret object was to compromise the royalist commanders, so as to leave them no other alternative than to unite with him in the cause of independence.

CHAPTER XIV.

Operations of a patriot detachment in the vicinity of Pisco.—It re-embarks.—Proceeds to Arica.—Unsuccessful attempts to land.—Morro de Sama.—Arica taken.—Property captured.—Affair of Mirabe.—Moquegua.—Calera.—Armistice.—Patriot prisoners released from slavery.—Character of La Tapia.—Mrs. Gago.—The patriots re-embark at Arica.—Sail to the northward.

THE object of the expedition to Pisco, which sailed from Huacho on the 13th of March, was to interrupt the communication between Lima and the southern provinces.

The viceroy being informed that a patriot detachment had landed, ordered Colonel Garcia-Camba, with a royalist division, to march against it. Garcia-Camba proceeded forty leagues along the coast, as far as Chincha Baja, situated eight leagues north of Pisco, where he fixed his head-quarters. Between these places are the rivers Chincha and Pisco, which, at a distance of four or five leagues from each other, run in parallel lines from the Cordillera to the sea, fertilizing the extensive valleys through which they flow. In the most northern valley, and not far from the right bank of the Chincha, stand the two pleasant villages of Chincha Alta and Chincha Baja; and on the south side of the other river is the town of Pisco. The intervening desert was patroled by the patriots, who nominally held possession of the left bank of the Chincha. Their infantry occupied the town of Pisco, and their cavalry the estate of Caucato, on the opposite side of the river.   This estate once belonged to the Jesuits, and, when the independents landed in 1820, contained upwards of 900 negro slaves, many of whom entered their army.   Of those that still remained, Miller permitted thirty of the most able-bodied to join him.   They acted as guides, and were particularly useful when detachments had occasion to cross difficult or dangerous fords.   Some of the most intelligent of these negroes were often sent, in disguise, within the royalist lines.   They signalized themselves in frequent skirmishes, and being dressed in scarlet caps and ponchos, soon obtained the name of the *infernales*.   The cattle and other provisions left at Caucato, when the royalist proprietor abandoned his estate, furnished an ample supply, not only for the troops on shore, but also for the shipping in the bay of Pararca.   Miller devoted a few hours every day to business in Pisco, and generally, a little before sunset, repassed the river to sleep at his outposts.

The river of Pisco is particularly dangerous, as it expands during two or three months in the year to upwards of 150 yards in width; while, during the dry season of the *sierra*, it is a shallow rapid about twenty yards in breadth.   A year never passes without fatal accidents occurring in the fords, which is equally the case in all the large rivers on the coast of Peru, when swollen by the melting of the snows, or the rains which fall in the interior.   The stream of the Pisco was, at the period of which we are now speaking, at its greatest height; the water being of a turbid

whitish colour, and, when the sun glistens upon the
surface, it shoots past like a flood of molten lead.
The passenger about to cross, takes his feet out of the
stirrups, lifts up his legs, clings by his heels to the
horse's sides, and keeps his eyes steadily fixed upon
some object on the opposite bank; for if they rest but
for a moment on the rushing fluid, a giddiness seizes
even the strongest head, the rider loses his seat, and
the lassos of the *vadeadores,* or river guides, cannot
always ensure his rescue from the sweeping torrent.
It requires considerable coolness and dexterity to
pass the river with safety, and the horses must be
accustomed to it.   Some of those belonging to Can-
cato had been trained for that purpose, and it was
astonishing with what sagacity, and pilot-like skill,
they stemmed the current, and felt their way so as
to avoid stepping out of their depth.   The animal
should be allowed to have his head, but he must be
gently kept towards the stream, so as to meet it without ever presenting his side to its full force.   It is
necessary to incline or zigzag, according to the shoals
and shifting sand-banks.   These difficulties are increased, by the deeper parts of the river being thickly
covered with huge rolling stones, which become
rounded by attrition, as, in the course of ages, they
are driven rumbling from the Andes.   If the horse
gets entangled among these boulders, he plunges, and
is sometimes, together with his rider, carried down
the stream.   In this case the rider allows the horse
to recover himself by his own efforts; or if washed
from his saddle, he catches hold of his horse's tail,
and is dragged on shore at some distant point below.

From daybreak until dark *vadeadores* are stationed on the river-side to conduct passengers across, but when they consider the ford impracticable they retire to their huts.

Miller sometimes arrived at the river after the *vadeadores* had quitted it, but his *infernales* were equally expert as guides. Some would ride before, others follow close behind, and one or two keep along-side of Miller's horse; all of them shouting to encourage and direct the horses, and at the same time twirling their lassos over their heads in order to be prepared against accident. Although Miller slept almost every night in his wet clothes, he preserved his health for several weeks under circumstances which excited general surprise. He had remained free from the intermittent fever at Huacho, where scarcely a man of the liberating army had escaped being in the sick list from this cause. He began to flatter himself that his constitution was ague-proof; but he was now attacked by a malignant tertian fever, which in a few days reduced him to a skeleton. This was accompanied by delirium; and, during the intervals of the fever, his mind was racked by continual reports of the enemy's approaching; and this at a time when he was not able to rise from the mattrass on which he was stretched. His medical attendance was not good, but this was compensated by the affectionate and attentive nursing of his faithful servant Ortega, who, together with Ildefonzo, one of the *infernales*, were constantly at his bedside. The fidelity and attachment of these worthy fellows could not fail to cheer the mind of the patient. The Señora Martinez,

her two amiable daughters, and several other families, were exceedingly attentive to Miller during his
illness. It so happened that the royalist commander
was also confined to his bed by fever at Chincha. The
respective seconds in command limited their operations to threatening movements, which brought on
occasional affairs of outposts; but both parties kept
essentially on the defensive.

Of six hundred men who landed with Miller,
twenty-two died within a month, and one hundred
and eighty were in hospital, if that name can be applied to places almost destitute of surgeons, medicine,
and proper attendance. Most of the sick were sent
back to Huacho. The rest of the troops were in a
very feeble and sickly state.

One hundred slaves, six thousand dollars' worth of
plate melted into bars by order of Miller, five hundred jars of brandy, one thousand loaves of sugar, a
quantity of tobacco, and various other articles, taken
from estates belonging to Spaniards, or from natives
serving with the royalists, were sent on board the
squadron.

On the 18th of April, Miller was conveyed in a
litter on board the admiral's ship. Lord Cochrane,
who had been absent on a cruise to Callao, and had
only returned to the bay of Pararca on the 17th,
showed much concern at his ghastly appearance.

The health of the men continuing to decline, it
was determined to abandon Pisco, and to endeavour
to recruit their strength by a sea-voyage. In pursuance of this object, the troops were re-embarked
on the 22d of April, in the San Martin, which sailed

to the southward, leaving the other vessels of the squadron to proceed back to Callao.

On the 6th of May, they were becalmed twenty-five or thirty miles from Arica. A part of the troops were ordered into the boats with Miller. They pulled along the coast for four hours without being able to make out a landing-place. A breeze then arising, the San Martin came up with them, and took them on board, much exhausted from the heat of the weather, and from having left the ship without a supply of water. The San Martin then made for the bay of Arica, and anchored out of range of the guns of the fort. A summons sent to the governor, inviting him to surrender, was treated with disdain. He had a garrison of from three to four hundred men, and the only landing-place was defended by a battery mounting six pieces of artillery. The swell was unusually great, so that a disembarkation appeared imprac-ticable. This was confirmed by information acquired from neutral vessels at anchor in the bay. Neverthe-less, an attempt was made a little to the southward, where Captain Wilkinson, of the navy, in his anxiety to see the patriot soldiers on shore before the riches of Arica could be placed out of reach, fancied he had discovered a spot favourable for disembarkation. Two hundred and fifty men got into the boats, and pushed off at midnight. The sea rolled in long surges, but the surface was unruffled. The stars shone bright enough to render visible a remarkable white patch on the coast that served as a land-mark. Wilkinson and Miller, with thirty men, led the way in the first launch. On nearing the shore, they backed in stern-

most; but on arriving within a few fathoms, they
were lifted on the crest of a huge roller, carried
along with

"The torrent's smoothness ere it dash below,"

and thrown, with the velocity of thought, into a yawn-
ing abyss formed by large black loose rocks.   Fortunately these rocks prevented the launch from being
drawn back by the receding surge, and for a few
moments it was left *high and dry*.   The men had
scarcely time to jump out and run, when a second
roller dashed the launch to pieces.   The breadth of
snow-white foam formed a terrific contrast with the
dark line of coast, and the water, which had previously
appeared to be smooth as a mill-pond, now bubbled
around rocks which, until then, had escaped observation.   The launches astern were warned to keep off,
and the nearest dropping a grapple, was apparently
encompassed with breakers.   The situation of Miller's
party became extremely critical.   The men had saved
their muskets, but their ammunition was rendered
unserviceable.   Re-embarkation did not seem to be
within the bounds of possibility, and their number
was too small to justify any hope of success from a
rash attempt to surprise the garrison.   Yet, upon
consultation, this last was considered to be the only
alternative, and it was decided that the party should
creep into the town, surprise the guard, get into the
fort, and hold out until succour could be obtained.
Accordingly the men formed, and a search was made
for a path, but it was found that the flat beach,
a few yards wide, extended only to a very short

distance either way, and was walled in by an almost
perpendicular cliff. After climbing and groping
about for nearly two hours, no outlet could be discovered in any direction. The party returned, and
sat down in a state bordering on despair. It was very
probable that the royalists had overheard the repeated
hailing from the launches, which still kept their
stations, and it was apprehended that daylight would
bring an additional misfortune, in the shape of an
enemy on the edge of the cliff, whence they could
despatch the patriots by a few volleys, or by hurling
down fragments of rock upon their heads. In this
desponding interval, Captain Wilkinson discovered
a ledge which projected some way into the sea. He
instantly brought into play the resources of his professional experience, and adopted a plan which, in
ordinary times, might have been considered an act of
madness. He ordered one of the launches to pull in,
and anchor as closely to the ledge as possible. This
was done, though with great peril to all on board.
A whale-boat was sent from the launch with a small
hawser, one end of which was thrown upon the rock
and made fast. By these means the whale-boat was
warped to and from the launch. Only two men could
stand at one time upon the ledge, to which they were
obliged to cling, drenched by the spray, until a lull,
which commonly occurs between every seventh or
ninth surge or breaker, enabled the whale-boat to
warp to the lee side of the rock, and to remain there
just long enough to allow the men to lower themselves by the hawser with the greatest celerity, and
drop into the boat. By this tedious process the party

was taken off, with the loss of only one man, who was
drowned.   At sunrise a party of the Spaniards was
seen on the brink of the cliff.

On the following night a second attempt was made
to the northward, when the same party was again entangled, and nearly swamped, amidst breakers, from
which they got clear only by dint of extraordinary
exertions.   The fatigue, the immersions, and the
anxieties of these two nights, completely exhausted
every man employed.

These attempts to land so near Arica ought, perhaps, not to have been made.   Persons from neutral
vessels had asserted that the disembarkation was
absolutely impracticable, but Cochrane, from past
experience of neutrals, doubted their information.
Droves of mules, heavily laden, were occasionally
seen to issue from the town, when every telescope
on board was eagerly caught hold of and pointed to
the moving convoy.   The *auri sacra fames* multi-
plying the number of animals, and converting their
cargoes from bales of merchandize into bags of dollars, gave rise to numberless suggestions for the soldiers to be sent on shore, and Cochrane's better judgment at last gave way to these importunities.   On
this occasion it was curious to contrast the serious
countenances of the troops destined to land on the
almost hopeless enterprise with the buoyant spirits
of the naval *lookers-on* from the ship.

The soldiers were next transhipped to two small
schooners, which had been made prizes of in the
course of the cruise, and sent to the Morro de Sama,
a miserable port, ten leagues to the northward of

Arica. The vessels had temporary rudders only, and were steered, even before the wind, with difficulty. The naval person who had charge of them was a petty officer, who had never been on the coast. Provisions and water for twenty-four hours were put on board; but it was two days before Miller, who was obliged to act as pilot, could make out the Morro de Sama, and even then he stood towards the inlet without being certain he was right; but the wind was light, the sea rolled very high astern, and absolute want left no other alternative than to get on shore somewhere. Though abounding with rocky dangers, it proved to be the desired haven, but was so fringed round with surf, that landing still appeared impracticable. Lord Cochrane having become uneasy for the fate of the detachment, sent Lieutenant Freeman, of the Chileno navy, to afford assistance. Freeman's launch entered the creek as the schooner came to anchor, and with his able and indefatigable assistance the men were got ashore. There was a small well at the Morro, but it was brackish; and there was scarcely enough water in it to quench the thirst of half a dozen people. They had then to march eight leagues before a good draught of water could be obtained. Upon landing, the knees of the men trembled under them, as they had not entirely regained their strength from the effects of ague, and they could not walk more than half an hour at a time without lying down on the sand to recover themselves.

Upon reaching the top of the mountain of Morro de Sama, which is too steep to ride, either up or down, and three miles to the summit by the winding

path, a delightful breeze fanned their faces; refreshed
the exhausted men, and each felt his strength increase as he went along.   The only guide was a soldier, who had travelled the road a few times.   He
was frequently alarmed by doubts as to being in the
right direction.   The anxieties of this night were
rendered perfectly agonizing.   Tormented by thirst;
knowing that no water could be obtained in the line
of road they had passed over; and uncertain whether the route they had taken was the right one, the
horrors of their situation were further aggravated by
the knowledge that men's lives were frequently lost
in those extensive deserts, where, for many leagues,
nothing is to be discerned but a barren sea of sand.
Nothing could exceed their joy when the guide discovered, by some remembered hillock, that he was
still in the right track.

A fatiguing march of thirteen hours brought the
patriots to the entrance of the valley of Sama (at
9 A. M.) in a very distressed state.   The sun, which
shone scorchingly, and reflected from a deep loose
sand, had deprived them of the invigorating effects
of the previous night breeze.   So soon as the party
caught sight of vegetation, every man rushed forward in search of water; some who could with difficulty but creep till this moment, now ran with the
celerity of greyhounds to the valley.

At Sama horses were procured for the commanding
officer and a few others.   On the next day the party
advanced to Tacna, a distance of twelve or fourteen
leagues, and about twenty from their place of landing.
Tacna contains a population of four thousand souls.

Miller rode on with ten or a dozen soldiers mounted,
and was enthusiastically received by the clergy, municipality, and inhabitants, who met him outside the
town.

About this time Don B. Landa introduced himself to Miller. He was nearly six feet in height, and
of a gaunt raw-bone figure, with rather a ruddy, but
lengthened, care-worn visage. After some conversation, he said, " You will hear numerous accounts of
me, and but few that are favourable. The patriots
will tell you that I was once a persecuting royalist,
and they will tell you the truth. They doubt the sincerity of my present intentions; but believe me, when
I assure you, that I have been for some time a bitter
and determined foe to the Spaniards; and if you will
trust me without slighting me (*sin desayrarme*), I
will not betray your confidence. You know nothing
of the localities of these provinces, whereas I know
every body, and every inch of ground. I know, too,
that you must greatly stand in need of a person of my
experience. Rely upon me, and I will serve you
well." There was an air of sincerity and good faith
in his frankness which led to his being immediately
employed; and his subsequent conduct fully justified
the ready confidence reposed in him. Landa had
been a lieutenant-colonel of militia, and the subdelegate of a province under the Spaniards. He was
allowed to retain the same military rank in the patriot
service.

Major Soler had marched from the Morro de
Sama by the coast to Arica, which was abandoned
at his approach. He overtook the fugitive garrison

in the valley of Asapa, and made about one hundred prisoners, most of whom, with four royalist officers, were admitted into the patriot service by Miller, whom Soler rejoined at Tacna. The naval force remained in possession of Arica, and many houses were plundered.

One hundred and twenty thousand dollars, in specie, were taken near Locumba by a detachment sent by Major Soler. This sum, and four thousand dollars found in the custom-house at Tacna, together with about three hundred thousand dollars' worth of merchandize, Spanish property, were conveyed to Arica, and there embarked. Original documents, sufficient to condemn the cargoes of the Lord Cathcart, Colombia, and Joseph, lying in the port, were found in the archives of Tacna; so that the false papers furnished by British merchants in Rio Janeiro to cover these cargoes became unavailable, and the fraudulent system of cloaking Spanish property sent to the Pacific was thus exposed.

Another instance of the same kind occurred with respect to the English vessels, the Lord Suffield and the Edward Ellice, which were seized about this time by the Chileno ships of war blockading Callao, and sent to Valparaiso for adjudication. It so happened, that Lord Cochrane had received information from London, proving that the cargoes of these two vessels were, *bona fide*, Spanish property, and pointing out the precise method by which false papers were to be obtained at Gibraltar. The vessels were justly condemned; but this decision was afterwards reversed, as it is believed, by some of the judges being bought

over; and Lord Cochrane is, at the present moment
(1829), bound over to answer to an action for da-
mages and demurrage.

During these operations of the patriots, General
Ramirez had ordered three detachments to march
against them. One, of three hundred and eighty
men, proceeded from Arequipa by the way of Moquegua, where it was augmented by one hundred
rank and file; another, from Puno, of two hundred
and eighty, and another from La Paz, both by way
of Tarrata. All three were to form a junction at
Tacna, and then "to drive the insurgents into the
sea." But, contrary to the calculations of Ramirez,
the patriots had advanced from Arica into the interior, as already stated.

The greatest part of the rich cargoes of the three
vessels before mentioned, consisting of Canton crapes
and other Indian goods; French wines and brandies;
English pale ale, brown stout, and other good cheer,
was found in the public warehouses of Tacna. A
part of this royalist property was immediately sent
to Arica, and shipped in the San Martin. The soldiers had scarcely time to taste these unusual luxuries,
when they were ordered away; but such was their enthusiasm, that the idea of marching to cross bayonets
with the enemy prevented a single expression of regret on leaving so many good things behind. The
keys of the storehouses were given up to commissioners appointed to continue the shipment of the
prize goods.

So soon as Miller ascertained the movements of
the royalist detachments, he determined to attack

them separately; for which purpose, he advanced
from Tacna to meet the party of Colonel La Hera,
sent from Arequipa.   Miller's force consisted of
three hundred and ten infantry, seventy cavalry, and
about sixty well mounted volunteer peasantry; with
which, on the 20th of May, he arrived at the hamlet
of Buena Vista, situated in a romantic spot, at the
foot of the Cordilleras, which a little higher up are
covered with snow.   The bracing and almost wintry
feeling of the weather was delightful to men who
had so lately been traversing scorching sands.   Here
the patriot commander, having, during the night,
learned that Colonel La Hera had changed his direction from Locumba, and marched towards Tica-
-pampa, determined to direct his own course with all
possible speed to Mirabe, in order to prevent the
royalist parties from La Paz and Oruro forming a
junction with that from Arequipa.   Soon after day-
break, the patriot division began its march; and to
prevent the possibility of royalist emissaries acquiring
correct information, Miller pursued a track as if he
intended going to another place.   Having proceeded
some leagues, he turned to the right, and took the
path which led to Mirabe.

The march from Buena Vista to Mirabe, a distance
of fifteen leagues, is across a stony desert entirely
destitute of water and vegetation; but Miller having
taken the precaution, before he left Tacna, of ordering
eight mules to be loaded with hollands *, a halt was

---

* This hollands had very fortunately been sent from Antwerp ready packed
in green cases, each containing six large quadrangular bottles.   These formed
very handy packages, eight of them being just a mule load.

occasionally made, and a reviving dram sparingly
served out. Thus moderately stimulated, men pushed
on in steady compact order, which they preserved
even after the darkness of night had thrown an additional horror over the cheerless, pathless, and, to
all but the guides, unknown waste. The march
was one of deep and anxious interest, and, with the
exception of Colonel Landa, no one was made acquainted with their destination. The officers medi-
tating upon the probability of attacking double numbers, they knew not where, nor how soon, felt the
hazardous nature of their position; and being con-
scious that there was no retreat, they mechanically
grasped the hilts of their swords as if by way of con-
firming their courage. It may appear strange or
exaggerated to record this; but it was so, and those
who have been placed in similar circumstances will
not consider it extravagant. The last two leagues
was a rapid descent amidst precipices and projecting
rocks, called the *mal paso*, or bad pass, and is so
narrow as to admit of advancing in single files only,
and on foot. After a toilsome march of eighteen
hours, the patriots reached, at midnight, the rugged
bank of a stream which rushes through the valley of
Mirabe. The royalists had, on the preceding afternoon, possessed themselves of the mud enclosures
around the cultivated grounds of the little hamlet of
Mirabe, situated in the hollow of the opposite or
right bank, where they awaited the arrival of their
expected reinforcements, which at that time had
halted only three leagues distant from them, up the
valley, and on the *left* bank of the river.

As the route from Sama to Mirabe was considered impassable for troops, the royalists had not the slightest idea of the proximity of their enemies; but the indiscreet zeal of a patriot officer in front announced to the Spaniards their unexpected approach. He had been sent on from the entrance of the *mal paso* with five mounted infantry and as many peasants, but he disobeyed orders by advancing too fast and too far in front. In the darkness of the night he came unawares upon a small royalist piquet, guarding four or five hundred horses and mules grazing in an enclosed field. A royalist officer, Lieutenant Callao, and two men, were made prisoners; but the remainder escaped and gave the alarm. The royalist division under La Hera, being at not more than a few hundred yards from the spot, were awakened from a sound sleep, and immediately opened a brisk, but random, fire. One of the patriot peasants, having advanced too far, was taken prisoner; the rest of the party, after discharging their muskets two or three times, retired with all practicable speed, and, without much caution, scrambled up the bank of the valley by the rough track they had just before descended. As they approached the head of the patriot column they vociferated, in the loudest and most ridiculous manner, *auxilio! auxilio!* help! help! Their noises, added to the fire of musketry, echoed and re-echoed among the mountains, gave birth to feelings of intense solicitude, soon however assuaged by the Spanish prisoners being brought before Miller, who ascertained from them the position of the royalists. Determining to attack before they had time for reflection, the march was instantly quickened, the drums beat, the bugles sounded, and the cavalry rushed on heedless of obstacles, and closely followed by the infantry, all uttering the Indian yell, until the progress of the latter was arrested by the rapid flood above described. The gallant Captain Hill with ten brave marines were alone enabled to cross, and even they were carried off their legs by the current; but the river was narrow, and they fortunately reached the opposite bank with no other accident than their ammunition being rendered unserviceable. The patriot horse, which had continued to advance, were driven back. They were not permitted to repass, but made to form above the ford. A rocket party, under the direction of Captain Hind, was detached to an eminence on the left, from which it occupied the attention of the enemy: for the same object another small party was sent to the right. Miller remained below with the rest of his men, who sat down in line on the bank of the torrent, unperceived and unheard by the enemy, who were not more than at pistol-shot distance; but the intervening space was covered with wood.

Whilst the royalists kept up an unceasing fire upon the rocket parties, Miller conveyed his infantry to the other side of the torrent by mounting a foot soldier behind each dragoon, who went and returned until the whole of the troops had effected the passage. During this operation Captain Hill was posted in a wood, close to the royalists, where he remained quiet, having orders not to suffer a musket to be fired unless the enemy sallied from his position, in which

case the patriot advance was to stand its ground at
all risks; and such was the determined spirit with
which Hill and his marines were animated, that it is
more than probable they would have perished sooner
than have given way. On Miller's crossing the river
a bright glimmering light was perceived. A peasant
guide, who had just been wounded in the shoulder,
said that it must proceed from some habitation. The
patriots immediately advanced, jumped over low mud
walls, threaded their way up entangled vineyards, and
reached the house to which the light had been a
beacon. Captain Plaza was now sent with a detachment to fire down upon the enemy, who had not
stirred from their parapeted position, and were not
aware that the patriots had effected the passage of
the river. Plaza mingled a great deal of well-timed
jocularity with his accustomed coolness, and told his
men that, having regaled themselves with excellent
water at the stream, they must now fight for a supper.
The royalists finding themselves unexpectedly as-
sailed on that side, withdrew to a short distance. A
good deal of random firing took place during the
night, and the patriots lost an officer and seventeen
men. Whilst this was going on, Miller placed his
infantry on a sort of mountain level, about a quarter
of a mile in width, which was flanked on one side by
the steep acclivity of the valley next the river, and
bounded on the opposite direction by a range of bold
hills: his cavalry was kept below in some lucern enclosures, where the jaded horses were allowed to feed.
The night was one of extreme anxiety, for the patriot
commander was ignorant of the precise position of the

enemy, and the nature of the ground whereon the
struggle of the following day was to take place. An
hour before daybreak he advanced on foot with Lieutenant Correa and an orderly, to reconnoitre as well
as the darkness would permit. They had not proceeded above a hundred yards when a slight rattling
of the orderly's sword startled a Spanish sentinel, who
challenged sharply. They instinctively held their
breath, and the listening vidette hearing no further
noise, naturally concluded that all was right, and gave
no alarm. They retired a few paces, and sending
Correa to the rear with orders, Miller, with his
orderly, lay upon the ground until the first faint
gray of morning enabled him to distinguish objects.
The first that caught his attention was what he
imagined to be a line of chalky cliff; but as objects
became rather more distinct, he perceived an occasional movement in this line, and thereby knew
that it must be the linen cover of the chacos of the
royalist army. On this discovery Miller withdrew.
Fortunately for the patriots, there was nothing that
could be easily discerned by that light about their
uniforms, as their accoutrements were dirty, and
their musket-barrels had lost their glitter. Besides
which their line was hidden in the deep shadows of
the ridge immediately behind them, so that they
were not perceived by the royalists for many minutes
after the latter had become distinctly visible. The
patriot cavalry, already in movement, agreeably to
previous orders, were hastened up from the pastures
below, and entered the arena, fresh and cheerily, just
in time to form on the right of the infantry, in a line

parallel to that of the royalists, and at the distance
from them of about two musket-shots. Upon perceiving this, the Spaniards faced to their left and
attempted to gain the ridge, but the patriot horse,
followed by the infantry in column, charged with
such celerity as completely to frustrate these intentions, and to cut off their retreat. Driven to the
edge of a precipitous ridge, they fought with desperate valour for fifteen minutes. Ninety-six were
killed on the spot, and one hundred and fifty-seven
taken prisoners, most of them wounded; four hundred mules were also taken. About sixty infantry
and eighty cavalry escaped. Immediately after the
royalists had given way, the expected reinforcement
from Puno and La Paz, mounted upon mules, appeared in sight, upon which the patriots were recalled to face a fresh enemy. A few rockets were
discharged at this party as it began to cross the river
at the place where, during the night, it had been
forded by the patriots. The reinforcement perceiving that it had arrived too late, instantly countermarched.

The conduct of the patriots throughout this incursion was most exemplary. The officers of the
small division were men really deserving of the name
of soldiers, and would have done honour to any service. Captain Don José Videla, a native of Mendoza, was a person of few words; but no officer understood his duty better, or enjoyed more popularity
than the sedate but brave and zealous Videla. Captains Marure and Aramburu, Lieutenants Asagra,
Dominguez, Ballejos, Vicente Suares, La Tapia, and

others, were officers of tried valour. The conduct of
Hind and Hill, both Englishmen, reflected credit on
their own country, and the cause they had espoused.
The latter was afterwards drowned at sea.

. In the affair of Mirabe, Mr. Welsh, private surgeon to Lord Cochrane, and who had volunteered
his services to accompany Miller on this occasion, was
amongst the slain. The loss of this fine young Scotchman was very much deplored. There was a liveliness of manner and a kindness of heart perceptible
in his assiduous attentions to the sick and wounded,
which won for him more than the esteem of all. The
soldiers wept over his remains; and such was the idea
of his worth in the minds of the inhabitants of Tacna,
that the news of his fall produced, in the principal
families, sensations of regret to an extent unusual
upon so short an acquaintance. Cochrane wrote that
he would sooner have lost his right arm; and Miller
had to lament a friend, whose unwearied attendance
had beguiled the irksome hours of a sick-bed and long
suffering from severe wounds. Welsh was mourned
alike by the soldiers and by the sailors, by his countrymen and by South Americans; and his early death
was a severe loss to the patriot service.

. On the afternoon of the 22d, Miller continued the
pursuit of the few cavalry and infantry of La Hera's
division to Moquegua, thirty leagues to the northward. On reaching Locumba they halted; the
friendly inhabitants brought out provisions, but the
soldiers were too much fatigued to cook them. The
calls of hunger were overpowered by drowsiness, and
they threw themselves down to sleep under the shade

of some trees. At the end of three hours they were
aroused to continue the chase. About midnight they
were met by two enthusiastic boys, each seventeen
years of age, who, on hearing of the landing of the
patriots, had ran away from college at Arequipa.
These spirited lads were immediately made cadets *.
Lieutenant-Colonel Landa, with a few armed peasants,
rode on ahead, and before daybreak gained the portillo,
or narrow pass, in the ridge that fringes the basin in
which Moquegua is situated; and thus prevented any
egress from the town by the eastern outlet. After a
most wearisome march, the patriots entered Moquegua
at 9 A. M. on the 24th of May. The fugitive royalists
had arrived only a few hours before. Their commander, La Hera, uninformed of the near approach of
his enemy, had proceeded towards Puno. The party
he left behind, having refreshed themselves, were on
the point of following, when Miller galloped into the
plaza with twenty dragoons under the brave Vicente
Suares. A skirmish ensued, but the royalists slowly
retreated in good order, until the zealous Major Soler
coming up with the rest of the patriot cavalry, a charge
was made half a mile outside of the town, when a
royalist officer and thirteen rank and file were killed,
and the rest made prisoners, with the exception of an
adjutant and his servant, who escaped the vigilance of
their pursuers, first by the goodness of their horses,
and then by disguising themselves in the *poncho* and
clothes of a peasant, whom they met accidentally on
the road, and murdered for the sake of obtaining his

---

* Both became highly deserving officers. One of them, Don Mariano
Rivero, was afterwards made a prisoner of war at Ica, and being of a feeble
constitution, he died from fatigue on his route to the depôt of Chucuito.

dress. Colonel Portocarrera, governor of the province
of Moquegua, passed over to the patriots.

The town of Moquegua contains nearly ten thousand inhabitants. They received the patriots with
every expression of unbounded satisfaction, and, as a
proof of their sincere attachment to the cause of
independence, voluntarily and cheerfully contributed
the means to strengthen and give full efficiency to
the little division.

On the 25th of May, Miller learned that from
two to three hundred Spaniards were passing the
heights of Torata, about five leagues distant. This
was the detachment which appeared in the rear of
the patriots at the conclusion of the affair of Mirabe,
and was now proceeding to Arequipa. The lieutenant-colonel, with a hundred and forty of his infantry upon mules, and a few cavalry, set out in pursuit. The brave Landa, with eighteen or twenty
well-mounted armed peasantry, accompanied the detachment. At sunset they reached Torata, an Indian
town, situated at the foot of a lofty ramification of
the Andes, where they learned that the enemy had
bivouacked the preceding night on the hills which
overlook the town, and had recommenced their
march at noon. The patriots halted for three hours,
and having eaten a good supper, and obtained some
fresh horses and mules, they continued their march
by a track which ran up and down, and along the
sides of tremendous mountains. The weather was
intensely cold; a good deal of soroche prevailed; the
night was very dark, and the march was as dangerous
as it was tedious and harassing. The party lost its

way for some hours, and three men fell, with their
animals, down a ravine.   A mule was killed, but the
men were not seriously injured.   More than half
the regular troops lagged behind from excessive fatigue; the rest reached Calera (fourteen leagues from
Moquegua, and sixty-three from Arica) at 9 A. M.
on the 26th of May, soon after the royalist party
had arrived by a shorter road, without being aware
that their pursuers were at hand.   They had scarcely
time to saddle, and fly from the place, when the
patriots entered.   In the course of a further pursuit, of three leagues, all were taken prisoners or
dispersed.   Of above six hundred royalists, who
composed the two detachments sent from Arequipa
and Puno, perhaps not above twenty rejoined the
Spanish army.   The garrison of Arica, about four
hundred men, had also been annihilated; so that in
less than a fortnight after the few patriots landed,
they had killed, made prisoners, or put *hors de combat*, upwards of a thousand of the royalist army.
This success was the result of long, difficult, and
forced marches, which the patriots underwent with
a cheerfulness and patience worthy the highest admiration.   Hunger and thirst in the desert and in
the mountain wilds were borne with uncomplaining
resignation ; but irresistible sleep often overpowered
the soldier, who fell as if in a trance from his mule
as he rode along, and was sometimes left to follow
as he could.

   During the march of the patriots, whenever they
fell in with Indians, they immediately engaged them
to scour the country and bring in the straggling

royalists, who, having thrown away their arms, for the most part quietly submitted. To encourage the Indians in this service, money was given to them, and now and then a jaded mule, which they were permitted to retain on their delivering a Spanish prisoner at Moquegua.

The Indians were assured that neither tribute nor sacrifices were required of them; that the patriots, their brethren in arms, came to liberate them from tyranny. Such assurances and conduct towards them produced an extraordinary and enthusiastic feeling of patriotism in these long outraged and oppressed aborigines. Miller organized a guerrilla party, and having waited for a moonlight night, that he might cross the desert with greater facility, he retired from Calera, leaving there an officer and six regulars. This place being situated near the regions of perpetual snow, his men had begun to suffer greatly from cold and difficulty of respiration.

After a most fatiguing march, he re-entered Torata, celebrated for the excellence of its bread, and situated at the foot of high mountains, over which the road to Calera winds. On the next day, the 29th, the patriot party, worn out with fatigue, re-entered Moquegua, hailed by the enthusiastic greetings of the inhabitants.

Moquegua is surrounded by high hills. Ague is very prevalent. The position was objectionable as a defensive one; and Miller, considering his force too weak to attack General Ramirez, who held Arequipa with seven hundred and fifty-four royalists, fell back, on the 4th of June, with the cavalry to

Santo Domingo, two leagues from Moquegua. The infantry were ordered to La Rinconada, five leagues in the rear.

On the same day, it was ascertained that La Hera was advancing from Santiago de Machaca with new reinforcements towards Tacna, to cut off the retreat of the patriots. The patriot sick were sent to Ilo. The inhabitants of Moquegua became a little alarmed at these ominous preparations; but were re-assured by seeing a guerrilla party, and a few regulars, despatched to approach as near to Arequipa as the commanding officer, Lieutenant La Tapia, judged it prudent.

On the 7th of June, the patriot infantry marched from the Rinconada. On the 8th, Miller overtook them at Sitana, a place consisting of half a dozen huts, two leagues west of Locumba. On the 9th, the cavalry arrived from Santo Domingo, and the whole division bivouacked on a commodious estate near Sitana.

On the 10th, Miller set out for Ilo. A ride of ten leagues over hill and dale brought him to the *Olivares*, an estate of olive-groves, celebrated for the fruit being nearly as large as pigeons' eggs, and reckoned superior in flavour to the olives of Seville. They are cured by being soaked in oil, which softens and swells the pulp. Small pieces of onion are often minced up and eaten with the olives, which, with good bread, make no contemptible repast, especially after a long ride over the desert. Continuing his journey for four leagues along the sea-coast, Miller arrived at Ilo, which, like most other places on the desert, is mud-built and miserable. He went on board three small brigs which Cochrane had sent to Ilo, to remain there as a resource, in case of emergency. He then visited about thirty sick men, placed under the care of a couple of elderly females; there being no medical officer with the patriots. Assistant-Surgeon Molloy, an Irish gentleman, who had been destined to replace the loss of Mr. Welsh, in attempting to land near the town of Ilo, was drowned, together with the boat's crew.

Miller having left some orders with the *alcalde* of the town, set out on his return to Sitana on the 11th, whence his division had been ordered to march, and which he came up with, at Sama, the same evening.

His guide on this journey was Captain Belasquez, of the militia, who had been brought up by a missionary. He spoke several Indian dialects with fluency, and was master of some curious acquirements: one of the most useful was, that of imitating the voices of different animals. He was often employed to go into the woods and enclosures of the valleys, where he would neigh like a mare; when, if any horses were hidden there by the royalists, they would neigh in answer, and soon became patriot property.

On the 12th, Miller rode to Tacna, eight leagues, where he received intercepted correspondence (announcing the armistice of Punchauca) from Ramirez to La Hera, who was supposed by Ramirez to have advanced to the coast: but having approached within four leagues of Tacna with eight hundred men, including the battalion of Gerona, commanded by Colonel Ameller, La Hera returned to Santiago

de Machaca, under the impression that the patriot
force was superior in numbers to his own. This
miscalculation arose from several letters from La
Hera being intercepted by Miller, who made many
of the persons they were addressed to sit down and
write such answers as best suited his views.

On the 14th of June, Miller concentrated his
small force at Tacna, excepting the small party in
advance at Moquegua. He sent an officer and some
montoneros in the direction of Santiago de Machaca,
and another to summon the governor of Tarapaca.
Miller sent Captain Hind to La Hera, informing
him of the armistice of Punchauca. Hind entered
Santiago de Machaca after sunset, unobserved by the
royalist sentries, and coolly entered the house of La
Hera, who was taking wine with some of his officers.
On recovering from their extreme astonishment at
being so broken in upon, Hind was received in the
most cordial manner, and entertained with good fare
and the best bed they could procure. The next morning it was agreed that the armistice of Punchauca
should be observed by the contending divisions in .
the Intermedios. After three days' countermarch,
Captain Hind reached Tacna with the preliminary
articles, which were afterwards ratified by Miller on
the part of the patriots, and by General Ramirez, at
Arequipa, on the part of the royalists.

Hostilities having ceased, and Lord Cochrane
thinking, no doubt, that they would not be renewed,
sailed from Ilo for Chorrillos and Ancon on the 2d
of July, to have an interview with San Martin. Miller had, at this time, pushed his advanced posts to

within fourteen leagues of Arequipa; to within twelve leagues of Santiago de Machaca; and to within a few miles of Iquique : so that the patriots held possession of the principal points of one hundred leagues of country from north to south, and thirty leagues from east to west.

He had augmented his force as far as the supply of arms taken from the enemy would allow. It consisted of nearly nine hundred rank and file, well clothed and equipped. Besides this, several montonero parties had been formed and spread over the country. A communication had also been opened with Colonel Lanza, a celebrated guerrilla chief in Upper Peru.

The two worthy patriots, Don Juan Agustin Lyra, and Señor de Lobaton, arrived from Majes at Arica, with letters from Colonel Don Domingo Tristan, and Doctor Cordova, *cura* of Salamanca, both possessing great influence in the province of Chuquibamba, soliciting the co-operation of the patriot division, and offering to support any movement by every exertion in their power. But as Miller had been left without adequate means to transport his men from point to point by sea, he was unable to take advantage of those favourable proposals.

In the course of these operations, the spirit of patriotism had been awakened, and it spread with enthusiastic rapidity. Even such of the inhabitants as were Spaniards, or attached to the Spanish cause, behaved in a manner the most friendly. Such was the orderly conduct of the patriot soldiers, that they acquired universal esteem; and such was their intrepidity and good fortune in the field, that the royalists, with double numbers, ceased to act upon the offensive.

The communications from the Spanish commanders to Miller contained expressions of personal esteem not common between opposing chiefs in that country. La Hera, who was beaten at Mirabe, always spoke of his successful opponent in terms of respect and regard.

The patriots had now a good opportunity of tasting the good things found in Tacna; and they not only did so, but Miller sent two mules laden with spirits, wine, and porter to La Hera at Santiago de Machaca, who courteously acknowledged the present. It is not to be supposed that good dinners were forgotten amongst other relaxations of the officers. One day, as the cloth was removing from Miller's table, a shock of an earthquake was felt; most of the company rose up and cried, *Temblor, temblor! misericordia!* Amongst the foremost to retreat into the street was the worthy Doctor Lazo; but Miller and others attempted to detain him. Other shocks succeeded, and they would willingly have followed the doctor, but having laughed at his alarms, they remained; not, however, without repenting their own ill-timed jocularity. The house was much shaken, the rafters cracked, and the plaster came tumbling down; but luckily the building was a very strong one, and nothing happened beyond frightening those who had made game of their wiser companions. Fourteen houses were either partially or entirely overthrown in the course of successive shocks, which took place during the space of four minutes. After this lesson,

Miller always ran into the street with the rest when he felt an earthquake.

During Miller's residence in Tacna he was, upon two occasions, attacked with violent fits of ague, and each illness confined him to his bed for eight or ten days. Tacna is not unhealthy, it being situated at some distance from the coast, and at the foot of mountains; but few persons remain any considerable time in the other valleys without being annoyed by the ague.

Amongst other interesting incidents which occurred at this time, we select the following.

Miller, upon his first landing, learned that many negroes and mulattoes formerly belonging to the Buenos Ayrean army, and who had been made prisoners at Sipe-Sipe, and other battles in Upper Peru, still existed in a state of slavery on the plantations in the Intermedios. It seems that these unfortunate soldiers had been *sold* by order of the Spanish general. Miller immediately ordered them to be released, and about thirty of them, all that could be found, were restored to freedom. Amongst these were two young men of colour, who had risen in the patriot service to the rank of commissioned officers, in consequence of their good conduct and bravery. But, having been confined for eight years in *galpones*, or slave huts; worked like beasts of burden; and associating only with *out-door* slaves, their minds had sunk under the debasing servitude, and they gave themselves up to drunkenness, and all the vices inseparable from a state of slavery. They were found to be so utterly irreclaimable that they could not be employed again.

Thus were two brave and naturally well-disposed men lost to the service, to society, and to themselves.

Amongst the Spanish prisoners taken at Moquegua was Captain Suarez, who was severely wounded. The royalist chiefs at Arequipa requested that their wounded friend might be permitted to go there for surgical treatment, engaging, at the same time, that he should return as a prisoner of war when cured of his wounds. Miller released the Spaniard *unconditionally*, and supplied him with the means of going to his friends. This trifling occurrence produced a remarkable effect amongst the royalists; for when Miller sent a flag of truce, some time afterwards, into Arequipa, the Spanish officers, discovering that the bearer was commissioned to make some little purchases, kindly undertook to procure the articles, and such as were not to be bought in Arequipa they sent for expressly to Lima; but, unluckily, before they were received, Miller had left the coast. With Old Castilian delicacy, the wounded officer did not again take arms upon his recovery, but accepted a civil employment in the custom-house.

The following adventures of Lieutenant La Tapia are given as illustrative of the nature of the contest, and of the characters of some of the opposing parties.

It has been stated, that when Miller retired from Moquegua towards Tacna, he sent La Tapia with a trumpeter, a few regulars, and a montonero party, with orders to approach as near as possible to Arequipa. Tired of the dreariness of this service, La Tapia longed to pay a visit to the city itself. Ac-

cordingly he presented himself one day at the royalists'
advanced post, under pretence of being a *parlamen-
tario*, or bearer of a flag of truce, and was conducted
to General Ramirez, then commanding in Arequipa.
Producing a paper, which had been fabricated for
the purpose, he said, "General, you will perceive
by this document that I am commissioned by Lieutenant-Colonel Miller, my commanding officer, to
communicate with your excellency." "Yes," answered the general, after looking at the paper; "but
what can you have to say now that the armistice has
taken place between the viceroy and General San
Martin?" La Tapia, to whom the news of the armistice was equally sudden and unexpected, and who
had prepared quite a different pretext, replied with
the utmost composure and readiness, "That is the
object of my mission, to inform your excellency of
that event, and to propose, in consequence, that
hostilities should cease at the same time between
the troops under your excellency's command and
those of the liberating division of the south." "It is
impossible," exclaimed the astonished general, "that
your commanding officer could yet have heard of the
armistice, for it was concluded at Punchauca only
eight days ago, which time it has taken the courier
to bring me the intelligence, and it has only just
arrived. How then could your commanding officer,
who is forty leagues farther off, have already received
the information?" La Tapia, perfectly unembarrassed,
answered, that he was not in the least surprised at
the astonishment expressed by the general, as indeed
the circumstance was almost incredible; that, how-

ever, he was not at liberty to divulge the means by
which Lieutenant-Colonel Miller received communications from General San Martin along the line of
coast occupied by the royalists; that he would, therefore, only observe, that such was the energy and patriotism exhibited by the inhabitants, that the agents
of the independents could perform their secret missions with such celerity as though they actually had
wings; that although the main body of Lieutenant-
Colonel Miller's division might be nearly forty leagues
distant, yet this officer was in the habit of riding to
his advanced posts, which his excellency well knew
were almost at the gates of Arequipa; and that it
was just as probable that communications should be
received at the one point as at the other.

Ramirez appeared, upon this reply, to recover in
some degree from his surprise, and invited La Tapia
to partake of a collation, during which he received
marks of the politest attention from the general and
his staff.

In the meantime the circumstance of the arrival
of the patriot officer occasioned a considerable sensation amongst the patriotic inhabitants of Arequipa,
and the interest became at last so ardent, that Ramirez thought it prudent to dismiss La Tapia without delay, which he did with the assurance that he
was willing to conform to the armistice, and that he
would send an officer on the following day to arrange
the terms.

La Tapia had left Arequipa six hours, when General Ramirez discovered how ingeniously he had
been played upon, by the arrival of an official com-

munication from Lieutenant-Colonel Miller upon the subject of prisoners, in which no allusion was made to the armistice or La Tapia's mission.

La Tapia was remarkable for his ready wit, his amazing fluency of speech, and for the quaint and amusing terms in which he could express his inveterate detestation of the Spaniards.

When an ensign, La Tapia had distinguished himself at the assault of Valdivia. The day after the western forts were captured he was left with a small guard in charge of the prisoners at the castle of Corral, whilst the remainder of the patriot troops were re-embarked to proceed against the forts on the opposite side of the harbour. La Tapia was no sooner left to himself than he determined upon shooting the whole of the prisoners. He was upon the point of commencing this operation at the moment Lord Cochrane's secretary went on shore to look at the castle. Observing the preparation for this massacre, the secretary went towards La Tapia, who congratulated him upon his having arrived in time to witness the execution of the *godos* (goths), who, he added, had shown a disposition to rise upon the guard. The secretary with some difficulty prevailed upon La Tapia to suspend the execution, and to allow him to examine into the matter. In the meantime he sent off word to the admiral, who was on board the frigate anchored under the guns of the castle. La Tapia was placed under arrest before he could accomplish the intended execution. He stated in palliation of the projected crime, that his father, mother, two brothers, and an almost infant sister

z 2

having been murdered in Colombia by the royalists, he had made a vow never to show them quarter; that the admiral might hang or shoot him if he pleased, but that he never could lose an opportunity of avenging the cruel massacre of his family. He then threw off his shoes, and pulling down his stockings, pointed to several deep scars upon his ankle. "These," said he, "were caused by the heavy irons which fettered me in a loathsome dungeon for eighteen months before I had attained the age of sixteen. Is it in human nature to forget or forgive such injuries? The sight of a Spaniard," he added, "throws me into a fever, and his harsh and guttural tones remind me of the insults I was compelled to bear when a prisoner. I know that I have done wrong in the eyes of the law, but I obey the law of nature."

In consequence of this affecting appeal, and of his very courageous conduct during the assault, La Tapia was, after a few weeks' imprisonment, liberated, with a severe reprimand.

When Cochrane approached Arica in May, his views were far more comprehensive than merely to cause a diversion in favour of San Martin. He had previously importuned the Chileno government to reinforce Miller with a thousand, or at least five hundred men, and to furnish a thousand stand of spare arms from the ample stores of Santiago. No part of this request was ever attended to; and Miller, thus unsupported, was unable to avail himself of excellent opportunities, arising out of the good will of the natives, to recruit. It may easily be imagined with what feelings of disappointment he relinquished the advantages already obtained, and at a time, too, when the fairest prospect appeared, not only of being able to maintain his ground, but also of taking possession of Arequipa, whose inhabitants were warmly disposed in his favour.   He might have augmented and organized his forces in that rich and populous city, and have marched towards Cuzco, and thereby placed the royalist army under the viceroy, at Huancayo and Xauxa, in an embarrassing situation.   That this is not an extravagant assumption will probably be granted, if it be remembered that Miller enjoyed the unlimited confidence of the inhabitants of the Puertos Intermedios *; that they unanimously pressed forward and made unsolicited sacrifices to assist him; and that the soldiery entertained an idea that he could not be beaten.

During this time General Ramirez had drawn from distant garrisons nearly two thousand men to act against Miller, who could now only muster four hundred effective men, about the same number being placed *hors de combat* by ague.

Previous to the expiration of the armistice, La Hera advanced from Santiago de Machaca with one thousand royalists, and took possession of Moquegua on the 10th of July; by which movement he formed a junction with a considerable reinforcement sent from Arequipa.   This breach of faith he alleged to be in retaliation, 1st, for Lord Cochrane's having taken, from the port of Ilo, a quantity of wheat, Spanish property, during the suspension of hostilities;

---

* The coast of Peru between Ocuña and Iquique is called *Los Puertos Inter- medios*, or, the intermediate ports.

2dly, for the patriots having taken possession of
Tacna; 3dly, for an irregularity committed by a
montonero party, which was explained to the satisfaction of General Ramirez; and, 4thly, upon the
unfounded pretext of not having a sufficiency of provisions at Santiago de Machaca, the position he
occupied.

The following are translations of letters which
passed on the subject. The first was brought by the
royalist flag of truce, Captain Don Ramon Burges,
who reached Tacna on the 9th of July, and who set
out with an answer on the following day.

" Express orders from the general in chief of the
national army in Peru having authorised me to occupy the town of Moquegua with the division under
my command, I believe that this movement, so far
from being construed into an hostile act, or an in-
fraction of the armistice of Punchauca, will be admitted to be founded upon bases legitimate and just.
Resolved not to vary my position until the expiration
of the armistice, or a definitive result, I have maintained myself in the midst of the most rigorous
wants, preferring to observe good faith in spite of
the injuries it might entail. But suffering has its
limits, and necessity is a law so imperious, that it
impresses the character of duty to actions which at
first sight appear to be in violation of acknowledged
rights. Any lengthened extension of the armistice
would prevent the possibility of preserving my division, if I adhered strictly to the articles of that
treaty. This determination is warranted by infrac-

tions such as the occupation of Tacna by you; the
excursion of a party to carry off horses from Caraquen; and the embarkation of wheat from Mollendo
in the San Martin, will justify, in the eyes of military
men (*en los ojos de todos los guerreros del globo*),
the instructions which my general has transmitted to
me. You know well the force of reasons as luminous
as they are unquestionable, to allow them to produce
a violation of the truce on your part. But if, in
spite of principle, you lend yourself to demonstrations leading to hostilities, I shall be obliged to act
with the energy and decision which the decorum of
the national arms demands, holding you responsible
for the event.

"God preserve you many years.

"(Signed)   José Santos de la Hera.

"To Lieut.-Col.   "Santiago de Machaca,
"Don Guillermo Miller.   "5 July, 1821."

"In answer to your letter of the 5th inst. I inform
you, that in Tacna I received intelligence of the armistice of Punchauca, several days after the military
commandant of this district had taken possession in
the name of the *patria**. The taking of the horses
from Caraquen has been explained to the satisfaction
of the most punctilious advocate for military etiquette,
as you will perceive by the accompanying copy of a
letter from your general. I believe you will not expect me to make myself responsible for the conduct
of the navy. You will act as you please, while I shall

---

* It is true, that while Miller was returning from Moquegua, La Hera advanced to within four leagues of Tacna, and the patriot governor did abandon
the town; but as the royalists did not approach any nearer, he re-entered in the
course of a few hours.

regulate my proceedings by what is dictated by my
duty in maintaining the honour of the division under
my command.

"God preserve you many years.

"(Signed)   GUILLERMO MILLER."

"To Colonel   "Tacna,
"Don José Santos la Hera.   "9 July, 1821."

On the 15th of July, Colonel La Hera announced
officially the recommencement of hostilities. Miller
drew in his scattered detachments.   His sick and
stores were sent to Arica. The three miserable craft
left at Ilo were also ordered to proceed to the same
place.   They made the attempt, but being unable
to beat up, ran down to leeward, and were seen no
more at the Puertos Intermedios.

On the evening of the 19th, Miller sent off his
infantry from Tacna towards Arica. Ten of the patriots could not be removed from the hospital. When
he went to take leave of them, and to supply them
with a few dollars, the poor fellows wept bitterly, and
assured their commander they would die faithful to
the cause.

The tailors, shoemakers, smiths, and others, who
had been employed by requisition, were ordered to
assemble an hour after sunset at Miller's quarters, to
receive what was due to them on account of work
done in the public service. All these people had
shown so much zeal and alacrity, that a few extra
dollars were given to each master to be distributed
among his journeymen as a token of Miller's satisfaction of their good conduct. Under the vice-regal
government it was the rule to embargo the services

of tradesmen, and to pay them at a rate below their ordinary earnings, or not to pay them at all, when employed on account of the public service.   The gratuity, therefore, to the tradesmen of Tacna was received with equal surprise and pleasure.   Not content with giving loud and repeated *vivas*, they embraced the *commandante*, and vowed, over and over again, that they would remain unchangeable patriots. The populace was indulged with a few cases of merchandize belonging to the royalists, which being placed in different streets, were unnailed, and every body allowed to help themselves.

At two A. M. on the 20th, Miller, with the cavalry, followed the infantry.   The inhabitants felt deeply the departure of the patriots.   They continued their kind offices to the last, and every soldier was shaken by the hand at least twenty times as they filed out of the town on the Arica road.

The venerable Don Agustin Sapata of Moquegua, the highly respectable families of Potrillo, Landa, Lazo, and several others, had departed for Arica on the day before, choosing rather to emigrate than to live again in Spanish bondage.   Others were equally willing to follow the fortunes of the patriots, but having young families, or from other causes, were obliged to remain.   Amongst these were Don Enrique Solar and Don N. Boteler, who had both compromised themselves by having accepted appointments.   Although Miller strenuously advised them to make their peace with the royalists by speaking against the patriots, they bade him farewell in the most dejected manner, which, joined to the weeping

of their afflicted families, added very much to the
embarrassment of this depressing separation.   Three
hours after this the royalists entered Tacna.

The tradesmen who had been employed by the
patriots shouted their *vivas*, and proceeded to hide
themselves in the valley, in order not to be embar-
goed to work for the royalists.   The expectation was
that Miller would fight; and he kept up this necessary illusion so completely, that the officer next to
him in command was not aware of his real intention
to embark.

The patriot division, after a harassing march of
eleven leagues in thirteen hours, over a hot desert of
sand, arrived at Chacalluta, and bivouacked on the
bank of a rivulet.

La Hera, who was also fully persuaded that Miller
intended to make a resolute stand, halted for twenty-
four hours at Tacna to refresh his men.   This delay
gave time to the patriots to secure the means of retreat by sea.   Arrangements had been secretly made
for withdrawing to the Sierra, in case the embarkation
could not be accomplished.   The hopes entertained
by the patriots of escaping by sea were founded upon
the casual presence of four merchant-vessels in the
roadstead of Arica, which they calculated upon getting possession of, either by persuasion or force.

The manner in which transports were obtained
will show how the course of events may sometimes
be changed by a trifling incident.   Previous to Miller's arrival, the governor of Arica had, with very
good intentions, sent two or three soldiers aboard a
very fine North American schooner, of three hun-

dred tons, to secure her. The master, disliking the
embargo, got ready to slip his cable and put out to
sea, intending to land the soldiers when and where
it suited his convenience. Being informed of the
circumstance, upon entering Arica, Miller instantly
went on board unaccompanied. He offered the most
liberal terms, which were pertinaciously rejected.
This refusal rendered the services of the other three
vessels unavailable, as they could not have taken off
the whole of the troops. During an animated conversation, Miller, as he paced the quarter-deck, recognised some men amongst the ship's company who
had formerly served with him in the Chileno squadron, and who were evidently attending with deep
concern to what was passing. It happened that
the seamen in the Pacific, whether British or North
American; whether serving in men-of-war or in merchant vessels, had always evinced the liveliest interest in the successes of the English leader. It was
a feeling which produced an important effect at the
present critical juncture. He turned round to them,
and made a short address. They all answered his
appeal by an animated declaration, that "a countryman *hard pushed* should not be forsaken." After
some unavailing remonstrances on the part of the
master, he indignantly threw up the command, and
went on shore. The chief mate prepared to follow,
but was prevailed upon to take charge of the vessel.
Thus were the patriots fortunately relieved from the
necessity of contending with the most fearful odds in
an untenable position.

When the patriots landed at Arica in May, the inhabitants were decided royalists. The pillage of the town by the sailors of the San Martin augmented this political feeling into a deadly hatred. Amongst the most violent was the young and beautiful wife of the late royalist governor, Colonel Gago. Her house had been stripped; even her piano-forte was taken on board; and she herself left without a change of apparel. She was subsequently often heard to say that she should only die happy if she could soak her handkerchief in the blood of an insurgent. However, the general good conduct of the officers and men of the division of the patriot army produced, in time, a complete revolution of opinion. Notwithstanding the unfavourable circumstances under which they re-entered Arica, the inhabitants came forward with the greatest good will, and assisted in the embarkation. They sent a thousand loaves of bread, and a proportionate quantity of fresh meat, for the use of the sick. Some of the most steadfast adherents to the king sent refreshments of coffee, chocolate, &c. to Miller during the night, whilst, knee-deep in surf, he superintended the difficult embarkation. Only three or four men could be conveyed at a time upon each *balsa* to the launches, which could not with safety approach nearer to the beach than twenty or thirty fathoms. At five P.M. on the 21st, the royalists were reported to have arrived within four leagues. Captain Belasquez, who had been despatched, well mounted, and with led horses, from Chacalluta, on the road to Tacna, had

reconnoitred the advancing enemy, and now brought
the report. He had left ten confidential men in observation until his return.

The shipment of the troops was rendered more
difficult by a hundred emigrants with their baggage.
The latter, as well as all those who had recently
adopted the patriot cause, were particularly anxious
to be the first on board.   The operation became
more complicated by the necessity of sending wood,
water, and provisions on board at the same time.
Fifty bullocks were killed, skinned, cut up on the
beach, and shipped before morning. This was another night of very hard work; but, with the valuable
assistance of Mr. William Cochran, an eminent English merchant, and the cordial co-operation of the
inhabitants, every difficulty was overcome, and Miller, in the last launch, pushed off only a few minutes
before the royalists appeared and formed upon the
beach.

Miller sent a boat on shore with a flag of truce, to
request that the sick left at Tacna should be treated
with humanity. Colonel La Hera returned a polite
answer, paying some compliments on the discipline
of the patriot force, and giving an assurance that the
few independent soldiers in the hospital should be
attended to in preference to his own men.

At two P. M. on the 22d, the vessels weighed
anchor and stood to the northward.

The good conduct of the patriot soldiers has been
mentioned as well as that of several officers.   It remains to enumerate some others whose names cannot
with justice be omitted. Colonel Landa, afterwards

taken prisoner at the battle of Moquegua and shot
by the royalists; Captain Aramburu, taken prisoner
at the same time, and drowned at sea on his passage
to Chiloe; Captain Carreño, killed on the day before
the battle of Ayacucho; and Lieutenant Don Vicente Suares, killed in 1824, in an affair of outposts
near Lima; all distinguished themselves for zeal and
valour.   Dr. Don José Lazo, a lawyer of superior
talents and warm patriotism, acted as *auditor de
guerra,* or judge advocate; he rendered important
services as a legal adviser, and acquired the confidence of his commander, and the consideration of
the Peruvian government.   He was subsequently in
a village near Chucuyto, having been left behind on
the dispersion of a patriot force.   He, however, continued to win the good graces of the royalists by
his poetical talents, and escaped being made a close
prisoner by writing complimentary verses upon some
of the royalist leaders.   In this dilemma his muse
proved to be his best friend.

CHAPTER XV.

Pisco re-occupied.—Ildefonso.—A Peruvian Meg Merrilies.—Copari.—Caguachi.—Character of Santalla.—General San Martin
enters Lima.—Atrocities of the royalists.—Independence proclaimed.—San Martin becomes protector.—Decrees.—Canterac
returns to Callao—retreats again—is pursued.—Puruchuco.—
Quiros.—Montoneros.

WHEN Miller sailed from Arica it was his intention to have landed at Quilca, and to have
marched rapidly upon Arequipa, which city was left
unguarded, Ramirez having sent the garrison to
Arica: but the wind was so boisterous that it was
impossible to effect a landing, and having only three
days' provisions and water on board, he was unable to
wait off the bad port of Quilca until the weather moderated. Ignorant of the situation of General San
Martin, he took upon himself to direct his course once
more to Pisco. The commander of the schooner
never having been on that part of the coast, Miller
acted as pilot, and entered the roadstead after dark
on the 1st of August, landed, and, before daylight on
the 2d, took possession of the town. Fifty royalist
cavalry, after exchanging a few shots, galloped off.

He detached small parties in every direction to
procure horses and mules, to mount a company
in pursuit of the garrison of two hundred men,
commanded by Colonel Santalla, who had seized

upon every horse and mule, not hidden away by the owners.

Amongst the casualties of this period was the loss of a negro youth, whose death should not go unrecorded. His condition was indeed lowly; but a noble mind is not restricted to colour or to station.

Ildefonso was born a slave at Chincha, near Pisco. He entered the patriot service as one of the *infernales* when Miller landed the year before, and shortly after became his servant. He brought himself first into notice by his shrewdness in discovering, and boldness in passing fords, where great skill in horsemanship and dexterity in throwing the *lasso* are sometimes the only means of saving the foremost to attempt the ford from being carried away by the torrent. Ildefonso was engaged in every affair that occurred in the Intermedios in the year 1821. He possessed all the good qualities of a soldier, being bold, obedient, and cleanly. To a tall and finely proportioned form, equal to any fatigue, and to any enterprise, were added a mild expressive countenance, teeth as white as ivory; and so pleasing were his manners, that he was as much beloved by his comrades, as he was admired by all for his extraordinary intrepidity. Trustworthy, and unceasing in his endeavours to please, nothing could ruffle the serenity of his temper but to see another person wait upon his master, at whose side he was constantly to be found in moments of danger. At the affair of Mirabe, Miller ordered him to the rear, under pretence of giving him charge of his horses. "No, sir," was the reply; "where there is danger, there will I be: where my master dies, there dies Ildefonso." *No, señor; donde hay peligro, ahi estaré yo; donde muere mi amo, ahi morirá Ildefonso.*

This brave negro lad deserved a better fate than that which now befell him. He had been sent into Pisco in disguise to acquire information, and, having indiscreetly delayed his return from the town until daybreak, he was seen and pursued by the Spanish cavalry. Unable to reach the patriot column that was advancing, he threw himself into the sea to avoid falling into the hands of his pursuers, who, calling upon him to surrender, received for answer that he would rather die a thousand deaths in the cause of *la patria* than again obey a Spaniard. The royalists then fired, and shot him through the neck. They themselves were made prisoners a few days afterwards, and related the last expressions of Ildefonso, whose body was washed ashore the next day, and consigned to the grave with military honours, amidst the deep regrets of his comrades.

Notwithstanding the enthusiastic exertions of the inhabitants, and the favourable disposition of the landed proprietors for twenty or thirty miles round, three days elapsed before the requisite means of transport could be obtained. In the interval, a *requa*, or drove, of fifty mules, arrived at Chincha from Lima. Miller gave an order to press them for the service; upon which the owner, a lady on the wrong side of fifty, whose hale, and not unhandsome, dark countenance and commanding figure might well become a queen of the gypsies, presented herself to the colo-

nel, and, with the imposing air of a *Meg Merrilies,*
displayed a passport and protection from General San
Martin, who had entered Lima just before she quitted
it.   On Miller's telling her that circumstances rendered it impossible to respect the general's safe conduct, she pompously exclaimed, that whoever could
act in defiance of that great man's signature must be
either the devil himself, or a wretch who could never
hope to reach the gates of heaven.   The patriot commander's determination to pursue the enemy could
not be shaken by the eloquence, or denunciations,
of the venerable dame, who was neither very choice
in the selection of her terms of reproach, nor very
sparing in their application.   He felt compelled to
take her mules, but gave her reason to hope that they
would be restored at Ica, and the detachment set out,
each soldier mounted on a mule.   The wary old lady
accompanied the party, grumbling most wofully, but
determined not to lose sight of her animals.   She
certainly had reason to complain of her ill fortune,
and to bewail her blighted prospects.   She explained
to the colonel, that the object of her long journey
had been to purchase brandy at Pisco, which at that
time was very scarce in Lima, in consequence of the
long investment of that place by the patriots.   She
might, at that moment, have procured it at eight
dollars the jar, and, providing she had been the first
speculator to enter Lima, would have sold it for
eighty.   The prospect of losing such a golden opportunity was ill calculated to reconcile her to the
forcible seizure of her mules.

The distance from Pisco to Ica is fourteen leagues:

the last ten are over a burning desert of very loose sand, thinly interspersed with clumps of palm trees.

The royalists retired from Ica as the patriots approached. The latter were enthusiastically received on the evening of the 5th of August, as they passed through, in pursuit of the fugitives. Santalla, already mentioned in describing the capture of Valdivia, had taken the route to Palpa, twenty-five leagues south of Ica. Only three hours were allowed for the patriots to rest at Garganta, two leagues beyond Ica, during which interval some fresh horses and mules were procured. They then continued the chase across the sandy desert, sixteen leagues, to Changuilla. At midnight on the 6th, the troops halted in the desert. For the purpose of protecting themselves against the heavy dews, each man excavated a sort of shallow grave, and lay down in it, and then scraped the sand over his body, leaving only his head above ground, which he wrapped up in his *poncho*. As it was important to observe the strictest secrecy, smoking was forbidden, lest the small twinkling lights should accidentally discover their approach to the enemy. The lady was the only person permitted to indulge in the solace of a cigar before she decorously tucked herself into a bed of sand, amidst the surrounding group of soldiers and muleteers. Thus, as it were buried alive, all slept as comfortably as if reposing on a bed of down, and so soundly that at daybreak it was difficult to rouse them from their delicious slumbers. The morning was foggy, as is very usual in these regions. They had marched about two leagues, when, the sun suddenly dispelling the mist, they discovered that, instead of advancing, they had retraced their route of the pre-vious night. To prevent the recurrence of similar mistakes, from that time, whenever they halted at night, they took the precaution to pile their muskets in such a way as to point out the proper direction.

The patriots reached Changuilla, on the 7th, at night, and cut off the retreat of Santalla, by the *direct* road, to Arequipa, from Palpa, where he was halting, unconscious of the approach of the patriots.

On the 8th, Santalla, perceiving the patriot party, retired with precipitation to the mountains; but Miller having already communicated with the Mo-ruchuco Indians, they rose *en masse*. The sides and summits of the hills were covered with these In-dians, and the air resounded with their yells and war-whoops.

Santalla could not escape by the road leading to Huancavelica with such enemies in front, and he could not return by the road he came without fight-ing with the party at his heels. At Copari, seven leagues from Palpa, a little skirmishing took place: a few of the royalists were killed, seventy or eighty made prisoners, and the rest took to a mountain so difficult of access, that the patriots, being unable from fatigue to climb it, returned by the valley through which they had advanced. Miller proceeded from Palpa back to Ica; but before he set out he detached Captains Plaza and Carreño, with twenty-three men mounted on fresh horses, in pursuit of Santalla, who had in all probability once more gained - the road leading to Arequipa. No more men could be sent forward, the rest being in a state of fever, in consequence of the late harassing marches. At midnight Plaza arrived at Caguachi, three leagues from Nasca, where he found ninety-six royalists, with their sentinels, all sound asleep in a *corral*. They were so worn out with fatigue that hallooing was not enough to awaken them. The patriots fired a volley, killed twelve, and wounded as many more. Amongst the latter was Lieutenant-Colonel Rada, a very brave Spaniard. Fifteen officers and sixty-seven rank and file were taken prisoners. The timid Santalla, and a few attendants, were the only persons who escaped; and this he effected in consequence of having taken the precaution of sleeping at a distance from his party, and galloping off at the sound of the first alarm. For this purpose their horses were kept saddled, and the bridles attached to the arms of the sleepers.

The *Iqueños* were so much exasperated with the troops of Santalla that many went out from Ica to waylay and murder the prisoners; but as they did not conceal their intentions, measures were taken, and their designs were frustrated.

During these long, dreary, and fatiguing marches, the aged damsel, already mentioned, rode by the side of Miller, but her resentful tone soon changed into such a good-humoured one, that she entered into the spirit of the expedition with the enthusiasm of an amazon. She declared that it did not signify *un pito* (a whistle) if all her mules were lost, provided she had the satisfaction to see the patriots triumph. She rode astride; wore large silver spurs; could manage the most restive horse; and was able to

throw the *lasso* as dexterously as any of her muleteers. Her voice was louder than a boatswain's, and
shrill as his pipe. The desert frequently rang with
the sound, as she hallooed to the men to encourage
them. Having accomplished the object proposed,
there was no longer any necessity to detain her, and
her mules were again put at her free disposal. Miller
presented the good old lady with twenty of those
taken from the Spaniards, but she would not accept
them. He then offered her a sum of money for the
service her mules had performed; but she could not
be induced to receive any species of remuneration.
She said she was amply recompensed by having witnessed the total overthrow of a party of royalists by
the "dear soldiers of the *patria.*" She, however,
thankfully accepted a letter to General San Martin,
certifying her services. When Miller read it to her,
she embraced him with tears of joy, and took leave
without repeating a word about the devil himself, or
the gates of heaven being closed. It is satisfactory
to add, that she was lucky enough, notwithstanding
her detention, to be the first to arrive with brandy in
Lima, where she realized all her expectations. This
most active and singular woman of business traded,
farmed, reared cattle, and let out *valenciennes* (ca-
briolets). She was accounted rich, and, though highly
disinterested in the above instance, fond of adding to
her wealth. Before taking our final leave of her, a
circumstance that occurred in the following year
(1822) may be mentioned here.

Miller happened to be riding towards the cantonments of his regiment at Lomo Largo, three

leagues south of Lima, in company with General Alvarado. The latter perceiving a well cultivated estate on the road-side, inquired of a countryman, who was passing, to whom it belonged. The man answered, that he was the major domo, or steward, of the estate, and that it belonged to Señor Miller. " To whom? to whom?" said Alvarado. " To Señor Miller," rejoined the man; "because my mistress has bequeathed it to him, and when she dies he will be the lawful owner." " And who," said Miller, " is that namesake of mine?" " No other," said the man, " than you yourself, sir : my mistress says she will have no other heir. When she delivered your letter to General San Martin, he received her so kindly, and has treated her so well ever since, that she considers you as the author of her good fortune." Miller's regiment, stationed within a mile of the estate in question, had been in the habit of sending thither to purchase vegetables, &c. and a good deal of surprise had always been excited by the major domo's invariably declining to receive any payment for them. He told them that his mistress would settle with the colonel for every thing which the officers and men had occasion to send for. The mystery was now cleared up, by the accidental meeting of the major domo as above described.

Having mentioned the royalist Lieutenant-Colonel Santalla more than once, and described his last signal discomfiture, we will now portray his character at some length, by way of contrast to that of the good Lima lady, who is still living, and as an exempli-

fication of the evils to which the Peruvians were exposed when the rod of iron was placed in the relentless
hand of an unprincipled poltroon.

When he first heard that the patriots had landed,
he bellowed forth to the assembled people in the
square of Ica, that if he discovered that a single individual communicated with the insurgent leader, he
would burn the city, and put every man, woman, and
child to death.   Upon overhearing this, his wife, a
Spanish woman, called out to him from the doorway
of the Marquess of Campo Ameno's house, " Santalla, all this ought to be *done*, instead of said. Why
not then burn at once a city whose inhabitants are
all rebels?" It will be presently seen that this fury
was reduced to implore upon her knees for the life
of her barbarian husband.

As commanding officer of the district of Ica, he
issued a barbarous circular, calling upon the landed
proprietors in that extensive valley to furnish three
hundred horses and mules within four hours of the
date of the order, in default of which they were to
be shot; their houses burned; their estates made
desolate; and their families put to the sword * !

* " Commandancia-general del sur,—Los hacendados de este valle, dentro
del perentorio, y preciso termino de *quatro horas*, presentarán en casa del Señor
Marques de Campo Ameno, tres cientos cavallos y mulas suyas, tomandolas
de qual-quiera persona que las tenga sin excepcion alguna, en inteligencia que
no verificandolo dentro de dicho termino serán irremisiblemente pasados por las
armas, quemadas y taladas sus haciendas, y pasadas à cuchillo sus familias.
                              " JUAN DE SANTALLA.
" Ica, à las 10 de la mañana de hoy 19 de Julio de 1821.
" Al Señor Don Fulgencio Guerrero."

(TRANSLATION.)

" Commandancy-general of the South,—The landed proprietors of this valley
will deliver up three hundred horses and mules at the house of the Marquess of
Campo Ameno, within the peremptory and precise time of *four hours*, taking

Many landowners resided upon their estates, which
were at such a distance from the town that it was
physically impossible to comply with the requisition
within the specified time.   But too many patriots
had already been put to death; too many women
violated by Santalla and his followers; too many old
men, and even children, punished with stripes and
imprisonment, to leave a doubt on the mind of any
one that he would hesitate to put his savage threat
into execution: in fact, he had taken one step to show
that he was in earnest.   The *alcalde* Sorillo, a rich
and respectable citizen, had concealed a beautiful and
favourite horse.   This was discovered by Santalla.
He immediately ordered Sorillo to be fastened to the
banquillo, or bench of execution, fixed in the square,
preparatory to being shot: but every minute brought
fresh intelligence of the nearer approach of the patriots from Pisco.   The assembled inhabitants, already
disposed to rescue their *alcalde* by force, increased in
numbers and boldness.   Santalla was only induced
by his fears to forego glutting his vengeance, and he
hurried away, to provide for his personal safety.

Santalla was a man of lofty stature, and in strength
a giant.   He was what is called double-jointed; and
could, with his thumbs and fingers, break a dollar in
two, and tear a pack of cards in halves.   But his pusillanimity was greater even than his personal strength.

them from any person who may have them, without any exception whatever; it
being understood that, in failure hereof within the said term, the defaulters will
be immediately shot, their houses pillaged and burned, their estates ravaged,
and their families put to the sword.

(Signed)   " JUAN DE SANTALLA.
" Ica, 10 A. M. 19th July, 1821.
" To Don Fulgencio Guerrero."

On retiring from Ica, he was informed that the
pursuing patriots were only one hundred in number.
His officers remonstrated against a disgraceful flight
before such an inferior force.   To justify himself in
their eyes, he forged a letter, and directed it to himself. It purported to be from a royalist in Ica, stating
the insurgents to be above four hundred. He showed
the paper to his officers, and they then acquiesced in
the propriety of further retreat.   This fact was related to Miller by Captain Matafuertes, who was
made prisoner at Caguachi, and who declared that
the letter was forged in his presence.

In his flight from Caguachi to Arequipa, Santalla
escaped being torn to pieces by having recourse to
the stratagem of speaking bad Spanish, and passing
himself off as a French officer in the patriot service,
sent forward to procure quarters and provisions. He
had also the address to persuade the priest of Yauca
to confide to his care a fine horse which *his Reverence*
had concealed with great care, for the purpose of
presenting to the first patriot chief who should pass
through the parish.

Notwithstanding the disguise which Santalla had
assumed, he was recognised at Chaparra, and the inhabitants of the valley having tied his hands and feet,
were about to treat him as he deserved; but his life
was spared through the tears and entreaties of his
wife, who was in the last stage of pregnancy, and who
gave efficacy to her prayers by a liberal distribution
of doubloons amongst the poorer people.

Upon his arrival at Arequipa, Santalla was put
under arrest for a few days, *on the charge of cow-*

ardice, but it never transpired that he was ever reprimanded for his *cruelties* and *extortions*. The contrary appears from his having soon afterwards received the civil appointment of sub-delegate of Arica! The system of shooting patriot inhabitants, and confiscating the property of the wealthy at the caprice of the commanding officer, was too common with the royalists.

Miller, who had been promoted to the rank of colonel *, assumed the civil and military government of an extensive district, of which Ica was the centre. His administration is still spoken of by the inhabitants in terms highly honourable to his character. He employed this opportunity in augmenting his military means, and in establishing montoneros, or guerrillas, to hover on the flank of the enemy, then in cantonments between Guamanga and Xauxa. The Marquess of Campo Ameno, the Señores Nestares, Guerrero, and other wealthy inhabitants, who long preserved their attachment to the royalist cause, now openly declared themselves in favour of the patriots; and cordially combined, in the most efficacious manner, to second the efforts of Miller to establish permanent order, and to give every possible support to his military operations. Amongst these Captain La Tapia was sent to surprise a royalist piquet at Huaitará, commanded by the sub-delegate ————, who made a desperate resistance. La Tapia grappled with him personally; both fell, and struggled together for several minutes on the floor of a room. The

* Immediately after the affair of Mirabe, Miller was advanced to this rank by Lord Cochrane. When at Ica he received the commission signed by San Martin.

sub-delegate managed to draw a dagger from his boot, and was about to plunge it in the body of La Tapia, when a patriot soldier came up to the assistance of his officer, and knocked out the sub-delegate's brains with the butt-end of his musket.

Miller having learned that Canterac had descended from his position at Xauxa, and that a general action was likely to take place near Lima, left Major Videla in command at Ica, and set out for the capital alone. After passing through Lurin, six leagues south of Lima, he observed, at the distance of two or three leagues, the Spanish columns in full march between him and Lima. Unable in consequence to proceed, he returned to Lurin, and wrote a letter to San Martin, signifying that he was at the head of a thousand followers, watching for an opportunity to pounce upon the rear-guard of Canterac. The despatch was put into the wallet of a well-mounted peasant, who was instructed to ride near enough to the royalists to attract attention, and to drop his wallet, as if by accident, when pursued. These orders were very cleverly executed, and the intercepted despatch appears to have produced an order from Canterac to hasten up stragglers. Miller reached Lima on the 12th, and was received with warm expressions of approbation by San Martin, two days after Canterac had entered Callao.

But before we proceed to describe the collateral events which occurred at this time, it will be necessary to revert to the 24th of June, when hostilities recommenced in the vicinity of Lima, on the expiration of the armistice of Punchauca.

The viceroy, unable to retain possession of the capital, invested as it was by montonero parties which hovered around and cut off regular supplies, abandoned that city on the 6th of July, and the patriots entered it on the 9th, amidst universal acclamations. One division of the royalists under Canterac took the way of Lunaguana, and the other, commanded by the vice-king in person, took the road to Yauyos, the ultimate destination of both being Xauxa.

During the retreat, desertion from the royalist ranks was so frequent, that the Spanish generals gave orders that every soldier found a hundred yards from the line of march should be shot, and many were in consequence executed. To increase their difficulties, the Indians rose in favour of the patriots, whilst the *montoneros* hung upon the rear, and cut off all stragglers.

If the liberating army, instead of going, as it did, into cantonments in the dissipated city of Lima, had seconded the efforts of those armed patriotic bands, it can hardly be doubted that the war would have terminated in a very few weeks: whereas, for want of timely energy, unhappy Peru continued to suffer, and her capital and provinces were alternately in the hands of the friends and foes to freedom. Each army, unavoidably oppressive even to its friends, was a scourge to those inhabitants who espoused the opposite side, and each party felt the scourge in turn.

Once, when the viceroy happened to be in Guamanga, a landowner of facetious humour waited upon his excellency, and represented that one party * having

* " *La madre patria.*"

eased him of his cash and valuables, and the other party* having taken away his cattle and crop, he humbly besought the viceroy to inform him to what party he ought to deliver over his *skin*, that being all that was left which he could venture to call his own.

The town of Cangallo, two days' march from Guamanga, was burnt by the royalists, and the viceroy issued a decree, dated 11th January, 1822, that the walls of the houses should be destroyed, and that the name of Cangallo should henceforth disappear from the list of towns. The villages of Ulcamayo, Huailly, Zancas, and some others, with many estates in the vicinity of Tarma, were burnt. The stores of the silver mines of Pasco were plundered five times by the royalists, and as often by the patriots. The wonder is how the works were kept going at all! In fact, they often stopped, or were worked upon so limited a scale as hardly to be worth the attention of either party.

When General Carratalà retreated from Pasco before the division of Arenales, meeting an Indian on a very fine brood mare, he ordered him to dismount, and to deliver it up. In vain the poor peasant represented, that to deprive him of the only animal he had in the world, was to take away the chief means of his support. The general was inexorable, the mare was taken, and the plundered Peruvian followed on foot with the troops. On arriving at the village of Moya, opposite to Concepcion, near Xauxa, the royalist division halted. The Indian, taking advantage of the bustle which prevails when soldiers

* " *El Padre Rey.*"

make good their quarters, suddenly threw himself across the best charger of Carratalà, and galloped off through four thousand people who at that moment crowded the Plaza and the streets. He was pursued to the river close by, and some muskets were discharged at him; but the man, being well acquainted with the ford, escaped untouched. Several Spaniards dashed into the water after him, and three of them were drowned. On arriving at the patriot bivouac on the opposite bank, the Indian received, in exchange for Carratalà's charger, a doubloon, and a mare as good as the one of which he had been robbed.

Lieutenant-Colonel O'Brien commanded the advanced guard on the following day; and entering the town of Carguancuanga, near the bridge of Iscuchaca, inquired for the priest of the parish, supposing that he could give the most correct information of the enemy: but as he had absconded, O'Brien next asked for the sexton. The Indians pointed in silence to a tree; and, upon approaching it, he beheld the sexton and his wife suspended by the neck from one of the branches. The crime of the unfortunate man was, the not being in attendance when one of General Carratalà's officers, on passing through the village, demanded the keys of the church, which he required to quarter his troops in. The crime of the woman was, in not revealing the hiding-place of her husband, which was, however, discovered, and both were immediately hanged. O'Brien saw their nine young children on their knees weeping most piteously, and praying to their lifeless parents to come down to them.

A day or two after this horrible cruelty had been committed, Carratalà sent a flag of truce, consisting of an officer, a trumpeter, and six privates. As they were passing through Carguancuanga, the inhabitants rose, and put every one of them to death. Their tongues were cut out, their bodies drawn and quartered, and then stuck upon poles.

The viceroy was fortunate enough to reach the valley of Xauxa, where he concentrated his forces. He, as well as Canterac and Carratalà, were still more fortunate in not having been attacked by Arenales, whose division consisted of the regiment of granaderos à caballo, and of the battalion of Numancia, Cazadores, Nos. 2 and 7; altogether four thousand three hundred and eighty-four men. With these Arenales re-crossed the Cordillera, and arrived on the Lima side of the mountains on the 26th of July. Thus the patriots abandoned the important provinces of the *Sierra*, of which the royalists took quiet possession, by isolated divisions. Thus this extraordinary oversight on the part of the patriots compensated the royalists for the loss of Lima.

The viceroy, on his departure from Lima, had left a garrison in the castles of Callao. They were invested by a patriot division under General Las Heras, while Lord Cochrane blockaded the port by sea. On the 24th of July, Captain Crosbie cut out, in the most masterly manner, three merchant vessels, and burnt four others. In this affair Captains Morgell and Simpson, of the Chileno navy, particularly distinguished themselves.

On the 26th July, a sortie was made from the

castle, but repulsed in the most gallant manner by Major Don Eugenio Necochea and Captain Raulet. The latter received a lance wound.

On the 28th of July, the independence of Peru was proclaimed, and the usual oath taken, with great pomp and rejoicings.

On the 12th of August, an attempt to surprise and take the principal castle of Callao (Real Felipè) failed.

On the 3d of August, San Martin declared himself protector of Peru, and assumed the supreme civil and military command.   He appointed Don Juan Garcia del Rio, Don Bernardo Monteagudo, and Dr. Don Hipolito Unánue, ministers respectively for foreign affairs, for war and marine, and for finance. General Don Juan Gregorio de Las Heras was appointed commander-in-chief of the army.

The following are early specimens of the legislation of the protectorate.

Of the 12th of August, 1821, a decree declaring that the children of slaves born in Peru subsequently to the 28th of July, 1821, should be free.

Of the 15th of August, declaring every individual, naval as well as military, who sailed from Valparaiso in the liberating expedition, to be considered as belonging to the service of Peru, and to be entitled to a pension, equal to half the amount of the pay he was in the receipt of, on leaving Chile; such pension to be paid even though the individual should fix his residence in a foreign country.

Of the 27th of August, abolishing the tribute, and forbidding the name of *Indians* to be applied to the aborigines, who were thenceforth to be called

Peruvians, which term was formerly confined to those born of Spanish parents, and their descendants.

Of the 28th of August, abolishing the *mita,* and every species of compulsory labour to which the Indians had been subjected.

The establishment of a national library was decreed on the same day.

In the month of October, the Order of the Sun, upon the model of the Legion of Honour in France, was established. It was divided into three classes: 1st, *Fundadores;* 2d, *Benemeritos;* 3d, *Asociados.* To the members of the first class, and to a certain number of each of the other classes, pensions were attached. It might have been rather better to have postponed the formation of an order of knighthood until after the Spaniards were expelled; but the institution was a popular measure, and it was politic, inasmuch as it enabled government to reward military and civil merit, at a cheap rate, although it was evidently a step towards the introducing of principles savouring strongly of monarchy *. The mode of con-

* In 1825 the congress passed a resolution abolishing the order. Although it did not receive the official assent of the executive, it goes far enough to show the narrow views which actuated some of the deputies on the question. It was unjust to attempt to deprive men of a decoration given for past services, and it was indelicate towards members of the order, who had called these very deputies into political existence, by services performed when many of them were languishing in obscurity, and groaning, in comparative insignificance, under the Spanish yoke.

One great cause of offence was, that the honour was almost exclusively restricted to those who had espoused the cause of independence, from principle, at an early period of the contest, and before it became *the safe side of the question.* Those who had done nothing to earn the distinction could not bear the sight of it when bestowed upon others.

As to the legality of the absolute abolition of the order, congress had no more power to pass laws having the retro-active effect of taking away from members the decorations and pensions, than it had to deprive them of medals given for victories, unless indeed that congress assumed the power of the Turkish divan; a fault it was not entirely free from when its labours were confined to petty legislation.

ferring the decoration on the military was impartial. A certain number of those who in each corps had established the fairest claims were recommended by a junta of general officers.

On the 19th December, property valued at 500,000 dollars was granted to twenty general and field officers of the liberating army, as a reward for past services, and was equally divided amongst them. Colonel Miller received 25,000 dollars for his share.

Canterac's division, united with that of Carratalà, entered Xauxa on the 25th of July. The viceroy reached the same place in the beginning of August.

On the 24th of August, Canterac again set out from Xauxa, with 3000 infantry and 900 cavalry; and, countermarching by the road of San Mateo, arrived on the 9th of September in sight of San Martin, encamped on the *hacienda* called Mendoza, a mile from Lima, on the Arequipa road.

The object of Canterac was to attack the patriots, and to succour the castles of Callao. He had probably been encouraged by information transmitted by Spaniards from Lima, as to the state of the patriot army; the composition and appearance of which was any thing but favourable, although it then exceeded seven thousand in number: but when Canterac beheld them strongly posted behind mud walls, and supported in the rear by the population of Lima, many of whom were on horseback, armed with sabres, knives, pikes, &c. he deemed it more prudent to pass on between Lima and the sea-shore, and to take shelter under the guns of Callao on the afternoon of the 10th.

The patriots changed their position, and took up
another equally strong at Mirones, a league and a half
from Callao, extending half a mile in length, and intersected by the Lima road.

San Martin has been severely censured for not
attacking the royalists upon this occasion: but when
it is considered that many of his troops consisted of
raw recruits, perhaps it may be allowed that he acted
wisely. The royalists, on the contrary, were veteran
soldiers, and well disciplined. It is curious that some
of the patriot chiefs most loud in condemning the in-
action of the protector were those who had shortly
before let pass the most brilliant opportunities to an-
nihilate the royalists when scattered in the Sierra, as
also when Canterac shortly afterwards retreated from
Callao towards Xauxa.

On the 14th of September, Miller was appointed
to the command of 700 men, being the light companies of the liberating army, to act as a column of
observation, and to be in readiness to move at a moment's warning.

On the 15th this party made a lateral movement,
in consequence of Canterac having commenced a retreat. Having reached the mouth of the river Rimac,
half a league from Callao, he suddenly countermarched; upon which the light companies, under
Miller, returned to their position at Mirones. The
colonel at this time suffered so much from ague that
he was obliged to be carried into Lima, where the
attentive nursing and kindness of the Baroness of
Nordenflidtch in two days restored him to health.

In the night of the 17th, Canterac effected his

escape across the Rimac at Bocanegra, leaving General La Mar in the castles with three days' provisions to make the best terms he could. Las Heras,
with the liberating army, was ordered to pursue the
royalists, but to avoid a general action. After advancing to the estate called Los Cavalleros, nine
leagues from Lima, Las Heras gave over further
pursuit. Miller's division, now consisting of 700
infantry, 125 cavalry, and 500 montoneros, were not
permitted to follow up until 9 A. M. on the 20th.
During this long, and apparently uncalled for, halt
of ten hours, his men were without provisions, and
were allowed to march onwards with empty haver-
sacks. Las Heras and the rest of the army countermarched; for many of the chiefs appeared to be less
eager to prosecute hostilities than to indulge in the
gayeties of Lima, where every officer and soldier had
been well received, and where each had formed friendships and attachments he was anxious to renew.

A march of three leagues brought Miller with the
light division to Macas, where they dined upon a
number of sheep, which the royalists left behind, ready
prepared for cooking. Lieutenant-Colonel O'Brien
and Captain Vidal skirmished with the rear-guard:
the latter was wounded. One hundred royalists deserted to the patriots in the course of the day's march.

It appeared that Canterac had prevailed upon his
men to quit the walls of Callao, under the persuasion
that they were to be led against the patriots, so soon
as they had cleared the country intersected by the
mud fences. He then promised them victory, and a
return to the capital. But when the men ascertained,
beyond a doubt, that their destination was for the

cordillera, such were the attractions of Lima that
discontents arose, and a mutiny was prevented only
by the active energy of Valdez, Loriga, and other
royalist chiefs, and by shooting an officer and nine
rank and file. At 5 P. M. the patriot infantry marched
three leagues, and bivouacked at the foot of the Cuesta
of Puruchuco. Miller having ridden in the dark a
quarter of a mile in front of his column, suddenly met
six Spanish deserters, headed by Serjeant Gineres,
who, supposing him to be a royalist officer, were preparing to despatch him : but upon his challenging
them, they luckily perceived, by his accent, that he
was no royalist, and gave themselves up. They described Canterac to be a league in advance, about half
way up the mountain. With the montoneros and half
a dozen trumpeters the royalist army might have been
put into commotion, if not dispersed ; but the montoneros had been unaccountably ordered, by superior
authority, to the rear from Macas, and the light division was too much fatigued to undertake the double
duty of alarming the enemy at night, and of performing long marches in the day. Indeed, so tired were
they, that not a man could have advanced a mile
farther.

At daybreak on the 22d, the division began to
climb a fatiguing ascent of two leagues of the *cuesta*,
or mountain side of Puruchuco, on which was discerned the royalist rear-guard. So narrow, rugged,
and steep was this zigzag track, that the patriots were
obliged to march in single files, their line extending
over half a league of ground. Upon gaining a small
level spot near the summit, the headmost files halted,
and the rest formed as they came up ; but they were

all so fatigued that they were allowed to lie down upon their arms. At no great distance in front, a few royalists were seen to come out from behind crags, covered with heath and brushwood. They called out that they wished to pass over to the patriots. O'Brien, accompanied by a trumpeter, rode forward to parley with them, but he had not proceeded far when the pretended deserters commanded him to halt *. At this time a royalist battalion issued from an ambuscade; but finding that the patriot party was not to be entrapped, they pursued their march to the summit of the mountain. The light infantry company of Numancia, commanded by the gallant Captain Saens, and some cavalry, were sent forward, under the orders of O'Brien, who skirmished for about an hour; but three royalist battalions having countermarched to support their rearguard, O'Brien was compelled to fall back, and the patriot division was drawn up so as to defend a strong pass; and they continued in this position all night, expecting to be attacked; but the royalists continued their retreat.

The montoneros having been permitted to rejoin, Miller with these, a company of the battalion No. 7, and the cavalry, marched, on the morning of the 22d, to the village of Puruchuco, situated in a recess on the eastern side of the mountain. From a high hill the patriots saw the royalists, in Huamantanga,

* In 1824, when Miller was on his passage from Valparaiso to Peru in a patriot brig of war, which captured a Spanish boat off Callao bound to Pisco, a royalist officer, with despatches, was taken. In a conversation with Miller he asked if he recollected the circumstance that occurred on the *cuesta* of Puruchuco, and said, that he commanded the very party which endeavoured to decoy the patriots into an ambush.

a small town on the crest of an eminence two leagues from Puruchuco.

The montoneros were sent to the front, whilst the cavalry and infantry bivouacked in some pasture grounds. Amongst the luxuries of Puruchuco, two loaves of bread were procured, and were an unusual treat. The rest of the division was marched back to Macas, as it was not without risk to have the whole light division unsupported so near the royalist army, which showed no disposition to move from Huamantanga.

On the 23d, Miller rode to within five hundred yards of Huamantanga to reconnoitre. He saw the enemy drawn up, as if in perfect readiness to make some movement. He rode back to Puruchuco; formed his company; and placed the montoneros, dismounted, in the ravines of the mountain side. He had no sooner done this than the royalists rapidly descended with the greater part of their force, consisting of the first battalion of the regiment imperial; second battalion of the 1st regiment; one hundred dragoons of the union regiment; and their granaderos à caballo of the guard; in all two thousand men. The montoneros were driven in, and Miller was expelled from his strong position, with the loss of fifteen killed, twenty-five wounded, and six missing. The Spaniards, in their official accounts, reckon the loss of the patriots at fifty in killed alone, and their numbers at five hundred infantry: whereas there were only one hundred and twenty-one regulars, all raw troops, and many of them boys from fourteen to seventeen years of age. O'Brien, with a small party of infantry, by a well-directed fire, kept the royalists in check, and enabled the patriots to make an orderly retreat. O'Brien and Miller were more than once on the point of being made prisoners. They were saved by the goodness of their horses, and galloped down declivities that, at another time, they would hardly have descended on horseback at a walk. Lieutenant-Colonel Davalos, commanding the montoneros, behaved exceedingly well, as did Captain Prieto of the battalion No. 7.   The patriots reached Macas at midnight, when Miller had the mortification to find that his next in command, Lieutenant-Colonel Capa Rosa, a Spaniard, had retired two leagues farther than his orders authorized him to do.

Finding his division insufficient in numbers to continue an effectual pursuit, Miller ordered it to Lima, with the exception of thirty picked dragoons. With these, and some montoneros, he and O'Brien marched on the 24th again to the front by a different route. They bivouacked the first night by the side of a stream, flowing through a few fertile fields in a grand and beautiful ravine.

On the 25th they joined a montonero party, commanded by a chieftain named Quiros; a man of great natural abilities, tried courage, and of extraordinary tact in command.   He had been, not long before, a captain of banditti, and had, on coming out of jail for the fourth time, been publicly whipped. At a former period he had reduced his highway exploits to so much system, that there were not wanting merchants and others who paid him tribute to exempt their muleteers and cargoes from plunder.   Had Quiros received a proper education, he must have become a shining military character.

His party consisted of men of lawless habits, wearing long beards, and dressed in the most grotesque manner. Halting at night, it was curious to hear the conversation of these fellows seated in groups around their fires. One avowed having committed seventeen murders; another having strangled a woman of seventy, and violated her daughter. Almost every one boasted of some deed of darkness. As most of them had been followers of Quiros in his former capacity, he preserved the most absolute authority, in spite of the familiarity which subsisted: and this party, one hundred and fifty strong, was the most daring and efficient of the montoneros. Quiros was afterwards wounded and taken prisoner in action near Pisco. His wife, who always accompanied him, fell fighting by his side. Quiros was shot by the royalists on the same day.

On the 26th, O'Brien proceeded towards Canta with the montoneros of Davalos. Miller, still suffering from ague, remained behind, in company with Quiros and his *delectable* associates.

The *quebrada*, or ravine, was most romantic. The grandeur of the mountain sides, studded with overhanging rocks; the torrent which foamed below; the huts at different elevations, in the midst of cultivated patches; and the narrow zigzag paths leading to them, imparted a picturesque air of mountain magnificence, whilst its loneliness, and the *Newgatonian* character and conversation of those around, gave a depth of interest equal to its novelty.

On the 27th, Miller ordered two montonero parties across the cordillera in observation of the enemy, who passed it on the 25th. One of them found the corpse of General Sanchez, who had been left in the rear by the retreating royalists, and who expired in a hut by the road-side. Sanchez was the officer who treated Miller with harshness at Talcahuano in 1818. Having no further object to induce him to remain in front, and the bracing air of the mountain having driven away his ague, Miller took leave of the montonero chieftains, Davalos and Quiros, and, on the 28th, returned to Lima, where he reported for cowardice the Lieutenant-Colonel Capa Rosa, who afterwards passed over to the royalists, but has since transferred his *valuable* services to Mexico.

Although the pursuit, by the light division, was not altogether successful in its object, it captured three hundred head of oxen, some horses and mules; obliged Canterac to destroy his military stores; and facilitated the desertion of above one thousand royalists, in spite of the exertions and severities of their chiefs.

San Martin has been greatly blamed for remaining before Callao with a single battalion (No. 4) and thirty cavalry, instead of placing himself at the head of the forces sent to molest the royalists in their retreat. The protector assigned as a reason, that he thought it necessary to preserve the direct communication opened with La Mar, governor of Callao, in order to prevent Lord Cochrane from obtaining possession of the castles, upon which it is said his lordship intended to hoist the Chileno flag, in opposition to the views and policy of the protector. A misunderstanding had existed for some time, and, without entering into the merits of conflicting statements, we shall notice the incident which rendered the breach irreparable. The admiral made a claim,

First. For arrears due to the squadron.

Secondly. A bounty equal to one year's pay for each individual of the squadron, agreeably to the promise made before sailing from Valparaiso.

Thirdly. Fifty thousand dollars, which had been promised to the seamen, in the event of their taking the Esmeralda; and

Fourthly. One hundred and ten thousand dollars, the estimated value of the frigate.

The protector contended, that the Chileno government was alone responsible for the first and fourth claim. He admitted the justice of the second and third, but required to have time allowed him to liquidate them. The admiral was highly dissatisfied with this answer. In the mean time, the royalist army approached the walls of Callao, when, as a matter of precaution, the coined and uncoined treasure belonging to government, as well as to private individuals, was removed from the Lima mint to transports lying at Ancon. The admiral sailed there, and seized the treasure to pay the squadron, and returned to the bay of Callao. His lordship stated the treasure so seized to have belonged to government, or to have been contraband, that is, silver sent on board unaccompanied by a document to prove the embarkation duty had been paid, and that the whole amounted to two hundred and five thousand dollars.

The protector, on the other hand, asserted that a great part of it was private property, and that the total sum was above four hundred thousand dollars.

The investment of the fortress presented the unfortunate spectacle of two chiefs, who ought to have acted in unison, offering terms separately to a third party, equally hostile to both. Callao surrendered on the 21st of September to the protector, upon terms highly favourable to the besieged. Colonel Don Tomas Guido was appointed governor of the castles.

On the 26th of the same month, the protector transmitted to Lord Cochrane a copy of that article of his private instructions, from the Chileno government, which authorized San Martin, as commander-in-chief of the liberating expedition, to employ *(disponer)* the whole, or any part, of the squadron as he might deem most expedient. In virtue of these powers he ordered the admiral, and the vessels under his command, to leave the coast of Peru. His lordship sailed, shortly afterwards, for California.

CHAPTER XVI.

Description of Lima.—Markets.—Vicinity.—Banditti.—Pantheon.—Bridge.— Baths.—Cathedral.—Palace.—Fountain.—Theatre.——Bull circus.——Bull fights.——Climate.——Routs.—Balls.—Uninvited spectators.—Tapadas.—Gaming.—Inhabitants.— Palanganas.—Ladies of Lima.—Costume.—Peruvian legion.— Patriot and royalist forces.—Supreme delegate.—Distress at sea.—Spanish ships capitulate.—Lord Cochrane returns to Chile.—Quits the service.—The surprise at Ica.—Battle of Pinchincha.—Interview between Bolivar and the protector.—Monteagudo banished.—Congress installed.—San Martin retires from public life.

THE viceroyalty of Peru formerly comprehended the whole of the Spanish dominions in South America. Lima, its capital, was the centre of riches, influence, political intrigue, and dissipation. The elevation of the subordinate governments of Buenos Ayres and of New Granada to vice-regal rank diminished the consequence of Lima, but it still retained its court, and continued to be the favourite resort of the wealthy and the sensual. The city, ten miles in circumference, is built on the left bank of the Rimac, in a plain near the foot of some of the lower branches of the Andes. Viewed from the bay of Callao, its numerous domes and towers give to it an air decidedly oriental. The prospect at sunset is particularly interesting, for when twilight has already thrown the landscape of the plain into deep shade, the domes of the city are still gilded by the departing sun, and when these also become shrouded in darkness, the peaky summits of the mountains continue for some time to be illumined by his lingering beams. The approach from Callao is by a fine road, the last mile of which is shaded by four rows of lofty trees, forming a handsome promenade, with benches. The entrance is by a noble gate built by the public-spirited viceroy Don Ambrosio O'Higgins, Marquess of Osorno.

The city was founded by Pizarro in 1535. It contains about seventy thousand inhabitants, three hundred and sixty streets, nearly four thousand houses, fifty-four churches, monasteries, and chapels, a theatre, and a university. The Moorish aspect does not altogether disappear on closer inspection. The houses, like those in most other Spanish American towns, are disposed in *quadras*, or square plots, and are generally one story in height, having a light and flat roof. The *quadras* are equal in size, and form straight streets, nearly forty feet wide, intersecting each other at right angles. The best residences are scattered amidst houses of a meaner sort. The description of one of the former may perhaps convey an idea of the usual plan of a mansion in any Spanish American city. A single building sometimes occupies half a *quadra*. A line of dead wall, relieved by a lofty gateway, forms the street front, except when it is converted into shops, which have no communication with the inner court. In consequence of the frequency of earthquakes, the houses consist generally of a ground floor only. The apartments occupied by the family, the offices, coach-houses, and

stabling, being in the same court-yard, which is divided in the centre by a suite of lofty and well-pro-
portioned reception rooms, capable of being thrown
into one by means of large folding doors, which are
in themselves very handsome, the upper part consisting of splendid panes of plate glass enriched with
highly burnished gilded mouldings.   The windows
are open to the ground, and are secured by iron bars
wrought in a manner highly ornamental, and partially gilded.   The centre suite of apartments commands a view through the gateway into the street.
Some of the houses are of two stories, with a balcony round the upper floor, whilst the exterior fronts
have large verandas, latticed in a fashion completely
Moorish.   The roofs are flat, and mostly formed
with rafters made of canes tied five together, and
covered with matting; others are built much stronger,
and being paved with bricks, form an agreeable promenade.

A shallow stream of water, of two feet in width,
runs through the centre of the principal streets, and
contributes much to carrying off impurities.   These
miniature canals are supplied by means of a dam
placed across the Rimac, by which a portion of the
water is diverted into them at some distance above
the city.   The streets are paved, but badly lighted,
and are patrolled by watchmen, who vociferate "*Ave
Maria purisima! viva la patria!*" and a serene,
or cloudy, sky; as if either the Virgin Mary or
patriotism had any thing in common with the hour
of the night, or the state of the weather.

In the less frequented parts of the city the eye is

offended by unsightly proofs of the total inattention of the police to general cleanliness. The markets are plentifully supplied with fish, fruit, vegetables, &c. The standings are usually under portable canvas awnings, of a circular shape, made fast to a long pole, like an umbrella. Monks, with wallets slung across their shoulders, go punctually round, and collect the offerings of the pious market-people, who have always something in readiness for the holy mother church. A remarkable feature in the market is the rows formed by the stands of the *mistureras*, or flower-women, who are at the same time venders of perfumery, for both of which there is a great consumption in Lima. The narrow avenues so formed are called *calles de peligro*, or paths of peril, and are much frequented by gallants, who make purchases of bouquets for those ladies on whom they are in attendance, the flowers of Lima being particularly beautiful. Such is the competition occasioned by these love-stricken swains, that seven or eight dollars have been frequently paid for a single carnation.

The walls of the town describe four-fifths of a circle, resting upon the river, having seven gates, and thirty-three bastions; but the ramparts are too narrow to admit of heavy ordnance being placed upon them.

Lima is situated in a plain about ten or twelve leagues in circumference, irregularly indented by gentle elevations, which, being above the level of irrigation, are condemned to irreclaimable sterility. Small hills are scattered over various parts of the plain, resembling barrows, which are covered with the ruins of villages. The fortress of Callao contains from two to three thousand inhabitants; and in the valley of the Rimac are also the fishing town of Chorrillos, the large villages of Miraflores, Magdalena, Surco, and some small hamlets. The rest of the valley is parcelled out into fine estates, some of which are worth from five hundred thousand to a million of dollars each. These are surrounded by high mud walls, called *tapias*, and subdivided by quadrangular fences of the same materials, four or five feet high. The principal produce is sugar, Indian corn, legumes, chirimoyas, oranges, olives, plantains, bananas, alligator-pears, apples, lucern, and various other fruits and vegetables common to the torrid and temperate zones. Fuel is exceedingly expensive; fires are seldom made but for culinary purposes, and then with the greatest parsimony. Charcoal is brought by the aborigines from great distances. A particular kind of willow is planted along the banks of the azequias, and underneath flowers the nasturtium, or nun of Peru. In a few swampy spots the wild cane runs up to a luxuriant height, and forms extensive clumps of airy elegance, giving variety to the verdant prospect. Could the reader imagine Milan placed within twenty miles of Duomo d'Ossola, he may form a clear idea of the circumjacent landscape, this land view of the lower ridges of the Andes bearing a strong resemblance to the Italian Alps in outline and in altitude.

The vicinity of the capital is occasionally infested by banditti, carrying on their operations in open day with

so much system, that all who chance to travel at that
time are sure to be relieved of their valuables.   These
robbers are composed chiefly of free mulattoes and
others of a mixed race.   The evil has existed from
time immemorial, and is of purely Spanish origin; for
Indian honesty, in retired villages, is so great, that
when a family for a time leaves its cage-like hut, the
latchless wicket is left ajar; a brush is placed on the
sill, and it would be worse than sacrilege for any one
to cross the threshold under any pretence.   It has
happened that the brigands, well armed and well
mounted, have assembled at distant and uncertain
periods within a mile of Callao.   They direct their
course towards Lima, stop all whom they meet, and
having very civilly lightened them of their purses,
oblige the plundered persons to accompany the robbers until all arrive near to the city gate, when the
bandits disperse.   Some ride boldly into the town;
many conceal themselves in the thickets of canes;
whilst others cut across the country, and return
quietly to their homes, to enjoy the spoil, or follow
their usual occupations.   The banditti, on such extraordinary occasions, amount to twenty or thirty in
number; and it has happened that they have had
about twenty carriages, besides persons dismounted
and made to lead their own horses, in the train,
which was regularly brought up by a rear-guard, while
the advanced scouts pushed on to secure fresh booty.
They seldom commit murder; and whenever it is
possible, they avoid robbing officers of the army, or
civilians in the employment of government.   Neither
do they, when acting in small parties, attack persons

of note. Foreigners and strangers are in general their usual victims. In 1822, two Chileno gentlemen, named Errazuris and Baras, were stopped. Errazuris told the chief bandit that the horse on which he rode was a borrowed one, belonging to an officer in the army, and so valuable that he could not replace it; he therefore entreated that the animal might not be taken. The robber replied, " We cannot give it up at present, as good horses are exactly what we are most in need of, being on the eve of a distant excursion ; but say where you live, and the horse shall be returned." A few mornings after, it was found in the court of the house of Doña Rosita Cortes (a descendant of the celebrated Hernan Cortes), where Errazuris had taken up his residence. The other gentleman, from whom a few thousand dollars had been taken, perceiving that the request of his friend was so readily complied with, told the robbers that he had no more money than what they had taken, and begged them to return enough for him to subsist upon in Callao. They asked him how much he wanted. He answered, a few doubloons; upon which the robbers refunded a hundred dollars, and all parties then took a polite leave of each other. To the practice of abstaining from personal violence, and to the discriminating exemption granted to influential persons, may be attributed in a great measure the degree of impunity enjoyed by these well-bred *chevaliers d'industrie*.

The pantheon, half a mile east of the city, is the general cemetery. It is a large circular enclosure, having a handsome entrance, and a well built chapel for the performance of the burial service. Behind

the chapel are seven double tiers of brick-work, divided into compartments, each of sufficient dimensions to admit a full-sized coffin, and which, when
occupied, is closed at the end, and a tablet with
the name of the deceased recorded on it. There are
thousands of these receptacles, but, as this mode of
interment is expensive, the poor are buried in long
and deep trenches, which are gradually filled by the
number of corpses daily deposited, and by the slight
covering of earth which is thrown upon them. Monks
are in constant attendance, and reprieved malefactors
are employed to perform the office of inhumation,
and to keep this great burial-ground in order.

A stone bridge over the Rimac leads to the extensive suburb of San Lazaro, at the eastern extremity
of which is a fine alameda, or public walk, above
half a mile in length, overlooking the river. This
conducts to the bull-ring, and to the baths of Antaza,
which are spacious and excellent. Not a great distance from thence, and leading to the Conventillo de
los Descalzos, is a small alameda, ornamented with
fountains and grottoes.

The cathedral is a large, handsome, though heavy
structure. The viceregal palace is a spacious building, but without architectural merit. There are inner courts, around which are offices for the treasury,
and ministers of the war and home departments. The
ascent to the state rooms is from the west front of
the palace, by a grand marble staircase. The most
interesting ornaments of these apartments are original
portraits of forty-four viceroys who governed Peru,
from Pizarro down to Pezuela. Each viceroy was

expected, on taking office, to have a painting of himself placed in the saloon, and it is remarkable that the
last vacant panel was filled by the portrait of Pezuela.
The head of Pizarro is classically shaped, his forehead
high, nose Grecian, complexion dark, and countenance much covered by a long, black, and martial
beard. The different shades of complexion, from the
Moorish down to the modern Spanish, as also the
gradual variety of costumes which these interesting
pictures display, furnish matter for curious con-
templation. Several of the paintings have been injured, though the South American rabble are less
prone to destruction than were the puritans of England, or the revolutionary mobs of France. The
Limeña populace is equally ardent, but less wanton,
than the destroying hordes of Europe, who boast of
her superior refinement.

The palace and cathedral occupy the northern and
eastern sides of the plaza, or great square; the town-
house and gaol, together with spacious houses consisting of two stories, ornamented by an arcade, complete the quadrangle. Shops and stalls are placed
under the arcade. In the centre of the square is a
handsome fountain, having bronze figures round the
reservoir. In the evening, numbers of persons assemble in front of the arcades, to regale themselves
with ices, orgeat, lemonade, sweetmeats, &c. The
proprietors of the adjoining coffee-houses place
benches and chairs for general accommodation, and
many people remain thus in the open air until midnight. The theatre is a well arranged and neat
building. The performances take place three times

a week, and are tolerably good. The head of the executive attends, in rather more than republican simplicity, his cavalcade consisting of a state carriage drawn by six horses or mules, attended by an escort and torch-bearers.

A captain's guard is on duty during the performance, and sentries are stationed in various parts of the house, as in continental theatres. In the pit, immediately under the government-box, are placed a corporal and six soldiers with carried arms. Adjoining the state-box is one skreened from public view, in which General San Martin was accustomed to grant interviews, especially to such of his secret agents as could not conveniently appear at the palace. They could glide into this private box, deliver in their reports, and receive fresh instructions, without attracting observation. Smoking at the theatre is now prohibited. Under the old régime it was permitted between the acts; when the viceroy withdrew from the front of his box, and was supposed to be absent, at which moment hundreds of pocket tinder-boxes were produced, and clouds of smoke arose. On drawing up the curtain, the viceroy resumed his seat, and every cigar was suddenly extinguished. The use of the cigar is still so prevalent, that it is frequently seen in the mouth of a woman, or placed in reserve behind her ear, in imitation of the pen of a shopman. Ladies rarely indulge avowedly in the practice, and the mere attempt at concealment proves that the custom is growing into disrepute.

The amphitheatre, in which the bull-fights are held,

is the best constructed and most convenient place of public amusement in Lima. The exterior wall is a circus of about half a mile in circumference : three, tiers of boxes enclose an uncovered arena. Above the ground tier, and in front of the middle one, which recedes, ten or twelve rows of benches are placed, which slope from the front of the boxes to the extreme edge of the roof of the lower tier. The seats accommodate ten thousand spectators, and, whenever this favourite diversion takes place, are crowded as well with beauty and rank as with the motley and variously tinged populace. In the centre of the arena is an escapade, composed of two rows of strong palisades, intersecting so as to form a cross. The stakes are wide enough apart to allow a man to pass between them.

The taste for bull-fights, introduced by the early Spaniards, is retained by their American descendants with undiminished ardour. The announcement of an exhibition of this kind produces a state of universal excitement. The streets are thronged, and the population of the surrounding country, dressed in their gayest attire, add to the multitudes of the city. The sport is conducted with an éclat that exceeds the bull-fights in every other part of South America, and perhaps even surpasses those of Madrid. The death of the bull, when properly managed, creates as much interest in the ladies of Lima as the death of the hare to the English huntress, or the winning horse to the titled dames at Newmarket or Doncaster; nor can the pugilistic *fancy* of Eng-

CHAP. XVI.   BULL-FIGHTS.   393

land take a deeper interest in the event of a prize
fight than the gentlemen of Lima in the scientific
worrying of a bull.

It is curious to observe how various are ideas of
cruelty in different countries. The English, for
instance, exclaim against the barbarity of the bull-
fight, as compared with the *noble* sports of cock-
fighting, badger-baiting, &c.; but their enlightened
horror could not exceed the disgust shown by a
young South American, who witnessed a casual box-
ing-match between two boys in Hyde Park, surrounded and encouraged, as he expressed himself,
by *well-dressed barbarians*. It is amusing to witness the complacency with which one nation accuses
another of cruelty, without taking a glance at customs at home.

The bulls destined for the ring are obtained principally from the woods in the valleys of Chincha,
where they are bred in a wild state. To catch and
drive them to Lima, a distance of sixty leagues, is a
matter of no inconsiderable expense. A bull is given
by each *gremio,* or incorporated trading company, of
the city. The gremios vie in decorating their donation, which is bedizened with ribands and flowers;
across its shoulders are suspended mantles, richly
embroidered with the arms of the gremios to which
it belongs, all of which becomes the perquisite of
the *matador* who slays the bull.

Early in the afternoon of the day fixed for a bull-
fight, every street leading to the amphitheatre is
crowded with carriages, horsemen, and pedestrians.
All are in the greatest glee, and in full dress. The

price of admission is four reales, or two shillings, but
an additional charge is made for seats in the boxes.
The managers pay a considerable tax to government
on every performance.

About 2 P. M. the business of the circus commences, by a curious sort of prelude. A company
of soldiers perform a *despejo,* or a military panto-
mime. The men, having been previously drilled
for that purpose, go through a variety of fanciful
evolutions, forming the Roman and Greek crosses,
stars, and figures describing a sentence, such as *viva
la patria! viva San Martin!* or the name of any
other person who happens to be at the head of the
government. As a finale, the soldiers form a circle,
face outwards, then advance towards the boxes, preserving their circular order, while they extend until
they approach close enough to climb up to the benches.
Every movement is made to the sound of the drum;
and the effect is exceedingly good. A band of music
is likewise in attendance, and plays at intervals.

The prelude being over, six or seven *toreadores*
enter the arena on foot, dressed in silk jackets of different colours, richly spangled and bordered with gold
or silver lace. One or two of these men are *matadores;*
they are pardoned criminals, and receive a considerable sum for every bull they kill. About the same
time various amateurs, well mounted on steeds gaily
caparisoned, fancifully and tastefully attired, present
themselves. When all is prepared, a door is opened
under the box occupied by the municipality, and a
bull rushes from a pen. At first he gazes about in
surprise, but he is soon put upon his mettle by the

waving of flags, and the throwing of darts, crackers, and other annoyances. The amateur cavaliers display their horsemanship and skill in provoking his ire, and in eluding his vengeance, in order to catch the eye of some favourite fair one, as well as to gain the applause of their friends and the audience. They infuriate the animal by waving a mantle over his head; when pursued, they do not allow their horses to recede more than a few inches from the horns of the angry bull. When at full speed, they make their horse revolve upon his hind legs, and remain in readiness to make a second turn on the animal. This operation is several times repeated, with equal agility and boldness, and is called *capear*. The amateurs then promenade around, to acknowledge the plaudits bestowed. This species of *sparring on horseback* with the bull is practised only in South America. Indeed, in no other part of the world is the training of the horses or the dexterity of the rider equal to the performance of such exploits. Effigies made of skin, and filled with wind, and others made of straw, in which are live birds, are placed in the arena. The bull tosses them in the air, but the effigies, being made heavy at the base, come to the ground, and always retain an upright posture. The straw figures are furnished with fireworks, which are made to take fire, on the birds escaping; and it often happens that the bull runs about with the cracking figure upon his horns. Sometimes he is maddened by fireworks being fastened on him, which go off in succession. The crackers being expended, the animal usually stands gazing around with rolling tongue, panting sides, and eyes sparkling with rage. He is then faced by the principal matador, who holds a straight sword in one hand, and a flag in the other. As the bull runs at him at full speed, the matador coolly, but with great celerity, takes one step to the left, holding the flag just over the spot he occupied when the bull took aim. Being foiled, he wheels round, and charges his tormentor a second time, who again skilfully eludes being caught on the horns. This is repeated about three times, to the great delight of the audience. At length the matador assumes a sort of fencing attitude, and, watching the proper moment, as the bull runs at him, plunges his sword into the animal's neck, near its shoulders, when it falls down dead at his feet. Handkerchiefs are then waved, and applauding shouts resound. Four horses, richly harnessed, next appear. The dead bull is quickly fixed to traces, and dragged out at a gallop, cheered by continued acclamations.

> "Four steeds that spurn the rein, as swift as shy,
> Hurl the dark bulk along, scarce seen in dashing by."—BYRON.

Other bulls are killed in the same way by successive matadores. One is generally despatched by means of a long knife, grasped by the matador, so that when his arm is extended, the blade is perpendicular to the wrist. The bull being worried for a time, the matador, instead of receiving him on the point of a sword, as before, steps one pace aside, as the bull runs at him, and adroitly plunges the knife into the spinal marrow, behind the horns, when the animal drops instantly dead. Another bull is next attacked by mounted *picadores*, armed with lances. Their

legs are protected by padding.   Their horses are of
little value, and cannot easily get out of the way of
the bull.   Neither do the riders often attempt it, as
to do so, is considered cowardly.   The consequence
is, the horses generally receive a mortal gore.   Part
of their entrails are frequently torn out, and exhibit
a most disgusting spectacle.   The riders run considerable risk, for their lances are inadequate to killing the bull, which, after being pierced and mangled,
is finally despatched by a matador.

> " Foil'd, bleeding, breathless, furious to the last,
> Full in the centre stands the bull at bay,
> Mid wounds, and clinging darts, and lances brast,
> And foes disabled in the brutal fray :
> And now the matadors around him play,
> Shake the red cloak, and poise the ready brand.
> Once more through all he bursts his thund'ring way—
> Vain rage! the mantle quits the cunning hand,
> Wraps his fierce eye—'tis past—he sinks upon the sand!"—BYRON.

The next bull, as he sallies from the pen, is encountered by six or eight Indians with short lances,
who kneel down, like the front rank of a battalion
to receive a cavalry charge.   One or two Indians
are usually tossed.   The others follow up the bull,
and when he turns upon them, they drop on one
knee, and receive him as before.   They are seldom
able to despatch him; and a matador steps forward
to end his sufferings.   Some of the Indians are often
much hurt.   They invariably make themselves half
drunk before they enter the circus, alleging, that
they can fight the bull better when they *see double*.

Again another bull is let into the ring, for the
lanzada, or trial of the lance, the handle of which
is very long and strong, fixed into a wooden socket
secured to the ground, and supported by an Indian

toreador. The head of the lance is a long blade, of
highly tempered steel, made sharp as a razor. Before the bull is permitted to leave the pen, he is
rendered furious by a variety of torments. When
he has been sufficiently maddened, the doors are
thrown open, and the animal makes a rush at the
Indian who is dressed in scarlet, and directs the
lance as he kneels on the ground. The raging bull
runs at him, but he steadily points the lance so as
to receive the bull on its point. Such is the force
with which he plunges at his opponent, that the
lance generally enters at the head, and, breaking
through skull and bones, comes out at the sides or
back.

Finally, a bull, with tail erect, comes bellowing
and bounding in, with a man strapped on his back.
The animal jumps and capers about, making every
possible effort to rid himself of his burden, to the
no small amusement of the spectators. The rider
at length loosens the straps, and the bull is attacked
on all sides by amateurs on foot and on horseback.
When a matador has killed a bull, he bows to the
government-box, to the municipality, and all around,
receiving plaudits in proportion to the skill he has
shown, and the sport he has afforded. Advancing
then to the box of the municipality, he receives his
reward from one of the members appointed as judge,
or umpire, on the occasion, which consists of a few
dollars thrown into the arena. When the spectators
are particularly gratified by the performance, they
also throw money into the arena.

Dryden has given so spirited and correct a de-

scription of a bull-fight, that we cannot refrain from
transcribing it in this place.

> " One bull, with curl'd black head beyond the rest,
> And dewlaps hanging from his brawny chest,
> With nodding front awhile did daring stand,
> And with his jetty hoof spurn'd back the sand;
> Then leaping forth, he bellow'd out aloud:
> The' amazed assistants back each other crowd,
> While monarch-like he rang'd the listed field;
> Some toss'd, some gored, some trampling down he kill'd.
> The' ignoble Moors from far his rage provoke
> With woods of darts, which from his sides he shook.
> Meantime your valiant son, who had before
> Gain'd fame, rode round to every mirador;
> Beneath each lady's stand a stop he made,
> And, bowing, took the applauses which they paid.
>   *   *   *   *
> Thus while he stood, the bull, who saw his foe,
> His easier conquests proudly did forego,
> And, making at him with a furious bound,
> From his bent forehead aim'd a double wound.
> A rising murmur ran through all the field,
> And ev'ry lady's blood with fear was chill'd :
> Some shriek'd, while others, with more helpful care,
> Cried out aloud, ' Beware, brave youth, beware !'
> At this he turn'd, and as the bull drew near,
> Shunn'd, and received him on his pointed spear.
> The lance broke short, the beast then bellow'd loud,
> And his strong neck to a new onset bow'd.
> The undaunted youth
> Then drew, and from his saddle bending low,
> Just where the neck did to the shoulders grow,
> With his full force discharged a deadly blow.
> Not heads of poppies (when they reap the grain)
> Fall with more ease before the lab'ring swain
> Than fell this head :
> It fell so quick, it did even death prevent,
> And made imperfect bellowings as it went.
> Then all the trumpets victory did sound;
> And yet their clangors in our shouts were drown'd."
>   CONQUEST OF GRANADA.

Notwithstanding that Lima is situated in twelve
degrees south latitude, Fahrenheit's thermometer
seldom rises to 70° in the shade. This low temperature is probably caused by the rays of the sun
being, for a great part of the year, intercepted by a
fleecy, or mottled veil of clouds, called by sailors a
mackarel sky. At one season of the year, *garuas*,
or heavy mists, prevail, which chill the air and moisten

the ground sufficiently to render the pavement slippery. With the exception of intermittent fevers,
Lima is subject to no epidemical disease. Those
who outlive fifty years generally attain the age of
eighty and upwards, for which reason Lima has been
called the paradise of the old.

In this city, as at Buenos Ayres, Santiago de
Chile, &c. families are *at home* every evening to
their friends, which is called the tertulia. The
only refreshments offered consist of liqueurs, sweetmeats, and a glass of water. People walk in and
out, and join the dance without ceremony. Nothing can be more agreeable than this unconstrained
intercourse, from which even strangers are not churl-
ishly debarred; whilst the circumstance of being a
foreigner is usually in itself a sufficient introduction.
If he understands the language tolerably well, and
makes himself agreeable, his future visits are encouraged, by the assurance, on his taking leave of the
hostess, that the house is at his disposal, which is
equivalent to a general invitation. The *baile de
convite*, or the set party, is an affair of no small
moment. Great preparations are made for many
days previous, nor is the *baile de convite* a matter
of indifference to the uninvited, as custom gives to
the populace the privilege of being spectators. A
porter usually takes his station at the gateway, but
does not dispute the entrance into the court-yard of
orderly persons of any class. These crowd about
the doors and windows in such numbers, that a lane
must be made for the guests as they arrive. These

lookers-on are not sparing in their observations, but
are careful never to utter a joke that can offend.
This privilege claimed, and pertinaciously exercised,
by the uninvited, is one which they would not quietly
relinquish. An English gentleman once shut his gate,
but it was forced, and the foreigner had the good sense
to quell the revolt by conforming good-naturedly to
a custom which he found himself unequal to set aside,
and which, he also discovered, was as agreeable to
the gazed-at, as to the gazers.   Indeed the distinguished beaux and belles would not only consider
it a flat evening unless admired by the crowd, but
the whole party would feel disappointed if there were
none to look on and vary the scene.   Besides these
threshold guests, there is another class of visiters
peculiar to South America, called *tapadas*, or muf-
fled-up females, who are frequently of a rank, or in-
timacy, to entitle them to an invitation, but who,
being elderly, or unprovided with a proper dress, or
not liking the trouble of dressing, or slightly indisposed, or in deep mourning, or from some other
cause, prefer to attend in the character of unseen
spectators.   Some go thus disguised in consequence
of not being of a rank in life to appear otherwise,
and it is maliciously supposed that some few attend
for purposes of flirtation.   The tapadas are accommo-
dated with seats in adjoining rooms, which have no
other light than what is thrown through the folding doors; they give a piquancy to these balls which
otherwise they would not possess.   They do not
always preserve their incognita very strictly, but chat
with such of their friends as come to them.   The

dancers, particularly the young men, frequently leave
the ball-room to converse with some veiled friend,
and many tender disclosures are made on these happy
opportunities. Balls were not very frequent at Lima
previous to the entrance of the patriots. When General San Martin established his head-quarters there,
he gave an assembly once a week at the palace. At
first the ladies who had been accustomed to minuets,
the *fandango*, *mariquita*, and *guachambai*, were not
perfectly *au fait* at country dances; but they were
apt scholars, and soon became graceful dancers, and
passionately fond of that amusement.

Gambling, the besetting sin of the indolent in
many countries, is ruinously general throughout
South America. In England, and other European
states, it is pretty much limited to the unemployed
of the upper classes, who furnish a never-ending
supply of dupes to knavery. In South America
the passion taints all ages, both sexes, and every
rank. The dregs of society yield to the fascination
as blindly as the high-born and wealthy of the old or
of the new world. Perhaps gaming ought not to be
subjected to legal restraints: so long as the gamester
is without family ties, and stakes but his own property, he is surely at liberty to fool it away as he
pleases. If the transfer benefits no third party, it
at least occasions the public advantage of dispersing
an overgrown patrimony. If any thing can be advanced in extenuation of the vice, as practised in
South America, it is the baneful policy of the Spanish system, which once almost totally shut out the
active and well-disposed mind from the resources

of reading, study, and honourable pursuits. Hence play was not merely an amusement, but an occupation. Fortunately, public opinion, the only efficacious check, is beginning to take a right direction. It speaks much in favour of the revolution, that this vice is sensibly diminishing in Peru, and to the unfortunate Monteagudo belongs the honour of having been the first to attempt its eradication. A noted gambler was once as much an object of admiration in South America as a six-bottle man was in England fifty years ago. The houses of the great were converted into nightly hells, where the priesthood were amongst the most regular and adventurous attendants. Those places are now more innocently enlivened by music and dancing. Buena Vista, a seat of the late Marquess of Montemira, six leagues from Lima, was the Sunday rendezvous of every fashionable of the capital who had a few doubloons to risk on the turn of a card. On one occasion, a fortunate player, the celebrated Baquijano, was under the necessity of sending for a bullock car to convey his winnings, amounting to above thirty thousand dollars: a mule thus laden with specie was a common occurrence. Chorillos, a fishing town, three leagues south of Lima, is a fashionable watering-place for a limited season. Here immense sums are won and lost; but political and literary coteries, formerly unknown, daily lessen the numbers of the votaries of fortune.

To show the effects of gaming amongst the soldiery, the following anecdotes are introduced. Two non-commissioned officers, who had been remarkable

for bravery and steady conduct, suddenly disappeared.
They were pursued, and, when brought back, con-
fessed that the motive which induced them to abscond
was, their having had an extraordinary run of luck
at play, by which, in the course of a few evenings,
they had won upwards of fifteen hundred dollars each.
Considering such sums ample fortunes, they resolved
to . quit the army, and, when taken, they were on
their way to establish themselves in their native villages. The patriot commander asked one of his
officers what punishment ought to be inflicted.
"Shoot them both," was the reply. "If I do so,"
answered the patriot general, "I ought to shoot
every gambler in the division; and in that case I
should hardly have an officer or private soldier left.
Besides, I ought, in justice, to begin with you, who
are notoriously addicted to play." The two offenders
were pardoned; but a second run of good fortune
having afterwards added to their ill-gotten wealth,
they took their measures more cautiously, and, deserting a second time, got clear off. So strong was
this ruling passion, that when the patriot army has
been closely pursued by the royalists, and pay has
been issued to lighten the military chest, the officers,
upon halting, would spread their ponchos on the
ground, and play until it was time to resume the
march; and this was frequently done even on the eve
of a battle. Soldiers on piquet often gambled within
sight of an enemy's advanced post. A Colombian
officer, intrusted with two or three months' pay belonging to Colonel Don Thomas Heras, lost the
amount, and, being unable to replace it, attempted

to pass over to the royalists, but being taken at a patriot outpost, he was shot, by order of General Bolivar, who at that period commanded the liberating army in Peru. Perhaps no other vice, singly, produced so many drawbacks to the patriot cause as the unfortunate propensity to play on the part of ministers, envoys, and officers of all ranks, who too frequently dissipated public property intrusted to their care. Insubordination, desertion, occasional defeat, and a prolongation of the miseries of war, were some of the natural consequences of the unhappy propensity. A generation or two must pass away before a habit so general and so inveterate can be altogether rooted out. It is but fair to add, that one of the greatest recommendations an officer, particularly if he were a foreigner, could possess, was the reputation of not being a gambler. Few things tended more to obstruct his rise to responsible commands than habits of gaming.

The majority of the men of Lima have the appearance of being feeble and emaciated. These physical defects are certainly attributable not alone to climate, but may be ascribed also to the general dissoluteness which characterized the old regime; in proof of which, those who have latterly grown to maturity showed themselves, during the campaigns, to be hardy, enterprising, and infinitely superior to their predecessors, who had been taught to cringe to Spanish satraps, and to familiarize their minds with every species of meanness. Hence the duplicity, dishonesty, shameful political inconsistency, and total want of public spirit evinced by some few who have

attained office since the overthrow of the all-debasing
European despotism.   From the rising generation in
Peru higher expectations may be formed.   The youth
generally possess great natural vivacity as well as
talent, and are impelled by an honest ambition to
render themselves useful to their country.   The climate of Lima seems to be favourable to the quicken-
ing of the intellectual faculties.

   The native mulattos have great aptitude for trades,
becoming excellent shoemakers, tailors, barbers, car-
penters, &c.   From the church and the bar they
were excluded by the laws of the Indies, but many
acquired a knowledge of medicine, and some of those
who received a regular education have risen to great
eminence.   Such is the extreme volubility of this
mixed race, and the ease with which they express
their ideas, that they have acquired the nickname
of *palanganas*, or chatterers.   Sermons, and their
preachers, are favourite objects of criticism, probably
because there is a never-failing source in Lima, which
abounds in altars ; and a sermon, or rather an eulogium
upon the life and miracles of the principal saints, is
given at their respective festivals.   On these occasions
the palanganas seldom fail to indulge in their critical
propensity.   They remember, with provoking accuracy, sermons preached several years before, and
when a friar repeats an old discourse, the palangana
manifests his detection by violent gesticulation.   One
day a clergyman smarting under this annoyance exclaimed from the pulpit, " Turn out that mulatto,
who disturbs me."   " That," said the palangana, with
characteristic readiness, " is the only thing that is

new; all the rest was preached two years ago by
Father Francisco, in the church of Santo Domingo."
Sometimes a palangana not only remembers an entire
sermon, but will versify it on the repetition. Mulatto
servants will occasionally repeat one, word for word,
as delivered, and often draw their master and his
family to become auditors. Notwithstanding the
mental vivacity of the palanganas, they do not make
as good soldiers as the Indians, in consequence of
their inferiority in bodily strength, and more especially in the power of resisting the cold of the mountains, which the following anecdote will demonstrate.

In 1780 a battalion of palanganas was raised, and
sent to the interior, under the command of Inspector
Valle, to assist in putting down the insurrection of
Tupac-Amaru. The latter, knowing the complexion
of his opponents, studiously avoided coming to close
quarters until a fall of snow should render them an
easy prey, by depriving them of the free use of their
limbs. Accordingly, Tupac-Amaru fell upon them
early in the first morning after a severe frost, when
they were so benumbed that they could not handle
their muskets. The palanganas called out when the
action commenced, "Wait, Indians, wait, until the
sun shines out;" but they of course turned a deaf
ear to the proposal, and most of the mulattos were
slain.

Perhaps the proportionable number of *very* handsome women is smaller in Lima than in Guayaquil,
and in some other South American towns; but there
is in the manner of the Limeña a spell which gives
her an influence over the other sex unknown else-

where.   In consequence of the power they exercise,
and the consideration they enjoy, Lima is called the
heaven of women*.

The Limeñas have black, resistless eyes, delicately
arched eyebrows, finely turned arms, pretty shaped
hands, and feet bewitchingly small.   Their stature
is short, and nothing sets off their supple forms more
enticingly than the *saya* and the *manto*.   The saya
is an elastic petticoat, usually of silk, which fits rather
closely, and lessens in circumference as it approaches
the ankle, so much so, that the wearer is obliged to
take short steps.   It is an expensive article of dress,
costing very frequently upwards of ten pounds; is
made by men; and the prevailing colours are black or
brown.   The manto is a piece of black silk, formed
into a skirt, open in front.   This, when the ladies
walk out, is turned over the head, and, taking a
corner of it in each hand, hold it across, just under
the chin, which forms the manto into a complete
hood, that conceals the whole of the face, with the
exception of one eye, an engine that seldom appears
to be idle.   It might be imagined that some of these
jetty piercers belong to the houris promised by
Mahomet to the faithful.   It has been remarked *by
the malevolent,* that a gust of wind rarely deranges
the manto, so as to discover the features, unless a
stranger happen to be passing, and the face beneath
more than usually pretty.   This unique dress is the
costume of ladies when they go to church, to the
promenade, or to pay morning visits.   It is a sort of
domino, of Moorish origin, and often gives oppor-

* It is also called the purgatory of husbands, and the hell of asses.

tunities to those who may wish to indulge in innocent adventure, without provoking the noisy tongue of scandal. The Limeñas are esteemed warm in their attachments, but somewhat inconstant.

Having endeavoured to make the reader acquainted with the Peruvian capital, we will resume the thread of the narrative.

Shortly after the retreat of Canterac, the Peruvian legion of the guard was formed, the chief command of which was given to General the Marquess of Torre Tagle. It consisted of a regiment of hussars, Lieutenant-Colonel Brandsen; a troop of horse artillery, Captain Arenales; and a regiment of infantry, Colonel Miller. From the deserters from the enemy Miller selected forty good non-commissioned officers, and from two to three hundred privates. An equal number of mulattos and mestizos were soon recruited at Lima, and six hundred Indians were sent from the interior. His regiment was to consist of two battalions, each of eight companies of one hundred and fifty rank and file per company. The colonel was permitted to propose his own officers for the approval of the protector; several of the most active and intelligent of whom had before served under Miller's orders, and now joined him, besides many of the distinguished youths of the capital. The organization of his regiment became a favourite object with Miller, who studiously endeavoured to give to it a national character; and he completely succeeded in the attempt to infuse an *esprit de corps*, which it ever after retained. The uniform was blue with red facings,

white edging and red lace. The grenadier company
had high bearskin parade caps; the light company
had caps similar to those worn by English riflemen,
and the other companies the French chakos.

The hussar regiment of the legion was composed
of four squadrons, or eight troops: each troop consisted of one hundred rank and file. The uniform
was similar to that of the English hussars.

The troop of artillery was composed of one hundred and twenty rank and file, with five four-pounders,
and one four-and-a-half inch howitzer. The uniform
was similar to that worn by the British horse artillery.

The retreat of Canterac; the capitulation of
Callao ; and the departure of Cochrane for California in quest of two Spanish frigates and a corvette;
gave the protector an opportunity to consolidate his
government, and to take further steps for the termination of the war.

The royalists were now few in number; not cordial
in council, and depressed by gloomy anticipations.
The protector had above eight thousand men in the
vicinity of Lima. Half of this force, if properly led
on, would have been sufficient to have driven the
last Spaniard beyond the Peruvian frontier. But,
unfortunately, the pleasures of a luxurious capital
had taken such a firm hold on the minds of the
chiefs and others, that, when the march of some battalions had been determined upon, obstacles were
raised, and pretences fabricated for delay. If such
irregularities and want of zeal had been punished in
one or two principal instances, San Martin might

not have had to pay the penalty of indecision, by
feeling himself, in a manner, compelled to retire
from public life when his fame was at its zenith.
Perhaps he might have avoided the latter alternative
if he had thrown off the shackles which bound him
to the *Logia*, an institution already described, and
which, at this time, pointedly supported the mal-
contents of the liberating army in every intrigue
directed against the power of the protector.

When *chiefs* are remiss in the performance of
duty, and inattentive to the claims and comforts of
their men, it is no wonder that the junior officers become lukewarm, and the soldiers discontented.

The inhabitants of Lima, who had received the
independent army with so much enthusiasm, grew
tired of their liberators, in proportion as discipline
relaxed; nor could a quick succession of balls and
entertainments prevent the growth of dissatisfaction
and murmurs. Lima began to feel severely the burden of an army kept unemployed, while an enemy,
whom the patriot chiefs affected to despise, retained
undisturbed possession of the interior.

Although the South Americans profess to be animated by a republican spirit, they in general retain
a strong bias towards some of the attributes of monarchy. Peru has the Order of the Sun, Chile the
Order of Merit, and Colombia that of Liberators.
All these confer privileges on their members, and
are held in high estimation. Military rank too, always so much coveted, was eagerly sought for and
often obtained by men of property, whose principal
merit consisted in their having declared for the

cause of independence. It might have been very politic to have bestowed nominal rank upon persons of this description, but they ought not to have been intrusted with commands for which they were glaringly incompetent. Disastrous results attended this lamentable oversight of the protector.

San Martin having agreed to meet Bolivar, the president of Colombia, at Guayaquil, delegated his civil and military powers to the Marquess of Torre Tagle, who was in consequence named *Supremo Delegado* on the 19th of January, 1822. San Martin sailed from Callao on the 8th of February, and, touching at Truxillo, learned that the visit of Bolivar had been postponed. He therefore returned to Lima on the 3d of March, but Torre Tagle retained his post of supreme delegate, as the protector still intended to proceed to Guayaquil to hold the projected conference with Bolivar.

Cochrane having, as before stated, sailed, in October 1821, with the O'Higgins, Valdivia, Independencia, and a small vessel, in pursuit of the Spanish squadron, ascertained, at Panama, that it had touched there. This enterprising seaman proceeded in his leaky and inefficient vessels to the coast of California, but, learning that the Spanish frigates had not gone in that direction, he returned to the coast of Peru. The dangers and privations endured on this cruise have seldom been surpassed. The crazy ships were tossed about in a tempestuous and unfrequented sea, while the ill-paid and discontented crews, suffering from great scarcity of fresh water and of provisions, were obliged to keep constantly working at the pumps.

At one time, after a long calm, and when ninety leagues from the nearest land, the stock of water in the whole squadron was reduced to less than a hundred gallons. The crews were in a state of consternation at the horrid death which seemed to await them, and which no human efforts could avert. Every eye was lifted towards heaven; fervent ejaculations were uttered, for, on such trying occasions, there are no unbelievers. The crews were a medley of all religions; but the same thoughts, the same fears, and the same hopes in the all-powerful Director of events, pervaded every breast. When the feelings of all were approaching to frenzy and despair—when they had arrived at that pitch of heart-rending agony, of which none, but those who have experienced similar calamities, can form any idea—at this critical period the sky assumed a threatening aspect; the lightning flashed on the horizon; black clouds arose; peals of thunder resounded through the air, and every thing indicated an approaching storm. The drooping spirits of the sufferers revived, and one and all earnestly looked for the speedy bursting of the tempest. Dangers which, at other times, would have been dreaded, in such shattered vessels, were now hailed with rapture. The rain soon fell in torrents, and, as if escaped from shipwreck, the men wept with joy. Every awning and sail that could be made available was spread. It continued unceasingly for twenty-four hours, and every cask was filled. The wind, boisterous at first, soon moderated into a fair steady breeze, and the trials and danger of the sufferers were forgotten.

In the meanwhile the Spanish naval commanding officer, Don José Villegas, fearing to come in contact with the patriot admiral, had made the best of his way from Panama to Guayaquil, where he capitulated to the Peruvian agents in that city on the 15th of February, 1822. During the progress of the negotiation the patriot authorities caused signals to be telegraphed, from the mouth of the river, that the squadron under Lord Cochrane had arrived within sight of the coast. This stratagem tended materially to hasten the termination of the business, by which the Spanish commanders were to receive a considerable sum. One of the frigates and the corvette remained in the river. The other frigate sailed for Callao, where she arrived on the 31st of March. All the vessels were delivered up to the Peruvian government. Cochrane arrived in the bay of Callao on the 25th of April, and demanded them as his prizes. The Peruvian government alleged that he had no right to them, and refused to comply with the demand. Some altercation took place, and the admiral sailed for Chile on the 10th of May, 1822*.

General Don Domingo Tristan had been appointed to the command of Ica, for the purpose of recruiting the patriot forces in that neighbourhood. He took with him two battalions from Lima, and his instructions were, that in the event of the approach of an enemy, however inferior, he was to retire without fighting. Colonel Gamarra was appointed, as second

* In December, 1822, Lord Cochrane received an invitation from the Emperor Don Pedro to take command of the Brazilian navy. On the 19th of January, 1823, the admiral sailed from Valparaiso for Rio Janeiro.

in command, to assist in the organization of the new
levies, for which he was well qualified.   Both these
officers had passed over from the Spaniards.   Tristan
had twice changed sides.   He was a worthy country
gentleman of large landed property, and had worn
the uniform of a colonel of militia.

The royalists, driven to a state of desperation, and
unable to augment their almost skeleton corps for
want of arms, decided upon attempting a *coup de
main* against Tristan, whom they calculated upon
being able either to surprise or intimidate.   Accordingly, on the 26th of March, 1822, Canterac put
himself in motion from the valley of Xauxa at the
head of fifteen hundred infantry, six hundred cavalry,
and three field-pieces.   After a march of above
seventy leagues, he arrived, on the 6th of April, at
Carmen Alto, within two leagues of Ica.   Tristan
was completely taken by surprise.   It is true he
heard rumours of some hostile movements, but he
neither knew the numbers of the enemy advancing
against him, nor the name of the general who commanded them.   Ica is a bad position.   Tristan ought
to have placed his division at the Molinos, four leagues
on the road to Xauxa; but as he seldom or never extended his rides beyond the suburbs of the town, it
is not very surprising that he did not avail himself
of the localities.

In the evening of the 6th, Canterac made a detour
to the Pisco road, and cut off the retreat of Tristan
by placing himself at Macacona, a league and a half
from Ica.   Tristan, though entirely ignorant of the
enemy's last movement, commenced his retreat; and

at one A. M. on the 7th was attacked whilst on his
march. His force dispersed immediately. Canterac
took one thousand prisoners, who went to swell the
ranks of the royalists, four pieces of artillery, and a
great number of horses, mules, and oxen. Lieutenant-Colonel Aldunate, a highly distinguished officer,
was wounded and taken prisoner. Major Gumer
(a German) was assassinated as he lay wounded on
the field by the dastardly Spanish Colonel Don Mateo
Ramirez. The circumstance of his being a foreigner
was the only reason given for this cold-blooded
murder.

On the 8th a squadron of lancers advanced from
Chunchanga to the neighbourhood of Ica, to reinforce Tristan, being in total ignorance of his defeat. They were attacked by Colonel Loriga: ten
were killed, and ninety taken prisoners.

The appointment of Tristan to an important command was not creditable to the usual discrimination
of the protector. It must have originated in the
misplaced hope that promotion and commands bestowed on men of rank, who passed over to the patriot
cause, would encourage other influential people to
follow their example, and thus in the end attach all
the country to the cause of independence, and settle
the question *without bloodshed;* a benevolent motive, but the source of incalculable mischief.

The immediate result of the unfortunate affair of
Ica was the capture, not only of nearly three thousand stand of arms thrown away in the flight, but
also of a large quantity of spare muskets, sabres, &c.
in depôt at Pisco; and for the want of which the

royalists had been much distressed.   The moral effect
was to dispel the idea, which until then had been
entertained, of the superiority of the patriots; and
to throw a damp over the mass of the population,
which had before this cheerfully lent its powerful
assistance.   Union was again restored in the royalist
councils, while the patriots were distracted by dissensions, and weakened by insubordination.

The only counterbalancing event at this time was
the victory of Pinchincha.   This battle was won on
the 24th of May, 1822, by the Colombian General
Sucre, with the assistance of an auxiliary Peruvian
division, composed of the battalion No. 2, the battalion of Piura, and two squadrons of cavalry, sent
from Truxillo under Colonel Santa Cruz.   The contending forces were about equal, each being from
three to four thousand men.   No. 2 of Peru bore
the brunt of the action; but being opposed to
overwhelming numbers, it began to give way, when
Colonel Cordova, with two Colombian battalions,
came up, and, gallantly charging the royalists, decided the fate of the day.   The battalion Albion,
commanded by the brave Colonel Mackintosh, distinguished itself particularly in another part of the
field.   Five hundred Spaniards and three hundred
patriots were either killed or wounded.   The remainder of the royalists capitulated.   By the event of
this battle the independence of Colombia was finally
secured.

The brilliant little affair of Rio-Bamba preceded
the battle of Pinchincha: and it is worthy of being
recorded.   Lieutenant-Colonel Lavalle, with his

squadron of granaderos à caballo, forming part of
Colonel Santa Cruz's division, having followed up
the enemy closely, found himself unexpectedly much
nearer to four hundred of the royalist cavalry than
was prudent: but to have attempted a retreat so near
to such superior numbers would, he knew, have led
to a complete dispersion of his men. He therefore charged with his few followers, and drove the
royalist cavalry back upon their infantry with considerable loss. Lavalle was obliged to retrograde;
and the royalists, having been reinforced, Lavalle,
whilst retreating at a trot, ordered his men to wheel
about, and then charged the enemy a second time in
the most determined and brilliant manner, killing
four of their officers and fifty-two rank and file,
and wounding many others, most of whom however
escaped under the fire of the infantry. Lavalle was,
during his active career, successful in every charge.
Captains Bruiz* and Sowersby, Lieutenant Latus,
and Cornet Olmos, highly distinguished themselves
in this affair, which took place on the 21st of April,
1822. The royalists were so awed by it, and their
consequent timidity was so evident, that, no doubt,
the event contributed in a great measure to the victory of Pinchincha.

San Martin again set sail from Callao for Guayaquil, where he met the Liberator Bolivar on the 26th

---

* A very gallant Frenchman, and son to the celebrated Admiral Bruiz. He
had been page to Napoleon. He met his death by accident in Lima. A
younger brother was shot through the heart in an action against the royalists in
Chile, and in which he had accompanied Bruiz as an amateur. The pre-
mature loss of these distinguished young men was universally lamented. Bruiz
had served in the Russian campaign. Latus, a spirited young Englishman,
formerly of the rifle corps, died at Lima of his wounds.

of July, 1822, who had arrived twelve days before. The interview, which took place between these two distinguished characters, does not appear to have been very satisfactory. The protector remained at Guayaquil only eight-and-forty hours, and then sailed for Callao, where he arrived on the 21st of August.

This province had preserved its independence from the time of its revolution in 1820, when the Señor Dr. Don J. J. de Olmedo, the celebrated poet *, a native of the city, was placed at the head of the government; but soon after Bolivar arrived there, he declared that Guayaquil belonged to the territory of Colombia, and that it should henceforward be in-corporated with that republic. The independent colours of the province were consequently supplanted by those of Colombia.

During the protector's absence from Lima, a com-motion took place in that capital on the 28th July. The inhabitants, aggrieved by some oppressive mea-sures of the unpopular minister of state, Don Ber-nardo Monteagudo, assembled in a riotous manner, and demanded through the municipality his imme-diate removal from office; which demand was acceded to by the trembling Supremo Delegado, the Marquess of Torre Tagle, who obliged Monteagudo instantly to resign. The military took no part in the affair: on the contrary, they were insulted; though many lawyers and learned "*doctores*" tampered with them, and gained over to their party some officers, who en-gaged to assist them, in case the general-in-chief,

* Amongst other works, Olmedo translated Pope's " Essay on Man" into the Spanish language.

Alvarado, should attempt to support the ex-minister. Men in a state of intoxication penetrated into the palace, and reviled the Supremo Delegado in the most abusive manner.

The people had just grounds for insisting upon the removal of Monteagudo. The harsh and uncourteous tone in which he addressed all who transacted business with him; the oppressive espionage which he had adopted; the cruel manner in which he had banished many highly respectable and extensively connected individuals, principally accused of royalism, together with his suspected views of establishing a monarchical government contrary to the wishes of the people, all served to render him an object of dislike and mistrust. The commotion was therefore a natural consequence of his despotic administration, and the feeble support which he received from the weak and dissolute Torre Tagle.

Monteagudo was sent to Callao under arrest, and embarked, not without some risk of assassination from the populace. He sailed for Guayaquil*.

The protector arrived at Lima on the 19th of August, and on the 21st reassumed the supreme command. Agreeably to a former decree, deputies had been elected, and the congress was installed with due formality on the 20th of September, 1822. The protector repaired in state to the hall of the deputies, where, divesting himself of the insignia of supreme power, he declared that, from that moment, congress was installed, and that he resigned all authority into

* Monteagudo resided in the city of Quito until 1824, when he returned to Peru, under the patronage and protection of Bolivar. He was assassinated at Lima in 1825.

the hands of the representatives of the people. He then withdrew, and immediately set out for his country house at Magdalena. Two hours afterwards a deputation of congress waited upon his excellency to communicate a decree of that body, expressive of the gratitude of the Peruvian people, and another conferring upon him the office of generalissimo of the Peruvian forces. San Martin consented to accept merely the title, but refused the exercise of the command, and embarked the same evening at Callao for Chile, leaving the following proclamation addressed to the Peruvians:—

" I have witnessed the declaration of the independence of the states of Chile and Peru. I hold in my possession the standard which Pizarro brought to enslave the empire of the Incas, and I have ceased to be a public man; thus I am more than rewarded for ten years spent in revolution and warfare. My promises to the countries in which I warred are fulfilled; to make them independent, and leave to their will the election of their governments.

" The presence of a fortunate soldier, however disinterested he may be, is dangerous to newly constituted states. I am also disgusted with hearing that I wish to make myself a sovereign. Nevertheless, I shall always be ready to make the last sacrifice for the liberty of the country, but in the class of a private individual, and *no other*.

" With respect to my public conduct, my compatriots (as is generally the case) will be divided in their opinions; their children will pronounce the true verdict.

" Peruvians! I leave your national representation established: if you repose implicit confidence in it, you will triumph; if not, anarchy will swallow you up.

" May success preside over your destinies, and may they be crowned with felicity and peace!

" Pueblo-libre, September 20, 1822.

" (Signed)   SAN MARTIN."

On the retirement of San Martin, General Don José de la Mar, Don Felipe Antonio Alvarado, (brother to General Alvarado) and the Count Vista Florida, were named by congress to form an executive, which was called the *Junta Gubernativa.*

The learned and eloquent Luna Pizarro, a native of Arequipa, remarkable for the dignified firmness, and for the political consistency of his character, had been chosen president of the congress. One of the first measures of that assembly was to decree that General San Martin should bear the title of FOUNDER OF THE LIBERTY OF PERU, and enjoy a pension of twenty thousand dollars per annum.

The actions of men who have conspicuously con- tributed to change the destinies of nations belong to history; and it is the duty of writers to put fleeting facts upon record, before the opportunity of correct- ing mistatements, or inadvertencies, shall have passed away. The eminent services of General San Martin to the cause of independence in the New World, are

SAN MARTIN

London: Published 1829, by Longman & Co.

Engelmann & Co lithog

of so commanding a character, as to render every
circumstance of his life a matter of public interest.

José de San Martin was born in the year 1778,
at Yapeyú, his father being at that time governor of
the *Misiones*, bordering on Paraguay. When eight
years old, San Martin was taken by his family to
Spain, and being destined for the military career, he
was admitted a student of the College of Nobles, in
Madrid. He served in the peninsular war, and was
aide-de-camp to Solano, Marquess of Socorro, then
governor of Cadiz. On that nobleman's falling a
victim to popular fury, San Martin narrowly escaped
assassination, being mistaken in the confusion for the
marquess, to whom he bore a strong resemblance.
San Martin distinguished himself at the battle of
Baylen in a manner which attracted the attention of
General Castaños, and his name was mentioned with
honour in the despatches. He was promoted to the
rank of brevet lieutenant-colonel, and served afterwards under the orders of the Marquess de la Romana
and General Coupigny. But the cry of liberty arose
in his native land; and he could not resist the holy
invocation. Without having more than a vague idea
of the true state of the contest in America, he resolved to quit Spain. By the kind interposition of
Sir Charles Stuart, now Lord Stuart de Rothesay, he
obtained a passport, and sailed for England, where
he remained for a short period. To the friendship of
Lord MacDuff, now Earl of Fife, he was indebted
for letters of introduction, as well as of credit; and
although he did not avail himself of the latter, he

always speaks of the generosity of his noble friend in
terms of grateful recollection *.

San Martin sailed from the Thames to the Rio
de la Plata in the ship *George Canning*. Soon after
his arrival at Buenos Ayres, he married Doña Re-
medios Escalada, a daughter of one of the most distinguished families of that city. San Martin, having
established his credit as a soldier on the banks of
the Paraná, and acquired the confidence of the Argentines, was appointed to an important command.
We have seen that to his persevering genius belongs
the honour of introducing a regular and scientific
system of operations for the emancipation of South
America; and of forming that army which, on the
heights of Chacabuco, and on the plain of Maypo,
gave to Chile her political existence. It was San
Martin who first raised the standard of liberty in
Peru, and there laid the groundwork of that great
plan which was so gloriously accomplished at Ayacucho. Having redeemed his pledge of allowing the
Peruvians to assemble in congress, to form a government conformable to the wishes of the people, San
Martin, emulating the example of Washington, retired from public life. The only riches he has
acquired, is the glory resulting from his great and

* Lord MacDuff was amongst the first of the British who took a part in the
war of Spanish independence. Being at Vienna in 1808, and hearing of the
events in the Peninsula, he immediately proceeded to embark at Trieste for Spain,
and was engaged in many affairs during the war. He was severely wounded,
made general in the Spanish service, and decorated with the military order of
San Fernando. Since the Earl of Fife's return to England, he has been made a
British peer, a knight of the Thistle, grand cross of the royal Hanoverian Guelphic
order, lord of the bedchamber, and lord-lieutenant of Banffshire. The friendship formed between his lordship and San Martin continues, with undiminished
mutual regard, to the present day.

patriotic labours during ten years of incessant exertion
both in the cabinet and in the field.   The eventful
operations which he directed have been detailed in
this narrative, sometimes, indeed, with qualified applause, but always with an uncompromising regard to
truth and justice.

The person of San Martin is tall and full-formed.
He has a dark attractive countenance, with black,
expressive, and penetrating eyes.   His manners are
dignified, easy, friendly, eminently frank, and prepossessing.   His conversation is lively, and that of
a man of the world.   His friendships are warm and
lasting.   Though economical and unostentatious in
his habits, yet he is of a most hospitable disposition.
He writes his own language well, and speaks French
·fluently.   Although he has had political enemies,
he has always been personally popular.   Even when
his army has pressed most heavily on the resources of
a province, the inhabitants have continued to speak
of him with respect and enthusiasm.   In the formation of the government of Peru, as well as previously,
he displayed the soundness of his judgment by selecting men of first-rate talent, such as Jonte, Monteagudo *, Guido, Garcia del Rio, and others.   If he
was sometimes less fortunate in the selection of his
military leaders, it could hardly have arisen from
want of discernment.   With regard to his political
bias, San Martin considered the representative mon-

* The talents, and not the conduct, of persons are here alluded to.   The arbitrary conduct of one of them has been already mentioned, but it was more than
counterbalanced by his eminent services, particularly in the early part of the revolution.

archical form of government, as best adapted to the
South Americans. Nevertheless, his principles are
republican, and it is the decided opinion of those
who have had opportunities of forming one, that he
never entertained the remotest idea of placing a crown
upon his own head, although it is believed that he
would have willingly assisted a prince of the blood
royal to mount the throne of Peru; but, even in this
case, it was to have been on the basis of absolute and
complete independence from Spain.

San Martin having had the misfortune, in 1822,
to lose his very charming wife, quitted his estate near
Mendoza, and sailed from Buenos Ayres to England,
where he remained sixteen months. He visited his
friend Lord Fife, in Scotland, and afterwards went to
Brussels to complete the education of an only child, a
beautiful and accomplished daughter. In November,
1828, he once more visited England, having left
his daughter at Brussels under the care of Miss
Phelps, a highly respectable English lady, resident
at that place. During the few days which the general
devoted to preparations for a long voyage, he paid his
friend Miller the compliment of going down to Can-
terbury to visit his mother. San Martin sailed from
Falmouth on the 21st of November, in the Countess
of Chichester packet, bound for Buenos Ayres.

APPENDIX.

(A.)

(Page 34.)

Letter from Captain Beaver to Sir Alexander Cochrane.

His Majesty's Ship Acasta, La Guayra, 19th July, 1808.

SIR,

EVENTS of singular importance occurring at present in the province of Venezuela, I have thought it necessary to despatch to you, without loss of time, the late French corvette, Le Serpent, in order that you might, as early as possible, be made acquainted with those which have already occurred, as well as be able to form some opinion of those which will probably follow. The latter port (La Guayra) I made in the morning of the 15th, and, while standing in for the shore, with the cartel flag flying, I observed a brig under French colours just coming to an anchor. She had arrived the preceding night from Cayenne with despatches from Bayonne, and had anchored about two miles below the town, to which she was now removing. I was never nearer than five miles to her, and could not have thrown a shot over her, before she was close under the Spanish batteries, and therefore I attempted not to chase; but I claimed her of the Spanish government, as you will perceive by my letter, No. 1. Just before I set out for the Caracas, and presented your despatches, the captain of the French brig returned exceedingly displeased (I was told), having been publicly insulted in that city. About three o'clock I arrived at the Caracas, and presented your despatches to the captain-general, who received me very coldly, or rather uncivilly, observing, that that hour was very inconvenient to him and to me; and that, as I had not dined, I had better go and get some dinner, and return to him in a couple of hours. On entering the city, I had observed a great effervescence among the

people, like something which either precedes or follows a popular
commotion; and as I entered the large inn of the city, I was
surrounded by inhabitants of almost all classes.

I have learned that the French captain, who had arrived
yesterday, had brought intelligence of every thing which had
taken place in Spain in favour of France; that he had announced
the accession to the Spanish throne of Joseph Napoleon, and had
brought orders to the government from the French emperor.

The city was immediately in arms; ten thousand of its inhabitants surrounded the residence of the captain-general, and
demanded the proclamation of Ferdinand VII. as their king,
which he promised to do the next day; but this would not satisfy
them; they proclaimed him that evening, by heralds, in form,
throughout the city, and placed his portrait, illuminated, in the
gallery of the town-house. The French were first publicly insulted in the coffee-house, whence they were obliged to withdraw; and the French captain left the Caracas privately, about
eight o'clock that night, escorted by a detachment of soldiers,
and so saved his life; for about ten o'clock his person was demanded from the governor by the populace; and when they had
learned that he was gone, three hundred followed him on the
road, to put him to death. Coldly received by the governor, I
was, on the contrary, surrounded by all the respectable people of
the city, the military officers included, and hailed as their deliverer. The news which I gave them from Cadiz was devoured
with avidity, and produced enthusiastic shouts of gratitude to
England.

Returning to the governor about five o'clock, the first thing I
demanded was the delivering to me the French corvette, or at
least the permitting me to take possession of her in the roads, in
consequence of the circumstances under which she had entered,
as stated in my letter to him, No. 1. Both these he positively
refused, as well as to take possession of her himself; but, on the
contrary, he told me he had given orders for her immediate
sailing. I made him acquainted with the orders I had given, to
seize her if she sailed, to which he assented; and I at the same
time told him that, if she was not in the possession of the Spaniards on my return, I should take her myself. He replied,

that he should send orders to the commandant of La Guayra to fire upon me if I did; to which I simply replied, that the consequence would fall upon him: and I further told him, that I considered his reception of me at Caracas as that rather of an enemy than a friend, while, at the same time, I had brought him information of hostilities having ceased between Great Britain and Spain; and that his conduct towards the French was that of a friend, while he knew that Spain was at war with France. He replied, that Spain was not at war with France: to which I asked him what he would consider as a war, if the captivity of two of his kings, and the taking possession of their capital, was not to be so considered? He only replied, that he knew nothing of it from the Spanish government, and that what your despatches informed him of he could not consider as official.

(B.)

(Page 81.)

Declaration of the Independence of the United Provinces of South America.

IN the well-deserving and most worthy city of San Miguel del Tucuman, on the ninth day of the month of July, 1816, the ordinary sitting being ended, the congress of the United Provinces resumed its previous deliberations respecting the grand, august, and sacred object of the independence of the inhabitants constituting the same. The cry of the whole country for its solemn emancipation from the despotic power of the kings of Spain was universal, constant, and decided; nevertheless, the representatives carefully dedicated to this arduous affair the whole extent of their talents, the rectitude of their intentions, and the interest with which they viewed their own fate, that of the people represented, and also of their posterity. After mature deliberation, they were asked, whether they considered it expedient that the provinces of the union should constitute a nation, free and independent of the kings of Spain and the mother country?

490   APPENDIX B.

Filled with the holy ardour of justice, they simultaneously answered in the affirmative by acclamations, and then, one by one,
successively reiterated their unanimous, spontaneous, and decided
votes in favour of the independence of the country; and, in virtue
thereof, they concurred in the following declaration: ·
· · We, the representatives of the United Provinces of South
America, in general congress assembled, invoking the Supreme
Being who presides over the universe, in the name and by virtue
of the authority of the people we represent, and protesting to
Heaven, and to the nations and inhabitants of the whole globe,
the justice by which our wishes are guided, do solemnly declare
in the face of the earth, .that it is the unanimous and indubitable
will of these provinces to break the repugnant ties which bound
them to the kings of Spain, to recover the rights of which they
were despoiled, and invest themselves with the high character
of a nation, free and independent of King Ferdinand VII., his
successors, and the mother country. In consequence whereof,
the said provinces, in point of fact and right, possess ample and
full power to assume for themselves such forms of government as
justice requires, and the urgency of existing circumstances may
demand. All and each one of them publish, declare, and ratify
the same, through us, pledging themselves, under the assurance
and guarantee of their lives, property, and honour, to abide by
and sustain this their will and determination. Let the same,
therefore, be communicated for publication, to whomsoever it
may concern; and, in consideration of the respect due to other
nations, let the weighty reasons which have impelled us to this
solemn declaration be detailed in a separate manifesto. Given
in the Hall of our Sittings, signed by our hands, sealed with the
seal of the Congress, and countersigned by our secretaries, also
members thereof.

(Signed) Francisco Narciso de Laprida, President and Deputy for
    San Juan.
Mariano Boedo, Vice-President and Deputy for Salta.
Dr. Antonio Saenz, Deputy for Buenos Ayres.
Dr. José Darregueyra, Deputy for idem.
Father Cayetano José Rodriguez, Deputy for idem.

Dr. Pedro Medrano, Deputy for idem.

Dr. Manuel Antonio Acevedo, Deputy for Catamarca.

Dr. José Ignacio de Gorriti, Deputy for Salta.

Dr. Andres Pacheco de Melo, Deputy for Chichas.

Dr. Teodoro Sanchez de Bustamante, Deputy for the city of Jujuy and jurisdiction thereof.

Eduardo Perez Bulnez, Deputy for Cordova.

Tomas Godoy Cruz, Deputy for Mendoza.

Dr. Pedro Miguel Araoz, Deputy for the capital of Tucuman.

Dr. Estevan Agustin Gazcon, Deputy for the province of Buenos Ayres.

Pedro Francisco de Uriarte, Deputy for Santiago del Estero.

Pedro Leon Gallo, Deputy for idem.

Pédro Ignacio Rivera, Deputy for Mizque.

Dr. Mariano Sanchez de Loria, Deputy for Charcas.

Dr. José Severo Malabia, Deputy for Charcas.

Dr. Pedro Ignacio de Castro Barros, Deputy for La Rioja.

Licentiate Geronimo Salguero de Cabrera y Cabrera, Deputy for Cordova.

Dr. José Colombres, Deputy for Catamarca.

Dr. José Ignacio Thomas, Deputy for Tucuman.

Father Justo de Santa Maria de Oro, Deputy for San Juan.

José Antonio Cabrera, Deputy for Cordova.

Dr. Juan Agustin Maza, Deputy for Mendoza.

Tomas Manuel de Anchorena, Deputy for Buenos Ayres.

José Mariano Serrano, Deputy for Charcas, and Secretary.

Juan José Paso, Deputy for Buenos Ayres, and Secretary.

MANIFESTO.

Addressed to all Nations of the Earth, by the General Constituent Congress of the United Provinces of South America, respecting the treatment and cruelties they have experienced from the Spaniards, and which have given rise to the Declaration of their Independence.

HONOUR is a distinction which mortals esteem more than their own existence, and they are bound to defend it above all earthly

benefits, however great and sublime they may be. The United
Provinces of the river Plata have been accused, by the Spanish
government, before other nations, of rebellion and perfidy; and
as such also has been denounced the memorable Act of Emancipation, proclaimed by the National Congress in Tucuman, on the
9th of July, 1816, by imputing to it ideas of anarchy, and a wish
to introduce into other countries seditious principles, at the very
time the said provinces were soliciting the friendship of these
same nations, and the acknowledgment of this memorable act, for
the purpose of forming one among them. The first, and among
the most sacred of the duties imposed on the National Congress,
is to wipe away so foul a stigma, and defend the cause of their
country, by displaying the cruelties and motives which led them
to the declaration of independence. This indeed is not to be
considered as an act of submission, which may attribute to any
other nation of the earth the power of disposing of a fate which
has already cost America torrents of blood, and all kinds of sacrifices and bitter privations: it is rather an important consideration we owe to our own outraged honour, and the decorum due
to other nations.

We wave all investigations respecting the right of conquest,
papal grants, and other titles on which Spaniards have usually
founded and upheld their dominion. We do not seek to recur to
principles which might give rise to problematical discussions, and
revive points of argument which have had defenders on both sides.
We appeal to facts, which form a painful contrast of our forbearance with the oppression and cruelty of Spaniards. We will exhibit a frightful abyss which Spain was opening under our feet,
and into which these provinces were about to be precipitated, if
they had not interposed the safeguard of their own emancipation.
We will, in short, exhibit reasons which no rational man can disregard, unless he could find sufficient pleas to persuade a country
for ever to renounce all idea of its own felicity, and, in preference,
adopt a system of ruin, opprobrium, and forbearance. Let us
place before the eyes of the world this picture, one which it will
be impossible to behold without being profoundly moved by the
same sentiments as those by which we are ourselves actuated.

From the moment when the Spaniards possessed themselves of

these countries, they preferred the system of securing their dominion by extermination, destruction, and degradation. The plans of this extensive mischief were forthwith carried into effect, and they have been continued without any intermission, during the space of three hundred years. They began by assassinating the monarchs of Peru, and they afterwards did the same with the other chieftains and distinguished men who came in their way. The inhabitants of the country, anxious to restrain such ferocious intrusion, under the great disadvantage of their arms, became the victims of fire and sword, and were compelled to leave their settlements a prey to the devouring flames, which were every where applied without pity or distinction.

The Spaniards then placed a barrier to the population of the country. They prohibited, under laws the most rigorous, the ingress of foreigners; and in every possible respect limited that of even Spaniards themselves, although in times more recent the immigration of criminal and immoral men, outcasts, was encouraged; of such men as it was expedient to expel from the Peninsula. Neither our vast though beautiful deserts, formed by the extermination of the natives; the advantages Spain would have derived from the cultivation of regions as immense as they are fertile; the incitement of mines, the richest and most abundant on the earth; the stimulus of innumerable productions, partly till then unknown, but all estimable for their value and variety, and capable of encouraging and carrying agriculture and commerce to their highest pitch of opulence; in short, not even the wanton wickedness of retaining these choice countries plunged in the most abject misery, were any of them motives sufficiently powerful to change the dark and inauspicious principles of the cabinet of Madrid. Hundreds of leagues do we still behold, unsettled and uncultivated, in the space intervening from one city to another. Entire towns have, in some places, disappeared, either buried in the ruins of mines, or their inhabitants destroyed by the compulsive and poisonous labour of working them; nor had the cries of all Peru, nor the energetic remonstrances of the most zealous ministers, been capable of reforming this exterminating system of forced labour, carried on within the bowels of the earth.

The art of working the mines, among us beheld with apathy

and neglect, has been unattended with those improvements which have distinguished the enlightened age in which we live, and diminished the attendant casualties; hence opulent mines, worked in the most clumsy and improvident manner, have sunk in and been overwhelmed, either through the undermining of the mineral ridges, or the rush of waters which have totally inundated them. Other rare and estimable productions of the country are still confounded with nature, and neglected by the government, and if, among us, any enlightened observer has attempted to point out their advantages, he has been reprehended by the court, and forced to silence, owing to the competition that might arise to a few artisans of the mother country.

The teaching of science was forbidden us, and we were allowed to study only the Latin grammar, ancient philosophy, theology, and civil and canonical jurisprudence. Viceroy Joaquin del Pino took the greatest umbrage that the Buenos Ayres Board of Trade presumed to bear the expenses of a nautical school: in compliance with the orders transmitted from court, it was closed; and an injunction besides laid upon us, that our youths should not be sent to Paris to become professors of chemistry, with a view to teach this science among their own countrymen.

Commerce has at all times been an exclusive monopoly in the hands of the traders of Spain, and the consignees they sent over to America. The public offices were reserved for Spaniards, and notwithstanding, by the laws, these were equally open to Americans, we seldom attained them, and when we did, it was by satiating the avarice of the court through the sacrifice of immense treasures. Among one hundred and sixty viceroys who have governed in America, four natives of the country alone are numbered; and of six hundred and two captains-general and governors, with the exception of fourteen, all have been Spaniards. The same, proportionably, happened in the other offices of importance; scarcely, indeed, had the Americans an opportunity of alternating with Spaniards in situations the most subaltern.

Every thing was so arranged by Spain, that the degradation of the natives should prevail in America. It did not enter into her views that wise men should be formed, fearful that minds and talents would be created capable of promoting the interests

of their country, and causing civilization, manners, and those excellent capabilities with which the Colombian children are gifted,
to make a rapid progress. She unceasingly diminished our population, apprehensive that, some day or other, it might be in a
state to rise against a dominion sustained only by a few hands,
to whom the keeping of detached and extensive regions was intrusted. She carried on an exclusive trade; because she supposed
opulence would make us proud, and inclined to free ourselves from
outrage. She denied to us the advancement of industry, in order
that we might be divested of the means of rising out of misery
and poverty; and we were excluded from offices of trust, in order
that Peninsulars only might hold influence in the country, and
form the necessary habits and inclinations, with a view to leave
us in such a state of dependence as to be unable to think, or act,
unless according to Spanish forms.

Such was the system firmly and steadily upheld by the viceroys,
each one of whom bore the state and arrogance of a vizir. Their
power was sufficient to crush any one who had the misfortune to
displease them. However great their outrages, they were to be
borne with resignation; for by their satellites and flatterers their
frown was superstitiously compared to the anger of God. Complaints addressed to the throne were either lost in the extended
interval of those thousands of leagues it was necessary to cross, or
buried in the offices at home by the relatives or patrons of men
wielding viceregal power. This system, so far from having been
softened, all hopes that even time would produce this effect were
totally lost. We held neither direct nor indirect influence in our
own legislation : this was instituted in Spain; nor were we allowed
the right of sending over persons empowered to assist at its formation, who might point out what was fit and suitable, as the
cities of Spain were authorized to do. Neither had we any influence over the administration of government, which might, in
some measure, have tempered the rigour of such laws as were in
force. We were aware that no other resource was left to us than
patience, and that for him who was not resigned to endure all, even
capital punishment was not sufficient, since, for cases of this kind,
torments, new and of unheard-of-cruelty, had been invented, such
as made nature shudder.

Neither so great, nor so repeated, were the hardships which roused the provinces of Holland, when they took up arms to free themselves from the yoke of Spain, nor those of Portugal, to effect the same purpose. Less were the hardships which placed the Swiss under the direction of William Tell, and in open opposition to the German emperor. Less those which determined the United States of North America to resist the imposts forced upon them by a British king; less, in short, the powerful motives which have urged other countries, not separated by nature from the parent state, to cast off an iron yoke, and consult their own felicity. We, nevertheless, divided from Spain by an immense sea, gifted with a different climate, possessing other wants and habits, and treated as herds of cattle, have exhibited to the world the singular example of forbearance amidst degradations, by remaining obedient, when, at the same time, we had the most favourable opportunities of breaking the bond, and putting an end to so unnatural a connexion.

We address ourselves to the nations of the earth, and we cannot be so rash as to seek to deceive them in what they have themselves seen and felt. America remained tranquil during the whole period of the war of succession, and waited the decision of the question then at issue between the houses of Austria and Bourbon, and with a view to follow the fate of Spain. That would have been a favourable moment to redeem herself from so many hardships: but she did not do it; rather she sought to arm and defend herself alone, in order to preserve herself united to the parent state. We, without having direct share or interest in the differences of the latter with other powers of Europe, have equally felt and partaken in her wars; we have experienced the same ravages, and, without repining, we have endured the same wants and privations, brought upon us by our weakness at sea, and the manner in which we were cut off from all communication with her.

In the year 1806 we were attacked. A British squadron surprised and occupied the capital of Buenos Ayres, through the imbecility and unskilfulness of the viceroy, who, although he had no Spanish troops, did not know how to avail himself of the numerous resources offered to him in defence of the town. At the end of forty-five days we recovered the capital, and the British, together with their general, were made prisoners, without

the viceroy having had the smallest share in the affair.. We implored the government at home to send us such aid as would protect us from another invasion, with which we were threatened;
and the consolation transmitted to us was, a revolting royal order,
by which we were enjoined to defend ourselves in the best manner
we could. In the following year, the eastern bank of the river
Plata was occupied by a fresh and stronger expedition, and the
fortress of Montevideo was besieged and surrendered. There
more British forces assembled, and an armament was formed for
the purpose of again attacking the capital, which, in fact, within
a few months experienced an assault; but fortunately the heroic
courage of the inhabitants and garrison overcame the efforts of
the enemy, and a victory so brilliant compelled him to evacuate
Montevideo, and the whole of the eastern bank.

No opportunity more favourable for rendering ourselves independent could have presented itself, if the spirit of rebellion and
perfidy had been capable of actuating our conduct, or if we had
been susceptible of those seditious and anarchical principles imputed to us. But why recur to pleas of this kind? We could not
be indifferent to the degradation in which we lived. If victory at
any time authorizes the conqueror to be the arbiter of his own
destiny, we could at any moment have secured our own; we had
arms in our hands, were triumphant, without a single Spanish
regiment among us capable of resistance; and if victory and force
do not suffice to establish a right, we had still other more powerful
reasons no longer to submit to the dominion of Spain. The forces
of the Peninsula were not to be dreaded by us; its ports were
blockaded, and the seas controlled by British squadrons. Yet,
notwithstanding fortune thus propitiously favoured us, we did not
seek to separate from Spain, conceiving that this distinguished
proof of loyalty would change the principles of the court, and cause
them to understand their real interests.

We miserably deceived ourselves, and were flattered with vain
hopes. Spain did not receive a demonstration so generous as a
sign of benevolence, but as an obligation rigorously due. America
continued to be governed with the same harshness, and our heroic
sacrifices served only to add a few pages more to the history of
that injustice we had uniformly experienced.

Such was our situation when the Spanish revolution commenced. Accustomed as we were blindly to obey all the arrangements of the Madrid government, we tendered our allegiance to Ferdinand de Bourbon, notwithstanding he had assumed the crown by ejecting his own father from the throne, through the means of a commotion excited in Aranjuez. We afterwards saw that he passed on to France, was there detained with his parents and brothers, and dispossessed of that throne he had just usurped. We beheld that the Spanish nation, every where overawed by French troops, was in a convulsed state; and that illustrious persons, who either governed the provinces with success, or honourably served in the armies, were assassinated by the people, in a state of open mutiny: that, amidst the oscillations to which the administration of affairs was exposed, distinct governments rose up, each one calling itself supreme, and each arrogating to itself the right of commanding over America in sovereignty. A junta of this kind instituted in Seville was the first that presumed to exact our obedience, and to it the viceroys compelled us to give in our acknowledgment and submission. In less than two months afterwards, another junta, entitled the supreme junta of Galicia, sought from us a similar acquiescence, and sent over to us a viceroy, with the generous threat that thirty thousand men would also come over if it should be necessary. The central junta was next instituted, yet without our having had any share in its formation; we instantly obeyed, and with zeal and efficacy complied with all its decrees. We sent over succours in money, voluntary donations, and aid of all kinds, in order to prove that our fidelity was in no danger, whatever might be the risk to which it was exposed.

We had been tempted by the agents of King Joseph Napoleon, and flattered by great promises of our situation being ameliorated, if we adhered to his party. We were aware that the Spaniards of the highest class and importance had already declared in his favour; that the nation was without armies, and divested of all vigorous guidance and administration, so necessary in moments of dilemma. We were informed that the troops belonging to the river Plata, which had been carried over as prisoners to England after the first expedition of the British here, had been conveyed to Cadiz, and there treated with the greatest inhumanity; that they had been compelled to beg alms in the streets, to avoid dying of hunger; and that, naked and without any relief, they had been sent to fight against the French. Nevertheless, amidst so many urgent and trying causes of complaint, we remained in the same position till Andalusia was occupied by the French, and the central junta dispersed.

In this state of things, an address was published, without date, and signed only by the archbishop of Laodicea, who had been president of the dissolved central junta. By it the formation of a regency was ordained, and three members who were to compose it were named. A measure as sudden as it was unexpected could not fail to surprise and alarm us. For the first time we were then placed on our guard, fearing that we should be involved in the misfortunes of the mother country. We reflected on her uncertain and vacillating situation, the French being already before the very gates of Cadiz and La Isla de Leon. We were apprehensive of the new regents, to us totally unknown, since the Spaniards of greatest credit had already passed over to the French, the central junta had been dissolved, and its members persecuted and accused of treason in the public prints. We were sensible of the informality of the decree published by the archbishop of Laodicea, and his total want of powers to establish a regency. We were ignorant whether the French had taken Cadiz, and completed the conquest of Spain, in the mean time that this same decree had been wafted over to us. We were moreover dubious whether a government rising out of the dispersed fragments of the central junta would not very soon share the same fate. Intent on the risks to which we were exposed, we resolved to take upon ourselves the care of our own security, until we acquired better information respecting the situation of Spain, and saw that the government there attained at least some degree of consistency. Instead of this, we soon beheld the regency fall to the ground, and various changes succeeded each other in moments of great public distress and confusion.

Meanwhile we established our own junta of government, on the model of those of Spain. Its institution was purely provisional, and in the name of the captive King Ferdinand. Our viceroy, Don Baltasar Hidalgo de Cisneros, immediately issued circulars to the interior governors, in order that they might prepare a civil war, and arm one province against the other. The river Plata was soon blockaded by a squadron; the governor of Cordova began to organize an army, that of Potosi, and the president of Charcas caused a division of troops to march to the confines of Salta; and the president of Cuzco, presenting himself with a third army on the margins of El Desaguadero, entered into a forty days' armistice, in order to throw us off our guard; but before its termination commenced hostilities, and attacked our troops, when a bloody battle ensued, in which we lost more than one thousand five hundred men. The human mind shudders at the recollection of the acts of violence then committed by Goyeneche in Cochabamba. Would to God it were possible to forget this ungrateful and bloody American, who, on the day of his entry into the above place, ordered the honourable governor and intendant, Antesana, to be shot; and, witnessing from the balcony of his house this assassination, in a ferocious manner cried out to the soldiery not to shoot him in the head, because he wanted this to place it on a stake; who, after cutting it off, ordered the lifeless trunk to be dragged along the streets; and who, by his barbarous decree, authorized his soldiers to become the arbiters of lives and property, allowing them, in possession of so brutal a power, uncontrolled to range the streets for several days!

Posterity will be astonished at the ferocity exercised against us by men interested in the preservation of America; and that rashness and folly with which they have sought to punish demonstrations the most evident of fidelity and love will ever be matter of the greatest surprise. The name of Ferdinand de Bourbon preceded all the decrees of our government, and was at the head of all its public acts. The Spanish flag waved on our vessels, and served to animate our soldiers. The provinces, seeing themselves in a bereft state, through the overthrow of the national government, owing to the want of another legitimate and respectable one substituted in its stead, and the conquest of nearly the whole of the mother country, raised up a watch-tower, as it were, within themselves, to attend to their own security and self-preservation, reserving themselves for the captive monarch, in case he recovered

his freedom. This measure was in imitation of the public conduct
of Spain, and called forth by the declaration made to America,
that she was an integral part of the monarchy, and in rights equal
with the former; and it had, moreover, been resorted to in Montevideo through the advice of the Spaniards themselves. We offered
to continue pecuniary succours, and voluntary donations, in order
to prosecute the war, and we a thousand times published the
soundness of our intentions and the sincerity of our wishes. Great
Britain, at that time so well-deserving of Spain, interposed her
mediation and good offices, in order that we might not be treated
in so harsh and cruel a manner. But the Spanish ministers,
blinded by their sanguinary caprice, spurned the mediation, and
issued rigorous orders to all their generals to push the war, and
to inflict heavier punishments; on every side scaffolds were raised,
and recourse was had to every invention for spreading consternation and dismay.

From that moment they endeavoured to divide us by all the
means in their power, in order that we might exterminate each
other. They propagated against us atrocious calumnies, attributing
to us the design of destroying our sacred religion, of setting aside
all morality, and establishing licentiousness of manners. They
carried on a war of religion against us, devising many and various
plots to agitate and alarm the consciences of the people, by causing
the Spanish bishops to issue edicts of ecclesiastical censure and
interdiction among the faithful, to publish excommunications,
and, by means of some ignorant confessors, to sow fanatical doctrines in the tribunal of penance. By the aid of such religious
discords, they have sown dissension in families, produced quarrels
between parents and their children, torn asunder the bonds which
united man and wife, scattered implacable enmity and rancour
among brothers formerly the most affectionate, and even placed
nature herself in a state of hostility and variance.

They have adopted the system of killing men indiscriminately,
in order to diminish our numbers; and on their entry into towns
they have seized non-combatants, hurried them in groups to the
squares, and there shot them one by one. The cities of Chuquisaca and Cochabamba have more than once been the theatres of
these ferocious acts.

They have mixed our captive prisoners among their own troops, carrying off our officers in irons to secluded dungeons, where during the period of a year it was impossible for them to retain their health; others they have left to die of hunger and misery in the prisons, and many they have compelled to toil in public works. In a boasting manner they have shot the bearers of our flags of truce, and committed the basest horrors with military chiefs and other principal persons who had already surrendered themselves, notwithstanding the humanity we have always displayed towards prisoners taken from them. In proof of this assertion, we can quote the cases of Deputy Matos from Potosi, Captain General Pumacagua, General Angulo and his brother, Commandant Muñecas, and other leaders, shot in cold blood many days after they had been made prisoners.

In the town of Valle-Grandé they enjoyed the brutal pleasure of cutting off the ears of the inhabitants, and sent off a basket filled with these presents to their head-quarters; they afterwards burnt the town, set fire to thirty other populous ones belonging to Peru, and took delight in shutting up persons in their own houses before the flames were applied to them, in order that they might be burnt to death.

They have not only been cruel and implacable in murdering, but they have also divested themselves of all morality and public decency, by whipping old religious persons in the open squares, and also women, bound to a cannon, causing them previously to be stripped and exposed to shame and derision.

For all these kinds of punishment they established an inquisitorial system, seized the persons of several peaceable citizens, and conveyed them beyond seas, there to be judged for supposed crimes; and many they have sent to execution without any form of trial whatever.

They have persecuted our vessels, plundered our coasts, butchered their defenceless inhabitants, without even sparing superannuated priests; and, by orders of General Pezuela, they burnt the church belonging to the town of Puna, and put to the sword old men, women, and children, the only inhabitants therein found. They have excited atrocious conspiracies among the Spaniards domiciliated in our cities, and forced us into the painful alternative of imposing capital punishment on the fathers of numerous families.

They have compelled our brethren and children to take up arms against us, and, forming armies out of the inhabitants of the country under the command of their own officers, they have forced them into battle with our troops. They have stirred up domestic plots and conspiracies, by corrupting with money, and by means of all kinds of machinations, the peaceful inhabitants of the country, in order to involve us in dreadful anarchy, and then to attack us in a weak and divided state.

In a most shameful and infamous manner they have failed to fulfil every capitulation we have, on repeated occasions, concluded with them, even at a time when we have had them under our own swords; they caused four thousand men again to take up arms after they had surrendered, together with General Tristan, at the action at Salta, and to whom General Belgrano generously granted terms of capitulation on the field of battle, and more generously complied with them, trusting to their word and honour.

They have invented a new species of horrid warfare, by poisoning the waters and aliments, as they did when conquered in La Paz by General Pinelo; and in return for the kind manner in which the latter treated them, after surrendering at discretion, they resorted to the barbarous stratagem of blowing up the soldiers' quarters, which they had previously undermined.

They have had the baseness to tamper with our generals and governors, by availing themselves of and abusing the sacred privilege of flags of truce, exciting them to act traitorously towards us, and for this purpose making written overtures to them. They have declared that the laws of war observed among civilized nations ought not to be practised towards us; and their general, Pezuela, after the battle of Ayoma, in order to avoid any compromise or understanding, had the arrogance to answer General Belgrano, that with insurgents it was impossible to enter into treaties.

Such has been the conduct of Spaniards towards us, since the restoration of Ferdinand de Bourbon to the throne of his ancestors. We then believed that the termination of so many sufferings and

disasters had arrived; we had supposed that a king schooled by
the lessons of adversity would not be indifferent to the desolation
of his people, and we sent over a commissioner to him, in order
to acquaint him with our situation. We could not for a moment
conceive that he would fail to meet our wishes as a benign prince,
nor could we doubt that our requests would interest him in a
manner corresponding to that gratitude and goodness which the
courtiers of Spain had extolled to the skies. But a new and unknown species of ingratitude was reserved for America, surpassing all the examples found in the histories of the greatest tyrants.

In the first moments of his restoration to Madrid he declared
us to be in a state of mutiny, but since then he has refused to
hear our complaints, to admit our requests; and, as the last favour
we could expect from him, he has offered to us unconditional
pardon. He confirmed the viceroys, governors, and generals,
whom at his return he found carrying on their works of butchery.
He declared it to be a crime of high treason for us to presume to
frame a constitution for ourselves, in order that the administration
of our own affairs might not depend on a tyrannic, arbitrary,
and distant government, under which we had groaned during
three centuries; a measure which could alone be offensive to a
prince, the enemy of justice and beneficence, and consequently
unworthy of governing.

By the aid of his ministers, he then applied himself to the
forming of large armaments, with a view to employ them against
us. He has since caused numerous armies to be conveyed over to
these countries, in order to consummate the work of devastation,
fire, and robbery. He has caused the first felicitations of the
potentates of Europe, on his return to Spain, to be used as pleas
in order to engage them to refuse us all aid and succour, and thus
behold us tear each other to pieces with an eye of indifference.
He has made special regulations for cruising against vessels belonging to America, containing barbarous clauses, and ordering
that the crews shall be hung. He has forbidden, with regard to
us, the observance of the laws of his naval regulations, framed
according to the rights of nations, and denied to us all that we
grant to his subjects when captured by our cruisers. He has sent
over his generals with certain decrees of pardon, which they

cause to be published for the purpose of deceiving weak and ignorant minds, and under a hope to facilitate their entry into the towns; but at the same time he has given to them other private instructions; and, authorized by these, as soon as possession is gained, they hang, burn, plunder, confiscate, and connive at private assassinations, plotting all kinds of injury against those thus feignedly pardoned. In the name of Ferdinand de Bourbon it is, that the heads of patriotic officers who have been taken prisoners are placed on the highways; that one of our commanders of a light party was killed with sticks and stones; and that Colonel Camargo, after also being murdered with blows by the hand of the villain Centeno, had his head cut off, which was sent as a present to General Pezuela, with this revolting notification, "that this was a miracle of the Virgin del Carmen."

Such is the extent and force of the evils and sufferings which have impelled us to adopt the only alternative left to us. We have long and deliberately meditated on our fate, and, casting our eyes every where around us, we have beheld nothing but the vestiges of those elements by which our situation was necessarily distinguished, opprobrium, ruin, and patience. What had America to expect from a king who ascends the throne animated by sentiments so cruel and inhuman? from a king who, before he commences his ravages, hastens to prevent any foreign prince from interposing in order to restrain his fury? from a king who with scaffolds and chains rewards the immense sacrifices made by his own subjects of Spain to release him from the captivity in which he lay? those very subjects, who, at the expense of their own blood, and under every species of hardship, had, without any intermission, fought to redeem him from prison, and till they had again placed the diadem on his head! If men to whom he is so much indebted, only for forming to themselves a constitution have received death and imprisonment as a return for their services, what could we suppose was in reserve for us? To expect from him and his butchering ministers benign treatment were to seek among the tigers of the forest the magnanimity of the eagle.

Had we hesitated in our resolve, we should have beheld repeated among us the sanguinary scenes of Caracas, Carthagena,

Quito, and Santa Fé; we should have implicated the ashes of eighty thousand persons who have been victims of the enemy's fury, whose illustrious memories would have risen up in judgment against us, and demanded vengeance; and we should have called down upon ourselves the execration of so many future generations condemned to serve a master at all times ready to ill-treat them, and who, owing to his impotency at sea, has been completely disabled from protecting them from foreign invasions.

In consequence whereof, and impelled both by the conduct of Spaniards and their king, we have constituted ourselves independent, and prepared for our own natural defence and against the ravages of tyranny, by pledging our honour, and offering up our lives and property. We have sworn to the King and Supreme Judge of the universe that we will not abandon the cause of justice; that we will not suffer that country which he has given us to be buried in ruins, and immersed in blood spilled by the hands of our executioners; that we will never forget the obligations we are under of saving our homes from the dangers by which they are threatened, and the sacred right vested in our country to demand from us every sacrifice, in order that it may not be polluted, crimsoned with blood, and trampled under foot, by usurpers and tyrants. We have engraved this declaration on our hearts, in order that in its behalf we may never cease to combat; and while we manifest to the nations of the earth the reasons which have so powerfully induced us to adopt the present measure, we have the honour to proclaim it as our intention to live in peace with all, even with Spain herself, from the moment she is desirous of accepting it.—Given in the Hall of Congress, Buenos Ayres, this 25th day of October, eighteen hundred and seventeen.

Dr. Pedro Ignacio de Castro y Barros, President.
Dr. José Eugenio de Elias, Secretary.

(C.)

(Page 317.)

[The following documents are inserted to elucidate the operations in the Puertos Intermedios. They are translations of intercepted letters, and of fictitious answers which were sent to them. The originals are in the hands of the author.]

Letter from General Ramirez to the Subdelegate of Tarapaca.

" The enemy, who re-embarked in Pisco on the 22d of April last, have directed themselves towards this part of the coast, and have steered for Arica, according to the information I have received.

" I have placed a combined expedition under the command of the subinspector-general of the army, Colonel Don José Santos de la Hera, to operate against them, and to oblige them to re-embark. As the amount of the enemy's force is only 500 infantry and 100 cavalry, it is merely sufficient for the purposes of plunder, and to satiate their avarice for pillage.

" As those persons who are attached to the opposing party are always raising rumours and forging lies, exaggerating circumstances according to their wishes, and detracting from our successes, and from whatever may be of advantage to the national cause, I communicate this to you for your government.

" God preserve you many years.

" Head-quarters in Arequipa, 7th May, 1821.

(Signed) " JUAN RAMIREZ.

" To the Subdelegate of Tarapaca."

(D.)

(Page 331.)

Letter from Don José Santos de la Hera, to the illustrious Constitutional Municipality of Tacna.

" As inspector-general of the army of Upper Peru, and commandant-in-chief of the division destined to regain possession

of this coast, I have received your official note, dated yesterday.
I shall only, at this moment, remark, that it is very singular
that we should not have received any information from your
illustrious municipality since the 13th of this month, on which
day the enemy entered your town, and that not one inhabitant
should have come over to join the national army, as they must
have had frequent opportunities of doing so.

" I am at the head of more than sufficient troops to drive the
enemy from the places he occupies, and in a very short time you
will see all the towns of the provinces of Arequipa subject to the
national arms, as are all those from Lima to Jujuy.

" I, in consequence, order, that from to-morrow you will inform
me daily of every thing that occurs, directing your communications to me at Tacora, that they may be forwarded from thence
towards Moquegua, where I am about to proceed by the direction
of which I have informed the commandant of the troops, who will
remain in that point, in conjunction with the forces. Should you
fail in attending to this order, or conceal from me the most trivial
particular that you may become acquainted with, you must not
be surprised if the inhabitants of Tacna are treated as enemies,
both in their persons and interests.

" It is also indispensable that in the course of an hour you
should send me, by a special messenger, an answer to the following questions :

" 1. What is the total amount of the force that the enemy has
landed on all parts of this coast ? Which are those that
they now occupy, and with what number of men ?

" 2. What cavalry has he, and of what description ?

" 3. Who are the enemy's chiefs, and of what rank ?

" 4. If the subdelegate, Portocarrero, has assisted them in
any thing, and if he is now with them.

" God preserve you many years.
" On the march, 1st June, 1821.

(Signed)   " JOSE SANTOS DE LA HERA."

(E.)

(Page 332.)

Letter from La Hera, commandant-in-chief of the Royalist Division, to Don Blas Mendoza.

" To Don Blas Mendoza.

" Dear Sir,

" In the course of a few days I shall have the pleasure of seeing you. Although I have information of all that is passing in your town, I desire that you will immediately send me an answer to the following questions. Your doing this will certainly decide as to your future fate, and I hope that you will prevent its being an unhappy one :

" 1. What is the total amount of the enemy's force, and what points do they occupy, distinguishing infantry and cavalry?

" 2. What other force has entered Moquegua, besides that which Miller brought with him from the attack of Mirabe? and if they have landed more troops?

" 3. How many negroes, and peasants of all classes, have joined them?

" 4. If they think of advancing upon Arequipa, what day? with what force? and by what route?

" 5. What part does Colonel Portocarrero play amongst them?

" I imagine that you will know who it is that writes to you, and the benefits that await you, if you fulfil my commands.

" The Commandant-General of the troops of the King, marching upon Moquegua."

Counterfeited Answer to the above, sent by Miller.

" Honoured and most respected Sir,

" I received last night the note which you were pleased to address to me, requiring information as to the enemies who unfortunately infest this coast. I did not answer you immediately, because, as I am known to be a royalist, and a good servant of the king, (whom God preserve!) their eyes are always fixed upon

me; and I have now got up before daybreak, and am dictating
this letter by candle-light, that I may not be observed by any body.
" I cannot tell you the precise number of the enemy's force,
because they are spread all over the coast. They say that in this
town there are a thousand and upwards, between cavalry and
infantry; but I do not conceive that they can have more than 900,
because people always exaggerate things. Three days ago this
garrison received reinforcements from Ilo, which were sent by
Cochrane. A Captain Quadros came with the troops, but as
they arrived in the night, we do not know how many he brought.
They say that more troops have landed in the Morro de Sama,
and at Arica, and that all of them are to march against you; and
that, with this intention, Miller will leave this place to-morrow
with all his force. They boast a good deal of the action at
Mirabe, which they say they gained; and also, that when they
have done with you, they will march to Arequipa, to salute his
excellency, General Don Juan Ramirez. There are, however, so
many reports afloat, that you must not consider it extraordinary,
that I cannot say any thing positive as to the operations of these
wretches. Portocarrero made use of every pretext not to take
any side until Miller told him that he must either publish a proclamation, declaring himself an enemy of the king, or consider
himself a prisoner. Portocarrero wished, in the first instance,
to go on board ship to see Cochrane, but Miller told him
that he should not move a single step till he declared himself,
which he did the same day; and he is now called a brigadier of
the patria, though it does not appear that they confide much in
him. Sr. Miller appears to place more confidence in the rebel
Bernardo Landa, and Don Agustin Sapata, than in Portocarrero.
Miller's second in command is Major Soler. They say there are
three other chiefs between Arica and Ilo. The infamous Captain
Carreño has passed over to them, and is already major of the
insurgents. Doctor Laso also plays a great part amongst them.
There are two lieutenants, who are called Francisco La Tapia,
and Vicente Suares, in whom Miller has great confidence. They
say that they are as brave as lions, and on this account are always
at the advanced posts, and they give no quarter. La Tapia has
under his orders about fifty peasants and a few regulars, and is

about to march on a secret expedition, some say to Arequipa, and others, to get into your rear.

" This is all the information I can give you; and you will know by whom it is dictated, and who remains

" Your faithful and loving servant,

" B. M.

" If you should write to me again, please to send your letter by a trustworthy person; because they would hang me without mercy if they discovered our correspondence."

(F.)

(Page 414.)

Translation of a Vote of Thanks from the Peruvian Congress to Lord Cochrane.

THE sovereign constituent congress of Peru, contemplating how much the liberty of Peru owes to the Right Honourable Lord Cochrane, by whose talents, valour, and constancy the Pacific has been freed from our most inveterate enemies, and the standard of liberty has been displayed on the coasts of Peru, resolves that the Junta of government, in the name of the Peruvian nation, do present to Lord Cochrane, admiral of the squadron of Chile, expressions of our most sincere gratitude for his achievements in favour of this country, once tyrannized over by powerful enemies, now the arbiter of its own fate. The Junta of government, obeying this, will command its fulfilment, and order it to be printed, published, and circulated.

Given in the Hall of Congress, Lima, the 27th September, 1822.

(Signed) Xavier Luna Pizarro, President.

José Sanchez Carrion,   } Deputies,
Francisco Xavier Marreatigui, } Secretaries.

In obedience, we order the execution of the foregoing decree.

(Signed)   José de La Mar.
               Felipe Antonio Alvarado.
               El Conde de Vista Florida.
By order of his Excellency,   Francisco Valdivieso.

Lord Cochrane's Proclamation on quitting Chile.

CHILENOS! You have expelled from your country the enemies of independence. Do not sully the glorious act by encouraging discord, and promoting anarchy, that greatest of all evils. Consult the dignity to which your heroism has raised you, and if you must take any steps to secure your national liberty, judge for yourselves; act with prudence; and be guided by reason and justice.

It is now four years since the sacred cause of your independence called me to Chile. I assisted you to gain it; I have seen it accomplished; it only now remains for you to preserve it.

I leave you for a time, in order not to involve myself in matters foreign to my duty, and for reasons concerning which I now remain silent, that I may not encourage party spirit. Chilenos! you know that independence is purchased at the point of the bayonet. Know also that liberty is founded on good faith, and is supported by the laws of honour, and that those who infringe them are your only enemies, among whom you will never find

(Signed)   COCHRANE.

END OF VOL. I.

LONDON:
PRINTED BY THOMAS DAVISON, WHITEFRIARS.

Ingram Content Group UK Ltd.
Milton Keynes UK
UKHW020757260423
420810UK00007B/396